D1204328

The Music of the
Moravian Church
in America

EDITED BY NOLA REED KNOUSE

UNIVERSITY OF ROCHESTER PRESS

ML
3172
.M87
2008

First published 2008

University of Rochester Press
668 Mt. Hope Avenue, Rochester, NY 14620, USA
www.urpress.com
and Boydell & Brewer Limited
PO Box 9, Woodbridge, Suffolk IP12 3DF, UK
www.boydellandbrewer.com

ISBN-13: 978-1-58046-260-0
ISBN-10: 1-58046-260-X

ISSN: 1071-9989

Library of Congress Cataloging-in-Publication Data

The music of the Moravian Church in America / edited by Nola Reed Knouse.
      p. cm. — (Eastman Studies in Music ; v. 49)
  Includes bibliographical references and index.
  ISBN-13: 978-1-58046-260-0 (hardcover : alk. paper)
  ISBN-10: 1-58046-260-X
  1. Church music—Moravian Church. 2. Moravians—United States. I.
Knouse, Nola Reed.
  ML3172.M87 2007
  781.71'4600973—dc22

                    2007024810

A catalogue record for this title is available from the British Library.

This publication is printed on acid-free paper.
Printed in the United States of America.

Contents

Illustrations

Figures

Foreword

To Moravians, music carries deeper meanings than that of casual entertainment. Whether composed by Moravians or adopted into their repertoire, during half a millennium music has helped build communal identity and differentiate Moravians from their neighbors, organize the rhythm of daily life, punctuate and extend the liturgy into every waking hour, and attract others to the brethren's ways. As the following chapters explain in detail, distinctive vocal and instrumental genres give flight to spiritual sentiments that, to Moravians, transcend words alone, allowing communication plainly and directly from the heart. This immediate, heartfelt expression, especially through uncomplicated hymns within range of any voice, instills in the brethren an inner sense of heavenly harmony and thus reinforces the strong urge for social concord that once also underlay Moravian pacifism.

Although such soothing yet sometimes emotionally cathartic music provides relaxation and aesthetic enjoyment, it also imposes discipline, energizes its hearers, and sharpens the mind's focus on tasks at hand. If much Moravian church music seems simple and spontaneous, it is seldom naïve. By being readily adaptable to circumstances—as in arranging hymns for outdoor performance by brass choirs, or creating new litanies from preexisting materials—it constantly reminds congregants, no matter where they are, of Jesus' presence, assures them that their labor and sacrifices are worthwhile, and formerly helped alleviate the anxiety experienced by children reared communally and by missionaries far from home, sometimes facing persecution and confronting hostility on Western civilization's frontiers.

Based chiefly on Jan Amos Comenius's inspirational ideals and on methods expounded by German theorists, notably Daniel Gottlob Türk (1756–1813)—whose didactic texts, well represented in Moravian libraries, remained influential far into the nineteenth century—the core Moravian repertoire has been enriched by stylistic influences of cultures from South Africa to Labrador. Hence, music among the Moravians is nothing if not eclectic and dynamic. Today as in the past, thoughtfully harmonized hymns and litanies in up-to-date as well as familiar, old-fashioned idioms, committed to memory through innumerable repetitions, reinforce faith-affirming continuity while strengthening religious purpose—the aim of all Moravian musicianship. Because traditional

Moravian belief blurs distinctions between sacred and secular and so sanctifies all aspects of life, even a piece of light parlor music becomes holy when played with genuine feeling.[1] The rich holdings of Moravian music archives illustrate keen interest, over generations, in popular *Hausmusik* as well as in serious works of great masters. In a sense, then, the music of the Moravians comprises many musics, all gratefully received and generously valued.

It cannot be overemphasized that Moravians traditionally regard music making, like every other endeavor, as an act of worship. Like Luther, Zinzendorf himself seems to have regarded music as the "fifth gospel." Moravians believe that the God-given gift of making music especially well imposes an obligation to use this talent for the good of the community, not to aggrandize the composer or the performer. Therefore, they have not sought virtuosity, which commonly involves extreme specialization, competition, and distraction. Rather, modest competence and self-effacing sincerity are hallmarks of Moravian musical practice. For this reason, many Moravian compositions are anonymous. Nevertheless, due largely to intensive childhood exposure, Moravians have produced more than their share of musicians whose gifts have been widely recognized. The Pennsylvania-born John Antes, for one, composed the chamber music by which he is best remembered while living abroad in the service of his church; typically, he did not include his full name on the published score.

In America particularly, the excellence of music training in Moravian schools has drawn pupils from many denominations. Since the 1740s, boys and girls have benefited equally from Moravian pedagogy. Some have gone on to fulfilling careers as church musicians, concert performers, composers, instrument makers, music historians, and educators. Exemplary among this coterie are the editor of this volume, Nola Reed Knouse, the renowned harpsichord builder Willard Martin, and the late Thor Johnson, who introduced innumerable student musicians, including this writer, to the rigors of professional-level orchestral work. The accomplishments of John Frederick Wolle, one of America's most influential Moravian musicians and teachers, still resonate in performances of the beloved Bethlehem Bach Choir, which he founded in 1898.[2] A century later, Moravian-trained players helped reconstitute the Civil War–era 26th North Carolina Regimental Band (Federal City Brass Band). Not to be forgotten is the contribution of Joshua, a native Mohegan, who under Moravian tutelage in Bethlehem in the mid-1750s learned to play the organ and later built a spinet (or perhaps a clavichord) for the Wyalusing congregation, which he served as chapel musician.[3]

Testifying to widespread recognition of Moravian musical values, during the first half of the nineteenth century some of the most discerning instrument manufacturers in urban America preferred to send their daughters or granddaughters to the Bethlehem Female Seminary for instruction. Among these girls were Elizabeth Taws (granddaughter of the Philadelphia piano maker Charles Taws); Elizabeth Loud (daughter of the British-born Philadelphia piano manufacturer Thomas Loud); Amelia Scherr (daughter of the Philadelphia organ, piano, and guitar maker Emilius N. Scherr, a Danish immigrant); Lisette, Sophie, Augusta, and Henrietta Eisenbrandt (daughters of the German immigrant Charles Heinrich Eisenbrandt, an instrument manufacturer and importer in Baltimore); Mary Lousia Erben (daughter of Henry Erben, New York's most prominent organ builder); and Lavinia Geib (granddaughter of the New York piano and organ builder John Geib, a German previously active in London)—not to mention four daughters of Bethlehem's own Henry G. Guetter.[4,5] Thanks largely to their enviable musical standards, nineteenth-century Moravian schools attracted a culturally diverse, cosmopolitan student body. These students went on to elevate their families' and the nation's taste.

Moravian music making has also had substantial economic impact. In later-eighteenth-century America, for example, printed sheet music, most of it imported, was costly and not always readily available (especially during the Revolutionary period). Copying music by hand was virtually a Moravian cottage industry, reliant on the prevailing high level of music literacy. Moravian account books of the period record frequent purchases of blank music paper used for copying and composing, and payments for binding finished scores. Purchases of instruments and supplies such as violin strings also added up to significant sums. For example, accounts of the Nazareth general store document the purchase in 1795 of a piano from the Philadelphia firm of Trute & Wiedberg for $110 in Pennsylvania currency, a very stiff price. That store also stocked the country's largest known assortment of iron and brass music wire in many gauges, necessary for maintaining the community's many clavichords and pianos and perhaps citterns, zithers, and spinets as well.[6]

Because missionary settlements outside Europe could not easily afford imported instruments, especially heavy bells and keyboard types that were hard to transport, inhabitants often relied on their own ingenuity to craft what they needed. In 1747, for example, the Society for the Furtherance of the Gospel paid Samuel Powell of Bethlehem £1, 11s. for materials for making a bell for the ill-fated Native American mission of Gnadenhütten. (Hostile natives destroyed the village in 1755.) On February 20, 1754, the Bethabara, North Carolina, congregation diary cited "our new trumpet, which we have made from a hollow tree, and no trumpet in Bethlehem has a better tone." An anonymous Germanic upright piano now in the Moravian Historical Society could be the oldest extant piano of American manufacture, making Pennsylvania the cradle of a major industry.[7]

Particularly noteworthy are the extant instruments of John Antes, Johann Gottlob Klemm, Christian Frederick Hartmann, and David Tannenberg, all pioneers of American musical artisanship whose work is now represented in museum collections.[8] By developing instrument making locally (partly to avoid import tariffs) and selling some of their output beyond their communities, Moravians gained cash, contributed to regional economies, and influenced taste. Tannenberg, in fact, seems likely to have introduced the modern tuning system known as equal temperament to America.[9] Not at all insular where music was concerned, Moravians also patronized "worldly" instrument makers such as John Huber of Northampton, Pennsylvania, who sold one of his pianos in 1796 to Gottlob Schober, a prosperous Moravian businessman in Salem, North Carolina; this elegant piano still survives as evidence of Schober's cultural aspirations.[10]

When they could afford it, Pennsylvania's Moravian settlers also led the nation in introducing fine European instruments: for example, a rare trombone dated 1761 by Johann Gottfried Leydholdt in Dresden, preserved today at the Moravian Historical Society, and an expensive *clavecin royale*, a new-fangled form of piano invented in Dresden about 1774 and possibly brought over by the minister and musician Johann Friedrich Früauff when he arrived from Germany in 1788. Sophisticated instruments such as these were heard not only by the brethren but also by interested visitors, some of whom, including Benjamin Franklin, wrote down their favorable impressions of Moravian musicianship. Eliza Bowne, a traveler from New York, was astonished by what she saw in Bethlehem in 1803: "[T]here is scarcely a house in the place without a Piano-forte; the Post-Master has an elegant grand Piano. . . . We went thro' all the different schoolrooms . . . and in every room was a Piano."[11]

Tuning and maintaining all these instruments and many others, from delicate violins to complicated church organs, took constant attention from a pool of skilled local technicians. Some of them became instrument makers and dealers themselves, whose activities extended far beyond Moravian circles.[12] In 1842, Charles A. Zoebisch, a Moravian importer and manufacturer mainly of brass instruments, established a thriving business that, from headquarters in New York, became known across the country. Among firms associated with C. A. Zoebisch & Sons was the famous guitar-making factory founded by Christian Frederick Martin, a latecomer to the Moravian Church. Martin's enterprise still flourishes in Nazareth, and, ironically, the brand "C. F. Martin" is probably the most widely recognized name of any Moravian associated with music.[13] Indeed, providing instruments of all kinds is arguably the greatest Moravian contribution to shaping and disseminating musical taste.

Of course, this influence has not been limited to America. For example, the renowned Moravian craftsman David Roentgen of Neuwied, Germany, one of the greatest eighteenth-century European furniture makers (Louis XVI conferred on him the title *Ebéniste mécanicien du Roi et de la Reine*), collaborated with other artisans to produce magnificent musical clocks and pianos for courts across Europe. In 1785 Russia's Grand Duchess Maria Feodorovna, daughter-in-law of Catherine the Great, acquired a precious Roentgen & Kinzing piano that was sold in 1987 for $209,000. (Roentgen had hoped to join his evangelical brethren in America but never made the journey.) The following chapters discuss many other Moravians who have advanced music and worship throughout the world. Notably, the modern South African brass band movement owes its vigor mainly to Moravian input.

When discussing music's many roles and meanings among the Moravians, it is important to point out functions that orthodox Moravians shunned. In "worldly" cultures, musical ability was once a social grace cultivated especially by young ladies for display in courtship. The sober old Moravian way of life, in which until 1818 marriage partners were often chosen by lot, had no use for such vanity. Also, in most other communities, possession of a prized instrument bolstered a family's status by underscoring its taste and wealth; not so among communal Moravians, although surely the Bethlehem postmaster's grand piano, say, might have sparked some pride or envy. Until about the mid-nineteenth century, however, most Moravians regarded their instruments as utilitarian appliances rather than status symbols, just as their compositions, even light-hearted ones, were set down for serious purposes.

This is not to deny the life-affirming pleasure gained from music, but as the following essays make clear, Moravians intended such enjoyment primarily to lift hearts and minds toward Jesus. As an aid to religious contemplation and even to induce ecstatic states, old-time Moravian performance practice seems to have favored slow, quiet affects. The eighteenth-century Moravian taste for mild organ stops and the predilection for clavichords, the most sensitive of keyboard instruments, reflect the meditative peacefulness that characterizes Moravian spirituality; this is hardly a church militant. Even trombones were played loudly only on special occasions. The "soundscape" of old Moravian settlements is hard to imagine, much less re-create, today.

Over the past half century, Moravian music has taken on another function, as a subject for academic inquiry. As this book shows, much fresh research on Moravian music comes from scholars born or educated outside the church's traditions. Such objectivity as this distance might allow provides opportunities for new insights, of which those offered here, as in the past by musicologists such as the late Marilyn Gombosi, are only a prelude. As more Moravian music is presented for hearing and analysis, as archives around the world continue to reveal untapped primary sources for examination, as iconography and other modern disciplines enter the picture, a fuller sense will emerge of what Moravian music means.

—Laurence Libin
The Metropolitan Museum of Art

Notes

1. A story is told of a young pastor who reprimanded some Single Brethren for playing serenades on the same instruments they used in church; an elder responded that the pastor used the same mouth for preaching as he used for eating sausages.

2. Paul S. Larson, *An American Musical Dynasty: A Biography of the Wolle Family of Bethlehem, Pennsylvania* (Bethlehem: Lehigh University Press, 2002).

3. John Heckewelder, *A Narrative of the Mission of the United Brethren among the Delaware and Mohegan Indians* . . . (Philadelphia: M'Carty & Davis, 1820), 414.

4. William C. Reichel, *Bethlehem Seminary Souvenir: A History of the Rise, Progress, and Present Condition of the Moravian Seminary for Young Ladies, at Bethlehem, Pa., with a catalogue of its pupils, 1785–1858*, 4th ed., revised and enlarged by William H. Bigler (Bethlehem: Published for the Seminary, 1901), *passim*.

5. Stewart Carter, "The Gütter Family: Wind Instrument Makers and Dealers to the Moravian Brethren in America," *Journal of the American Musical Instrument Society* 27 (2001): 48–83.

6. Laurence Libin, "Music-Related Commerce in Some Moravian Accounts," in *"Pleasing for Our Use": David Tannenberg and the Organs of the Moravians*, edited by Carol A. Traupmann-Carr, 79–115 (Bethlehem, Lehigh University Press, 2000); and "Commercial Accounts of Early Moravian-American Music" in *Land Without Nightingales: Music in the Making of German-America*, ed. Philip V. Bohlman and Otto Holzapfel, 99–110 (Madison, University of Wisconsin Press, 2002).

7. Laurence Libin, "Nazareth Piano May Be Among America's First," *Moravian Music Journal* 33/1 (Spring 1988): 1–6.

8. On Antes and Hartmann, see Frederick R. Selch, "Some Moravian Makers of Bowed Stringed Instruments," *Journal of the American Musical Instrument Society* 19 (1993): 38–64. For Tannenberg's background, accomplishments, and influence, see Raymond J. Brunner, *"That Ingenious Business": Pennsylvania German Organ Builders* (Birdsboro, Pennsylvania, Pennsylvania German Society, 1990), especially chapters 8–11. For an overview of instruments used by Moravians in America see Curtis S. Mayes, "A Descriptive Catalogue of Historic Percussion, Wind, and Stringed Instruments in Three Pennsylvania Museums" (MM thesis, Flordia State University, 1974).

9. Laurence Libin, "New Insights into Tannenberg's Clavichords," *De Clavicordio VII: Proceedings of the VII International Clavichord Symposium, Magnano, September 6–10, 2005* (Magnano: Musica Antica a Magnano, 2006): 129–55.

10. Laurence Libin, "John Huber's Pianos in Context," *Journal of the American Musical Instrument Society* 19 (1993): 5–37.

11. Eliza Southgate Bowne, *A Girl's Life Eighty Years Ago* (New York: Charles Scribner's Sons, 1887), 173–74.

12. Paul Larson and Carol Traupman-Carr, eds., *The Square Piano in Rural Pennsylvania 1760–1830.* (Catalogue of an exhibition, Payne Gallery, Moravian College, Bethlehem, October 19–November 26, 2000).

13. Philip F. Gura, *C. F. Martin and His Guitars, 1796–1873* (Chapel Hill and London: University of North Carolina Press, 2003).

Preface

When asked once to give a presentation on "small groups in the Moravian Church," my colleague C. Daniel Crews responded, "The whole Moravian Church is a small group!" This being so (the membership of the Moravian Church world-wide is approximately eight hundred thousand), the Moravian Church has nonetheless had a significant impact in all corners of the world, particularly in education, in worldwide mission endeavors, and in music.

Donald M. McCorkle's ground-breaking doctoral dissertation, entitled "Moravian Music in Salem: A German-American Heritage" (Indiana University, 1958), as well as his other publications and presentations, sparked a great deal of interest in research into the music of the Moravians, especially in North America. As the first director of the Moravian Music Foundation, Dr. McCorkle set a high standard for research. Although I did not know Dr. McCorkle, I am proud to follow in his footsteps. It is no exaggeration to say that all research into the music of the Moravians in America has been grounded on the firm foundation he laid.

Over the past fifty years, many students and scholars have completed a great many research projects dealing with aspects of Moravian music. What has been lacking, however, is a general introduction to this rich and varied musical culture, reflecting current research. Each of the following essays introduces and explores a facet of this music. Should reading these essays raise more questions and spur more research, this book will have succeeded.

No project of this complexity is completed without the aid of many persons. E. Allen Schultz, the former executive director of the Moravian Music Foundation, reviewed the first beginnings of an outline for this book and has provided invaluable encouragement, friendship, and sage advice for nearly fifteen years. Karl Kroeger, another former director, worked with me on my master's thesis (my first Moravian musical research project) and has been a mentor and guide throughout my years at the Moravian Music Foundation. Philip Dunigan, a former member of the foundation's Board of Trustees, has applied his keen intellect to various aspects of Moravian musical research for more than twenty-five years now, and has contributed insights, a broader perspective, and unflagging enthusiasm to many areas of my work. Richard Crawford, editor-in-chief, and James Wierzbicki, executive editor of the American Musicological Society's MUSA (Music of the United States of America) series, assisted in making portions of chapters 1 and 7 far better than they could have otherwise been. The careful proofreading of the manuscript by Graham and Sybil Rights contributed much to its clarity and completeness. I am grateful for the assistance of Jayson Snipes in setting the musical examples, and for that of David Holston in the photographs for chapter 3.

The first Bethlehem Conference on Moravian Music took place in the fall of 1995, with a symposium on the life and works of David Tannenberg; subsequent conferences on a variety of topics followed in 1996, 1998, 2000, 2002, 2004, and 2006. The presenters and attendees at these conferences have built relationships beneficial to Moravian musical scholarship, exchanging ideas, questions, and information on a truly international level. Although I had long seen the need for a book introducing the wealth of the Moravian musical culture to a wider audience, the magnitude of the task was daunting, until I realized, during a break at the conference of 2002, that there were already many experts in various aspects of the music of the Moravians, and that a book of essays on selected topics would be a most effective introduction. All of the authors of these chapters have been regular presenters at the Bethlehem Conferences on Moravian Music, and other contributors are cited freely in notes. Their research and their willingness to write and revise these chapters has made this work possible. Their collegiality has made the work a joy.

Funding for this project has been graciously supplied by the Center for Moravian Studies, housed at Moravian Theological Seminary in Bethlehem, Pennsylvania; the Wachovia Historial Society; and by the Lee Shields Butterfield Revolving Publication Fund of the Moravian Music Foundation.

The Board of Trustees of the Moravian Music Foundation generously provided a six-month sabbatical in 2005 so that I might focus on this project. As the project has progressed, the staff of the Moravian Archives of the Southern Province and the Moravian Music Foundation have provided consistent and gracious support, generously sprinkled with good humor and patience. They have all fielded phone calls and greeted visitors on my behalf, helping me to secure the quiet time necessary for writing and editing. I owe them an immeasurable debt of gratitude: Moravian Music Foundation Assistant Director Albert H. Frank, Administrator and Development Director Bart Collins, and Executive Assistant Beth Wall; Assistant Archivists Richard Starbuck and Nicole Blum; and especially Archivist C. Daniel Crews, fellow band member, co-translator of hymns and anthem texts, co-presenter of workshops and scholarly papers, and faithful friend. His contributions to this project extend far beyond the one chapter that bears his name.

Of course, one cannot work on a project this fascinating without taking it home at night and on the weekends. Even if one isn't actually editing, one is always thinking of it, and puzzling over the best way to handle a particular passage. My family—my mother, Joyce Reed; my sister and brother-in-law, Betsy and

David Bombick; my mother-in-law, Polly King Knouse; and especially my dear husband, Paul—have maintained admirable patience with me, and for that I am deeply grateful.

The musical heritage of the Moravians is 550 years old now, and continues to grow from deep roots. To all who have taught and learned, composed and edited, sung and played, and worshiped with this music, past and present, and to those who will do so in our future, this work is humbly dedicated.

—Nola Reed Knouse
December 2006

Acknowledgments

Appreciation is expressed to the following copyright holders for permission to reproduce the following materials in whole or part herein:

Carl Fischer, Inc., 62 Cooper Square, New York, NY 10003, for:

Johann Friedrich Peter, *Kindlein, bleibet bei ihm*, Copyright © 1975. International Copyright Secured. All Rights Reserved. Reprinted By Permission.

Johann Christian Geisler, *Ehre sey dem*, Copyright © 1978. International Copyright Secured. All Rights Reserved. Reprinted By Permission.

Georg Gottfried Müller, *Ihr seyd theuer erkauft*, Copyright © 1978. International Copyright Secured. All Rights Reserved. Reprinted By Permission.

Johann Friedrich Peter, *Uns ist ein Kind geboren*, Copyright © 1976, 1977. International Copyright Secured. All Rights Reserved. Reprinted By Permission.

David M. Henkelmann, for *Feed Us, Jesus*, Copyright © 1975.

Hinshaw Music Company, P.O. Box 470, Chapel Hill, NC 27514, for:

Johannes Herbst, *Unser Keiner lebt ihm selber* (*None among Us Lives to Self*), Copyright © 1999. International Copyright Secured. All Rights Reserved. Reprinted By Permission.

Johannes Herbst, *Freuet euch und seyd fröhlich*, Copyright © 1997. International Copyright Secured. All Rights Reserved. Reprinted By Permission.

Christian David Jaeschke, *Die mit Tränen säen*, Copyright © 1990. International Copyright Secured. All Rights Reserved. Reprinted By Permission.

Johann Christian Geisler, *So spricht der Herr*, Copyright © 1999. International Copyright Secured. All Rights Reserved. Reprinted By Permission.

Larry Lipkis, for *Des Herren Wort*, harmonization Copyright © 1978.

Music Sales Corporation, for David Moritz Michael, *Hearken, for I Bring to You Great Joy*, edited by Andy Moore, Translation by C. Daniel Crews and Nola Reed Knouse. Copyright © 2004 by Fostco Music Press, A Division of Shawnee Press, Inc. International Copyright Secured. All Rights Reserved. Reprinted by Permission.

The Moravian Music Foundation, Inc., for:

Christian Gregor, *Ehre sey Gott in der Höhe*, Copyright © 2006.

Chapter One

The Moravians and Their Music

Nola Reed Knouse

Why a Book on Moravian Music?

The breadth, depth, and significance of the worldwide Moravian musical culture is unknown to most, and a mere curiosity to many others.[1] The musical life of the Moravians has been one of artistry, integrity, and harmony with their spiritual and moral values. From the beginning of the Unitas Fratrum in the middle of the fifteenth century through the beginning of the twenty-first century, music has greatly enhanced the Moravians' ability to worship with the heart as well as the mind, to express and teach their faith to each other, to strengthen their communities, and to go around the world in mission and service. As the Moravian Church spread from its modest beginnings in Bohemia and Moravia into a worldwide unity, its musical culture traveled as well, adapted in each new settlement to local needs but retaining a surprising coherence with its roots. This musical story, spanning five hundred fifty years and circling the earth, deserves to be known.

Music history texts of the mid-twentieth century deal with the Moravians only in passing, and then principally with regard to their American settlements. Those few that do make mention of the Moravians in Europe refer to the early hymnals published by the Unitas Fratrum rather than to the rich classical musical culture of the eighteenth century. Indicative of the lack of awareness of Moravian musical culture in Europe through the mid-twentieth century is the fact that the 1949–51 edition of *Die Musik in Geschichte und Gegenwart* has no listing for any of the names by which the Moravian Church has been known.[2] There

The section of this chapter entitled Moravian History and Moravian Faith, and portions of chapter 7, are based on the essay I prepared for *David Moritz Michael: Complete Wind Chamber Music*, ed. Nola Reed Knouse (Recent Researches in American Music 59; Music of the United States of America 16. Middleton, WI: A-R Editions, Inc., 2006). My thanks to Editor-in-Chief Richard Crawford and Executive Editor James Wierzbicki for their assistance.

is a brief biography of Zinzendorf, which mentions his hymn writing, the emphasis on hymn singing in the Renewed Moravian Church, and the fact that some Moravians settled in Pennsylvania. Although musicologists such as Gilbert Chase, Paul Henry Lang, Donald Jay Grout, and John Tasker Howard were aware of the musical life of the eighteenth-century American Moravian settlements, they were also unanimous in their judgment that the Moravians had no effect on the American musical landscape. Moreover, none of the works surveyed acknowledged, even in America, the continuation of Moravian musical life beyond the end of the eighteenth century. A few examples of the judgments passed on the American Moravians are these:

Paul Henry Lang, writing in 1941, says about the Moravians in America: "[I]n a country dominated by English thought and customs, a little band of foreigners, absorbed in themselves, could not be expected to make a lasting impression; the music of the Moravians will therefore always remain an episode interesting to the historian but of little importance to the musical destinies of the country at large."[3] Hans T. David, in his introduction to the New York Public Library's series of publications of Moravian music, gives a very brief overview of Moravian history, moving quickly to America, whose Moravian settlements he describes as "distinguished by a musical life of amazing intensity."[4] David does not explore any possible Moravian influence on the wider American musical landscape.

In 1954, John Tasker Howard briefly discussed some of the Moravian composers working in America and concluded:

> From an American standpoint, it must be admitted that these composers and their works are not of importance, even though they are superior in workmanship to those of our first native composers. That the works themselves were influenced entirely by the German school would not in itself make them unimportant, but the fact that they were not known very far beyond Bethlehem's limits prevents the possibility of their exerting any marked influence on our musical life. The Moravians at Bethlehem were complete unto themselves, and well might they be musically; there was little mingling with other colonies with whom they would have little in common. Consequently, the most advanced musical settlement did the least for the cultural advancement of the country as a whole.[5]

Gilbert Chase discusses the Moravians within the context of the conversion of John Wesley and his later influence on hymn singing in America; Chase makes some mention of the Moravians' own compositions, but pays no attention to the underlying reasons that the Moravians settled in America or to the role of music in their lives and worship.[6]

More recently, Ronald L. Davis's 1982 *A History of Music in American Life*, volume I: *The Formative Years, 1620–1865* shows a good understanding of the Moravians' life and culture; however, he shows little knowledge of the breadth of American Moravian musical culture beyond Bethlehem, Pennsylvania, and again, no understanding that this musical culture continued after colonial times. The most recent edition of Donald J. Grout's *History of Western Music* (2006) includes a paragraph acknowledging the sophistication of eighteenth-century Moravian musical life in Pennsylvania and North Carolina. However, neither of these two recent texts recognize that this musical culture continued after colonial times.[7]

Finally, several significant publications make no mention whatsoever of the Moravians or their music. *The Age of Enlightenment, 1745–1790*, volume VII of *The New Oxford History of Music*, published in 1973, has a section entitled "Choral Music in Protestant Germany," in which the Moravians are not mentioned.[8] And most recently, Richard Cullen Rath's *How Early America Sounded* discusses music of the Quakers and the Puritans, shape-note singing, and other sacred music of European settlers—but not of the Moravians at all.[9]

It is no wonder that the Moravians and their music are so little known.

Remarkably, despite this sad state of affairs, approximately fifty doctoral studies on Moravian musical topics have been completed within the past seventy years in the United States. Roughly half are limited to aspects of the music of the Moravian settlers in early America. Fewer than 10 percent deal with Moravian music and worship beyond American borders, and the remainder are studies of the music of one composer. Only one explores more than a single aspect of Moravian musical life: Donald M. McCorkle's ground-breaking *Moravian Music in Salem: A German-American Heritage* (University of Indiana, 1958), the single most influential study of the music of the Moravians to date. In the fifty years since he completed his dissertation, the music in the American Moravian collections has been organized and cataloged, and much more information has become available about the history and life of the Moravians in America, in Europe, and beyond. Still, McCorkle's work has not been made irrelevant; rather, it is simply out of date.

Many of the composer studies mentioned above are more limited in their usefulness than is McCorkle's work. Most were completed before the fall of the iron curtain and the consequent easing of restrictions on international travel and study; the research for these earlier studies was often limited to sources available in America. Since Herrnhut, the center of the worldwide Moravian Church and home of the Unity Archives, is in the former East Germany, many researchers found it extremely difficult or impossible to obtain the information they needed to make their studies complete.

Music editions included in these studies (and published commercially beginning in the 1950s) were prepared according to the editing standards of the mid-twentieth century, and it was often considered acceptable to "correct" things that were better left as the composer wrote them. Early editions of Moravian anthems, for instance, often changed the voicing from the original SSAB to SATB. Others made even more drastic changes, adding introductions and changing harmonies and even texts, since these editions were most often presented with only an English version, not the original German. Probably the best-loved Moravian anthem is Johann Friedrich Peter's *It Is a Precious Thing*, edited by Clarence Dickinson and published in 1954 by H. W. Gray. The work as published begins with a duet for soprano and baritone, followed by a four-part a cappella chorale. An examination of the five manuscript sources for this work reveals that Peter intended it as a duet for two sopranos.[10] A manuscript source for the four-part chorale included in the Dickinson edition has not been located. However, this chorale shares the same melodic and harmonic structure as the duet, with different meter and rhythm, leading to the conclusion that Dickinson may well have added this chorus to make the duet marketable as an SATB anthem. Conclusions drawn from these early editions are thus highly questionable.[11]

The literature concerning music of the Moravians elsewhere is even more sparse. A highly significant study by the Moravian musicologist and theologian Anja Wehrend, *Musikanschauung, Musikpraxis, Kantatenkomposition in der Herrnhuter Brüdergemeine*, focuses on the musical life of the Moravians in relation to their theology during the "formative period" from 1727 to 1760 in Germany.[12] This book should spark much more interest in the music of the Moravians in Europe, and it provides much-needed background to studies of the music of the Moravians worldwide.[13]

The Scope of This Book

The musical life of the Moravians spans the more than five hundred years of their existence as a separate Christian church body. From the earliest known published Protestant hymnal of 1501, which contained a number of hymns by the Moravian theologian Lukáš of Prague, through the "golden era of Moravian music" of the late eighteenth and early nineteenth centuries, to the continuing writing of anthems, organ works, and hymn texts and tunes through the beginning of the twenty-first century, Moravians have placed a high priority on the expression and communication of their faith through music.[14]

Moravian musical life includes hymns (texts and tunes), sacred vocal music for choir and soloists, organ music and organ building, a brass music tradition based on the *Stadtpfeifer* practices of the seventeenth century, a lively secular instrumental music life flowing from the *collegium musicum* practices of central Europe, and an enduring emphasis on music education in home and school. Moravians wrote music for each of these aspects and adopted music of the surrounding culture as they saw fit.

The singing and writing of hymns is a continuous tradition, with members of each generation both writing new hymn texts and tunes and reaching back to retain hymns from the past. Thus chapter 3, "Moravian Hymnody," spans five hundred fifty years, and the English translations included are those in current use.

The other chapters have a more restricted temporal focus. Chapter 2, "Moravian Worship: The Why of Moravian Music," focuses on the worship practices that arose in eighteenth-century Herrnhut as the practical and theoretical basis for sacred vocal music and for the use of hymns from the eighteenth century onward. Chapter 4, "Moravian Sacred Vocal Music," puts the anthems and solos of the eighteenth and nineteenth centuries into the context of the European classical tradition as it intersected with pietist theology and practice. Chapters 5 and 6, on Moravian organ and brass music, explore the way the organ and the brass ensemble support and enrich the community's worship and life. Anthem translations are those crafted with the creation of the modern edition.

Chapters 7 through 9 focus more narrowly in location as well as in time. Chapter 7, "The *Collegia musica:* Music of the Community," explores the secular instrumental practices of the Moravians in Europe and America in relation to the seventeenth- and eighteenth-century military and civilian instrumental music traditions in central Europe. Chapter 8, "Music in Moravian Boarding Schools Through the Early Nineteenth Century," discusses the boarding schools for both boys and girls in the eighteenth and nineteenth centuries, using those in Bethlehem, Nazareth, and Lititz, Pennsylvania, as examples. Chapter 9, "The Piano Among the Moravians in the Eighteenth and Nineteenth Centuries: Music, Instruction, and Construction," explores piano music and piano building among the Pennsylvania settlements of the Unitas Fratrum. Chapter 10 raises questions for further study, along with preliminary reflections concerning the appropriate context for the study of the music of the Moravians.

Throughout their long history, as the Moravians expanded their missionary outreach, they took with them their musical practices as an essential expression of their faith. The musical life of the Moravians in early America has been more thoroughly explored than that of other geographical regions, even central Europe. Until very recently the music of Moravian communities in other regions—South Africa, Labrador, Tanzania, the Caribbean—has been almost completely ignored. Even now far too little information about these former "mission provinces" is available. Thus the chapters of this book focus on America and the European continent, with only limited reference to Britain and other areas.

Names and Places

Many names have been applied to the Moravian Church throughout its five hundred fifty years, including these:[15]

- "Unitas Fratrum," still the official name of the worldwide Moravian Church, is the Latin form of the Czech *Jednota bratrská*, the name chosen by those who separated from the Roman Catholic Church in the mid-fifteenth century.

- The "Unity of the Brethren" is the English translation of Unitas Fratrum, not to be confused with the Unity of the Brethren in Texas, which also counts Jan Hus as its forefather.
- The "Ancient Unity" refers to the Unitas Fratrum from its founding through the seventeenth century, when it was driven underground and nearly extinguished.
- "Bohemian Brethren" is another term applied to the early Unitas Fratrum, because of its geographic origin.
- The "Unity" is one of the more frequently used terms for the worldwide Moravian Church throughout its entire history.
- The "Renewed Moravian Church" refers to the Unitas Fratrum as it was reborn in Saxony in the early eighteenth century, when refugees from Moravia were given refuge on Count Zinzendorf's estate and, over time, renewed their former Church.
- "Herrnhuters" was the name given by "outsiders" to the renewed Moravian Church in the eighteenth century, because of their residence in Herrnhut, Germany. This was in general not a term of respect.
- "*Evangelische Brüdergemeine*" (or simply "*Brüdergemeine*") is the German name for the Moravian Church today.[16]
- *Brüder-Unität*, usually rendered as "Brethren's Unity," means the worldwide Moravian Church (both male and female members).
- *Kreuzgemeine*, "congregation of the cross," was used by Moravians, especially in the eighteenth century, to signify their Church, emphasizing their total dependence on "Christ and him crucified."

In addressing or writing about people, Moravian practice is to refer to other members of the Moravian Church as "Brother" and "Sister." For those not members of the Moravian Church, titles such as "Mr." or "Reverend" are used. In minutes, diaries, and correspondence, then, it is possible to determine a person's relationship to the Church by the form of address used. As someone's relationship to the Church changes, so does the form of address; one might be "Brother" at one time and "Mr." at another. In the ensuing chapters, this Moravian practice is followed.

The Moravian Church had its beginnings in what is now the Czech Republic. Its renewal in 1727, however, took place in the southern corner of far eastern Germany, very close to the borders with Poland and the Czech Republic. Many of the places named in the history of the Moravian Church have remained quite small; many are not shown on readily available maps.[17] Some of the more significant places in Moravian history, especially in eighteenth-century Europe, are these:

- Herrnhut, which remains the center of the world-wide Moravian Church, is a small town to the east of Dresden. It is about eighteen miles southeast of Bautzen, between Zittau and Löbau, close to the borders of Poland and the Czech Republic.

- Berthelsdorf is about a mile northeast of Herrnhut. Count Zinzendorf, the Moravians' eighteenth-century patron, had a home there, and Berthelsdorf was the site of the Lutheran Church where the residents of Herrnhut initially worshiped.
- Groß Hennersdorf is about six miles east-southeast of Herrnhut and the home of Zinzendorf's grandmother, where he was raised.
- Herrnhaag was a beautiful and prosperous Moravian settlement some thirty miles northeast of Frankfurt.
- Niesky is eleven miles north-northwest of Görlitz, near the Polish border. The Moravian school for young boys and the theological seminary were transferred between Niesky and Barby several times in the mid-eighteenth century.
- Barby, the home of the Renewed Moravian Church's publishing house, is fifteen miles southeast of Magdeburg and some ninety miles west-southwest of Berlin.
- Marienborn, some fifty miles north-northeast of Frankfurt, is the site of an estate leased by Count Zinzendorf, the castle of which was the home of various synods of the Renewed Moravian Church.
- Ebersdorf is some thirty-nine miles south-southeast of Weimar.

Moravian History, Moravian Faith

The Moravian Church traces its origins to the followers of Jan Hus (ca. 1369–1415), a Czech priest and reformer who was martyred in 1415. Hus paid attention to "the practical things which needed to be done to reform the church from top to bottom."[18] His execution, ordered by the Council of Constance, sparked a firestorm of protest, leading to the Hussite wars of the 1420s. In 1457, a number of his followers, dissatisfied with the state of the church, organized a society called the "Unity of the Brethren" (Unitas Fratrum) that was devoted to simplicity of life, strict piety, and congregational participation in worship.

For about two hundred years this group led a precarious existence, mainly in Bohemia, Moravia, and Poland. Its first priests were ordained in 1467, and over the next forty years the Unity of the Brethren strove to create and understand its identity. The Brethren struggled with questions about the proper use of worldly power, the role of the nobility in the church order, and the relationship between faith and works in attaining salvation. An extended period of persecution began early in the sixteenth century, yet throughout the century and into the first half of the seventeenth century the Brethren arrived at their own approach to hymnody, theology, and education.

Throughout its history, the Unity saw the destruction that arose from conflicts over theological understanding. The Brethren sought, therefore, to avoid unnecessary disputes, and they distinguished between things "essential" to salvation, things "ministrative" to salvation, and things that are merely "appropriate" or "incidental."[19] All of the "essential" things were understood to be gifts of God, and were divided into two parts, those on the part of God and those on the part of humanity. The "essentials on the part of God" are (1) the good will of God the Father for all that he has made; (2) the saving work of Christ; and (3) the gifts of the Holy Spirit. The "essentials on the part of humanity" are the responses to God's actions in faith, love, and hope. These three are "gifts by which a person is given a share in the objective work of God."[20] Salvation is gained not by one's own works, but by the gifts of God. This theological understanding is one of the Unity's most significant contributions to Christian thought.

Early in its history the Unity recognized the importance of maintaining clear and accurate records of its actions, and it first organized its archives (*Akty*) in 1551. The Moravian Church's emphasis on preserving and making available to all readers the documents of its faith, its hymnody, and its history has continued into the twenty-first century.

Committed to literacy and education, in the first decade of the sixteenth century the Unity owned three of the five printing presses in Bohemia and produced fifty of the sixty works printed in Bohemia and Moravia. Among the works published by the Unity are numerous confessions of faith, including one from 1535 with an introduction by Martin Luther; the Kralice Bible;[21] more than twenty hymnals in Czech, German, and Polish (with multiple reprints and revisions); and a Czech grammar and Czech speller.[22] Even this early in the Unity's existence the members saw hymnody as the primary means of expressing and transmitting their faith and doctrine.

Two particularly important contributions of the original (and highly persecuted) Moravian church were the only music treatises known to have been written by Czech Protestants during the Renaissance and Reformation years. The first, *Musica* (1558), was the work of Jan Blahoslav (1523–71), a bishop of the Unitas Fratrum who also served as "an archivist, editor, diplomat, musician, educator, publisher, grammarian, and translator."[23] The second, *Muzika* (1561), was attributed to "Jan Josquin," most likely a pseudonym for Václav Solín (1527–66), who collaborated with Blahoslav on the printing of hymnals in 1561 and 1564. In studying these treatises, Thomas Sovík tracks the connection between the Unity's music theoretical studies and those originating in Wittenberg, noting the significance of these publications in the evolution of music in the Czech kingdom, in Central Europe, and indeed in Western Europe as a whole.[24]

Rejoicing at the rise of other bodies of believers who separated from the Roman Catholic Church, the Unitas Fratrum worked hard to establish cordial relationships with the new Lutheran and Reformed churches. Throughout the sixteenth century the members of the Unity recognized their own calling and consistently refused to relinquish their faith. Largely because of quarreling between the Lutherans and the Calvinists, in 1561 the Unity resolved to remain separate from both those denominations. The Unity also made approaches to Tsar Ivan IV of Russia (Ivan the Terrible) and to the Eastern Orthodox church, but without result.[25]

For a brief period, from 1609 to 1618, the Unity enjoyed a respite from persecution, being allowed to hold public worship services in Prague. With the beginning of the Thirty Years' War in 1618, however, the Unity was once again driven underground. Following the victory of the emperor Ferdinand at the battle of White Mountain (November 8, 1620), the Unity's churches in Prague were confiscated in 1621. In 1624 the Unity's priests, along with those of the Lutherans, were banished from Bohemia and Moravia. Inhabitants were forced to "convert" to Roman Catholicism by such means as the seizure of churches, the prohibition of gatherings, compulsory attendance at Catholic services, fines, imprisonments, the forcible presence of military men in homes, the removal of books, and so on. The estates of lords known to be members of the Unity were confiscated and given not only to Czech nobles loyal to the Catholic church, but to those nobles from other lands as well. Many members of the Unity (estimated at between five and six thousand) fled to Poland; others were unable to flee and remained behind, either submitting to Catholic authority or continuing to practice their faith in hiding. Insofar as possible, priests of the Unity traveled in secret to these small pockets of Brethren, providing such comfort as they could by their own ministrations and by bringing books written out of the need of the times.[26]

The most significant figure for the preservation of the Unity's history, church order, and hymnody through this difficult period and beyond was John Amos Comenius (Jan Amos Komenský, 1592–1670).[27] A bishop of the Unity, he found exile in Lešno (Lissa), Poland, along with other leaders of the Unity. His sorrow over the state of his nation, along with great personal losses (the deaths of his first wife and children, the loss of his personal library) did not crush his spirit; rather, he dedicated himself to extensive literary activity. His writings include a series of books, in Czech, focusing on pastoral care, comfort, and hope. He reflected on the state of the Unity after the battle of White Mountain, urging the priests, and in fact all in authority, to reform their own lives so that they might more worthily serve their members. His hope for a brighter future led him to push for preparation by education and reform of schools. His writings on education, in Latin, brought him renown throughout Europe.

As hope for the survival of the Unitas Fratrum in its homeland diminished, Comenius "lifted his voice in a book full of grief and dignity, with melancholy leave-taking of a better past and uncrushed hope."[28] Published in 1650, after the Peace of Westphalia (1648) made no provision for the Unity, this *Testament of the Dying Mother, the Unity of Brethren* presents the "last will and testament" of the dying church, with advice to those members still living, yet with hope for the Czech nation in the future.[29] Comenius continued to hope that this "death" would not occur. He published, in both Latin and Czech, a history of the Unity, calling members to return to the moral example of their ancestors.

Comenius' hopes blinded him to the worsening political situation in Poland, and he was unprepared for the burning of Lešno in April of 1656. Once again he lost his possessions to fire, including his own manuscripts. After a period of refuge in Silesia, he found a home in Amsterdam, where he continued to write and publish for the remnant of the Unity, using a printing press that had been rescued from Lešno. He published a reprint of the Unity's large catechism in 1661, and made a revision of the Unity's hymnal in 1659. This book includes a preface discussing the role of music in worship. In 1662 he published the Unity's confession of faith in Czech; he also prepared a revision of the Unity's German hymnal that was printed after his death. He also printed the Latin *De bono unitatis et ordine* ("Regarding the property and order of the Unity"), basing this work on an earlier (1616) comprehensive description of the Unity's church order and organization.[30] Before his death he made provision for the preservation of the Unity's episcopate, seeing that two priests were consecrated as bishops.

The tumultuous political upheavals in the seventeenth century resulted in the near destruction of the Unitas Fratrum. The tensions did not ease with the end of the Thirty Years' War in 1648; the struggle for ascendancy between the Austrian Hapsburgs and the royal house of France resulted in repeated military actions in German territories. Determined to stabilize the situation, Prussian rulers over the next century strove to concentrate their political power in a centralized government, using religion as a unifying force.[31]

One of the most significant social trends to arise during this period of continual turmoil was the religious movement known as Pietism. Although this movement is difficult to define concisely, most scholars identify its beginning as the publication in 1675 of Philip Jakob Spener's *Pia Desideria*.[32] Pietism was "in many ways a reaction to the perceived failure of the Lutheran church to improve the spiritual life of individuals and the social life of Germany."[33] It has also been described as a "moral reaction against the decadence resulting from the devastating Thirty Years' War . . . [which was] religiously divisive, morally subversive, economically destructive, socially degrading, and ultimately futile in its results."[34] Pietism was a social movement marked by the formation of small prayer and study groups whose members had a sense of separation from the world, not for the sake of utopian isolationism but rather in the hope of finding more intimate connections between Christian faith and active service to others.[35]

Into this tumultuous time was born Nicholas Ludwig, Count von Zinzendorf (1700–1760). Raised by his grandmother in a household of unusual piety, and trained in law as befitted a count of the Holy Roman empire, Zinzendorf was a "preacher, hymn writer, patron of Christian missions, advocate of religious toleration, and social critic" who became "one of the most famous (and controversial) figures in Germany."[36] In 1722, Johann Andreas Rothe, the Lutheran pastor at Zinzendorf's estate at Berthelsdorf in Saxony, introduced Zinzendorf to Christian David, a young carpenter from Moravia who was seeking a place of refuge for some of the descendants of the Unitas Fratrum. Zinzendorf agreed to help, not anticipating that the refugees would actually build homes on his property; but Christian David returned to Moravia and quickly found two families who were ready to make the two- to three-day journey on foot to a new home. The first refugees arrived at Berthelsdorf on June 8, 1722, and erected a cottage. Zinzendorf's first contact with them was in December of 1722, when he and his new bride came to stay at his Berthelsdorf home. Being the impulsive and extremely devout man that he was, he immediately knelt and prayed with them, and not only allowed them to stay, but devoted the rest of his life to their well-being.[37]

Along with other religious refugees, mostly also from Moravia, they built a town called Herrnhut ("the watch of the Lord"). Because of the diversity of backgrounds and beliefs, dissension arose within the community. Matters came to a head in early 1727, and Zinzendorf gave up his state duties in Dresden to come to live within the community and address the problems. On May 12, 1727, Zinzendorf issued a set of "Manorial Injunctions and Prohibitions" which the residents signed, acknowledging him as their feudal lord. A second document, known as the "Brotherly Agreement," was also presented and signed by those who wished to remain part of the Herrnhut community, defining their relationships with each other.[38] During the summer, Zinzendorf met with each family, leading them in Bible study and prayer.

On Sunday, August 10, 1727, during the weekly afternoon worship service in Herrnhut, Pastor Rothe was present along with Zinzendorf. The Herrnhut diary reports that when

he and the congregation prostrated themselves before God, they felt transported. The meeting continued until midnight with prayer, hymn after hymn, brotherhood, unity of purpose, and with weeping and supplication. The remaining separatists were completely brought over.[39]

The experience was not to end here, however. On Monday morning, Pastor Rothe invited the Herrnhuters to a service of Holy Communion to be held at Berthelsdorf on Wednesday, August 13. On Tuesday, August 12, Zinzendorf visited house to house throughout Herrnhut to prepare the people for Communion. On August 13, they spoke quietly with each other on the walk to Berthelsdorf. In the church, after an opening hymn and a blessing by Pastor Rothe, the congregation again prostrated themselves, singing and weeping at the same time. The diary reports that several of the brethren prayed for guidance on the true nature of the church. The diary continues, "Now after the inner anointing had flowed over us all and we were not far from Him, we prayed in certainty of faith that He should draw powerfully to our community our two elders, Christian David and Melchior Nitschmann, who for good purpose were in Sorau, and let them experience what we had experienced."[40] Indeed, on David and Nitschmann's return to Herrnhut, the diary records that they immediately asked what had taken place on the morning of August 13, as they had been powerfully drawn to prayer for the community at Herrnhut.[41]

In his three-volume biography of Zinzendorf, August Gottlieb Spangenberg (1704–92) describes these events and quotes the diary of David Nitschmann, who was later to become the first bishop of the renewed Unitas Fratrum, concerning this time:

> From this time on Herrnhut became a living congregation of Jesus Christ; from then on the members bound themselves anew with one another, to be faithful to the Savior with their whole hearts, and to serve him where and how he would have them. . . . In short: we were altogether almost beside ourselves with joy; we felt a new and almost heavenly family relationship with one another, which old and young were able to enjoy.[42]

Zinzendorf was later to describe this day as "a day of the outpouring of the Holy Spirit upon the congregation," as its Pentecost.[43] This date continues to be celebrated as the "birthday" of the Renewed Moravian Church.

Among modern historians there are varying opinions on the connection between the pre-Reformation Unitas Fratrum and the eighteenth-century Moravian Church. Moravian historians have most often written of the two as if the only tie between them is the fact that the eighteenth-century church chose to name itself after the former body. No continuous history of the Moravian Church has been written that includes both eras; rather, historians have written either the history of the "Ancient Unity" or the history of the "Renewed Moravian Church."[44] Moravian history courses at Moravian Theological Seminary remain divided into "Ancient Unity" and "Renewed Unity" semesters.

Recent scholarship in Moravian history, however, leads to a different conclusion. The Pietist leaders at Halle (where many who were to become leaders in the Renewed Moravian church studied, including Zinzendorf himself) knew of Comenius and his writings.[45] In 1727 Zinzendorf became acquainted with Comenius's *Ratio Disciplinae* at the library at Zittau, near Herrnhut, and he himself was struck by the similarities between the discipline of the old Unity and that of the emerging community at Herrnhut.[46] Examination of the theological writings of the two reveals a similar emphasis on the person and works of Christ, as well as the nature of salvation.[47]

The pietistic movement, moreover, is an effective bridge between the early Unitas Fratrum and the Renewed Moravian Church. The following characteristics are shared by the two bodies:

(1) emphasis on reading of the Bible, both individually and in small groups;
(2) making the priesthood of all believers effective through small groups within the church;
(3) recognition that Christianity is a matter of practice, not of knowledge;
(4) avoidance of destructive religious controversies;
(5) reformation of ministerial training in order to teach piety in addition to doctrine; and
(6) preaching of simple and edifying sermons for the laity.[48]

Almost from its renewal in 1727, the Moravian church was highly evangelical. Within a thirty-year span, the Moravians sent missionaries to St. Thomas (1732), Greenland (1733), North America (Georgia, 1735), Suriname (1735), South Africa (1736), the Gold Coast (1736), Russia (1737), Algeria (1740), Ceylon (1740), Persia (1747), Egypt (1752), Labrador (1752), and Jamaica (1754).[49] In addition, they organized smaller fellowships within the state churches in the Baltic region, Poland, England, the Netherlands, Switzerland, Germany, France, and Scandinavia.[50] The Moravians saw an urgent need for their own ordained ministry to administer the sacraments in far-flung locations where there were no other ministers. After much thought and prayer, and putting the question to the lot,[51] they turned to one of the two remaining bishops of the old Unitas Fratrum—Daniel Ernst Jablonski, the grandson of Comenius, now serving in Berlin. He consecrated David Nitschmann a bishop on March 13, 1735, thus authorizing Nitschmann to baptize converts, administer Holy Communion, and—most important—ordain others to the ministry.[52] This renewal of the epis- copal succession from the old Unity is yet another link between the two.

In addition to its wide-ranging missionary activity, the Renewed Moravian church established a number of settlement congregations (*Ortsgemeinen*) in both Europe and America. Their first settlement on the American colonial mainland was in Georgia in 1735. This settlement proved unsuccessful, partly because of war between Protestant England and Catholic Spain in Florida. In accepting the invitation of the evangelist George Whitefield in 1741 to relocate their colony to Nazareth in Pennsylvania, the Moravians were moving to a colony that offered religious liberty to a degree unknown in most of the other American colonies.[53] Their relationship with Whitefield deteriorated, but they were able to purchase five hundred acres approximately eight miles south of Nazareth, where they established their settlement, named Bethlehem in December 1742 by Zinzendorf himself during his 1741–43 visit to America. Soon thereafter they were able to purchase the Nazareth property itself from Whitefield.

In a move that had far-reaching consequences for the Moravians in Britain and the New World, in 1749 the British Parliament passed an act recognizing the Moravian Church as "an antient Protestant Episcopal Church." With this act, the Moravian Church became much more widely known and respected in British society; the church was acknowledged to be not a sect, but an interna- tional organization and a legitimate church.[54] Following the passage of the act, the Moravians received several offers from British noblemen seeking reputable settlers for their lands in such places as Nova Scotia, Scotland, North Carolina, Maryland, and Ireland. The Moravians negotiated an agreement with the earl of Granville to purchase one hundred thousand acres in North Carolina.[55] They established their first settlement in North Carolina in November 1753; their principal North Carolina town of Salem was begun in 1766. Also because of this act, Moravians in America were allowed to make payments in lieu of military service; in England and Ireland as well as in America, they were allowed to "affirm" rather than swear an oath.

The Moravian expansion to the American colonies addressed problems that the brethren had had in Europe. Although the Moravians were not overtly persecuted in Germany, they were acutely conscious of the fragility of relationships between themselves and their society. The loss of one of their most beautiful settlements, Herrnhaag, through no fault of their own, pointed up their precarious state.[56] The financial impact of this loss was crippling, and the Moravians hoped to recover some of their losses through the sale of land they had purchased in North Carolina. And not least important was their never-flagging commitment to communicate the gospel to the Native Americans and to other settlers in America.[57]

Near the middle of the eighteenth century the Moravian church faced a difficult and painful experience that came to be called the "Sifting Period" or "Sifting Time." The emotional intensity of this period was expressed in language marked by excesses of childishness and use of diminutives, sexual imagery, and a fascination with the physical sufferings of Christ that far exceeded the more normal Moravian "blood and wounds" theology. Craig Atwood describes the facts as follows:

> The term itself comes from Luke 22:31 ("Simon, Simon, behold, Satan demanded to have you, that he might sift you like wheat"), which refers to being tested. In Moravian historiography, the Sifting Time was a period of fanatical excess originating in the Herrnhaag community in Germany in the 1740s. At that time, the *Brüdergemeine* faced the real possibility that it would become a fanatical sect or what some today might call a "cult." In 1749 Zinzendorf was made aware of the situation in Herrnhaag and issued a long letter of reprimand. He also removed his son Christian Renatus from his office as head of the Single Men's choir. A special synod was called to deal with the problems in Herrnhaag and the resulting negative publicity. Hymnals, litany books, and many collections of Zinzendorf's sermons were edited and reissued.[58]

After the church was able to recover its balance, church authorities destroyed some of the documents from this period. The Sifting Time thus remains a problematic subject in Moravian scholarship; nevertheless, the middle of the eighteenth century must be recognized as a time of almost overwhelming creativity and passionate devotion to Christ as the suffering Savior, marked by a prolific outpouring of hymns, devotional poetry, and visual art.

The two great mid-century hymnals published by the Renewed Moravian Church, one in German (1753) and one in English (1754), were among the publications issued as the church returned to more orthodox theology.[59] These two hymnals were organized in similar fashion, demonstrating to both Moravians and others that the Moravian Church based its theology firmly on scripture; that the Moravian Church saw itself as part of the one universal church; that the Moravians saw themselves as closely connected with the

Protestant Reformation; and that the Moravians also saw themselves as heirs of their own venerable tradition, a tradition continuing to the present day. Both of these hymnals, then, were a vital part of the eighteenth-century Moravian Church's search for an understanding and appropriate expression of its own identity.[60]

For more than a half century, the Moravian settlements were primarily closed communities, serving both as places where the Moravians could live the life they chose and places from which they could send out missionaries. The meticulous records of the Moravians show that in the early years they preferred to maintain a significant degree of separation from their neighbors, but they did not form a separatist, monastic, or utopian society, and they were much more involved in the world around them than were the Shakers and similar groups.[61] Examination of their religious and social structures provides the context necessary to understand the role of music in their life and worship.

The center of the worldwide Moravian Church was in Herrnhut in eastern Germany. With their strong centralized church government and commitment to communication, Moravian pastors and administrators traveled a great deal, not only within a given country but throughout the entire Moravian world. They placed a high value not only on record keeping within each congregation or settlement but also on communication among the settlements. Each congregation kept a diary and periodically sent a copy to Herrnhut. Excerpts from these diaries were hand copied, assembled into reports known as the *Gemein-Nachrichten*, and sent back out to the congregations so that Moravians in every location could be informed of the activities of their brothers and sisters worldwide.[62] The result was a strong and peculiarly "Moravian" culture that transcended geographic and linguistic boundaries.

18th-century Moravian culture displays a remarkable degree of internal uniformity and coherence. Despite the fact that Moravian congregations and mission stations were scattered across four continents, they still formed one organic whole, committed to the same basic norms and inspired by the same vision. Except for minor local variations, all Moravian congregations shared in the same overarching tradition. A Moravian traveling from Lititz, Pa., to Neuwied on the Rhine, or from Herrnhut, Saxony, to Sarepta in Russia, would find the same familiar customs, the same style of worship, the same liturgical calendar, and the same order and organization of the community. This unity and uniformity of Moravian life and worship corresponded to the Moravians' sense of communion across all geographic and political boundaries and was carefully fostered well into the middle of the 19th century.[63]

Although the Moravians maintained contact and trade with their neighbors as well as with Moravians in other communities and lands, no one who was not a member of the Moravian Church could live within a Moravian settlement. This entailed agreeing to abide by the church rules, but before anyone could be accepted as a member, he or she had to be approved by the drawing of the lot.

The most distinctive feature of Moravian social structure was its choir system. The entire community was divided into "choirs" based on age, gender, and marital status (little girls, little boys, older girls, older boys, single sisters, single brothers, married people, widows and widowers). This was not for any musical purpose; rather, it was a "practical expression of Zinzendorf's theory that the earthly existence of the Son of God has sanctified all aspects of human life."[64] The members of each choir reflected on a different aspect of Jesus' earthly life as guidance for their own lives. In some communities the choirs had separate living quarters; in all communities, they had separate choir meetings for worship and study, for the development of close interpersonal relationships, and for mutual support and growth in the life "in Christ." The goal was to prevent the division of life into separate realms of the "sacred" and "secular," for according to the Moravians all of life was to be a liturgy, an act of worship, and a means of remaining in intimate contact and identification with Christ.

The Renewed Moravian Church maintained the emphasis on education that had been one of the hallmarks of the early Unitas Fratrum. The Moravians established schools in every new settlement and in many mission outposts. These schools had the practical benefit of caring for the children, both girls and boys, of members who were then freed for missionary service. Their academic quality was high enough, however, that before long, "outsiders" began applying to the Moravians to teach their children as well.

Although Zinzendorf and the Moravians were accused of opposing the use of human reason, they were not averse to education or the exercise of understanding. They were, however, opposed to *meaningless* speculation. They recognized that no matter how hard they tried to make the Christian experience into an organized, rational system, their faith would always have aspects that they felt reason alone could not explain. "One of [Zinzendorf's] most significant contributions was his discovery that the heart may know what the mind cannot understand."[65] The Moravians' worship combined a Lutheran sensitivity for liturgy and devotion with a pietist spirituality, enriching, and enriched by, their communal life.

The Moravians' single-minded devotion "allowed the Brethren to view all matters spiritual and social with breadth, with charity, and with catholicity. It was this synthetic spirit . . . which allowed for the cultivation of an aesthetic nature of the highest order."[66]

Music, which Zinzendorf saw as the best means of communicating directly to the heart, became an ever-present part of life. Through hymns, Zinzendorf's more abstract concepts were expressed in down-to-earth, more easily understandable terms. As was the case with the early Unitas Fratrum, the Moravians' passionate devotion to Christ poured forth in thousands of new hymns in dozens of printed text-only hymnals. The Herrnhut *Gesangbuch* of 1735 was followed by twelve appendices and four supplements. The 1753 *Alt und Neue Brüder-Gesang* included hymns by contemporary Moravians as well as a large number and wide variety of hymns from various periods of Christian history, including the Unitas Fratrum. Many other text-only hymnals were printed, and the Synod of 1775 assigned Christian Gregor the task of organizing and editing this immense body of hymns. His work resulted in the *Gesangbuch* of 1778, which, in reprints with some supplemental hymns, remained in use in German-speaking congregations for about a century. Copies of all of these hymnals were sent to Moravian congregations worldwide, and many privately owned copies survive in Moravian archives in Winston-Salem, Bethlehem, and Herrnhut.

Tune books or "chorale books" were also prepared for the organists. A number of manuscript tune books from the 1730s are in the Moravian Archives in Herrnhut. The largest and most significant manuscript chorale book is that prepared by Johann Daniel Grimm (1719–60) in 1755. Recognizing the need to standardize the versions of tunes used in the many congregations around the world, the Synod of 1782 assigned Christian Gregor the task of preparing a chorale book for publication. Gregor dropped tunes that were no longer in use, revised others, and composed a number of his own. Published in 1784, this book also remained a standard, not only in German-speaking congregations but also around the Moravian unity; chorale books published in England, America, South Africa, and elsewhere used Gregor's work as their foundation.[67]

Hymn singing was of utmost importance, and heavy emphasis was placed on memorization. From the Synod of 1750 comes the following declaration: "A congregation of the Savior must be able to sing without a book, for they should live in the matter. One passes a hymnal to a stranger."[68] Thus the printed hymnals were intended for the use of visitors, for the introduction of new hymns, and for private devotions, rather than for weekly or daily worship by the congregation. The Moravians' most characteristic worship service was the *Singstunde*, a service composed entirely (or almost entirely) of congregational hymn singing. The *Singstunde* was composed of hymn stanzas, carefully selected and ordered from a number of different hymns to convey some theme or aspect of Christian life and faith. There was no spoken sermon; the message was in the words of the hymns sung by the gathered congregation.

The Moravians considered hymn singing to be the most important means of communicating and expressing what they regarded as the spiritual truth. Writing in 1811, in the introduction to his *Anthems for One, Two, or more Voices performed in the Church of the United Brethren*, the Moravian pastor and mission administrator Christian Ignatius LaTrobe (himself a composer of no mean ability and accomplishment) described the Moravians' attention to hymn singing:

As a great portion of this service consists in the singing of hymns, they endeavoured to make it uniform and harmonious, by encouraging all to join, but checking any disposition to vociferation in individuals, and have thereby, in some of their settlements, acquired a degree of perfection in congregational singing, which is not attainable where there is no attention to general effect, but where every one is left to suit the strength of his voice, however grating, to the ardour of his feelings, or the vanity of his mind. The organ is directed to accompany the congregation so as not to overpower it, but only to complete and support the harmony of the whole.[69]

Christian Gregor (1723–1801) is perhaps the most central figure, aside from Zinzendorf, in the development of the musical heritage of the Moravians. He has been called "the first outstanding musical personality in the Renewed Moravian church,"[70] as well as the "father of Moravian music."[71] Along with serving the church as organist and minister, Gregor held important positions as a church administrator, visiting Pennsylvania and North Carolina in that capacity between 1770 and 1772. He is credited with introducing concerted anthems into Moravian worship.[72]

The incorporation of newly composed pieces (anthems, solos, duets) into the services for festival days is the context for what is most characteristically known as "Moravian music." Over the next hundred years, Moravian composers—most often pastors and teachers—wrote thousands of sacred vocal works, mostly accompanied by strings and occasional wind instruments, for their worship services. LaTrobe characterized Moravian anthems as follows:

> It will be easily perceived, that neither in the vocal, nor instrumental parts, any attempt is made to exhibit the skill of the performers by a display of extraordinary powers of execution, which might lead the attention of the congregation into an improper channel. More elaborate compositions are reserved for exercise at home. Vocal fugues, also, are not used in the Church, as being unintelligible to the congregation, who wish to understand the words of the Anthem, after which they generally sing a suitable response in a verse or hymn, treating of the same subject.[73]

Music and its proper place in worship was of great concern in the eighteenth century Moravian Church. For instance, as Colin Podmore discusses in his *The Moravian Church in England 1728–1760*, the music in the Moravian worship services was known to be beautiful, and the fear arose that many strangers were coming "for the music's sake only, and not seeking the Saviour."[74] After much discussion, the congregation "resolved to discontinue the music for the present, which probably attracts many strangers."[75] Also of note is the fact that for the worship service on Easter of 1778, the Elders' Conference in Salem chose not to go to God's Acre (the graveyard, as was customary at dawn on Easter Sunday) "on account of so many visitors. . . . [A]fter most of the visitors had gone home we held our Easter Liturgy in the Saal, at 3 o'clock in the afternoon, in the blessed peace of God."[76] Thus, although music was of great significance in Moravian worship, the brethren were careful not to allow it to become of *essential* importance.

Even so, Moravian composers were certainly aware of their musical gifts and accomplishments, but their *Lebensläufe* show that they were careful to keep them "in check."[77] Jeremias Dencke (1725–95), the composer of perhaps the first instrumentally accompanied sacred vocal works written in America, makes reference only to his organ playing, not to his composing. The composer and teacher Jacob Van Vleck (1751–1831) makes but one reference to music in his *Lebenslauf*, and that was to his pleasure in studying organ and playing for worship. Johann Friedrich Peter (1746–1813), certainly one of the most prolific of the Moravian composers in America, makes two references to music: one in a statement of thanksgiving to Christ for blessing the use of his musical gift in beautifying the worship services during his 1780–90 tenure in Salem, North Carolina, and the other in an ambiguous passage in which he praises Christ for bringing him through a difficult period of temptation during which he wrestled with his musical gift as something valued by the world. The Moravians believed that musical ability, like every other gift, was to be used in praise of Christ and for the good of the community, not for the benefit of the individual.

Throughout the history of the Moravian church, instruments have been used consistently in worship as well as in entertainments. LaTrobe's comment on the role of instruments in Moravian life and worship stresses practical more than spiritual concerns:

> In most of the Brethren's settlements, there is likewise a small band of vocal and instrumental performers, composed of persons voluntarily engaging their services. They sometimes meet for practice, and on particular occasions, enliven the service by the performance of the following, or similar Anthems, suited to the subjects under contemplation.
>
> The practice of Instrumental Music is recommended by the Brethren, as a most useful substitute for all those idle pursuits, in which young people too often consume their leisure hours; and since its application as an accompaniment and support to the voice is calculated to produce the most pleasing effect, its use in the Church has been retained.[78]

This commitment to making music required a significant commitment to music education. All students in Moravian schools received a thorough grounding in vocal music. Children in schools sang hymn tunes and chorales as part of their instructional program. They were also encouraged to learn to play instruments, including keyboard, winds, and strings.[79] Both girls and boys received this musical education. In general, the girls studied clavier and stringed instruments; the boys studied organ and wind instruments as well, filling the continuing need for organists and orchestral players for worship. (Women played instruments in their choir houses or at home, but not in public.)

A recent study by Pauline Fox has also shown that music instructional materials used in the pious communities of Bethlehem and Lititz, Pennsylvania, included both secular and sacred music: American patriotic songs, for example, as well as arrangements of British folk songs and dances, and songs from the British theater.[80] The instructors at these Moravian schools, mostly Moravian clergy, made use of selected aspects of the musical culture of the young country, rejecting neither the values of their faith nor things from beyond their own borders that they saw as both good and useful.[81]

Music among the Moravians in America in the eighteenth and nineteenth centuries was generally considered the property of the community, not of individuals. When a composer or musician moved from one location to another, he generally did not take all of his compositions with him; at least some of them remained in the music collection of the community where the composer had lived and worked. In many cases the same works are found in the collections of two or more Moravian settlements; it seems that copies of useful or beloved works were made and shared among communities.

Preservation and Rediscovery

The 1930s saw the beginnings of new explorations into the music of the American Moravians. Dr. Albert G. Rau, the dean of the Moravian Theological Seminary, collaborated with Dr. Hans T. David, a music scholar for the New York Public Library, in cataloging, researching, and publishing some of the music preserved by the Moravians in Bethlehem. In 1937, the Moravian Seminary and College for Women (now Moravian College and Theological Seminary) received a grant from the Penrose Fund of the American Philosophical Society to support research in Bethlehem for a year. Rau and David's *Catalogue of Music by American Moravians, 1742–1842*, was instrumental in bringing this music into the public eye, limited though it was to the music written by Moravians in America and preserved in Bethlehem. About two hundred fifty compositions were listed in this catalog.[82]

Other scholars in the 1930s added their research to the growing pool of knowledge. Through the efforts of Dr. Carleton Sprague Smith, chief of the Music Division of the New York Public Library, a set of ten vocal solos, at least one Moravian anthem, and the string quintets of Johann Friedrich Peter were published by C. F. Peters Corporation for the New York Public Library.

The growing interest among scholars working with the Moravian Archives and Central Moravian Church in Bethlehem, Pennsylvania, attracted the interest of Moravian clergy and lay people, who organized the first Early American Moravian Music Festival held in 1950 in Bethlehem. Dr. Thor Johnson, the conductor of the Cincinnati Symphony Orchestra and himself the son of a Moravian minister, served as music director and conductor. A second such Festival was held in 1954, and a third in 1955.[83]

Meanwhile, in 1954, Salem College in Winston-Salem, North Carolina, received a grant from Mr. Charles H. Babcock, Jr., to support musicological research into the history and significance of the music of the Moravians in America. Donald M. McCorkle was chosen to undertake this immense project, and he completed a number of articles and a doctoral dissertation within a very few years.

The success of the first three Early American Moravian Music Festivals led to the realization that an organization was needed to prepare music for those festivals, as well as to supervise the expanding research into that music. Again, Moravian clergy and lay persons collaborated, and the Moravian Music Foundation was chartered in 1956 for the purpose of studying, preserving, and disseminating knowledge of the music of the Moravians in America, with Donald McCorkle as its first director. Since that time, a major cataloging project was completed, with the support of the National Endowment for the Humanities; the total known body of music of the early American Moravians is closer to ten thousand manuscripts and early imprints than to Hans David's estimate of two hundred fifty. This includes both music by Moravian composers and works by other European composers that they copied and preserved in America, vocal and instrumental, manuscript and printed.

The full significance of the active musical life of the Moravians, even in America, cannot yet be evaluated. As the chapters that follow make clear, only portions of that musical life have been exhaustively researched. "Collected works" in scholarly editions simply do not exist for Moravian composers, even those few thought to have written all of their music in America, much less for the many more whose works were composed in Europe with copies brought to the American settlements.[84] Some highly significant studies have been made of the music education in Moravian schools; but the "ripple effect" of Moravian musical education has yet to be explored. How many of the non-Moravian students who learned music from the Moravians became teachers in other institutions? If, as musicologists in the mid-twentieth century believed, the actual *music* written and performed by the Moravians in America had little influence on the development of music in America, to what extent did the *music education* of the Moravians influence future generations of performers and composers?

If this is the case in America, research into the music of the Moravians elsewhere is still in its very infancy. Although several of the essays in this book focus primarily on aspects of Moravian music in America, I hope that the questions raised will spark research worldwide into the breathtaking richness and depth of the musical culture of the Moravians.

Notes

1. The term *curiosity* is taken from Ronald L. Davis's evaluation of the significance of the Moravians to the musical life of America, in his *History of Music in American Life*, vol. I, *The Formative Years, 1620–1865* (Malabar, FL: Robert Krieger Publishing Company, 1982), 31.

2. *Die Musik in Geschichte und Gegenwart* (Kassel and Basel, Bärenreiter, 1949–51).

3. Paul Henry Lang, *Music in Western Civilization* (New York: W.W. Norton, 1941), 692.

4. Hans T. David, "Introduction," in *Ten Sacred Songs for Soprano, Strings, and Organ*, edited by Hans T. David (New York: C. F. Peters Corporation for the New York Public Library, 1947), ii.

5. John Tasker Howard, *Our American Music*, 3rd ed. (New York: Thomas Y. Crowell, 1954), 29.

6. Gilbert Chase, *America's Music, from the Pilgrims to the Present* (New York: McGraw-Hill, 1955), 44–47, 58–60.

7. Davis, 26–31, 40–41, 51; J. Peter Burkholder, Donald Jay Grout, and Claudia V. Palisca, *A History of Western Music*, 7th edition (New York: W. W. Norton, 2006), 504–5.

8. Egon Wellesz and Frederick Sternfeld, eds., *The New Oxford History of Music*, vol. VII, *The Age of Enlightenment* (London: Oxford University Press, 1973), 328–32.

9. Richard Cullen Rath, *How Early America Sounded* (Ithaca, NY: Cornell University Press, 2003). Rath focuses his attention on the English-speaking settlers, as well as Native Americans, African Americans, and sounds of nature.

10. Salem Congregation Collection 37.1; Bethlehem Congregation Collection 174.4, 682.1, and 841.2; Bethlehem Scores 20.3.

11. In 1997, the Moravian Music Foundation adopted a music editorial policy that follows the trends in scholarly music editing shown in editions of Haydn (Joseph Haydn, *Works*, ed. and intro. by Jens Peter Larsen [Köln: Joseph Haydn-Institut; Munich: G. Henle Editions, 1958–], and *Kritische Ausgabe sämtlicher Symphonien*, ed. and intro. by H. C. Robbins Landon [Vienna: Universal Edition, 1965–68]); Sammartini (Bathia Churgin, ed., *The Symphonies of G. B. Sammartini* [Cambridge, MA: Harvard University Press, 1968]); Benda (*Six Sonatas for Solo Violin and Continuo*, ed. Douglas A. Lee, vol. XIII of *Recent Researches in the Music of the Classical Era* [Madison: A-R Editions, 1981]); Vanhal (*Six Symphonies*, ed. Paul Bryan, vols. XVII–XVIII of *Recent Researches in the Music of the Classical Era* [Madison: A-R Editions, 1985]); Rosetti (*Five Wind Partitas: Music for the Oettingen-Wallerstein Court*, ed. Sterling E. Murray, vols. XXX–XXXI of *Recent Researches in the Music of the Classical Era* [Madison: A-R Editions, 1989]); and C. P. E. Bach (*Carl Philip Emanuel Bach Edition*, Rachel W. Wade, general ed., E. Eugene Helm, coordinating ed. [Oxford and New York: Oxford University Press, 1989]). Over the past fifty years, the music editing community has developed the assumption that *the composer knew what he or she wanted*, and we should let his (or her) work shine through with minimal intervention from the editor.

12. Anja Wehrend, *Musikanschauung, Musikpraxis, Kantatenkomposition in der Herrnhuter Brüdergemeine* (Frankfurt am Main: Peter Lang, 1995).

13. Interest is growing in Moravian music beyond American borders. In 1999 a conference titled "In himmlischer Harmonie: Musik in der Geschichte der Herrnhuter Brüdergemeine" was sponsored by the Unitäts-Archiv in Herrnhut, Germany, partly with the goal of stimulating new research on Moravian music among European scholars. German-language research on Moravian music topics is listed in a bibliography by Peter Vogt, "A Bibliography of German Scholarship on Moravian Music," *Moravian Music Journal* 42/2 (Fall 1997): 15–22, and also "Bibliographie und Discographie zur Herrnhuter Musik," *Unitas Fratrum* 47 (2001): 128–36. The majority of German-language research publications date since 1965. (I am grateful to Alice Caldwell for the information in this footnote.)

Five Moravian brass musicians from South Africa attended the Twenty-First Moravian Music Festival held in Winston-Salem, North Carolina, in 2003. Their participation established relationships that have resulted in correspondence with the Moravian Music Foundation, revealing that in Moravian collections in South Africa are manuscript copies of some of the same sacred vocal music from the eighteenth and early nineteenth century that is found in Moravian collections in Europe and America.

Also of interest is the cataloging of the music collections of Moravian settlements in Labrador. Again, copies of eighteenth-century Moravian sacred vocal music are present. These instances raise questions regarding other areas, questions that will likely be answered only by a researcher traveling and examining the surviving records in person.

14. Donald M. McCorkle, *Moravian Music in Salem: A German-American Heritage* (PhD diss., Indiana University, 1958), 34.

15. See C. Daniel Crews, *Moravian Meanings: A Glossary of Historical Terms of the Moravian Church, Southern Province*, 2nd ed. (Winston-Salem: Moravian Archives, 1996).

16. The older spelling, *Gemeine*, is intentionally retained in place of the modern *Gemeinde*.

17. The locations and distances of several of these towns are taken from J. Thomas and T. Baldwin, eds., *Complete Pronouncing Gazetteer, or Geographical Dictionary, of the World* (Philadelphia: J. B. Lippincott & Co., 1855).

18. Rudolf Říčán, *The History of the Unity of Brethren*, trans. C. Daniel Crews (Bethlehem and Winston-Salem: Moravian Church in America, 1992), 5.

19. See Amédeo Molnár, "The Brethren's Theology," in Říčán, 390–420, for an overview of the history and main points of the Unity's theological understanding.

20. Molnár, "The Brethren's Theology," 408.

21. What Říčán calls "the loftiest literary and theological work which the Unity of Brethren produced" was the publication of the entire text of the Old and New Testaments in a new Czech translation in six parts printed in Kralice between 1579 and 1594. The entire translation (which had been prepared by a number of the Unity's theologians and writers) was published in a single volume in 1596. This translation achieved the status of the King James Version. In the nineteenth century, it was dubbed the Kralice Bible (Říčán, 270).

22. Thomas Sovík, "Music of the American Moravians: The First Tradition," *Czechoslovak and Central European Journal* (formerly *Kosmas*) 9, no. 1/2 (Summer/Winter 1990): 35–36.

23. Thomas Sovík, "Music Theorists of the Bohemian Reformation: Jan Blahoslav and Jan Josquin," *Journal of Czechoslovak and Central European Studies* (formerly *Kosmas*), Jan. 1989: 105–45.

24. Sovík, "Music of the American Moravians," 44.

25. Říčán, 248–49, 294–95.

26. Říčán, 343–48.

27. See Matthew Spinka, *John Amos Comenius: That Incomparable Moravian*, rev. ed. (New York: Russell and Russell, 1967).

28. Říčán, 363.

29. *Kšaft umírající matky Jednoty bratrské*; see Říčán, 363. See also John Amos Comenius, *The Bequest of the Unity*, tr. and ed. Matthew Spinka (Chicago: National Union of Czechoslovak Protestants in America, 1940).

30. This work, the *Řád církvení Jednoty Bratří českých* (Church Order of the Bohemian Brethren), was itself based on older documentation of the Unity's life and

organization, as well as current practice. It included expectations of members, priests, and church leaders, and was published in Lešno in 1632.

31. F. Ernest Stoeffler, *German Pietism During the Eighteenth Century*, vol. 24 of *Studies in the History of Religions* (Leiden: E. J. Brill, 1973), 39–41; Dale Brown, *Understanding Pietism* (Grand Rapids: William B. Eerdmans, 1978), 22.

32. Brown, 12.

33. Craig D. Atwood, *Community of the Cross: Moravian Piety in Colonial Bethlehem* (University Park: Pennsylvania State University Press, 2004), 28. For the early development of Pietism among English Puritans and on the European continent, see F. Ernest Stoeffler, *The Rise of Evangelical Pietism*, vol. 9 of *Studies in the History of Religions* (Leiden: E. J. Brill, 1971).

34. Brown, 21.

35. Atwood, 28.

36. Atwood, 6.

37. F. Ernest Stoeffler, *Continental Pietism and Early American Christianity* (Grand Rapids: William B. Eerdmans, 1976), 126–27; Stoeffler, *German Pietism*, 137–38.

38. Stoeffler, *German Pietism*, 139. The "Brotherly Agreement," with various revisions, has been a part of Moravian life since that time; in the twentieth century it was renamed the "Covenant for Christian Living."

39. Diary of Herrnhut, August 10, 1727. Cited in Hans-Christoph Hahn and Hellmut Reichel, *Zinzendorf und die Herrnhuter Brüder: Quellen zur Geschichte der Brüder-Unität von 1722 bis 1760* (Hamburg: Friedrich Wittig Verlag, 1977), 105. Translated in Gerhard Reichel, *The Story of the Thirteenth of August 1727*, trans. Douglas L. Rights (1927; rev. ed., Winston-Salem: Moravian Archives, 1994), 32. "[W]eil er zugleich sich vor Gott niederwarf, die mit ihm dahin fallende Gemeine fast außer sich selbst war. Es wurde mit Gebet, aneinander hangendem Gesang, Verbindung, Bereinigung zu einem Zweck und mit Knien und Flehen bis in die Mitternacht angehalten, die übrigen Separatisten vollends dahingezogen."

40. Diary of Herrnhut, August 13, 1727. Cited in Hahn and Reichel, 106. Translated in Reichel, *The Story*, 34. "Nachdem nun die innigste Salbung über uns alle ausgeflossen und wir nicht ferne von Ihm waren, baten wir in Glaubens-Gewißheit, er solle unsre beiden Ältesten, Christian David und Melchior Nitschmann (die aus guter Meinung, aber mit betrübtem Ausgang in Sorau waren), kräftig in unsre Gemeinschaft ziehen und erfahren lassen, was wir erfuhren."

41. Diary of Herrnhut, 28 August 1727. Cited in Hahn and Reichel, 107–8.

42. August Gottlieb Spangenberg, *Leben des Herrn Nicolaus Ludwig Grafen und Herrn von Zinzendorf und Pottendorf* (Barby: Zu finden in der Brüder-Gemeinen, 1772–74), 1:439. "Von der Zeit an ist Herrnhut zu einer lebendigen Gemeine Jesu Christi worden; von da an verbanden sich die Geschwister aufs neue mit einander, dem Heiland von ganzam Herzen treu zu seyn, und Ihm zu dienen, wo und wie Ers würde haben wollen. . . . Kurz: wir waren allezusammen voll Freuden fast wie ausser uns, fingen eine neue, und fast himlische Haushaltung unter und mit einander an, welche alte und junge zu geniessen krigten."

43. Reichel, *The Story*, 36.

44. The standard texts on Moravian history are Říčán, *The History of the Unity of Brethren*, covering the fifteenth-century Czech Reformation through the end of the seventeenth century; Edmund deSchweinitz, *History of the Unitas Fratrum* (Bethlehem: Moravian Publication Office, 1885), covering the same period; and J. Taylor Hamilton and Kenneth G. Hamilton, *History of the Moravian Church: The*

Renewed Unitas Fratrum, 1722–1957 (Bethlehem and Winston-Salem: Interprovincial Board of Christian Education, Moravian Church in America, 1967). At its 2002 meeting, the worldwide Moravian church's governing body, the Unity Synod, called for the writing of a history of the Unity.

45. Říčán, 382–83.

46. Hamilton, 32.

47. See Amédeo Molnár, "The Brethren's Theology," in Říčán, 390–420; also the following recent studies by the Moravian archivist and theologian C. Daniel Crews: *Confessing our Unity in Christ: Historical and Theological Background to the "Ground of the Unity"* (Winston-Salem: Moravian Archives, 1994); *This We Most Certainly Believe: Thoughts on Moravian Theology* (Winston-Salem: Moravian Archives, 2005); and "Questions of Moravian Identity," in *TMDK (Transatlantic Moravian Dialog-Korrespondenz)* 9 (July 1996): 26–32.

48. Atwood, 29.

49. Hamilton, 52–118.

50. Atwood, 4.

51. "In the eighteenth century Moravians made very frequent use of the Lot in an effort to determine the course of action which the Lord desired them to follow in any given instance. . . . After prayer, one of three Lots, usually slips of paper containing a Scripture verse, was drawn as the Lord's answer to the question at hand. One verse had a positive message, one a negative, and the other had a neutral statement which meant 'wait.' The use of the Lot lessened and finally disappeared as the nineteenth century developed. In the church records, an asterisk was often used to indicate that a decision had been submitted to the Lord through the Lot." C. Daniel Crews, *Moravian Meanings*, 2nd ed. (Winston-Salem: Moravian Archives, 1992), 18. See also Hahn and Reichel, 246–49.

52. Hamilton, 62–63.

53. See William Warren Sweet, *The Story of Religion in America* (New York: Harper & Brothers, 1950), 98–99; Edwin Scott Gaustad, *A Religious History of America*, rev. ed. (San Francisco: Harper & Row, 1990), 90–98.

54. Colin Podmore, *The Moravian Church in England, 1729–1760* (Oxford: Clarendon, 1998), 228. Podmore's informative book contains a chapter describing the events leading up to the 1749 act as well as its consequences for the Moravians.

55. Podmore, 263.

56. The loss of Herrnhaag is one of the saddest stories of eighteenth-century Moravian history. The overlord of Herrnhaag, well known for his policy of religious toleration, had been a supporter of Zinzendorf. His son, however, succeeded to his seat in 1749 and ordered the residents of Herrnhaag to swear allegiance to him alone and to repudiate Zinzendorf or face banishment. More than a thousand residents of Herrnhaag chose to vacate their homes and leave rather than show disloyalty to Zinzendorf, causing significant financial difficulties for the Moravian Church worldwide and for Bethlehem, since some two hundred of the Herrnhaag residents moved directly to Bethlehem. The story is significant not only because of the financial implications, but also for what it reveals about the Moravians' determination to remain faithful to their own identity and purpose, which they saw as given by Christ. See Atwood, 17.

57. Hamilton, 83; Sweet, 107.

58. Atwood, 11. Atwood (11–19) explores the various explanations that have been given of the Sifting Time and evaluates its significance for the Moravian Church.

59. *Alt- und neuer Brüder-Gesang von den Tagen Genochs bisher, für alle Kinder und Seelen Gottes* (London, 1753); *A Collection of Hymns of the Children of God in All Ages, From the Beginning till now. In Two Parts Designed chiefly for the Use of the Congregations in Union with the Brethren's Church* (London, 1754).

60. The preface to the German hymnal includes the following: "Ich glaube, daß dieses Gesangbuch in Effectu für eine Kirchen-Historie dienen kan, wenn sich der Leser die Mühe nimmt, das Ganze in einer Suite zu beaugen." In a parallel column, the following English version is given: "I think this Hymn-Book, when a Reader will review the Succession of the Whole, contains a Kind of Church-History in Effect." (*Alt- und neue Brüder-Gesang*, n.p.) From the preface to the English hymnal of 1754 comes this: "Considering it all together, it is a continued Series of godly and Christian Sentiments, both doctrinal and practical, thro' all the Ages of the Church; and consequently a Kind of Eccelsiastical History, with regard to the State of Piety and Devotion." (*A Collection of Hymns*, n.p.). See chapter 3, pp. 47–48, 51, for a discussion of these hymnals.

61. See Beverly Prior Smaby, *The Transformation of Moravian Bethlehem: From Communal Mission to Family Economy* (Philadelphia: University of Pennsylvania Press, 1988), 99ff, 105–20; Elisabeth W. Sommer, *Serving Two Masters: Moravian Brethren in Germany and North Carolina, 1727–1801* (Lexington: University Press of Kentucky, 2000), 35–39; C. Daniel Crews and Richard W. Starbuck, *With Courage for the Future* (Winston-Salem: Moravian Church in America, Southern Province, 2002), 48–49. For implications for music in particular, see Pauline Fox, *Reflections on Moravian Music: A Study of Two Collections of Manuscript Books in Pennsylvania ca. 1800* (PhD diss., New York University, 1997), 217, 224–27.

62. Hamilton, 113, 180. See also Carola Wessel, "Connecting Congregations: The Net of Communication among the Moravians as Exemplified by the Interaction between Pennsylvania, the Upper Ohio Valley, and Germany (1772–1774)," in *The Distinctiveness of Moravian Culture: Essays and Documents in Moravian History in Honor of Vernon H. Nelson on His Seventieth Birthday*, ed. Craig D. Atwood and Peter Vogt (Nazareth: Moravian Historical Society, 2003), 153–72.

63. Peter Vogt, "Introduction," in Atwood and Vogt, *The Distinctiveness of Moravian Culture*, 3–4.

64. Atwood, 176.

65. Arthur J. Freeman, *An Ecumenical Theology of the Heart: The Theology of Count Nicholas Ludwig von Zinzendorf* (Bethlehem and Winston-Salem: Moravian Church in America, 1998), 67. Chapter 1, "Zinzendorf and His Context," provides a helpful analysis of the various influences on Zinzendorf's theological thought, including the Enlightenment, Pietism, Lutheranism, and mysticism.

66. Harry H. Hall, *The Moravian Wind Ensemble: Distinctive Chapter in America's Music* (PhD diss., George Peabody College for Teachers, 1967), 53.

67. Christian Gregor, ed., *Choral-Buch* (1784). A facsimile edition was published by the Moravian Music Foundation Press in 1984.

68. Synod results, 18 November 1750. Quoted in Hahn and Reichel, 222: "Eine Gemeine des Heilands muß ohne Buch singen können, denn sie soll in der Sache leben. Einem Fremden reicht man ein Gesangbuch . . ."

69. Christian I. LaTrobe, *Anthems for One, Two, or more Voices performed in the Church of the United Brethren, Collected and the Instrumental parts adapted for the Organ or Piano Forte, Composed by various Authors* (London: Printed for the Editor, 1811), 2. For most of his life, LaTrobe served in England, where the music and worship of the Moravian congregations was quite similar to those in Germany, with their use of instruments

along with the organ. See Karl Kroeger, "A Preliminary Survey of Musical Life in the English Moravian Settlements of Fulneck, Fairfield, and Ockbrook During the 18th and 19th Centuries," *Moravian Music Journal* 29/1 (Spring 1984): 20–25, and Podmore, 150. The English Moravian churches had music collections similar to those of the German congregations, making it unlikely that LaTrobe's publication was intended for the Moravian congregations. This introduction, then, explains Moravian music and worship practice to those outside the Moravian Church.

70. Hans T. David, *Musical Life in the Pennsylvania Settlements of the Unitas Fratrum* (*Transactions of the Moravian Historical Society*, 1942; repr., Winston-Salem: Moravian Music Foundation Publications No. 6, 1959), 9.

71. James Boeringer, "Sources for the Moravian Tunes in Gregor's 1784 Choral-Buch," in *Choral-Buch*, ed. Christian Gregor (1784; repr., facsimile ed. 1984), 40.

72. See chapter 2., pp. 36–37.

73. LaTrobe, 3.

74. Podmore, 151.

75. Podmore, 151. Citations are for the Pilgrim House Diary 1742–48: October 20, 1748, July 19, 1745, April 10, 1747, and October 27, 1748. The reporting of dates through the middle of the eighteenth century can be confusing, since Germany had adopted the Gregorian calendar by 1700, while Great Britain (and America, then a British colony) did not do so until September of 1752. Dates according to the Julian calendar are referenced as "old style" (o.s.), while those in the Gregorian calendar are "new style" (n.s.). See William Bridgewater and Seymour Kurtz, ed., *The Columbia Encyclopedia*, 3rd ed. (New York and London, Columbia University Press, 1963), 317.

76. Salem Diary, April 19, 1778, in Adelaide L. Fries, *Records of the Moravians in North Carolina* (Raleigh: North Carolina Historical Commission, 1926), 3: 1228.

77. A significant part of the spiritual life of Moravians was the writing of a *Lebenslauf*, a spiritual autobiography that was completed after death by the pastor and then read at the funeral. These documents, filed in the archives of the Moravian Church, reveal a great deal about the spiritual struggles of individuals and contain much factual and genealogical evidence. The *Lebensläufe* of prominent Moravians were printed and distributed to congregations worldwide. This custom continues today, in somewhat modified form. Most present-day "memoirs" are prepared by the pastor after the subject has died; they rely on information supplied by the family rather than on the deceased's own reflections.

78. LaTrobe, 2.

79. Hall, 70–71. For an extensive study of Moravian musical education in Pennsylvania, as evidenced by the manuscript music books used by teachers and students, see Fox, *Reflections on Moravian Music*, especially 34–41.

80. Fox, 4.

81. Fox, 2.

82. Albert G. Rau and Hans T. David, *A Catalogue of Music by American Moravians, 1742–1842* (Bethlehem: Moravian Seminary and College for Women, 1938). See McCorkle, 8; David, "Introduction," *Ten Sacred Songs*, iii.

83. Moravian Music Festivals continue to this day, sponsored by the Moravian Church in America. The twenty-second Moravian Music Festival was held in Columbus, Ohio, in July 2006.

84. For instance, David Moritz Michael (1751–1827) lived in America from 1795 to 1815. During that time he composed two large woodwind suites, fourteen woodwind *Parthien*, and a number of vocal solos and anthems. Although he received his

musical training in Europe and worked in Germany after leaving America, he is not known to have composed any music other than during his twenty years in America. Similarly, Johann Christian Bechler (1784–1857) lived in Europe for the last twenty years of his life; but although he composed many anthems (and one woodwind suite) in America, he is not known to have composed any music while in Europe.

Chapter Two

Moravian Worship

The Why of Moravian Music

C. Daniel Crews

Those who have studied the music of eighteenth- and early nineteenth-century Moravian composers have been impressed with the skill and artistry of many of them. As with anything else, however, the full explication and appreciation of their music and gifts requires some knowledge and understanding of the context, the matrix, within which they wrote, and for Moravian composers that necessarily leads to a consideration of Moravian worship.

A musicologist who knows nothing of the Moravian Church or of its theology and life in the eighteenth century can, of course, analyze and certainly appreciate Moravian music. In reality, though, that approach is similar to observing a prehistoric honeybee preserved in a block of amber. The carcass of the bee is there to behold, and one can provide a description, even a minute analysis, of the bee: its size, wingspread, coloration, and all the rest. This can give only the vaguest idea of the essence of the bee, however. It cannot begin to fathom the full life of the bee: the meadows in which it lived, its relation to its fellow bees, the beauty of its soaring flight in a fleeting dawn millennia ago.

Of course, the case of this music is not exactly like that of the bee in amber. We are not restricted merely to a fossilized determining of the most frequent key signatures and characteristic harmonizations. We are fortunate to be able to get more than a lifeless appreciation of Moravian music simply by playing it or hearing it played. That is certainly an advance over the petrified insect, though even this is still somewhat like thinking we one may know all about a prehistoric bee by seeing a live one buzzing around in a cage. It still is not the same as experiencing reality with the bee in its natural habitat.

Naturally, we cannot conjure up the eighteenth century Moravian Church to experience its music fully in its essential setting—its "natural habitat"—any more than we can conjure up that bee's prehistoric meadows and flowers. Still, the more we know about those meadows and flowers, the more we can more fully appreciate and understand the bee and its enrichment of all of life. Similarly, the more we know of the Moravian Church—its life, and particularly its worship in the eighteenth century—the richer and more helpful will be our appreciation and understanding of that music. After all, it was for use in Moravian worship services that almost all of this music was written (except for a few instrumental works). Moravian worship, then, is the *why* of Moravian music.

Fortunately, because of the Moravians' penchant for recording the crucial factors in their lives, and for preserving these records in their archives, we have ample means of knowing in depth the context in which these Moravian musicians lived, wrote, and performed.

In Zinzendorf's thought, and in that of the Moravians of his time, all of life was "liturgical." That is, every aspect of life, even the most mundane, was a sort of worship to be offered to God, after the example of Christ himself. An entry in the *Jüngerhaus-Diarium*, the diary of Zinzendorf's official household, for April of 1760 describes the liturgical life:

> The liturgical state of being is a certain fixed, solid essence, which is ever present, so that if it is called to a holy, godly action it never first needs to collect itself, but can always remain in a natural state which belongs to it anyway, and can thus go and do whatever is to be done. For this essence proceeds in a liturgical course with the soul, and it never comes out of its liturgical mode. A person becomes accustomed to this little by little: to do all one's affairs, sweeping out, cleaning house, whatever one may call it and whatever may be produced, from the greatest to the least and lowest act—to do this with a dignity, whereby one's likeness to Jesus shines forth and loses nothing thereby. That is what liturgical means.[1]

For this reason, such normally "secular" matters as beginning a new business or reaping the fields had a religious connotation.[2]

To give this ideal of life concrete expression, and to nurture the souls of those who would live it, practical realities naturally led to the development of various worship services and devotions that gave the Moravian communities a character of their own.[3] As the Moravian theologian Craig Atwood observes in his dissertation on Moravian life and liturgy in mid-eighteenth century Bethlehem in Pennsylvania: "Nearly every aspect of life was incorporated into the communal rituals in an attempt to bring the secular into the sacred sphere by connecting daily life to the life and death of Jesus."[4] As Bishop Kenneth Hamilton stated:

> Ample provision was made for the cultivation of the religious life in early Herrnhut. Daily services brought the adults together soon after dawn; brief devotions followed for the aged and infirm at 8:30 o'clock and for the children at 10. Each day closed with common worship.[5]

At first, the Moravians had continued to worship in the Lutheran parish church at Berthelsdorf. It became customary to repeat on Sunday afternoons in Herrnhut the sermon that Pastor Rothe preached in the morning at Berthelsdorf. Zinzendorf or another layman would read the sermon for those who had not been able to attend the parish service.[6] Gradually other people from the area started attending this afternoon gathering, and it became known as the *Fremdenstunde*, the strangers' service. In the evening, however, another service "specially designed to edify souls assured of their relationship to the Savior" was held for the Moravians alone. This was known as the *Gemeinstunde*, or congregation service. Other services were added to these, specifically the *Bettag* or *Gemeintag*, "a monthly festival, devoted especially to the reading of reports or letters from Christian friends—later from missionaries in various fields of labor. These services did much to foster enthusiasm for missions."[7] Beginning in 1730, baptisms were also celebrated in Herrnhut, as was the Holy Communion after 1731. Other characteristic Moravian services made their appearance as well, the Easter dawn service in 1732, and the Watchnight service at New Year's Eve in 1733. As Moravians spread to new settlements across the world, their worship patterns continued to resemble closely those of Herrnhut.

Among the materials developed for Moravian worship services, the litanies and liturgies occupy a central role. The distinction between a liturgy and a litany was not always clearly maintained in Moravian statements about them, and the two terms are often used interchangeably. In general, however, "A litany is a church prayer and is more or less standardized. 'Liturgy' is a less precise term. It may refer to the entire worship service or a long hymn, sometimes called a liturgical hymn, on a single theme."[8]

Best known among the litanies were the large Church Litany (adapted from that of Martin Luther) and the Litany of the Wounds. The Church Litany, essentially a long responsive intercession for the church and the world, was generally sung on Sundays, not as part of a preaching service, but as a separate occasion for worship on its own. It was an all-encompassing prayer, and it is significant that other concerns and rituals in the life of the congregation were incorporated into it as appropriate. Thus, at the prayer for travelers, the names of congregation members who were on a journey might be mentioned. Names of individual missionaries could be added at the prayer for missions. In addition, the sacrament of baptism for infants might be celebrated in conjunction with the prayer for children; marriages might be celebrated at the prayer for homes; and ordinations might be administered at the prayer for ministers.[9] In the Church Litany, both symbolically and actually, the whole life of the congregation in the broadest context was incorporated into a formal act of worship.

The Litany of the Wounds was another favorite litany in the mid-1700s. As the name suggests, it focused on the sufferings of Christ the Redeemer. In 1753 this was divided into two parts: the Litany of the Life, Suffering, and Death of Christ; and the Hymn of the Wounds.[10] This litany was used on various occasions, such as the Sunday a week before Holy Communion was to be celebrated, or during an evening service, particularly on the weekends. This was appropriate, since throughout the year the Friday-through-Sunday progression was a minicelebration of the Passion-Resurrection event, mirroring each week the great annual Good Friday to Easter festival.[11]

The liturgies were generally shorter services, sometimes consisting of a hymn with verses that were sung in turn by various groups within the congregation (leader, men, women, etc.). An account that Traugott Bagge prepared in 1778 in Salem, North Carolina to give to "visitors of distinction" says that the men and women sang the liturgies antiphonally as well as together.[12] The Passion Chorale (*O Sacred Head, Now Wounded*) was used as a "liturgy" in this way and was a favorite for Friday evenings, which naturally recalled the Crucifixion. Other liturgies were addressed to the Father, the Son, and the Holy Spirit. Of course, given the centrality of Christ in Moravian theology, more than one was addressed to Christ, and even the one to the Father speaks mostly of God as the father of Christ. Certain liturgies were assigned for the use of particular "choirs."[13] All these liturgies were used in a variety of services, generally being assigned to the weekday devotions in a regular order.

Another significant addition to Moravian worship materials was made with the introduction of the *Losungen*, or Daily Texts, in 1728. These texts could be private devotionals, but they also assumed corporate congregational importance as well. Bishop Kenneth Hamilton describes the origin of the Textbook as follows:

> It had been Zinzendorf's custom to deliver addresses in the singing meetings each evening, either on a text of Scripture or on a hymn stanza. On the third of May [1728] he proposed that the stanza which had served as his theme become the *Losung*, or watchword, for the congregation on the following day. Thereafter he continued to do this each evening, and a record of these watchwords was preserved. Toward the end of the year and early in the following, Zinzendorf made a collection of suitable Scripture texts with the help of the elders. It was completed on June 29. From it an elder drew a text at the evening service. On the following morning each household received this text as the watchword for that day. Often a brief exhortation would be added. This practice continued in 1730. In 1731 a collection of texts for the entire ensuing year was printed.[14]

From that time on, Moravians throughout the world, whether in Germany, North America, or Africa, used these texts as a daily devotional guide, either in private devotions or in the brief morning or evening services for the whole congregation or a specific part of it. The Moravians took great comfort from the fact that wherever they were, they were using the same texts as their brothers and sisters far away. Of course, given the state of eighteenth-century travel, deliveries of textbooks could not always be made on time. In such cases the people simply used the texts for the year before until the new ones arrived, or else they used those for an earlier year in which the days of the week and dates corresponded to the current year.[15]

We can also note that although the eighteenth-century *Losungen* were generally drawn from scripture texts, they might also consist of a hymn stanza or a portion of one. This was characteristic of the Moravian Church, for the church expressed its theology most frequently and visibly in its hymnody and music. Unlike the Lutherans, whose main theological tenets received official expression in the Augsburg Confession and the other confessional documents of the Book of Concord, the Moravians tended to profess the core of their belief in their liturgies and hymns. We should also remember that the Renewed Moravian Church was actually born in a worship service, namely the communion service of August 13, 1727, sometimes called the Moravian Pentecost, when the brethren's former divisions and diversity of purpose were so welded into one that the life and mission of the church could have a new beginning.[16] "Zinzendorf insisted that the truest language for heart religion is song. . . . For Zinzendorf and the *Brüdergemeine* in Bethlehem, the truths of the Christian religion are best communicated in poetry and song, not in systematic theology or polemics."[17] With characteristic understatement, Bishop Hamilton says, "[T]he Moravian Church had given to hymn singing a prominence in worship not to be met within the traditions of other communions."[18] Zinzendorf himself had encouraged hymn singing. In the early days of Herrnhut, when the community did not yet enjoy a large repertoire of hymns, he conducted singing classes in which he taught not only the hymns, but something of the life and purpose of the author.[19] A large hymnal was produced in 1735, and many more texts were added in its numerous appendices. Slightly more manageable collections were made in 1754 and 1767. In 1778 the extremely influential hymnbook of Christian Gregor appeared, which remained in use among the German-speaking congregations for about a century. This contained 1,750 hymns, 308 of them written or recast by Gregor himself. Gregor's procedure in compiling these hymns is also instructive: "In many instances he had taken familiar stanzas from originally different hymns and combined them, often weaving them together with additional stanzas of his own composing."[20]

Gregor's procedure of recombining and adding to the stanzas of hymns may sound a bit unusual. In fact, however, that was a very "Moravian" thing to do. Indeed, this sort of approach, which combined new and old hymn stanzas in creative ways, was central to that most characteristic of Moravian services, the *Singstunde*. In speaking of Zinzendorf's care for the worship life of the Moravians, Hamilton writes:

He actively cultivated within the Herrnhut congregation an appreciation for the spiritual power of hymnody and gradually developed a unique kind of service called the *Singstunde*, which became in time his favorite form of public worship. In it the brother in charge selected with care individual stanzas from various hymns in such a manner that they would develop some Christian truth as the singing progressed. The congregation, which possessed an unusual command of the hymnal, would fall in with the leader before he reached the end of the first line of each stanza, singing by heart. No address was given on such occasions; none was needed.[21]

The beginning of the *Singstunden* appears to have been in the summer of 1727 when it became customary to sing a number of hymns relating to the theme of the day following the Sunday catechism instruction.[22] This soon led to the practice of weaving together appropriate verses from several hymns into one service. The preface to the hymnal of 1735 gives a further description: "One does not sing entire hymns of ten or twenty stanzas, but rather out of so many hymns half and whole stanzas, as the cohesive nature of the matter requires them."[23] As Hans-Christoph Hahn and Hellmut Reichel rightly observe, this progression from stanza to stanza or half stanza and melody to melody led to a new unity of these diverse parts, which then formed a real *Liederpredigt* (sermon in song).[24] For Zinzendorf, the singing of a congregation was a crucial indication of its spiritual life, and the members were expected to know many hymns by heart so as to be able to participate fully in the service: "A congregation of the Savior must be able to sing without a book, for they are to live in the matter itself."[25] Zinzendorf also remarked in 1754 that "the *Singstunden* are a remarkable beauty of our church. It is a defect if regular daily *Singstunden* are not held."[26]

Wherever they went, Moravians took the practice of *Singstunden* with them, and they were held regularly in Moravian churches throughout the world. In Herrnhut in the early years they were a standard feature of evening devotions.[27] In Bethlehem in 1747, for example, the weekly liturgical schedule called for a *Singstunde* to be held on Saturdays.[28] Similarly, *Singstunden* formed a part of the regular daily devotions of the Moravian settlers during their first year in North Carolina.[29] This continued in the following years, though by 1770 *Singstunden* were supplemented in the evening devotions with Bible readings, *Nachrichten* (reports from Moravians around the world), and collections of sermons read for edification.[30] They remained, however, a major factor in the worship life of the Moravian Church.

Important as the *Singstunden* themselves were, their form also had a great influence on the structure of two other important types of Moravian worship services. These were Holy Communion (*Abendmahl*) and the lovefeast (*Liebesmahl*).

Holy Communion, of course, is a central act of worship for all Christians, and it should come as no surprise that it was also highly esteemed in the Moravian Church. Zinzendorf referred to it as the "most intimate of all connection with the person of the Savior."[31] The real presence of Christ was thankfully received, though, typically, the Moravians refrained from delving too much into the precise way the Savior was sacramentally present.[32]

The sacrament was celebrated at first four times a year, and later monthly. Its administration was a very solemn event. Preparations for it began on the Sunday before, when the Litany of the Wounds was usually prayed.[33] During the week before the celebration, members met individually with their choir leaders for *Sprechen* (Speaking), during which they earnestly examined the state of their souls. Generally, beginning in the 1740s there was a lovefeast (*Liebesmahl*) before the communion service itself, and one of the Christ litanies might also be prayed at this time. Immediately preceding the communion itself there was an absolution. This is described by Craig Atwood:

> Communion itself began with a long process of absolution which sealed the confession to their choir leader. The congregation lay prostrate before the communion table, which often had a painting of Christ hanging on the wall behind it, and prayed silently while the liturgist offered a corporate prayer of confession. Those things which were deemed destructive to the soul of the brothers and sisters and to the communal mission were symbolically transferred to Christ who acted as the scapegoat for their sin. . . . This confession could be very emotional, but the emotions were generally a blend of shame and sorrow for having displeased the Savior and joy over having been forgiven. . . . Following the absolution and reconciliation through the kiss of peace, the elements were consecrated through the singing of Jesus' words at the Last Supper.[34]

In the earliest Moravian communion celebrations, the elements were distributed in the Lutheran manner, with groups of communicants coming to the front of the church to receive them. Beginning about 1742, however, modifications were introduced so that finally the usage came to be for the communicants to remain in their seats and for the ministers to bring the elements to them. Hymns were sung during the distribution of the elements, which were then shared by all at once.[35]

It is in the singing of hymn stanzas during the distribution of the communion elements that the influence of the *Singstunde* form on the *Abendmahl* service appears. The stanzas selected focused on the themes of redemption, Christ's sacrifice, and the heavenly banquet that the faithful would share at the end of time.[36] This, of course, sounds like the way a *Singstunde* was compiled. Indeed, we might say that the Moravian *Abendmahl* service was actually a *Singstunde* with the sacrament incorporated into it. Of course, this was a very special *Singstunde*, and we have seen all the other elements (litanies, "Speaking," lovefeast, absolution, kiss of peace) that were combined to form the entirety of the Moravian experience of Holy Communion. The actual service of Holy Communion itself, however, bore a decided resemblance in form to the *Singstunde*.

The same is true of the Moravian lovefeast (*Liebesmahl*), which has become perhaps the most widely known of special Moravian services. The origin of Moravian lovefeasts, following the renewing experience of the communion service at Berthelsdorf on 13 August 1727, is well known. Bishop Spangenberg's account tells the story simply:

> Upon the return of the congregation on August 13 from the Lord's Supper it had celebrated at Berthelsdorf, it met without prearrangement in seven separate groups. So that

they might be able to remain together without being disturbed, the count sent each of them some food from his kitchen for dinner. This they partook of together in love.[37]

Having once experienced the spiritual nourishment of the sharing of a simple common meal, the Moravians quickly came to see the value of continued similar experiences in a worship context.

> At first lovefeasts were limited to private groups. These gatherings represented conscious imitation of the *agapai* of the primitive church. On days of special significance or on Sunday evenings or in connection with weddings they would be conducted at Zinzendorf's house, with only a small group participating. The elders also had their lovefeasts. Later the custom spread to other groups, and finally to the congregation as a whole. Not until the Wetteravian period [1740s] did it become customary to hold such services preparatory to the Holy Communion. Often water and bread were served on these occasions in the early years, or water only. The service itself consisted of singing, free conversation, and the narration of religious experiences.[38]

It hardly needs to be noted that the "free conversation" mentioned above was quite different from a chance to gossip.

> Frequently the participants would have the opportunity to talk during the lovefeast; however, "worldly talk" was not permitted. Worshipers were expected to discuss their personal religious experience or other religious themes and concepts. New hymns were debuted and significant events were discussed but through it all the theme of twofold communion, with Christ and the *Gemeine* was stressed.[39]

The relation of the form of the *Liebesmahl* to that of the *Singstunde* is evident. Various hymn stanzas were selected to develop a theme for the day. If Holy Communion can be characterized as a *Singstunde* with the sacrament included, then the lovefeast can be characterized as a *Singstunde* with a simple fellowship meal included.

By the 1750s the lovefeasts had come to be celebrated in the church with hymns and the serving of a beverage and a simple bread or bun. As noted, in time some lovefeasts preceded Holy Communion. Others celebrated annual choir festivals, congregational anniversaries, etc. They might also be used at weddings or on birthdays, or to welcome travelers.

Indeed, by 1756 the lovefeast had often become the high point of the celebration of major festivals in the Moravian Church.[40] To enrich the celebration of these important festival days for the choirs or congregation, the hymn stanzas of the lovefeast were supplemented by the inclusion of anthems written by Moravian composers or borrowed from others. Bagge's 1778 explanation of the Moravians describes these services as follows:

> For the festivals of the Christian Church in general, and for the festal memorial Days peculiar to the Brethren's Church, some Psalms and Cantatas have been composed and

printed from time to time. These are performed by a musical choir in each Congregation, with gentle Music on Instruments, & the Congregation accompanies the same with singing at intervals Choruses suitable to the matter.[41]

In the context of this description, the "Psalms" would be the "odes" or orders of service for the lovefeast, including the hymn and anthem texts, and the "Cantatas" would be the choir anthems. The "Choruses" are hymns, and these orders of service (thousands of which are extant) are characterized by the alternation of anthems and hymn stanzas, all suited to the theme of the service. Indeed, except for hymns, most of the pieces we know today as "Moravian music" are the anthems written for these special celebrations, which generally included lovefeasts. On occasion, though, a festival *Singstunde* might be enriched with an anthem, as on January 1, 1784 in Salem: "In the evening there was a *Singstunde* for praise and thanksgiving, at the beginning of which a chorus sang: *The mountains shall depart . . . but my mercy shall not depart from thee.*"[42] In her *Catalog of the Salem Congregation Music*, Frances Cumnock states that an anthem or two were usually sung at the conclusion of the Sunday preaching services.[43] She also notes that anthems were sung during funeral services.[44] However, at least as far as research has shown to date, the festal lovefeasts seem to have been the major occasions for the composition of new anthems.

Writing in his memoir (*Lebenslauf*), Christian Gregor spoke of his part in composing musical works for such services:

> From the year 1759 I felt in me a special leading to prepare now and then a Psalm for the festival days of the *Gemeine* and its choir divisions, and sometimes to set to music the biblical texts occurring in them, and at times to use for these other appropriate compositions—with a few necessary modifications. I continued with this for several years, as much as time allowed me.[45]

The scripture texts of which Gregor spoke were frequently the *Losungen* (Daily Texts), and quite often the odes for festivals contain an anthem setting of the *Losung* for the day. The manuscripts of many of the anthems themselves note that they were written for the *Losung* of a particular day. Of course, particularly at the major festivals of the Christian year, many additional appropriate Scripture texts might suggest themselves, and these might be used instead of the *Losung* specifically assigned. Then, too, an anthem written for one anniversary or festival might do just as well for another (sometimes with slight or more extensive rewriting to fit the local occasion). Such variations were completely acceptable. We can take Gregor's practice of recombining materials in new ways as typical of other Moravian composers of the period.

Especially in the eighteenth and early nineteenth centuries, Moravian services tended to be simple in comparison to those of some other denominations. Still, festal lovefeasts, with anthems and organ and chamber ensemble accompaniments, could at times verge on the more elaborate. Yet the Moravian worship ideal called on members never to forget the basic purpose of all services: to promote devotion to the Savior and love to one another. As Christian David[46] said in describing the lovefeasts in 1735: "The purpose of our lovefeasts is to awaken love among the Brethren and to obtain a proper confidence towards one another in order always to become still more in fellowship with one another."[47]

This did not mean that Moravian worship forms were static throughout the period. Indeed, Zinzendorf insisted that they not become so.[48]

These rituals were intended to foster the Christocentric heart religion of Zinzendorf; thus there were changes from time to time so that they would continue to "speak to the heart." This was true to Zinzendorf's assertion that "in a congregation [*Gemeine*] of Jesus nothing should be done apathetically and by half measures but everything should go on with constant uniformity and conscientiousness." Things could be dropped or altered in a *Gemeine*, unlike in the established religions where "once anything is introduced, it endures in spite of there being neither spirit nor power in it any longer." However, even with changes in practice, the rituals in Bethlehem had a core that remained constant.[49]

This idea is also quite in keeping with a theological statement that the Moravians made at the "doctrinal synod" held at Marienborn, Germany, in 1740:[50]

Every church and every dispensation has insights of its own. If one puts them in writing they become a confession of faith, like the one we presented to the King of Sweden in 1735. We, however, make no symbol of them as the Lutherans (1577), which may not be altered. We want to retain freedom, so that our Saviour may enlighten our doctrine from time to time.[51]

In this, theology and worship went hand in hand. Worship forms might change somewhat as doctrine was "enlightened." This "enlightenment" was more in the sense of fine tuning rather than radical revision, however. Just as the essential core of the doctrine remained constant, so the basic nature of the worship services remained firm.

The Moravian worship ideal left little space for the egos of the preparer and leader of those services. Not only the ordained clergy, but all who held any office in the church, were seen as fulfilling a ministry and call of God.[52] Therefore, they were to be respected. This did not mean, however, that being granted a position in the church was for the glory of the individual. Respect was to be given to the office, not to the individual who held it.[53]

It is in this regard that Craig Atwood, in citing a report from 1757 in Bethlehem, can say that the religious purpose of music in the *Gemeine* was so vital that the leaders in Bethlehem could assert that the position of organist is also an office of the Holy Spirit and must be led by the Holy Spirit.[54] So crucial was it that the worship be a living voice of the Spirit, that Zinzendorf insisted that anyone who was not in a proper frame of mind should not undertake to lead a service.[55] Indeed, he went so far as to say that someone who held a service without the proper devotion "prostituted" himself.[56]

All that has been said before provides the context in which Moravian composers wrote their music. We tend to concentrate our attention on their anthems, but as we have seen, though the anthems tended to be used on the festal days of the church, they were only a portion of those services. We must also take into account the broad range of weekly, monthly, and annual services as described above that composed the broader whole of Moravian worship in the eighteenth and nineteenth centuries.

Neither should we forget that writing anthems was only a limited part of the duties of most of these musicians in the church. Like Gregor, they were to write music "as much as time allowed." In Salem for example, besides composing music, Johann Friedrich Peter helped in compiling orders of service, played the organ, taught music, taught in the boys school, preached, baptized, served communion, and served as secretary and congregational diary keeper. He also frequently held services in the outlying "country congregations" as well, where besides preaching and administering the sacraments, he sometimes played the organ and sang the anthems himself if a choir was not available. And in all of this, his purpose was supposed to be not to seek his own glory, but to serve Christ and the church. It is no accident that in recording the "Psalm of Joy" celebration at the end of the American Revolution the diarist (Peter himself) did not mention that it was he who had put the service together.[57]

This certainly in no way diminishes the value and beauty of Peter's or other Moravian composers' sacred compositions, or their musical artistry. It does, however, allow us to see these compositions better in the context in which they were written, to view them more in the way we might expect Moravians of the time to see them. In so doing, we begin to bring that hypothetical honeybee a little farther out of its block of amber.

Within the full context of Moravian worship, music was intended to strengthen the whole fabric of interconnecting services that fostered the hallowing of all of life to God. Anthems were expected to join in the greater harmony of Moravian spirituality, not to stand out as independent gems on their own. This sheds light on a troubling passage in Johann Friedrich Peter's *Lebenslauf*, in which he describes his spiritual struggle with his musical gift.

> The problem was not with the music itself—rather, it was going almost too well. The people received his efforts gladly and with praise. It was, in fact, this praise which worried Peter. As he says, "Namely, my musical gift could soon have become dangerous to me; I noticed that this was valued by the world and it was secretly affecting me." He was obviously concerned about getting a swelled head and being distracted from more usual sorts of humble service. Fortunately, he was able to overcome this tension, and his playing and composing of music continued.[58]

Peter's music was better than good, and it is not unreasonable to think that he and some other Moravian composers could have made a name for themselves in circles outside the church had they chosen to do so. The best of them might well have attracted to themselves a good deal of fame and glory. But that was not what these musicians were about. Their aim was not to glory themselves, but to serve, specifically in the worship of the church. That is the "why" of their music.

Notes

1. *Jüngerhaus-Diarium*, 20 April 1760. II, 228. Cited in Hans-Christoph Hahn and Hellmut Reichel, *Zinzendorf und die Herrnhuter Brüder* (Hamburg: Friedrich Wittig, 1977), 212f: "Liturgisch ist ein gewisses, gesetztes, solides Wesen, das sich immer gegenwärtig ist, das, wenn es zu einer heiligen, göttlichen Handlung berufen wird, niemals erst eine Fassung braucht, sondern allemal in seiner naturellen Situation bleiben kann, wie ihm ohnedem ist, und so hingehen und tun kann, was zu tun ist. Dann geht's in einem liturgischen Gang mit der Seele, und sie kommt nie aus ihrem liturgischen Fach; der Mensch gewöhnt sich nach und nach: alle seine Handlungen, auskehren, Häuser waschen, wie man's nennen mag und was vorkommen kann, von der größten bis zur kleinsten und niederträchtigsten Verrichtung mit einer Dignität [Würde] zu tun, dabei die Jesushaftigkeit herausblickt und nichts dabei verliert. Das heißt liturgisch." Copies of the *Jüngerhaus-Diarium* were sent to Moravian centers throughout the world to be read in congregation meetings.

2. Gillian Lindt Gollin, *Moravians in Two Worlds* (New York: Columbia University Press, 1967), 20.

3. See Hahn and Reichel, 217.

4. Craig Atwood, "Blood, Sex, and Death: Life and Liturgy in Zinzendorf's Bethlehem" (PhD diss., Princeton Theological Seminary, 1995), 164.

5. J. Taylor and Kenneth G. Hamilton, *History of the Moravian Church* (Bethlehem: Interprovincial Board of Christian Education, Moravian Church in America, 1967), 37. Kenneth Hamilton was a Moravian bishop who revised his father J. Taylor Hamilton's original work. This revision, here cited, is the standard history of the Renewed Moravian Church. See also Beverly Smaby, *The Transformation of Moravian Bethlehem* (Philadelphia: University of Pennsylvania Press, 1988), 14–22.

6. Zinzendorf did not receive Lutheran ordination until 1735. He was consecrated a Moravian bishop in 1737.

7. Hamilton, 37.

8. Atwood, 146.

9. Atwood, 146.

10. Atwood, 151n.

11. Atwood, 149.

12. Adelaide Fries, ed., *Records of the Moravians in North Carolina* (Raleigh: North Carolina Historical Commission, 1926), 3:1011f. Bagge's work is actually an English translation of an earlier work by Bishop Spangenberg.

13. See chapter 1, p. 16, for a description of the Moravians' "choir system."

14. Hamilton, 38f.

15. More than 1.5 million copies of the 2007 *Moravian Daily Texts*, noted as the two hundred seventy-seventh year, were printed in fifty-one languages and dialects. (*Moravian Daily Texts*, Bethlehem and Winston-Salem: Moravian Church in North America, 2006, v.)

16. See chapter 1, pp. 11–12.

17. Atwood, 136f.

18. Hamilton, 173; see chapter 3 below.

19. Otto Uttendörfer, *Zinzendorfs Gedanken über den Gottesdienst* (Herrnhut: Gustav Winter, 1931), 41.

20. Hamilton, 173.

21. Hamilton, 37.

22. Uttendörfer, 41.

23. Cited in Hahn and Reichel, 221: "Man singt nicht ganze Liedern von zehn, zwanzig Versen, sondern aus so vielen Lieder halbe und ganze Verse, wie sie der Zusammenhang der Sache erfordert."

24. Hahn and Reichel, 220. They also note that Zinzendorf often composed new hymns for these services, lining them out to the congregation as he went, though only a small number of these outlived the occasions for which they were made.

25. Synod of November 18, 1750, cited in Hahn and Reichel, 222. "Eine Gemeine des Heilands muß ohne Buch singen können, denn sie soll in der Sache leben."

26. *Jüngerhaus-Diarium*, 14 May 1754, cited in Uttendörfer, 42f: "Die Singstunden sind eine aparte Schönheit unserer Kirche. Es ist ein Defekt, wenn nicht ordentliche, tägliche Singstunden gehalten werden."

27. Uttendörfer, 43.

28. Atwood, 148.

29. Fries, 1:105.

30. Fries, 1:418; 3:1009.

31. London Sermons, cited in Dieter Meyer, *Der Christozentrismus des späten Zinzenforf* (Frankfurt: Peter Lang, 1973), 182: "[D]ie allerinnigste connexion mit der person des Heilandes."

32. For a comprehensive discussion of the theology and practice of the Holy Communion service among Moravians in Zinzendorf's day, see Helmut Hickel, *Das Abendmahl zu Zinzendorfs Zeiten* (Hamburg: Ludwig Appel, 1956).

33. Atwood, 149.

34. Atwood, 177f.

35. For a detailed description of these developments, see "Die Entwicklung der liturgischen Form des Abendmahles in der Brüderkirche" in Hickel, 17–25.

36. For a listing of some typical stanzas, see Atwood, 179.

37. Hamilton, 38, n12 (655). The original is in Spangenberg's life of Zinzendorf, Part I, 446: "Als die Gemeine am 13 August von dem in Berthelsdorf gehaltenen Mahle des Herrn zurükgekommen war; fanden sich, ohne daß man es angestellt hätte, sieben verschiedene kleine Gesellschaften zusammen. Damit nun diese ungestöret beysammenbleiben könten, schikte unser Graf einer jeden derselben etwas aus seiner Küche zur Mittagsmahlzeit; das genossen sie mit einander in Liebe." See appendix 1, p. 283, for a biography of Spangenberg.

Note, however, that Bishop Hamilton also cites Joseph Th. Müller's article in the *Zeitschrift für Brüdergeschichte*, 1912, 66, which says that in his home in Dresden, Zinzendorf had even earlier held something like a lovefeast after the example of the New Testament *agape* meals.

38. Hamilton, 38.

39. Atwood, 170.

40. Uttendörfer, 53.

41. Fries, 3:1013.

42. Fries, 5:2009: "Abends war noch eine Lob und Danksingstunde, zu deren Eingang der Chorus musicus sang: 'Es sollen wol Berge weichen—aber meine Gnade soll nicht von dir weichen.'" Two settings of this text (Isaiah 54:10) are found in the music collection of the Salem Congregation, one by Christian Gregor and one by Johannes Herbst. According to the date of this service, and the history and organization of the Salem Congregation Collection, it seems most likely that the Gregor setting (originally written for the Single Sisters Choir Festival, May 4, 1759) was used in 1784.

43. Frances Cumnock, ed., *Catalog of the Salem Congregation Music* (Chapel Hill: University of North Carolina Press, 1980), 6. See also Marilyn Gombosi, *A Day of Solemn Thanksgiving: Moravian Music for the Fourth of July, 1783 in Salem, North Carolina* (Chapel Hill: University of North Carolina Press, 1977), 4f.

44. Cumnock, 7.

45. *Lebenslauf* in *Nachrichten aus der Brüdergemeine*, 1818, 458. Cited in Hahn and Reichel, 230: "Vom Jahr 1759 an empfand ich einen besonderen Antrieb in mir, zu den Festtagen der Gemeine und deren Chor-Abteilungen dann und wann einen Psalm zu verfertigen und mitunter auch die darin vorkommenden biblischen Texte teils selbst in Musik zu setzen, teils andere schickliche Kompositionen—mit wenigen erforderlichen Abänderungen—dazu zu benutzen. Damit fuhr ich mehrere Jahre fort, so viel mir's die Zeit erlaubte."

46. Christian David (1690–1751), born of Roman Catholic parents in Moravia, grew up to become a carpenter. His contacts with both the remnant of the Unitas Fratrum and with Zinzendorf led to the emigration of these exiles from Moravia and Bohemia to Zinzendorf's estate, beginning in 1722.

47. Cited in Hahn and Reichel, 237: "Der Zweck von unseren Liebesmahlen ist, die Liebe bei Brüdern zu erwecken und ein rechtes Vertrauen zueinander zu kriegen, um immer noch gemeinschaftlicher zu werden."

48. See Hickel, 6f.

49. Atwood, 164. Reference is made here to remarks in the Bethlehem Diary for Oct. 31/Nov. 11, 1742. See chapter 1, p. 27, n75, for an explanation of the "old system" and "new system" calendar. See Kenneth G. Hamilton, trans., *The Bethlehem Diary Volume I 1742–1744* (Bethlehem: Archives of the Moravian Church, 1971), 105.

50. Marienborn, northeast of Frankfurt, is the site of an estate leased by Zinzendorf, the castle of which was the home of various synods of the Renewed Moravian church.

51. Translated in Hamilton, 157 from Johannes Plitt, "Denkwürdigkeiten aus der Geschichte der Brüder-Unität," ¶ 199: "Jede Gemeine und Oeconomie hat ihre Einsichten. Schreibt mans auf, so wirds ein Glaubensbekentnis wie unsers an dem König von Schweden 1735. *Wir* machen aber kein Symbolum daraus, wie die Lutheraner (1577), das man in künftigen Zeiten nicht mehre andern kann. Wir wollen die Freiheit behalten, daß der Heiland von Zeit zu Zeit unsere Lehre aufklären kann." Johannes Plitt, Unity Archivist from 1836 until his death in 1841, worked on this manuscript for some thirty years. See Hamilton, 183, 198.

For the specifics of the Moravian approach to theology, see C. Daniel Crews, *Confessing our Unity in Christ: Historical and Theological Background to "The Ground of the Unity"* (Winston-Salem: Moravian Archives, 1994). See also Crews, *This We Most Certainly Believe: Thoughts on Moravian Theology* (Winston-Salem: Moravian Archives, 2005).

52. See Ben van den Bosch, "Die Entstehung und Entwicklung der Posaunenarbeit der Brüdergemeinen in Deutschland und aller Welt," translated as *The Origin and Development of the Trombone-Work of the Moravian Churches in Germany and All the World* by C. Daniel Crews (Winston-Salem: Moravian Music Foundation, 1990), 1.

53. Bethlehem Diary, August 27/September 7, 1742. Hamilton translation, 79.

54. Atwood, 136f., citing "Gemein und Chor-Committee Bericht von dem Engern Synodo gehalten in Bethlehem in Januario 1757, 14 January 1757" (Bethlehem: Moravian Archives).

55. Conference on September 11, 1754, cited in Hahn and Reichel, 219.

56. Conference on September 10, 1754, cited in Uttendörfer, 9. "[W]enn man es einmal nicht mit der nötigen Andacht tut, so prostituiert man sich."

57. This celebration, held on July 4, 1783, is the earliest documented celebration of Independence Day in the United States. See Gombosi, *A Day of Solemn Celebration.*

58. C. Daniel Crews, *Johann Friedrich Peter and his Times* (Winston-Salem: Moravian Music Foundation, 1990), 17. The German text is problematical. It reads: "Es hätte mir nämlich meine musicalische Gabe bald gefährlich werden können; ich merkte, dass dieselbe von der Welt geschätzt und mir heimlich zugesetzt wurde."

Chapter Three

Hymnody of the Moravian Church

Albert H. Frank and Nola Reed Knouse

In the preface of the 1569 Polish edition of the Brethren's hymnal, Bishop Andrew Stefan (1528–77) of the early Unitas Fratrum wrote, "Our fathers have taught us not only to preach the doctrines of religion from the pulpit, but also to frame them in hymns. In this way our songs become homilies."[1] When we consider the tens of thousands of hymns and single stanzas that Moravian writers have composed since 1457, the truth of Stefan's statement becomes obvious.[2] As the Moravian Church has spread around the world and the need for worship materials in additional languages has been realized, new hymns have multiplied, so that any study of Moravian hymnody must acknowledge that it will be limited and incomplete. Yet a broad survey is possible. After an overview of hymnals produced by the Moravians beginning in the early sixteenth century, we will first consider five reasons that Moravians have continued to write new hymns. We will then present a chronological survey of Moravian hymn text writers and composers.

An Overview of Moravian Hymnal Publications

Moravian hymnody itself had already begun with the dawn of the sixteenth century. What has been hailed as the "first Protestant hymnal," containing eighty-nine hymns, was printed in 1501 in Prague. It has long been claimed as a hymnal of the Unitas Fratrum, but its connection with the Unity is tenuous, although it did contain eleven hymns by Lukáš of Prague, the most influential theologian of the Unity.[3] In his *History of the Unity of Brethren*, Rudolf Říčan asserts: "More definitely belonging to the Brethren, and more safely associated with Lukáš, were the hymnals of 1505 and 1519."[4] The 1505 hymnal is reported to have contained some four hundred hymns, but no surviving copy is known to exist today. The 1519 hymnal was actually edited by Lukáš; but again, no copy is known to survive. In these hymnals, Lukáš incorporated into the Unity's repertoire some Latin hymns of the Catholic church, translating them into Czech; this is but one example of his position that not everything from the Catholic church was harmful and deserving of rejection.[5]

Over the next 160 years, the Unitas Fratrum printed some eleven different hymnals in Czech, German, and Polish, most including tunes as well as words. In addition, Joseph Theodor Müller documents twenty-eight publications that are revisions or expansions of one of those eleven.[6] After the 1501 hymnal (again, with its tenuous connection to the Unity), these were not small books; the first German-language Unity hymnal (1531, edited by Michael Weisse) had 157 hymns with tunes, and the 1561 Czech hymnal, edited by Jan Blahoslav, contained 735 hymn texts and over 450 melodies. Clearly, the Unity certainly took its hymn singing seriously.

Hymnals were reworked both to add new hymns and to revise existing ones. For instance, Weisse's 1531 hymnal incorporates his own theological leaning toward an interpretation of Holy Communion as symbolic rather than incorporating the real presence of Christ. This escaped the elders' notice in their pre-publication review of the book. A revision of the 1531 hymnal was produced in 1544, edited by Jan Roh, to reshape this theological tendency as well as to add new hymns. Three copies of this 1544 book are known to exist, one of which is in the collection of the Moravian Music Foundation.

The 1566 German-language *Kirchengesang*—edited by Petrus Herbert, Michael Tham the Elder, and Jan Jelecký—contained 348 hymns in its main body as well as an appendix containing an additional 108 hymns by Lutheran authors. The book was dedicated to the emperor Maximilian, to whom it was intended to prove the Unity's orthodoxy.[7] This highly significant book was reprinted in 1580; later editions were issued in 1606, 1639, 1661 (edited by Jan Amos Comenius), and 1694.

Central Europe was rocked in 1618 with the beginning of what was to become the Thirty Years' War. After the defeat of the Protestant forces at the battle of White Mountain in 1620, the Unity was forced into bitter exile, reduced to the most fragile existence underground. Further development of hymnody among the Brethren was naturally curtailed; but these hymns and hymnals were not all lost. In fact, one of the most poignant items in the collection of the Moravian Music Foundation is a copy of the 1618 Czech hymnal, given to the foundation by the Czech province of the worldwide Moravian Church in 1967. The authors of the hymn texts are identified in manuscript notations in the margins, starting at the beginning of the book (see fig. 3.1). Sadly, the annotations cease around the middle of the book, giving rise to questions: What happened to the annotator? Was he captured? Imprisoned? Killed? Did he hide his book somewhere and still live to old age? How did this book survive?

Jan Amos Comenius is known as a true pioneer in the field of education. A well-traveled, well-educated, thoughtful man, he was primarily a minister and bishop of the Unity, and from his exile in Amsterdam he edited and produced the last of the Czech-language hymnals of the Bohemian Brethren in 1659. Its byl zprawowán/w swědomj,w naděgi chowán. ¶ Toě geſt paſtwa ney libegſſj/ každė w tě wěřjcý duſſi/ tebe řádně poſjwati/z toho w dobrém pracowati, ¶ Až do žiwota ſkonánj: neb ſlibugeš ſetrwánj/ pomozýš w miloſti ſtátj/ iádem twým ſe zprawowati: ¶ A když ſe k nám zaſe wrátjš/poſelſtwj konec včinjš/wzad s ſlužebnjků ſeganeš/ s lidem wěrným w nebe půgneš: ¶ Tuě ſe giž nebudem báti/abychom měli padati: neb

těla náſſe oſtawjš/w způſob Angelſký proměnjš.
¶ Z toho předrahého djla/budiž tobě Kryſte chwála/od ſwatých Angelů w nebi/y od nás lidj na zemi: ¶ Neb ſy s Otcem toho hoden/y s Duchem ſwatým Bůh geden/aby tě twogi chwálili/ na wěky wěků ſtawili, ¶ W té dokonalé radoſti/kdež nenj žádné žaloſti/ než rozkoš a wěſſenj: ó deyž w nj Kryſte bydlenj.

3 Jan Auguſta

Nebo Boha wſſemohaucýho/kázeň Otce nebeſkého/

proti kaž dé ne prawoſti/wedlé ge ho ſpra we dlno ſti,

¶ Wyprawůgmež k předeſſenj/miloſti geho k hledánj/dokuž ſe chce ſmilowati/ dijw než ſaud zaěne konati: ¶ Gehož Prorok hněwiwého/widěl, přewelmi hrozného/an hněw geho ze mj zatřéſt/ základy hor pohybowal, ¶ Z chjpj geho deym wycházel/z vſt oheň z jiragjcý ſſel/z Mageſtátu hromobitj/a ohniwé krupobitj: ¶ Sám on dj, Gá gſem Bůh ſylný/ ſprawedliwý, a zůřiwý/mſtě pro hřjch otců na ſynech/w pokolenjch třech, y čtyřech. ¶ Na Adama hněw ſwůg puſtil/ když genju pro hřjch zkořčil/kterýž po wſſechněch lidech gde/s mnohých na wěky neſegde. ¶ Kaina od Otce zahnal/ a w žádoſti ſwěta wydal/zbawiw důſtogného kněžſtwj/y práwa přwrozenſtwj: ¶ Swět w/

ſlecken hrozně zatopil/wodami žaloſtně zkázyl/wylil hněw ſwůg y na Cháma/zlého ſyna Noelowa, ¶ Národy co moře baujj/a gedny druhými kazy/tepe hladem,morem,ſſelmau/neduhy, nemocý těžkau: ¶ Wſſech národů nechal we tmách/ a Izraelſkých w mrákotách/ wſſecky pauſtěl w ohawnoſti/podlé ſrdce gich liboſtj. ¶ Totoť geſt přehrozná rána/že hřjſſnj kům proſpěch dáwá/aby ſwau wůli prowedli/že ſau Bozj za to měli: ¶ Stůl gich byt gim byl w oſýdlo/pokog,wěčné ſmrti hrdlo/maudroſt ge oſlepowala/ſluch od prawdy odwracela: ¶ Vwodjě ge y w ſwau prawdu/ byt gi dáwali w potupu/ ctitele gegj hubili/ tak ſe Bohu protiwili, ¶ Vſigůie Egypt treſtal/ y w ſwa:

Figure 3.1. *Písně duchovné evangelické* (Kralice, 1618), sample page. Photo by David Holston.

relatively small size is explained by Comenius' thought that the hymnal ought to be small enough to carry in one's pocket, so that one could use it as a devotional guide wherever one was.[8] This hymnal also contains a preface discussing not only the use of hymns, but also the role of music in general in the church.[9]

While the Unity of Brethren was driven underground, dispersed, and nearly destroyed, Comenius and others took care to see that its writings survived. In 1722, when some of the German-speaking descendants of the Brethren found refuge on the estate of the Lutheran nobleman Nicholas Ludwig von Zinzendorf in Saxony, they brought with them their love of music, their instruments, and their hymnody. From their two-hundred-year heritage of producing hymnals in the Unity, they were accustomed to hymns with theological depth and significance. They were used to producing hymnals. And they were moving into a region (and under a patron) already rich with a hymn-singing tradition, with the hymns of Luther and Gerhardt, and highly influenced by the pietistic movement.

Zinzendorf himself had published hymnals in the 1720s, and the first Moravian hymnal published for the congregation at Herrnhut was printed in 1735, with the title *Gesangbuch der evangelischen Brüder-Gemeinen in Herrn-Huth.* This "*Herrnhuter Gesangbuch*" marks the beginning of a two-hundred-year practice of printing the "hymnal" (*Gesangbuch*) separately from the "tune book" (*Choralbuch*), a practice that continued in Germany through the end of the twentieth century. The 1735 text-only hymnal contained 999 hymns, of which 208 were by Zinzendorf himself, with only two hymns from the earlier Unity. This hymnal was followed over the next twenty years by twelve appendices and four supplements. This prodigious output of hymns and hymnals was part of the overflowing creativity of the Sifting Period in the middle of the eighteenth century.[10] The twelfth appendix, in particular, was filled with extremes of imagery regarding Christ's wounds, as well as "excessive use of diminutives and childish, not just childlike, language in referring to God."[11]

A momentous effort to organize this body of hymns was made in the publication of *Alt und Neuer Brüder Gesang*, printed in London in 1754–55. This thick book was in two parts: a chronologically arranged collection of 2,168 German hymns from many eras and 1,096 hymns by the Moravians themselves, for a total of 3,264 hymn texts. However, the publication of a new hymnal was not only a way of organizing the materials at hand; it was also a means of helping to correct the excesses of language and bring Moravian theology back to the center.

This hymnal is fascinating for a number of reasons, not the least of which is the printing of the preface in both German and English in parallel columns. It is organized not by season or topic, but by the sources of the hymns: canticles and psalms from scripture; metrical paraphrases of other biblical texts; texts "aus der alten Kirche" (from the ancient church), translated from Greek and Latin; hymns of the old Unity; hymns of the sixteenth-century Reformation and seventeenth-century Protestant authors; and finally, hymns produced in the eighteenth-century Moravian Church. This very arrangement demonstrated to both Moravians and others that the Moravian Church based its theology firmly on scripture; that the Moravian Church saw itself as part of the one universal church; that the Moravians saw themselves as closely connected with the Protestant Reformation; and that the Moravians also saw themselves as heirs of their own venerable tradition, a tradition continuing to the present day.[12] This hymnal, then, was a vital part of the eighteenth-century Moravian Church's search for an understanding of its own identity.

By Zinzendorf's death in 1760, still other shorter hymnals had been published, and the need for a smaller hymnal (and one more useful for worship planning) was seen. At the Synod of 1775, Christian Gregor was assigned the task of organizing and editing this immense body of hymns. The resulting hymnal, published in 1778, has only 1,750 hymn texts. Of the more than three thousand hymn texts from which Gregor had to select, he dropped those not in current use or with questionable theology or language; he combined stanzas from others to create hymns with a different focus; he recast a large number of others; and he added some that he himself had written.[13] This hymnal, with its many reprints and supplements, remained in use in Germany for roughly a century.

The synod must have been happy with the results, for in 1782 it assigned Brother Gregor the task of preparing a chorale book to accompany the 1778 hymnal. He finished this in 1784, and, "along with the 1778 hymnal, it brought lasting stability to the hymn repertory of the Moravian Church."[14] Gregor thus played a major role in shaping the hymn singing, and therefore both the theology and the musical "ears," of the Moravians, an influence that continues today.

The use of tune numbers has been characteristic of Moravian tune books since the eighteenth century. Although the hymnals of the Bohemian Brethren contained numerous tunes, no numerical arrangement was provided for them. Moreover, although the 1735 manuscript tune book attributed to Tobias Friedrich contains two hundred tunes, there is no organized numbering system for them.[15] Several other manuscript chorale books, preserved like Friedrich's in the Moravian Archives in Herrnhut, are characterized by a metrical organization of the tunes. In each of these manuscript books, tunes with the same metrical structure (same number of lines, same number of syllables in each line, and similar accentuation pattern) have the same *number* and are distinguished from each other by a *letter*—e.g., 22 A, 22 B, and so on.

The tune numbers in use today date to the large manuscript chorale book prepared by Johann Daniel Grimm in 1755. Christian Gregor's 1784 *Choralbuch* simplified Grimm's system by omitting tunes not in current use and changing the numbering of others for a more consistent system. In general, the shorter the tune, the lower its number (tune 1, for instance, only has two lines, and tunes 2 and 3 have three lines). Many tunes have four lines, and these are organized logically as well—those with shorter lines, again, have lower numbers. This system is not totally consistent, but enough so that if we see, for instance, tune

Figure 3.2. *Wachet auf, ruft uns die Stimme*, tune 230, from Gregor *Choralbuch* (1784), 186. Photo by David Holston.

number 221, we can safely assume that it is longer and more complex than tune 14. Whatever the number, however, all the "tune 14s" have the same metrical structure, which is different from that of, for instance, the "tune 22s." Gregor assigned chorale numbers through 575. Tunes were printed with soprano and bass lines, with figures indicating inner parts (see fig. 3.2).

Gregor's 1784 *Choralbuch* was followed by a number of later tune books printed in Germany and England. The *Auszug aus dem bisher in den evangelischen Brüder-Gemeinen gebräuchlichen Choral-Buche mit ausgeschriebenen Stimmen der Choral-Melodien* was printed in 1831, with a dual purpose.[16] Melodies not in common usage were omitted, shortening the book considerably, and inner parts were included to eliminate the challenge of playing from the figured bass. These inner parts were added in close position, except where the soprano part is very low (see fig. 3.3).

The undated *Choralbuch* of Heinrich Lonas (1838–1903) contained known and new tunes for use in the German congregations, largely following Gregor's numbers but introducing new numbers as well.[17] By the late nineteenth century, the Moravian Church in Germany recognized the need for a new hymnal. A number of the hymns in the 1778 *Gesangbuch* had fallen out of use, either because of their obsolete texts or because of the difficulty of their associated tunes. This led to the publication of the *Kleine Gesangbuch der Brüdergemeine* in 1870.[18] The *Kleine Gesangbuch* came to be used in a number of congregations alongside the 1778 *Grosse Gesangbuch*. A second edition of the *Kleine Gesangbuch*

Figure 3.3. *Wachet auf, ruft uns die Stimme,* tune 230, from *Auszug . . . aus dem Choral-Buche* (1831), 103. Photo by David Holston.

was prepared beginning in 1891, but in recognition that this was indeed the book in use among the congregations, the designation *kleine* was dropped, and thus the 1893 edition was known simply as the *Gesangbuch der Brüdergemeine.*[19] A companion *Choralbuch* was printed in 1893, including the tunes needed for the 1893 *Gesangbuch* and the liturgy book printed in 1873.[20] New settings were prepared for some of the tunes, but Gregor's harmonies were retained wherever possible. All of the tunes are printed with four-part harmony, with soprano and alto on the treble staff and tenor and bass on the bass staff. An appendix contains thirteen chorales with different harmonizations intended for the *Sängerchor* (singers' choir), including some by Mendelssohn and J. S. Bach. The 1927 *Choralbuch* added many new tunes and more pieces for the *Sängerchor.*[21]

The 1960 German *Choralbuch* departed from the Gregor numbering in order to use a common identification pattern with the Evangelical Church in Germany with which the German Moravian congregations are in a close working relationship. That *Choralbuch* includes listings with both old and new tune numbers to facilitate the transition for the brass players, who play directly from the *Choralbuch.* This system enables Moravian and Lutheran brass to perform together more easily for brass festivals and other ecumenical events.

Moravian hymnody in other languages had its specifically "Moravian" roots in this strong German tradition. In each location the Moravians also adopted (and adapted) hymns from their surroundings. The first Moravian hymnal in Britain was published by James Hutton in 1742, containing 187 hymns.[22] This, like Zinzendorf's early hymnal publications, was not an official hymnal of the church but rather more of a personal collection. Supplements were published in 1746 and 1749, containing a number of hymn texts marked by excesses of enthusiasm and devotion that naturally led to careful and corrective measures later on.

The first official Moravian hymnal in English was *A Collection of Hymns of the Children of God in All Ages . . .* (1754).[23] This large book (containing 1,055 hymn texts) is organized in similar fashion to the 1754 German hymnal discussed above. Its contents include scripture hymns; hymns of the early church; many hymns translated from German, with fifty-one from the old Unity; and English hymns from earlier years and by contemporary authors such as Isaac Watts, Charles Wesley, John Cennick, and others. However, the Moravians in Britain did not take over these English hymns with no alterations; for example, Charles Wesley's hymn "Ye Servants of God, Your Master Proclaim" had to be altered slightly to fit a tune known by the Moravians, to begin "Ye Servants of God, your *great* Master proclaim," by adding a syllable to each of the first two lines.

The British hymnal of 1789, containing 887 hymns, was edited by John Swertner (1746–1813), the son of a Dutch Moravian pastor. He greatly altered the older translations from the German; in many cases he provided newer translations. This may have been in response to the excesses of language mentioned earlier, in conjunction with the eighteenth-century British tendency toward "respectability." However, in some of these translations the passion and power of the original German were lost.[24]

The British province also printed tune books based on Gregor's 1784 *Choralbuch.* In the preface to *Hymn-Tunes sung in the Church of the United Brethren* (1826), Christian Ignatius LaTrobe acknowledged his debt to Gregor, while noting that "some tunes peculiar to our English hymns are added; and as several new metres have been introduced into the Hymn-Book published in 1789, I have endeavoured to supply the Tunes wanted according to my best abilities."[25] Like the later German editions, LaTrobe's English tune book includes inner parts, printed in small notes in the treble staff in close position. Peter LaTrobe's mid-century revision of this book added more tunes and divided the inner parts between treble and bass staves, noting that this was "for the use of choirs."[26]

Later British Moravian hymnals were published in 1801, 1809, 1826, 1849, 1886, 1911, and 1975, the latter two including music for the hymns. The 1975 book took a unique approach to the selection of tunes. If a tune was familiar beyond the Moravian Church, the editors of this hymnal chose the more familiar "ecumenical" setting rather than a peculiarly "Moravian" setting of the tune. Each tune is identified by a tune name, and for each the meter is noted (either with a standard metric notation such as C.M. or with the syllable count such as 10.10.10.10), but no tune-numbering system is used. Moreover, the editors made a conscious attempt to include as many tunes as possible, stating in the preface to the hymnal that

> Our general aim has been to provide a different tune of high quality for every hymn. This rule has of necessity been relaxed in some instances on account of the nature of the hymn or the oddness of the metre. Some repetition then does occur. Our method has occasionally meant the wedding of a new tune to an old hymn, and in our opinion this has proved to be a gain. However, if needs must, a more familiar tune may be discovered elsewhere in the Book.[27]

Until the middle of the nineteenth century, Moravians in America used German and English hymnals from Europe. A Moravian hymnal was printed in Philadelphia in 1813, but the first independently edited American English-language hymnal was published in America in 1851.[28] It was similar to the British hymnal of 1849, but its American editors omitted some hymns and added others. It was printed again in 1853, and subsequent printings were made in 1866, 1872, 1875, and 1876, when a new, revised edition was issued. At this time the Moravians were feeling pressured to conform to other Christian denominations and "to smooth out the peculiarities of their hymnody."[29]

Meanwhile, in 1836, the composer and pastor Peter Wolle published *Hymn Tunes, Used in the Church of the United Brethren*, adding further tunes and introducing some significant innovations.[30] He commended this book not only to the Moravians, but also to "Christians of other persuasions," certain that "many will be found who approve of our church music, the slow and solemn movement observed throughout being in their estimation best suited for the holy worship of the Lord."[31] Unlike Gregor's earlier book, Wolle's tune book uses quarter notes rather than half notes throughout; he is careful to point out, however, that "this change is not designed in the least to accelerate the time to be observed in singing these tunes, which on the contrary require throughout a slow movement."[32] Wolle's other innovations are also designed to make the book more user friendly; he writes out parts for all four voice ranges, so that the book is useful for the choir as well as for the organist; and "to facilitate the adaptation of these tunes to hymns contained in the collections used by other Christian denominations," he notes the relationship between the Moravian tune-number system and a poetic metric system.[33] He observes that C.M. (common meter) corresponds to the Moravian tunes 14, 590, and 593; L.M. (long meter) corresponds to the Moravian tunes 22 and 166; and S.M. (short meter) corresponds to tunes 582 and 595.

The 1876 American hymnal remained in use until the 1923 *Hymnal and Liturgies of the Moravian Church (Unitas Fratrum)* was produced.[34] An "unofficial" hymnal, designed for use in churches and Sunday schools, Bible classes, the seminary, and various sorts of prayer meetings, was published in 1891, under the title *Offices of Worship and Hymns*.[35] It had 1,564 hymns, and in this book music was included in the same volume, for the first time since the old Unity hymnals of the seventeenth century.[36] Interestingly enough, this book was organized not by topic, but by metrical structure, with tunes of the same meter printed at the top of successive pages and texts of that meter below (see fig. 3.4).

The 1923 *Hymnal and Liturgies* took the inclusion of printed music a step farther. Hymns were arranged topically, and each hymn was assigned to a specific tune, with the first verse interlined in the music. This hymnal too had a long (and still quite revered) "pew life." Some congregations retained it long after the production of a revised *Hymnal and Liturgies of the Moravian Church* in 1969.[37] In the 1969 book, up to four verses were placed between the musical staves. It included a few new hymns, but had three hundred fewer hymns in total than the 1923 hymnal. The American provinces produced a truly "new" hymnal in 1995, the *Moravian Book of Worship*.[38]

As the Moravians established their mission work around the world, they made every effort to produce hymnals in the languages of the peoples among whom they lived and worked. Especially fascinating is *A Collection of Hymns for the Use of the Christian Indians, of the Missions of the United Brethren, in North America*, published in 1803 in Philadelphia.[39] With hymns in the Delaware language, this hymnal was edited by the Moravian missionary David Zeisberger and contains the following introductory letter, which articulates the Moravians' reason for providing hymnals in so many languages:

To the Society of United Brethren for propagating the Gospel among the Heathen.
Dear Brethren,

I beg leave to dedicate to you a collection of Hymns in the Delaware language, translated from the newest German and English hymnbooks of our Church, and request the favor of you to cause it to be printed for the use of the Indian congregations.

As the singing of psalms and spiritual songs has always formed a principal part of the divine service of our Church, even in congregations gathered from among the heathen, it has been for many years my ardent wish, to furnish, for the use of the Christian Indians, a regular and suitable hymnbook, wherein the grand subjects of our faith should be recorded and set forth in verse, which is so easily imprinted in the memories, particularly of young people. All our converts find much pleasure in learning verses with their tunes by heart, and frequently sing and meditate on them at home and abroad.

Some of these hymns contained in this collection have been for many years in blessed use among us; these have been carefully revised and amended; others have been in later years translated by myself. The chief care in translating has been, to preserve the true sense of the originals, which has caused, in some instances, an alteration of the tune or metre, or a necessity of extending one verse into two.

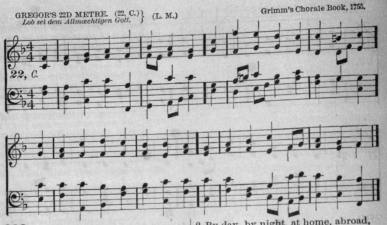

GREGOR'S 22D METRE. (22, C.)}
Lob sei dem Allmæchtigen Gott. (L. M.)

Grimm's Chorale Book, 1755.

22, C.

293 Tune 22.
Awake, my soul, in joyful lays,
And sing Thy great Redeemer's praise,
He justly claims a song from thee,—
His loving-kindness, oh, how free!

2 He saw me ruined in the fall,
Yet loved me notwithstanding all;
He saved me from my lost estate,—
His loving-kindness, oh, how great!

3 When trouble like a gloomy cloud,
Has gathered thick, and thundered loud,
He near my soul has always stood,—
His loving-kindness, oh, how good!

4 Often I feel my sinful heart
Prone from my Saviour to depart;
But though I oft have Him forgot,
His loving-kindness changes not.
                              Samuel Medley, 1738-99.

294 Tune 22.
The Saviour lives, no more to die;
He lives, the Lord enthroned on high;
He lives, triumphant o'er the grave;
He lives eternally to save.

2 He lives, to still His servants' fears;
He lives to wipe away their tears;
He lives, their mansions to prepare;
He lives, to bring them safely there.

3 Ye mourning souls, dry up your tears;
Dismiss your gloomy doubts and fears;
With cheerful hope your hearts revive,
For Christ, the Lord, is yet alive.

4 His saints He loves and never leaves;
The contrite sinner He receives;
Abundant grace will He afford,
Till all are present with the Lord.
                              Samuel Medley, 1738-99.

295 Tune 22.
Great God! we sing that mighty hand,
By which supported still we stand;
The opening year Thy mercy shows;
Let mercy crown it till it close.

2 By day, by night, at home, abroad,
Still we are guarded by our God;
By His incessant bounty fed,
By His unerring counsel led.

3 In scenes exalted or depressed,
Be Thou our Joy, and Thou our Rest;
Thy goodness all our hope shall raise,
Adored through all our changing days.

4 When death shall interrupt our songs,
And seal in silence mortal tongues,
Oh, may Thy praise our lips employ
In the eternal world of joy.
                              Philip Doddridge, 1702-51.

296 Tune 22.
To Thee, Lord Christ, all praise be given,
For Thy ascending up to heaven:
Support us while on earth we stay,
And lead us in the narrow way.

2 Though seated on Thy Father's throne,
Thou ne'er wilt cease Thy flock to own,
But always in their midst appear,
When in Thy Name assembled here.

3 For us to heaven Thou didst ascend,
To plead our cause, and to attend
To all our wants, yea, to prepare
A place for us, Thy bliss to share.

4 At parting from Thy little fold,
Thy second coming was foretold;
Therefore we wait with eagerness,
Lord Jesus, to behold Thy face.
                              John Swertner, 1746-1813.

297 Tune 22.
To Thee be glory, honor, praise,
  Jesus, Redeemer, Saviour, King!
Inspired with joy at Thine approach,
  Thy children loud hosannas sing.

2 Hail, Israel's King! hail, David's Son!
  Hail, Thou That in Jehovah's Name
Didst come Thy people to redeem,
  And comest now Thy crown to claim!

64

Figure 3.4. *Offices of Worship and Hymns* (1891), sample page. Photo by David Holston.

The litanies and liturgical hymns, used at baptisms, burials, &c. are taken from the newest liturgies of the Brethren's Church.

The contents of the several divisions of this hymnbook are expressed both in English and Delaware.

It was conceived unnecessary to add an Index. The Indian converts would make no use of it, and others will not easily become acquainted with the first lines of all the verses. The hymns have the same numbers placed over them, and are in nearly the same order, under which they are arranged in the German hymnbook, by recurring to which therefore they may easily be found, with their tunes.

May God our Saviour, who is the Saviour also of the heathen, grant His blessing to this work, that a people who formerly did not know Him, but now, through the power of His saving name, has been turned from darkness to light, and from the power of Satan unto God, and has received forgiveness of sins, and an inheritance among them which are sanctified by faith that is in Him (Act 26, 18.), may be the more excited to bring Him praise, honor and adoration for the grace and mercy which He has conferred upon them!—I am confident, dear Brethren, that you will esteem this a sufficient recompense for the expence of publication.

DAVID ZEISBERGER.
Goshen, River Muskingum,
September 30th, 1802.[40]

Evidently the Society did so esteem, as the book was indeed published in 1803; a revision, printed in 1847, contains the same introductory letter.

Over the years, the Moravian Church has printed hymnals in a great many other languages, including (but not limited to) such languages as Afrikaans, Danish, Dutch, French, Inuit (Greenland), Inuktitut (Labrador), Miskito, Welsh, and Yup'ik (Alaska), in addition to the more "expected" Czech, German, and English.

The Why of Moravian Hymnals

In consideration of the hundreds of Moravian hymnals published over five hundred years, it is obvious that the Moravians have been strongly motivated to write sung religious poetry in the interests of their faith community. Among the factors sparking new hymn texts are the following:

1. Hymns are written to give an outlet for and to preserve spiritual experiences of the writers. Writing in 1824, James Montgomery reflected on his experience of worship in these lines:

> To your temple, Lord, I come,
> for it is my worship home.
> This earth has no better place,
> here I see my Savior's face.

> While your ministers proclaim
> peace and pardon in your name,
> through their voice, by faith, may I
> hear you speaking from the sky.
>
> From your house when I return,
> may my heart within me burn,
> and at evening let me say,
> "I have walked with God today."[41]

In a similar vein, Henriette Luise von Hayn (1724–82) could write of her personal experience of Jesus Christ:

> I am Jesus' little lamb;
> ever glad at heart I am;
> for my Shepherd gently guides me,
> knows my need and well provides me,
> loves me every day the same,
> even calls me by my name.
>
> Day by day, at home, away,
> Jesus is my staff and stay.
> When I hunger, Jesus feeds me,
> into pleasant pastures leads me;
> when I thirst, he bids me go
> where the quiet waters flow.[42]

2. *Hymns are written to fill a need.* Incorporating into their worship gatherings Jan Hus's principle of vernacular congregational singing, the Brethren began to publish hymnals beginning in 1505. New occasions called for additional resources. In the eighteenth-century Herrnhut community, two daily worship services were held in addition to the Sunday gatherings. Often one of these was in the form of a *Singstunde*, a half hour gathering devoted to singing hymn stanzas developing a scriptural theme that was often determined by the daily Watchwords (*Losungen*).[43] The *Singstunden* necessitated more hymns from which to choose, and led to the memorization of hymns, still a characteristic in European Moravian congregations where weekly *Singstunden* are held. Adaptations of the basic *Singstunde* form provide the structure for the Holy Communion liturgies, lovefeasts, and the Christmas Eve Vigils during which lighted candles are distributed to the congregation.[44]

3. *Hymns are written to teach theology.* During dialogue sessions between the Evangelical Lutheran Church in America and the Moravian Church, the Lutheran delegates soon understood that Moravians "do theology" by telling

stories or singing hymns.[45] The eighteenth-century leader Count Nicholas Ludwig von Zinzendorf wrote a hymn of 162 stanzas on the Augsburg Confession.[46] Earlier, Bishop Jan Roh (1490–1547) taught the doctrine of the coming of Christ both at Bethlehem and the second coming in this hymn:

> Once he came in blessing all our sins redressing,
> came in likeness lowly, Son of God most holy;
> bore the cross to save us, hope and freedom gave us.
>
> Still he comes within us, still his voice would win us
> from the sins that hurt us; would to truth convert us
> from our foolish error, ere he comes in terror.[47]

Still in the twentieth century, we find the doctrine of the atonement and following joy taught in

> Lord Jesus, you are worthy for all on earth to praise;
> our hymns in glad thanksgiving in gratitude we raise,
> for all you did on Calv'ry when suff'ring on the tree—
> the world from sin's dominion most wondrously set free.
>
> And I, unworthy sinner, when kneeling at your feet,
> can see that my redemption in you is now complete:
> in faith I now would serve you through all my earthly days,
> and then in heav'nly glory my hallelujahs raise.[48]

4. *Hymns are written to mark special occasions.* James Montgomery wrote a seven-stanza text, "The God of your forefathers praise," to commemorate the centennial of the Pentecostal experience of August 13, 1727.[49] Several hymns were written before the quincentennial celebrations of the Unity in 1957. Some pastors have written a hymn each year to celebrate the anniversaries of the congregations they serve. The list can go on endlessly.[50]

5. *Hymns are written for services that focus on the sufferings and death of the Savior.* Zinzendorf prepared a harmonization of the Gospels, parts of which were read in worship services, interspersed with hymn stanzas to allow worshipers time to reflect on what the Savior had done for them. Hymns were written to provide appropriate stanzas. A second harmonization was done by Samuel Lieberkühn in 1769 and became the basis for the services of the eight to ten days before Easter. These services continue throughout the Moravian Church in various formats and occasionally inspire new hymn texts.[51] Herrnhut also had regular weekly services in which a Passion liturgy was sung, utilizing many of these stanzas.

Christian Gregor (1723–1801) was not only a Moravian bishop and administrator, and the editor of the 1778 *Gesangbuch* and the 1784 *Choralbuch*, but also a composer and poet in his own right. Of his numerous hymns on Christ's Passion, two are particularly noteworthy. In 1765, he wrote an antiphonal hymn setting of Matthew 21:9, "Hosanna, blessed is he that comes in the name of the Lord." Although originally intended for children's and adult choirs, it is used in a variety of two-part arrangements. It introduces the Advent season and is again sung on Palm Sunday to celebrate the triumphal entry of Jesus into Jerusalem.[52]

Dating from 1759 is Gregor's stanza used with the narrative of Jesus' agony in Gethsemane, requiring the believer's response in adoration and commitment:

O there's a sight that rends my heart,
nor can it from my mind depart,
how thou on Olivet didst languish;
O Lord, for thy soul's agony,
when wrestling there with death for me,
make me a trophy of thine anguish.[53]

While editing the 1995 edition of the *Readings for Holy Week*, the present American Moravian harmonization of the gospel accounts of Jesus' passion, Albert Frank struggled to find a stanza that is a good amplification or response to the parable of the talents, as recorded in Matthew 25:14–30. Finding none that filled the need, he penned these lines in 1995:

Help us, O God, to use our gifts
in service day by day,
that what you give us we may share
and work as well as pray.[54]

These five broad reasons do not explain all of the hymns that are often classified as "Moravian," partly because the total collection can never be assembled in any one place and partly because of the difficulty of defining a "Moravian" hymn. In a narrow sense, a Moravian hymn is one that was written by a member of the Unitas Fratrum for corporate or personal use. The examples cited in this chapter fit that definition. Yet in the broader sense, a Moravian hymn is one that is used in worship anywhere in the worldwide Unitas Fratrum. Because of the long history of Moravian involvement in ecumenical affairs and the desire of many Moravians to use worship materials that are common in their locales, the body of such hymns is limitless.

Authors and Texts, Composers and Tunes:
A Chronological Sampling

The Ancient Unity

Among the earliest hymns available to the Unitas Fratrum was a communion hymn text penned by Jan Hus in about 1410. The original Latin text was newly translated in 1993 by Dirk French for the *Moravian Book of Worship*. An earlier versification of the themes of this text was made by Martin Luther in 1524 and has appeared in previous hymnals of the American Moravian Church, mistakenly identified as the "oldest Moravian hymn known."[55] Its first English appearance was a translation by Christian Ignatius LaTrobe in the 1789 British *Moravian Hymn Book*.[56] In the 1995 *Moravian Book of Worship* (*MBW*), Luther's hymn appears with the LaTrobe translation for stanzas 1, 3, and 4, with a new translation of stanza 2 by Dirk French.[57]

The earliest known hymn of the Unitas Fratrum is actually *Radujme se vždy spolecně*, attributed to either Matěj (Matthias) of Kunwald in 1457 or Gabriel Komarovsky in 1467.[58] The Czech hymnal of 1954 notes only Matěj as author; this is also the judgment of Joseph Theodor Müller, who cites notes made by Jan Blahoslav (1523–71) in the 1561 hymnal.[59] However, in his later history of the ancient Unity, he is not so certain.[60] Known as the "ordination hymn of the Ancient Unity," this hymn is clearly indicative of the struggles of the Hussites from 1415 to 1457 and of the first years of denominational existence of the Unitas Fratrum from 1457 to 1467, when its ordained ministry was organized. This text was translated into German by Michael Weisse (1480–1534) in 1531 and translated into English by Evelyn Renatus Hassé (1855–1918), for the British *Moravian Hymn Book* of 1911, clearly capturing the ordination sense of the text:

> Come, let us all with gladness raise
> a joyous song of thanks and praise
> to God who rules the heav'nly host,
> God, Father, Son and Holy Ghost.

> For God, in grace and tenderness,
> regarded us in our distress;
> yea, to our aid himself he came;
> let all adore God's holy name.

> God gave us faithful ones to lead
> and help us in our time of need;
> but, Lord, all pow'r is yours alone,
> and you the work must carry on.

Father in heaven, fulfill your word;
grant us the Spirit of our Lord,
that through your truth, which cannot fail,
we may o'er every ill prevail.

And in your love may we abide,
estranged from none by wrath or pride,
among ourselves at unity
and with all else in charity.

Thus may our lips your praises sound,
our hearts in steadfast hope abound;
till you to heaven our steps shall bring
where saints and angels hail you King.[61]

This text is most often used with a harmonization of the tune that appeared with the German translation in the 1531 hymnal (see ex. 3.1).

Example 3.1. *Freuen wir uns*, tune and setting as in *Moravian Book of Worship* 519.

An anonymous hymn that first appeared in 1904 was long thought to be another translation of this same text; this hymn, however, was written anew based on the theology and ideals of the Ancient Unity. Included here because of its traditional linking to the Ancient Unity, the hymn contains this verse:

One our Master, one alone, none but Christ as Lord we own;
"brethren of his law" are we—"As I loved you, so love ye."
Branches we in Christ the Vine, living by his life divine;
as the Father with the Son, so, in Christ we all are one.[62]

Both of these hymns clearly express the essentials of the faith identified by the Unitas Fratrum.[63] Although the first is regularly used in the ordination services of

Example 3.2. *Gaudeamus pariter*, tune and setting as in *Moravian Book of Worship* 525.

the church, the second has become a favorite for any celebratory occasion, with its association with a joyful, memorable tune from the 1544 hymnal (see ex. 3.2).

Lukáš of Prague (1458–1528) was the leading theologian of the Unity during his life and contributed a number of hymn texts to the publications of the church. Although only one, "Christ the Model of the Meek," is included in the *Moravian Book of Worship*, a second text, representative of the Unity's view of death and resurrection, appeared in English in the 1923 *Hymnal and Liturgies*. This text is set to a tune from Georg Rhaw's *Neue deutsche geistliche Gesänge* of 1544, a tune that has become associated with a number of Moravian hymns.

> Now lay we calmly in the grave
> this form, whereof no doubt we have
> that it shall rise again that day
> in glorious triumph o'er decay.
>
> His soul is living now in God,
> whose grace his pardon hath bestowed,
> who through his Son redeemed him here
> from bondage unto sin and fear.
>
> Then let us leave him to his rest,
> and homeward turn, for he is blest.
> And we must well our souls prepare,
> when death shall come, to meet him there.[64]

Říčan describes Lukáš's hymns as "truly ecclesiastical. They sing about the church, which recognized and honored God's salvation in Christ, rejoiced in the message of the gospel, truly instructed the singer and the listener in the faith, and warned against Antichrist."[65] Unfortunately, very few of Lukáš's hymns have been translated from the original Czech into English.

Jan Augusta (1500–1572), a bishop and hymn writer, spent sixteen years of his life and episcopacy in prison. Müller noted that he contributed 141 hymns to the hymnal of 1561, of which two are in use today.[66] A paraphrase of Psalm 84 was in the American hymnals through 1969; German Moravian congregations still use the German translation of this hymn.[67] A Lenten text from Augusta's pen, "How Shall We Thank You, Christ, Our Lord," sounding the notes of thanksgiving and salvation, was recently translated and is included in the 1995 *Moravian Book of Worship*.

Jan Blahoslav (1523–71) was the historian and hymnal editor for the Unity during his years of activity. He contributed sixty-five hymns to the 1561 hymnal, forty-eight of which were his own texts, with the other seventeen being revisions of older Bohemian hymns.[68] Although none of his texts appear in the current German- or English-language hymnals, eight of his texts can be found in the Czech Moravian hymnal of 1954.[69]

Petrus Herbert (d. 1571) was a bishop of the Unitas Fratrum and one of the three editors of the 1566 German hymnal of the Brethren in which ninety of his hymns appeared.[70] Müller noted that his hymns were "distinguished by simplicity and beauty of style."[71] His text on the scriptures was traditionally thought to have been regularly used before the sermon:

> The word of God, which ne'er shall cease,
> proclaims free pardon, grace, and peace,
> salvation shows in Christ alone,
> the perfect will of God makes known.

> This holy Word exposes sin,
> convinces us that we're unclean,
> points out the wretched, ruined state
> of humankind, both small and great.

> It then reveals God's boundless grace,
> which justifies our sinful race,
> and gives eternal life to all
> who will accept the gospel call.

> It gently heals the broken heart
> and heav'nly riches does impart,
> reveals redemption's wondrous call
> through Christ's atoning death for all.

O God, in whom our trust we place,
we thank you for your word of grace;
help us its precepts to obey
till we shall live in endless day.[72]

In earlier American Moravian hymnals this text was set to a later German chorale tune, but in the 1995 *Moravian Book of Worship* it has been reunited with its original tune, in a harmonization by Larry Lipkis (see ex. 3.3).

Example 3.3. *Des Herren Wort.* Harmonization © Larry Lipkis (1978). Used by permission.

Jan Amos Comenius (1592–1670) was not only an editor of hymnals in both Czech and German, but also a capable hymn writer. A number of his hymns were translated from the original Czech into German at the time of the four hundredth anniversary of his birth.[73] To date few of his hymns have been translated into English.

Among the many thousands of hymns produced by the Unitas Fratrum in its first two hundred years, some common characteristics have been noted. C. Daniel Crews, in a paper presented at the Fourth Bethlehem Conference on Moravian Music in October of 2002, has described a "common structure" that many of these hymns share:

Very often, a hymn would begin with several stanzas giving a versified version of a story from the Bible. Then there would be several more stanzas giving applications to the church in the modern (16th or 17th century) world. There often followed a prayer to

God to let the lessons derived in the earlier stanzas become lived out in the believers' lives. Quite often these sections within a hymn were marked off [in the printed hymnal] by the symbol of a hand with a pointing finger.[74]

The Renewed Moravian Church: The Eighteenth Century

The renewal of the Unitas Fratrum in the 1720s on the Saxon lands of Nicholas Ludwig von Zinzendorf brought new opportunities for worship and new needs as additional worship forms developed. Beginning in 1732, a worldwide mission enterprise was undertaken that has carried the modern Moravian Church into its present locations and structure. Now that structure is itself undergoing change as global balances shift from North to South, and former "mission provinces" assume roles and responsibilities on a par with those of the older "home" provinces. Consequently, this overview of Moravian hymnody is only partial, since newer materials from the former mission provinces are not yet readily available.

The Zinzendorf era was a time of immense hymn output. The count (1700–1760), his wife Erdmuth Dorothea von Reuss von Zinzendorf (1700–1756), and their son Christian Renatus (1727–52) all wrote hymns. Of the count's more than two thousand hymns, one of his earlier ones is illustrative of his piety and devotion to the Savior:[75]

Jesus, still lead on, till our rest be won;
and although the way be cheerless,
we will follow, calm and fearless;
guide us by thy hand, to our fatherland.

If the way be drear, if the foe be near,
let not faithless fears o'ertake us,
let not faith and hope forsake us;
for through many a foe to our home we go.[76]

A second early Zinzendorf hymn similarly expresses his devotion to Christ:

Christian hearts, in love united, seek alone in Jesus rest;
has he not your love excited? Then let love inspire each breast.
Members—on our Head depending, lights—reflecting him, our Sun,
brethren—his commands attending, we in him, our Lord, are one.

O that such may be our union as thine with the Father is,
and not one of our communion e'er forsake the path of bliss;
may our light break forth with brightness, from thy light reflected shine;
thus the world will bear us witness that we, Lord, are truly thine.[77]

The countess was raised in a pietist household in Ebersdorf, Thuringia, and developed a personal spirituality as richly deep as her husband's. Eleven of her hymns are still found in the German Moravian *Gesangbuch* of 1967. Although her work is not currently represented in the American *Moravian Book of Worship*, older American hymnals did contain a few translations. She wrote the following verse in celebration of the immediate headship of Jesus Christ in the Moravian Church:

> Thus our bliss will last forever; while we enjoy thy love and favor,
> and safe beneath thy shadow rest,
> we with joyful acclamation adore thee as thy congregation,
> thou art our Head and Lord confessed.
> To thee, Ancient of days,
> be honor, power and praise now and ever;
> Lord, grant that we eternally may put our trust alone in thee.[78]

This text is used with the tune *Wachet auf, ruft uns die Stimme*, discussed below.

Although he died at age twenty-four, the Zinzendorfs' son Christian Renatus wrote two of the most characteristic hymn stanzas of Moravian theology from the period. *Das einige notwendige* was written in 1747 for his father's forty-seventh birthday and was recast by Christian Gregor in 1754 into its current form.

> 'Tis the most blessed and needful part to have in Christ a share,
> and to commit our way and heart unto his faithful care;
> this done, our steps are safe and sure,
> our hearts' desires are rendered pure,
> and naught can pluck us from his hand which leads us to the end.[79]

The second stanza, taken from a Holy Week hymn of three stanzas, states clearly the theme of Moravian worship of the period:

> Lamb of God, you shall remain forever
> of our songs the only theme;
> for your boundless love, your grace and favor,
> we will praise your saving Name;
> that for our transgressions you were wounded,
> shall by us in nobler strains be sounded,
> when we, perfected in love,
> once shall join the church above.[80]

The unity of the church militant and the church triumphant was a favorite theme of Moravian life and worship. The *Saal* and the God's Acre were organized similarly with men's (brothers) and women's (sisters) sides.[81] The *Saal* was painted white, with the idea that its adornment would be the people who gathered therein. The anticipation of the time when members should be received into the "upper congregation" (in heaven), with which they felt themselves in constant communion, held no terror for the believers. This prospect regularly found liturgical expression, as it still does in the communion liturgies. Johannes von Watteville (1718–88), one of the sons-in-law of the count and countess, expressed this theme in the following stanza often used at the conclusion of communion liturgies in Germany:

> Amen, yea, hallelujah! Watch for him expectantly;
> trust the Lord, who is not far; soon the hall will ready be
> for the Lamb's great wedding feast where, adoring at his feet,
> Jesus' Bride beholds him then; come, Lord Jesus, come! Amen.[82]

Two other hymn-writers of the Zinzendorf era deserve special attention. Christian Gregor not only wrote music but also texts, influencing the music and worship of the entire church in the eighteenth and subsequent centuries. Henriette Marie Luise von Hayn (1724–82) was leader of the Older Girls and Single Sisters at Herrnhut. Her three-stanza hymn based on Psalm 23, written for the birthday of one of the sisters with whom she had close contact, is used in the European congregations as a children's text, in Britain as a communion hymn, and in the American congregations as an "all-purpose" hymn of devotion and joy:

> Jesus makes my heart rejoice,
> I'm his sheep and know his voice;
> he's a Shepherd, kind and gracious,
> and his pastures are delicious;
> constant love to me he shows,
> yea, my very name he knows.
>
> Trusting his mild staff always,
> I go in and out in peace;
> he will feed me with the treasure
> of his grace in richest measure;
> when athirst to him I cry,
> living water he'll supply.
>
> Should not I for gladness leap,
> led by Jesus as his sheep?
> For when these blessed days are over
> to the arms of my dear Savior
> I shall be conveyed to rest.
> Amen, yea, my lot is blest.[83]

The tunes used for the hymns of the eighteenth-century Renewed Moravian Church share the vitality of the Lutheran chorale tradition. In the tunes they adopted from their surroundings, the Moravians used or adapted versions readily "singable" by the congregation, often with more harmonic interest than contemporary Lutheran versions.[84] For instance, one of their most frequently used tunes was Philipp Nicolai's 1599 tune *Wachet auf, ruft uns die Stimme*. Christian Gregor's 1784 *Choralbuch* includes the setting shown in figure 3.2, or, with its Moravian realization, as in example 3.4.

Example 3.4. *Wachet auf,* tune 230, harmonized from Gregor *Choralbuch* setting.

Example 3.5. *Wachet auf,* setting from Freylinghausen *Geistreiches Gesang-Buch* (1741).

The Lutheran composer and hymn writer J. A. Freylinghausen's setting, from the *Geistreiches Gesang-Buch* of 1741, is shown in example 3.5.[85]

Although the two settings share a simplicity and directness apt for congregational song, Gregor's harmonization has more variety and interest. The contrast between these two settings and that of J. S. Bach, intended for use by a trained choir with the music in front of them, is apparent (see ex. 3.6).

Not only did the eighteenth-century Moravians adopt tunes from their Lutheran neighbors, they also adapted tunes from their own heritage. In a significant percentage of instances, when the eighteenth-century Moravians preserved a text from the sixteenth- or seventeenth-century Unity, they also preserved its tune, often in a simplified form.[86] Dramatically revised with regard to rhythm, but still recognizably the same tune, is the tune *Frew dich heut o Jerusalem,* shown here in from the 1531 hymnal and the 1784 Gregor *Choralbuch* (see figs. 3.5 and 3.6).

The eighteenth-century Moravians also wrote hymn tunes as needed. For many of these, no composer has been conclusively identified, but Tobias Friedrich (1706–36) is identified as the probable composer of some twenty tunes in the *Choralbuch* of 1784.[87] The first organist of Herrnhut, he was known for his great musical gifts in accompanying congregational song. Both as a composer and organist, he is credited with establishing the firm foundation for Moravian hymnody in the renewed church.

Example 3.6. *Wachet auf*, J. S. Bach harmonization.

The Renewed Moravian Church: The Nineteenth Century

Among nineteenth-century Moravian hymn writers are Christian Ignatius LaTrobe (1758–1836) and James Montgomery (1771–1854). LaTrobe was an English Moravian mission secretary and the editor of the Moravian tune books of 1790 and 1826. A number of his tunes and translations of German texts remain in use today. One Lenten stanza in particular well expresses his theological orientation:

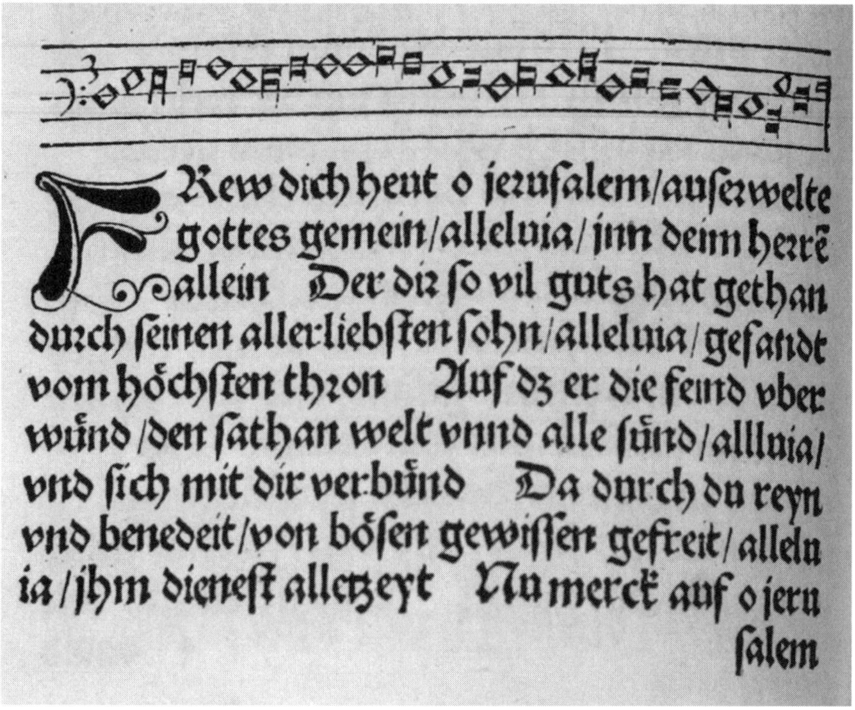
FRew dich heut o jerusalem/außerwelte
gottes gemein/alleluia/ jnn deim herrē
allein Der dir so vil guts hat gethan
durch seinen aller liebsten sohn/alleluia/ gesandt
vom hoͤchsten thron Auf dz er die feind vber
wuͤnd /den sathan welt vnnd alle suͤnd/alllnia/
vnd sich mit dir verbuͤnd Da durch du reyn
vnd benedeit/von boͤsen gewissen gefreit/ alleln
ia/ jhm dienest alletzeyt Nu merck auf o jeru
salem

Figure 3.5. *Frew dich heut O Jerusalem* from *Ein New Gesengbuchlen* (1531), B vii. Photo by David Holston.

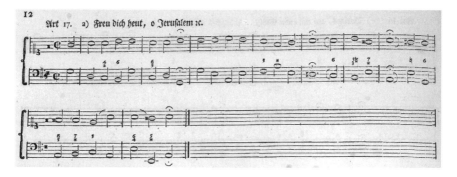

Figure 3.6. *Freu dich heut, o Jerusalem,* tune 17a, from Gregor *Choralbuch* (1784), 12. Photo by David Holston.

For our transgressions you were wounded;
our sins, O Lord, on you were laid;
your sufferings, O what love unbounded
for guilty ones the debt have paid!
With humble thanks we now adore you;
your cross our glory shall remain;
yet oft ashamed we weep before you,
that we by sin the Lord have slain.[88]

The earliest known appearance of its associated tune is in Grimm's 1755 manuscript chorale book, here in its customary harmonization in the Gregor *Choralbuch* (see ex. 3.7).

Example 3.7. *Saxony*, tune 184 B, harmonized from Gregor *Choralbuch* setting.

James Montgomery, the son of missionary parents, was a poet with a deep commitment to Sunday school and mission work. Among his many hymns are texts well known far beyond the Moravian church, including "Angels from the realms of glory," "Prayer is the soul's sincere desire," "Hail to the Lord's anointed," "According to thy gracious word," and the following Holy Week text, which deals with the "final incidents in the life of Jesus . . . to pray, to bear the cross, to die . . . and to live anew."[89]

Go to dark Gethsemane,
all who feel the tempter's pow'r;
your Redeemer's conflict see,
watch with him one bitter hour.
Turn not from his griefs away;
learn of Jesus Christ to pray.

Follow to the judgment hall,
view the Lord of life arraigned;
O the wormwood and the gall!
O the pangs his soul sustained!
Shun not suff'ring, shame or loss;
learn of him to bear the cross.

Calv'ry's mournful mountain climb;
there, adoring at his feet,
mark that miracle of time,
God's own sacrifice complete.
"It is finished!" hear him cry;
learn of Jesus Christ to die.

Early hasten to the tomb,
where they laid his breathless clay;
all is solitude and gloom;
who has taken him away?
Christ is ris'n—he meets our eyes!
Savior, teach us so to rise.[90]

This is sung to a somber tune by LaTrobe, shown in figure 3.7.

Figure 3.7. *LaTrobe*, tune 581 A, from C. I. LaTrobe, *Hymn-Tunes* (1826), 71.
Photo by David Holston.

Montgomery also continued the focus on the adoration of the victorious Lamb
of God in his hymn "Come, let us sing the song of songs." The final stanza of that
five-stanza hymn summarizes his own attitude toward eternity, which was existen-
tially vital, since his parents had both died shortly after the beginning of their service in the eastern Caribbean, leaving James and two younger brothers orphaned.

Long as we live, and when we die,
and while in heaven with him we reign,
this song, our song of songs shall be:
"Worthy the Lamb, for he was slain!"[91]

As noted with regard to Peter Wolle's 1836 tune book, during the nineteenth century, the American Moravian Church faced a certain impetus to conform, to use the best of "contemporary music." This was of particular concern to an influential American Moravian composer later in the century. In a memorial to the 1893 Northern Province Synod of the Moravian Church in America, the now-revered, but in his own day quite controversial, Francis Florentine Hagen (1815–1907) harshly criticized those who would hold to the "old" ways, including certain rituals, forms of decoration, and music:

> Some are wont to lay particular stress on singing ancient German chorales to the utter exclusion of American melodies, many of which are far more germane to the sense of some beautiful hymns than the German tunes. The slow, dull, soporific *tempo* of the latter, strongly suggests a corresponding spiritual *status* in those who most strongly affect them.[92]

In a footnote, Hagen goes on to write that

> German chorales properly belong to German churches, who sing them well. Having but little melody or rhythm, chorales are insipid, unless sung in 4-part harmony. . . . By forcing upon English-speaking American Churches foreign tunes, which but few are able to sing properly, we estrange from our services the very people among whom God has placed us to work. Need we wonder at our stunted growth?[93]

Hagen's own compositions, especially his organ preludes, reflect both his classical musical training and the influence of contemporary gospel music.[94] He remains best known, however, as composer of a tune to Johann Scheffler's 1657 text *Morgenstern auf finstre Nacht* (*Morning Star, O Cheering Sight*). First published in 1836 as a work for solo and chorus with piano, it was arranged in chorale style and included in the 1891 *Offices of Worship and Hymns*. It has become a favorite with American Moravian congregations (see ex. 3.8).

This was one of the many tunes added to the American Moravian repertoire in *Offices of Worship*, with tune numbers assigned in an attempt to continue the Gregor system.

The Renewed Moravian Church: The Twentieth Century

The spread of Moravian mission activity and development of the church far beyond its homelands has resulted in a variety of new hymns by many twentieth-century authors and composers. It is premature to make a general evaluation of their works so early in the twenty-first century, but some representative examples may be noted. Arthur James Lewis (1914–90) of the British Province served both as a pastor and an educator.[95] A collection of his hymns, *Some Malmesbury Hymns*, was privately printed in 1984; one of these was included in the British

Example 3.8. *Hagen*, tune 310 B, text and music from *Hymnal of the Moravian Church* (1969), 51.

Hymn Book of 1975.[96] The poetry of Wilhelm Jannasch (1888–1966) exemplifies the continuing tradition of hymn writing in the European Continental Province. Jannasch was also the author of a biographical study of the Countess Erdmuthe Dorothea von Zinzendorf.

Although the American Moravian provinces published three hymnals in the twentieth century (1923, 1969, and 1995), the first two were largely revisions of earlier hymnals. The 1995 *Moravian Book of Worship*, intentionally a "new" hymnal, includes a larger percentage of hymns by contemporary authors and composers. A text and tune by David M. Henkelmann (b. 1932) exemplify a newly emerging trend in Moravian hymnody of using a refreshing musical style with a text that maintains the primacy of an intimate personal relationship with Christ (see ex. 3.9).

Example 3.9. *Feed Us, Jesus. Moravian Book of Worship* 418. © David M. Henkelmann. Used by permission.

New texts by Moravian hymn writers recognize the changing nature of the worship experience in the North American congregations. New texts continually appear in the Caribbean area and the African provinces as well, enriching the tapestry of Moravian worship. As did Hagen's tunes a century ago, tunes by American Moravian composers of the late twentieth century continue to reflect the influence of classical training, the sound of traditional Moravian hymns, and a concern for contemporary-sounding music.[97]

Conclusions

Four conclusions and a question arise at the close of this brief history and survey of Moravian hymnody.

First, for more than five hundred years, the Unitas Fratrum has placed a very high value on congregational song. The production of hymnals, even under the most adverse circumstances and in the widest variety of obscure languages, has remained a high priority. These hymnals have contained both new and old hymns, written both by Moravians and by members of other Christian bodies.

Second, the hymns contained in Moravian hymnals exhibit a remarkable consistency of theological focus on the person and work of Jesus Christ. Even when Moravian theology shifted off center during the sixteenth century with Michael Weisse and again with the mid-eighteenth century Sifting Period, it was only a few years before a revision of the hymnal both aided and communicated the Moravians' intentional move back to the center of their theology.

Third, the hymnal editors and compilers have retained an awareness of the Moravian Church (Unitas Fratrum) both as part of the larger Christian church and as the heir and beneficiary of a long hymnic tradition of its own. Since the sixteenth century, the prefaces of Moravian hymnals have shown their compilers' awareness that these hymnals would be known and used far beyond Moravian congregations. These hymnals have consistently included hymns from the wider Christian church as well as hymns by Moravians. Moreover, the editors have made alterations in their own hymns as well as to those by others, to bring these hymns into agreement with their contemporary theological understanding as well as to make them fit the tunes available to the Moravians.

Fourth (and this follows directly from the preceding point), the Moravians have continually made use not only of materials from the past but also of contemporary expressions. They have recognized that the eternal truths of the past can be expressed in fresh language and can be sung to fresh, new music without threatening the security of the faith tradition.

The remaining question concerns the former "mission provinces" in Africa and other regions of the Moravian Unity. As noted above, the music and texts used in week-to-week worship in these regions are not easily available for study. What music is used, and what is the general theology of the texts? Given the 550 years of Moravian history and the 275 years of Moravian missions, it is reasonable to anticipate that, when these hymns and songs are studied, we will find that they express the same core values, using music that is unique to each area.

The Moravian Church has consistently understood the purpose of its hymns and hymn singing. In the preface of every English-language Moravian hymnal since 1789, the following prayer has been included. Similar injunctions appear in the prefaces of hymnals in other languages:

May all who use these hymns experience, at all times, the blessed effects of complying with the Apostle Paul's injunction (Ephesians 5:18,19), "Be filled with the Spirit, speaking to yourselves in psalms, and hymns, and spiritual songs, singing and making melody in your heart to the Lord." Yea, may they anticipate, while here below, though in an humble and imperfect strain, the song of the blessed above, who, being redeemed out of every kindred, and tongue, and people, and nation, and having washed their robes, and made them white in the blood of the Lamb, are standing before the throne, and singing in perfect harmony with the many angels round about it (Revelation 5:9–12 and 7:9–14), "Worthy is the Lamb that was slain, to receive power, and riches, and wisdom, and strength, and honor and glory, and blessing, forever and ever. Amen!"[98]

Notes

1. Cited in Edmund de Schweinitz, *History of the Unitas Fratrum* (Bethlehem: Moravian Publication Office, 1885), 402.

2. Throughout this chapter, the term *hymn* refers primarily to the text, not the music. When we are discussing the music, we will use terms such as *tune, chorale,* and so on. Also, hymn texts and tunes are printed separately rather than with the text interlined as in contemporary hymnal publications, in order to facilitate clear reading of the texts.

Many of the hymn texts cited in this chapter have been revised over the years since their composition; the most recent revisions in use are quoted. Unless otherwise noted, the German texts cited are also the most recent revisions in use.

3. Joseph Theodor Müller, *Hymnologisches Handbuch zum Gesangbuch der Brüdergemeine* (Herrnhut: Verlag des Vereins für Brüdergeschichte in Kommission der Unitätsbuchhandlung in Gnadau, 1916), 155.

4. Rudolf Říčan, *The History of the Unity of Brethren,* trans. C. Daniel Crews (Bethlehem and Winston-Salem: Moravian Church in America, 1992), 104.

5. Říčan, 104.

6. Müller, *Hymnologisches Handbuch,* 1–20.

7. Říčan, 220. Like some of the other hymnals printed by the Unity, this one was intended for use beyond the Unitas Fratrum.

8. We should recall that Comenius himself was twice driven into exile and his personal library was burned.

9. Jan Amos Comenius, ed., *Kancionál* (1659). Reprint ed. and introduction by Olga Settari (Kalich: Kultur Kontakt, 1992).

10. See chapter 1, p. 14, for information about the Sifting Period.

11. C. Daniel Crews, "The Hymnal of 1754: A Search for Identity and Respectability," unpublished paper presented at the Fourth Bethlehem Conference on Moravian Music, October 2002. Filed at the Moravian Music Foundation, 3–4.

12. Crews, "The Hymnal of 1754," 7–9.

13. See chapter 2, pp. 33–34, for a discussion of Gregor's practice of combining separate stanzas into a "new" hymn.

14. Martha Asti, introduction to facsimile edition of the Christian Gregor *Choralbuch* of 1784, ed. James Boeringer (Winston-Salem: Moravian Music Foundation Press, 1984), 24.

15. The German Moravian minister Julius Emil Bauer also noted this fact in his *Choralbuch der Brüdergemeine von 1784, nach seiner Abfassung und seinen Quellen mit dazu gehörigen biographischen Notizen* (Gnadau, 1867), 8.

16. *Auszug aus dem bisher in den evangelischen Brüder-Gemeinen gebräuchlichen Choral-Buche mit ausgeschriebenen Stimmen der Choral-Melodien* (Gnadau: Evangelische Brüder-Unität, 1831), 103. A second edition of this chorale book was printed in 1845.

17. Heinrich Lonas, *Choralbuch der evangelischen Brüdergemeine, enthaltend 123 der bekanntesten Melodien mit Text und als Anhang neun der Beliebsten Arien* (Gnadau: n. p., n.d.).

18. *Kleine Gesangbuch der Brüdergemeine* (Gnadau: Verlag der Unitätsbuchhandling, 1870).

19. *Choralbuch der evangelischen Brüdergemeine* (Gnadau: Verlag der Unitätsbuchhandling, 1893), iii–iv.

20. *Liturgienbuch der evangelischen Brüdergemeine* (Gnadau: Verlag der Buchhandlung der evangelischen Brüder-Unität, 1873).

21. *Choralbuch der evangelischen Brüdergemeine* (Gnadau: Verlag der Unitätsbuchhandlung, 1927).

22. James Hutton, *The tunes for the hymns in the collection with several translations from the Moravian hymnbook* (London: Bible and Sun, [1742]; part II, 1746; part III, 1749).

23. *A Collection of Hymns of the Children of God in All Ages, From the Beginning till now. Designed chiefly for the Use of the Congregations in Union with the Brethren's Church* (London: n.p., 1754).

24. For instance, the second half of one stanza of the great Zinzendorf hymn "Herz und Herz verein zusammen" reads:

> Und wenn eurer Liebeskette
> Festigkeit und Stärke fehlt,
> O so flehet um die Wette,
> bis sie Jesus wieder stählt!

In the 1789 English hymnal that half-stanza has been translated as:

> And should our love's union holy
> firmly linked no more remain,
> wait ye at his footstool lowly
> till he draw it close again.

where it might be more literally translated, still retaining the metrical structure, as:

> And should bonds of love which join you
> lose their strength and prove unreal,
> drive yourselves in prayer to Jesus
> till he turns love's bonds to steel.

This is not patient, passive waiting for someone else to fix a problem—this is a refusal to admit any reason for disunity among the Brethren!

25. Christian Ignatius LaTrobe, ed., *Hymn-Tunes sung in the Church of the United Brethren, Collected by Chrn. Igns. LaTrobe. A New Edition revised & corrected with an Appendix* (London: Printed for the Editor, 1826), i.

26. Peter LaTrobe, ed., *Hymn-Tunes sung in the Church of the United Brethren, First Collected by Chr. Ign. LaTrobe. An enlarged edition, Arranged in Parts for the Use of Choirs* (London: William Mallilieu, ca. 1854).

27. *The Moravian Hymn Book and Liturgy* (London: Moravian Book Room, 1975), xiv.

28. Henry L. Williams, "The Development of the Moravian Hymnal," *Transactions of the Moravian Historical Society* 18/2 (1962), 261.

29. Williams, 262.

30. Peter Wolle, *Hymn Tunes, Used in the Church of the United Brethren, Arranged for Four Voices and the Organ or Piano-Forte; to which are added Chants for the Litany of that Church, and a Number of Approved Anthems for Various Occasions* (Boston: Shepley and Wright, 1836). A second edition was printed in 1872.

31. Wolle, iii.

32. Wolle, iii.

33. Wolle, iii.

34. *Hymnal and Liturgies of the Moravian Church (Unitas Fratrum)* (Bethlehem: Board of Elders of the Northern Diocese of the Church of the United Brethren in the United States of America, 1923).

35. *The Offices of Worship and Hymns of the American Province of the Unitas Fratrum* (Bethlehem: Moravian Publication Concern, 1891). This book's popularity is evidenced by its reissue in a combined publication only seventeen years later under the title *The Liturgy and the Offices of Worship and Hymns of the American Province of the Unitas Fratrum* (Bethlehem: Moravian Publication Concern, 1908).

36. Williams, 262. See also Williams, "Centennial of a Transitional Hymnal: The Offices of Worship and Hymns, 1891," *Moravian Music Journal* 37/1 (Spring 1992), 3ff.

37. *Hymnal and Liturgies of the Moravian Church* (Bethlehem and Winston-Salem: Moravian Church in America, 1969).

38. *Moravian Book of Worship* (Bethlehem and Winston-Salem: Moravian Church in America, 1995), also cited as *MBW*. See Albert H. Frank, *Companion to the Moravian Book of Worship* (Winston-Salem: Moravian Music Foundation, 2004).

39. David Zeisberger, ed., *A Collection of Hymns for the Use of the Christian Indians, of the Missions of the United Brethren, in North America* (Philadelphia: Henry Sweitzer, 1803).

40. Zeisberger, v–vii.

41. *MBW* 553, verses 1, 4, 5.

42. *MBW* 723, verses 1 and 2, anonymous translation. The German original is found in *Gesangbuch der Evangelischen Brüdergemeine* (Herrnhut and Bad Boll: Direktionen der Evangelischen Brüder-Unität, 1967), 826:

Weil ich Jesu Schäflein bin,
freu ich mich nur immerhin
über meinen guten Hirten,
der mich wohl weiss zu bewirten,

der mich liebet, der mich kennt
und bei meinem Namen nennt.

Unter seinem sanften Stab
geh ich aus und ein und hab
unaussprechlich süsse Weide,
dass ich keinen Hunger leide;
und so ift ich durstig bin,
führt er mich zum Brunnquell hin.

43. See chapter 2, pp. 32–33, for a discussion of the Daily Texts.
44. See chapter 2, pp. 35–38, for a discussion of the lovefeast.
45. Arthur Freeman in conversation with Albert Frank; see also the discussion on the Unity's "ordination hymn" on pp. 59–60 below.
46. *Das Gesangbuch der Gemeine in Herrnhuth* (1737), *Anhang* XII, hymn 2034. Each article is treated with several expository stanzas and a collect.
47. *MBW* 270, stanzas 1 and 2, trans. Catherine Winkworth. *Gesangbuch* (1967), 43:

Gottes Sohn ist kommen uns allen zu Frommen
hie auf diese Erden in armen Gebärden,
daß er uns von Sünde freie und entbinde.

Er kommt auch noch heute und lehret die Leute,
wie sie sich von Sünden zur Buß sollen wenden,
von Irrtum und Torheit treten zu der Wahrheit.

48. *MBW* 774. © Albert H. Frank. Used by permission.
49. *Supplement to the Moravian Hymn Book*, 1911 ed. (London: Moravian Book Room, 1940), 909.
50. Perhaps the best example is what has come to be known as "the ordination hymn of the Ancient Unity," discussed below.
51. Frank, *Companion*, 268–69.
52. Frank, *Companion*, 270. Gregor's *Hosanna* is one of the few Moravian tunes to be widely published in nineteenth-century American tunebooks.
53. *Hymnal and Liturgies* (1969), 122, verse 1. The German (1967 *Gesangbuch*, 146):

O Anblick, der mir's Herze bricht!
Herr Jesu, das vergeß ich nicht,
wie du am Ölberg für mich büßtest.
O daß du für die Seelenangst,
in der du mit dem Tode rangst,
nun ewig mit mir prangen müßtest!

54. *Readings for Holy Week* (Bethlehem: Interprovincial Board of Communication, 2000), 52. © Albert H. Frank. Used by permission. *Companion,* 275.

55. *Hymnal and Liturgies* (1923), 304.

56. *A Collection of Hymns for the Use of the Protestant Church of the United Brethren.* (London, 1789). LaTrobe, John Swertner, and Frederick William Foster were the editors of this hymnal.

57. *MBW* 416, identified as "inspired by the Communion Hymn of John Hus."

58. *MBW* 519.

59. John Julian, *A Dictionary of Hymnology,* 2nd ed. (New York: Dover Publications, 1907), 1:395.

60. Joseph Theodor Müller, *Geschichte der Böhmischen Brüder, I Band 1400–1528* (Herrnhut: Verlag der Missionsbuchhandlung, 1922), 132–33.

61. *MBW* 519. The entire Czech original is found in *Písně duchovné evangelické* (Kralice, 1615), J xv (p. 351).

Radůgme se wždy společně
chwálu wzdáweyme ochotně
Bohu Otcy nebeskému
Synu zy Duchu swatému:

Nebot' gest račil shlednauti
na nás z swé Božské milosti
w tento čas přenebezpečný
bud'mež toho wssickni wděčni.

Wzbudil k potřebné pomocy
wůdce wěrné w tyto časy:
ó Pane náš wssemohaucý
rač to swé djlo konati,

Kteréž sy ráčil začjti
z swé přewewliké milosti
myt' vsáme w tobě Pane
že twé djlo předce stane.

☞O obnow swé swaté sliby
nebo sy w nich wždycky wěrný
včinto pro swau dobrotu
a vwed' lid swůg w gednotu.

Kterýž gest welmi rozptylen
a scestným včenjm sweden
ó Pastýři předůstogný
nawsstěw lid swůg rozptylený.

Račse k tomu přičiniti
lidi zesna probuditi
swětlo prawdy swé zgewiti
a temnosti zapuditi.

At'by prawdu twau znagjce
bludům neslaužili wjce
než tobě Bohu samému
na wěky požehnanému:

Nebos ty Pánem nad Pány
v také Králem nad králi
roztrniž swau Božskau mocý
vkrutnost té swětské mocy.

At'by twogi wywolenj
w tomto swětě nezhynuli
račiž Pane pospjsliti
mocně lid swůg ochrániti.

☞O deyž nám Otče nebeský
Ducha swatého swýlosti
at'bychom w twé prawdě stáli
wssemu zlému odolali:

A tak w lásce twé stogjce
y bližnj swé milugjce
s sebau wždycky w vpřijmnosti
přebýwali po wsse časy.

Činje djky tobě Bohu
naděgi magjce žiwau
že ty nás spolu dowedeš
tam kdežs Angely kralugeš.

Amen.

The German is verses 1–3, 11, 10, and 12 of the twelve printed in *Ein New Gesengbuchlen*, ed. Michael Weisse (1531; reprint, ed. Wilhelm Thomas [Kassel: Bärenreiter, 1931]), J xi.

Frewen wir uns all inn ein
geben lob unn preis allein
got dem vater unn dem Sohn
zu gleich der dritten perschon

Denn er hat barmherzikeyt
zur zeyt grosser ferlikeit
uns beweist und sein gesetz
geschrieben inn unser herz

Auch hat er inn seiner krafft
trewe diener uns verschafft
o herr hilf mit deiner gab
dz dein wreck einn fortgang hab.

O ewiger got gieb krafft
hielff das dein wort inn uns haft
und wir dem selben nachgehn
also vor dir wol bestehn

Hilff dz dein volck auserwelt
nicht so kleglich werd gekwelt
sonder aller ubel frey
dich lob unnd gebedeney.

Verley das wir all zu gleich
inn dir leben tugentreych
darnach dort funden zu lohn
eyn unuergengliche kron.

62. *MBW* 525, verse 2. Members of the early Unitas Fratrum often referred to themselves as "brethren of the law of Christ."

63. See chapter 1, pp. 7–8, for a discussion of the "essentials" as described by the Unitas Fratrum.

64. *Hymnal and Liturgies* (1923) 720, verses 1, 2, and 3. The English here cited was translated by Catherine Winkworth from Michael Weisse's 1531 adaptation of the Czech original (*Ein New Gesengbuchlen*, 1531, M v). The German translation has continued in use and is included in the 1967 *Gesangbuch* (1002, 1, 3, 7). Müller cites the first appearance of the Czech original as being in the 1519 hymnal; it seems to have dropped out of use in the Czech congregations of the Unitas Fratrum, as it does not appear in the 1615 hymnal, nor has it reappeared in the Czech hymnal of 1954 (*Bratrský Zpěvník* [Nové Pace, Jednota bratrská]). See Müller, *Hymnologisches Handbuch*, 186–87. The German is as follows:

Nun last uns den leib begraben
bey dem wir keinen zweifel haben
er werd am letztenn tag aufstehn
und unverrücklich erfür gehn.

Seine seel lebt ewig inn got
der sie allhie aus seiner gnad
von aller sünd und missetat
durch seinen bund gefeget hat.

Nu lassen wir ihn hie schlaffen
unnd gehn alsampt unser straffen

schicken uns auch mit allem fleiss
denn der todt kompt uns gleicher weiss.

65. Říčan, 104.
66. Julian, 156.
67. *Hymnal and Liturgies* (1969) 301.
68. Julian, 156.
69. *Bratrský Zpěvník.*
70. Müller, *Hymnologisches Handbuch*, 16.
71. Müller, in Julian, 512.
72. *MBW* 509, translated by Louis F. Kampmann (1876). The German is from the 1778 *Gesangbuch* (16):

Des Herrn Wort bleibt in Ewigkeit,
und schallet in der Gnadenzeit,
lehrt Christum, unsers Heiles Grund,
und macht uns Gotten Willen kund.

Zeigt an die böse Art und Sünd,
straft die an aller Menschen Kind,
treibt damit das Gewissen ein,
verdammet beyde groß und klein;

Schickt drauf sein Trostwort und Botschaft,
welch's ist ein' sondre Gotteskraft,
die alle ewig selig macht,
bey welchen es nicht wird veracht't.

Das ist das Evangelium,
der unerforschliche Reichthum,
das Sühnwort und Geheimniß groß,
welch's Christus bracht aus Vaters Schooß.

Lob und Dank sey dir, euer Hort,
für dein heilsames Gnadenwort:
Hilf, daß wir darnach allezeit
hier leben bis in Ewigkeit.

73. *Dir, o Herr, sei Lob gegeben: Mit Comenius singen und beten* (Herrnhut: Direktion der Evangelische Brüder-Unität, 1992).

74. Crews, "The Hymnal of 1754," 12. A significant part of this paper deals with the hymns from the early Unity that are contained in this eighteenth-century hymnal. This "pointing finger" can be seen in figure 1, column 2.

75. See Albert Knapp, *Geistliche Gedichte des Grafen von Zinzendorf . . . Mit einer Lebensskizze und des Verfassers Bildniss* (Stuttgart and Tübingen, ca. 1843).

76. *Hymnal and Liturgies* (1923) 696, verses 1 and 2, trans. Jane Borthwick (1846). 1967 *Gesangbuch*, 710:

Jesu, geh voran auf der Lebensbahn,
und wir wollen nicht verweilen,
dir getreulich nachzueilen;
führ uns an der Hand bis ins Vaterland.

Solls uns hart ergehn, laß uns feste stehn
und auch in den schwersten Tagen
niemals über Lasten klagen;
denn durch Trübsal hier geht der Weg zu dir.

77. *MBW* 673, verses 1 and 4, anonymous translation. See note 15 above for a discussion of verse 2 of the same hymn. 1967 *Gesangbuch*, 674:

Herz und Herz vereint zusammen, sucht in Gottes Herzen Ruh.
Lasset eure Liebesflammen lodern auf den Heiland zu!
Er ist's Haupt, wir seine Glieder, er das Licht und wir der Schein,
er der Meister und wir Brüder, er ist unser, wir sind sein.

Laß uns so vereinigt werden, wie du mit dem Vater bist,
bis schon hier auf dieser Erden kein getrenntes Glied mehr ist.
Und allein von deinem Brennen nehme unser Licht den Schein;
also wird die Welt erkennen, daß wir deine Jünger sein.

78. *Hymnal and Liturgies* (1923) 797, verse 2. The English translation first appeared anonymously in the 1789 British Moravian Hymn Book. This is part of a six-stanza hymn written for November 13, 1741. 1967 *Gesangbuch*, 336, 6:

Also sind wir innig fröhlich und halten uns für ewig selig,
dein Hirtenamt ist unsre Ruh.
Darum schallt in dieser Stunde aus unser aller Herz und Munde:
Glück zu dem Ältesten, Glück zu!
Dem Vater aller Zeit
sei bis in Ewigkeit Preis und Ehre!
Der Sünderschar ist's Elend klar,
drum läßt sie sich dem Heiland gar.

79. *MBW* 768, verse 1. The English translation was made by Philipp Heinrich Molther and altered for the 1789 British Moravian Hymn Book. 1967 *Gesangbuch*, 673:

Das einige Notwendige ist Christi teilhaft sein,
und daß man ihm behändige Geist, Seele und Gebein.
Dann geht man seinen Gang gewiß
und weiß, daß man durch keinen Riß
sich von der Hand, die nie läßt gehn, getrennet werde sehn.

80. *MBW* 346, verse 3. John Swertner's English translation, made for the 1789 British *Moravian Hymn Book*, catches the sense of the original, but not the literal phraseology. 1967 *Gesangbuch*, 147, verse 4:

> Darum du, O Herze ohnegleichen,
> du in deiner Todesschön,
> sollst uns nie aus unsern Augen weichen,
> bis wir dich auf immer sehn.
> An dem Liede: Jesus ist verschieden,
> sollen unsre Kehlen nie ermüden
> bis sie eingestimmet sein
> in die obere Gemein.

81. *Saal* is a German term for a gathering room including sanctuaries, auditoriums, etc., in contrast to the more formal *Kirche*, or church. God's Acre is the Moravian term for a cemetery or burial ground.

82. 1967 *Gesangbuch*, 1036, verse 5, trans. C. Daniel Crews, Nola Reed Knouse, and Roy Ledbetter (2005). The German is as follows:

> Amen ja, Halleluja! Seid stets auf ihn bereit und wacht!
> Harrt des Herrn, der nicht mehr fern; schon wird zur Hochzeit zurecht
>   gemacht,
> zu dem grossen Abendmahl, da ihn im Vollendungssaal
> seine Braut von nahem schaut. Komm, Herr Jesu! Ruft die Braut.

83. *MBW* 662, trans. Frederick William Foster (1789). *Companion*, 164–65. An alternate translation of the source of this hymn, *Weil ich Jesu Schäflein bin*, is "I am Jesus' little lamb"; see p. 56 and n42 above for verses 1 and 2. Verse 3 follows (1967 *Gesangbuch*, 826):

> Sollt ich nun nicht fröhlich sein,
> ich beglücktes Schäfelein?
> Denn nach diesen schönen Tagen
> werd ich endlich heimgetragen
> in des Hirten Arm und Schoss.
> Amen, ja, mein Glück ist gross!

Additional eighteenth century Moravian hymn-writers are listed and discussed in Joseph Theodor Müller's article on Moravian hymnody in Julian's *Dictionary of Hymnology*.

84. See chapter 5, pp. 137–38, for Gregor's instructions to organists regarding accompanying congregational hymn singing.

85. Johann Anastasius Freylinghausen, *Geistreiches Gesang-Buch, den Kern alter und neuer Lieder in sich haltend* (Halle: In Verlegung des Wäysenhauses, 1741), 34.

86. In fact, of the fifteen hymns from the 1531 hymnal that are included in the 1778 Gregor-edited hymnal, ten use the same tune as in 1531, although revised.

Further study of other hymnals from the early Unitas Fratrum is likely to result in a similar finding. For a study of one hymn (text and tune) from the sixteenth century and its use in the eighteenth century hymnals and tune book, see Nola Reed Knouse, "Recovering a Treasure: A Translation and Musical Setting of 'Gott sah zu seiner Zeit' from the 1544 *Gesangbuch der Brüder in Behemen und Merherrn*," in *The Distinctiveness of Moravian Culture: Essays and Documents in Moravian History in Honor of Vernon H. Nelson on His Seventieth Birthday*, ed. Craig D. Atwood and Peter Vogt (Nazareth: Moravian Historical Society, 2003), 9–17.

87. James Boeringer, "Sources for the Moravian Tunes in Gregor's 1784 *Choralbuch*," in Christian Gregor, *Chorabuch* (1784), facsimile ed., 36, 41.

88. *MBW* 340, verse 1.

89. See *MBW* 293, verses 1–4, *MBW* 749, *MBW* 263, *MBW* 422, and Frank, *Companion*, 56.

90. *MBW* 349.

91. *MBW* 469, verse 5.

92. Francis Florentine Hagen, *Unitas Fratrum in Extremis; or, Thoughts on the Past and Present Condition of the Moravian Church in America, Respectfully Submitted to the Provincial Synod of 1893, at Bethlehem, Pa.* (Bethlehem: Moravian Publications Office, 1893), 10.

93. Hagen, 10, note 1.

94. See chapter 5, p. 147, for a discussion of Hagen's organ music.

95. Frank, *Companion*, 89–90.

96. *The Moravian Hymn Book* (London: Moravian Book Room, 1975).

97. See Frank, *Companion*, 5–6, for a profile of the *Moravian Book of Worship* and a list of Moravian hymn writers represented in that hymnal.

98. *MBW*, iii.

Chapter Four

Moravian Sacred Vocal Music

Alice M. Caldwell

Although hymns made up the bulk of documented musical activity by the Moravians from their beginnings through the eighteenth century, independent sacred vocal compositions for soloists and choirs flourished especially during the period of approximately 1750 to 1830. During this time, Moravian composers wrote choral music, accompanied by instruments, that was heard or performed by members of Moravian congregations week in and week out throughout the church year. Although the Moravian Church worldwide has maintained a continuous tradition of vocal and instrumental music to the present day, the period 1750–1830 stands apart for the sheer intensity and volume of music making, as well as for its stylistic continuity throughout. From the vantage point of today, we can consider it the "golden age" of Moravian music. After a period of relative neglect in the later nineteenth and early twentieth centuries, scholars, particularly in America, began to rediscover the music of the earlier Moravians, and modern scholarship in Moravian music has existed since the 1930s.[1] Thanks to the work of these scholars, now in the third generation, we have at our disposal large quantities of Moravian music in modern editions, some of it recorded. An awareness of the contribution of Moravian composers has also entered mainstream scholarship and transcends religious denominations in America today. A recent discussion of the past, present, and future of American choral music among prominent American choral conductors pointed out the importance of the Moravians in establishing the foundations of the American choral tradition in the eighteenth century, along with the New England composers and the singing school movement.[2] In Europe, appreciation for the distinctly Moravian musical heritage has developed only recently, partly because of the rich context of the musical culture surrounding the Moravians in Germany, and partly because of the difficulties inherent in researching religious music in eastern Germany during the years of the German Democratic Republic, 1945–90.[3] Today, scholars working in the field are building on the accomplishments of the past several decades and are striving toward a more holistic understanding of Moravian music in its musicological, cultural, and theological context.

Thanks to the work of numerous cataloguers, the unpublished holdings of the major Moravian music collections are accessible to the modern researcher. These holdings are dauntingly vast by any standard of measurement: in the United States alone, about ten thousand documents, primarily from four congregation collections, are available.[4] In Herrnhut, Germany, the principal European repository of Moravian music, about thirty discrete collections representing congregations, schools, and musical institutions contain works by about 225 Moravian and non-Moravian composers, for a total of about three thousand manuscripts.[5] The congregation at Zeist in the Netherlands also had an extensive music collection, with over fifteen hundred pieces of music, vocal and instrumental. That collection, along with the archives of the Moravian congregation at Zeist, resides at the State Archives (Rijksarchief) in the province of Utrecht.[6] Other congregational collections in Great Britain, Europe, South Africa, and Labrador have been at least partially inventoried.

It is perhaps the sheer volume of Moravian music manuscripts that has led researchers to favor the preparation of modern editions over historical or stylistic commentary on the genre as a whole. Only with an adequate number of musical works readily available, representing a cross section of the total output of Moravian composers, could scholars undertake a historic-analytic overview. With modern editions of Moravian music now in circulation for some forty years, it is certainly time to begin the comprehensive study of the repertoire as a whole, with the eventual goal of understanding the origins, development, and flourishing of Moravian sacred vocal music not only as a genre but also by composer, region, and time period. This essay seeks to summarize those topics on the basis of work by previous scholars as well as this writer's own familiarity with some of the repertoire and to indicate directions where continuing research is needed.

An understanding of Moravian sacred vocal music begins with a look at the music of non-Moravian composers who inspired Moravian musicians to compose their own works and examines the works themselves on the basis of their manuscript sources. A survey of the repertoire and its style characteristics will consider choral anthems, arias, and duets. An overview of the sources available for study in the various Moravian archival collections will orient the reader to the documentary basis for modern editions and to the limited evidence at hand for historical performance practice.

Background and Context

Scholars of German church music in the eighteenth century have referred to the latter half of the century as a period of "decline" when measured against the sacred music of Johann Sebastian Bach and his contemporaries.[7] A combination of the secularizing influence of the Enlightenment, institutional decline, and a change in aesthetic values may well have led to a rejection of the musical depth and complexity of the baroque, but those same influences provided Moravian communities with the context for developing their own musical culture, one that could thrive not only in the historic/artistic continuity of Europe but also in the isolated, unsupportive environment of colonial America.

With the passing of the era of counterpoint came a new compositional ideal of melodic simplicity.[8] Daniel Gottlob Türk, who is represented by choral and keyboard pieces in Moravian collections, in 1787 dismissed J. S. Bach's *Canonic Variations on "Vom Himmel hoch"*—a veritable treatise on the art of counterpoint—as "music for the eyes."[9] In place of counterpoint, a new aesthetic of beautiful, clearcut melody supported by simple homophony emerged. Works in this style by Telemann and Handel were held up and emulated by later composers such as Johann Adolph Hasse, Carl Philipp Emanuel Bach, Johann Friedrich Doles, Johann Heinrich Rolle, Gottfried August Homilius, Johann Gottlieb Naumann, Friedrich Wilhelm Rust, and Johann Abraham Peter Schulz, all represented by works in Moravian music collections. This shift toward greater simplicity may have been influenced by the decline in the institutions—namely, choir schools—that had previously cultivated the art of complex vocal polyphony.[10] Enlightenment emphasis on a more secularized, scientific curriculum cut into the time once devoted to music instruction, leading to a neglect of choral music in schools.[11] Perhaps church music became simpler partly because the rigorous training and practice required to perform repertoire as demanding as the Bach cantatas was no longer cultivated.

But spiritual aims also influenced the trend toward a simpler aesthetic. Church music in the latter part of the eighteenth century sought primarily to "edify," that is, to awaken devotional feelings in as direct and accessible a way as possible.[12] Contrapuntal complexity with its severe intellectual demands did not fulfill this role; rather, a single, clear-cut, prominent melody with subordinate accompaniment allowed even the least-educated listener to participate in a form of "edification." Doles, a neighbor of the Saxon and Thuringian Moravians at the Thomaskirche in Leipzig (and a non-Moravian composer whose works are well represented in Moravian collections), described the ideal church music style in 1790: "rhythm that is orderly and easy to grasp, simple and powerful harmony, and heart-melting melody."[13] The goal of a "heart-melting" melody is to edify, or to bring the listener to a higher level of spiritual development. Moravian composers worked within this aesthetic, which, as we will see, was ideally suited to the role of music in Moravian worship and to the musical institutions in Moravian communities. What, then, were some of the specific sources and influences on which Moravian musicians drew in the development of a Moravian repertoire?

German Oratorio, Passion, Cantata, and Opera

As abundant and detailed as they are, Moravian congregation records nevertheless make virtually no reference to specific works of music by name or composer and thus provide minimal help in forming a theory of how Moravian music developed. We must draw conclusions from the collections of music manuscripts themselves. A close examination of the contents of the various collections allows a number of patterns to emerge and yields the beginnings of a hypothesis regarding the origins of Moravian music. The single work that is perhaps most valuable as a starting point because of its overwhelming popularity throughout Germany, as well as its ubiquity in Moravian music collections, is the Passion oratorio *Der Tod Jesu* by Karl Heinrich Graun.[14]

The Moravian Church grew and developed during a time of musical transition from the baroque to the classical. One of the leading figures in that transition, Graun was a significant influence on the development of Moravian composition, largely through his *Tod Jesu*. He was educated at the Kreuzschule of Dresden, geographically and culturally close to the beginnings of the Renewed Moravian Church in Saxony. Although Graun is chiefly associated with the flourishing of Italianate opera in Germany, in the field of sacred music *Der Tod Jesu* towered over all others in the estimation of the later eighteenth century, and well into the nineteenth. Modern observers have described *Der Tod Jesu* as having the significance that Bach's *St. Matthew Passion* later had in Germany, or Handel's *Messiah* in England and America.[15] In addition, the subject matter of Graun's oratorio fitted neatly into the theology of the Moravians, with its emphasis on contemplating the sufferings and death of Jesus as a means for individual and group devotion.[16] Frequent liturgical gatherings, not only during Holy Week, had the Passion of Christ as their theme and provided ample opportunity for performance of appropriate music.[17]

Composing at a time when the graphic and even violent musical depictions of the baroque Passion were considered too extreme for sensitive listeners, Graun used a text by Karl Wilhelm Ramler that toned down the vividness of the biblical texts, replacing them with sentimentalized poetry.[18] In Protestant Germany, the dramatic Passion of the baroque had been replaced with the simple reading of the Bible by the pastor, interspersed with congregational chorales. Musical "edification," in the spirit of the time, was provided instead by the lyrical Passion oratorio, or cantata as it was sometimes called, with the directness of the Bible story moderated by lyrical poetry and music aimed at the listener's "sensitivities" (*Empfindungen*).

The development of the oratorio in the eighteenth century, and the career of *Der Tod Jesu* in particular, appear circumstantially to be closely linked with the development of the Moravian anthem. Of course, the oratorio was not the only type of sacred music composed at this time; mainstream composers also wrote cantatas, motets, anthems, arias, and duets. But the frequent appearance of oratorio movements by other composers in Moravian collections strongly suggests that these works provided a model for Moravian composers developing their own repertoire.

An oratorio was a large-scale, multimovement work on biblical themes meant to "edify" in accord with the religious mind set of the time. A contemporary definition of *oratorio* by Johann Abraham Peter Schulz (1747–1800; a composer represented in Moravian collections) can be a starting point for extrapolation to the Moravian context:

> *Oratorium.* (Poetry; music.) A spiritual, but completely lyric and short drama, which is performed with music, for use in divine service on high feast days. . . . The oratorio assumes various personages who are strongly moved by the noble religious subject of the feast that is being celebrated and who express their sentiments [*Empfindungen*] about it, now singly, now together, in a very emphatic manner. The purpose of this drama is to penetrate the hearts of the listeners with similar sentiments [*Empfindungen*].[19]

If we paraphrase and reduce the scale of the above statement (remembering that "short" is a relative term; these works are long by modern standards), it is not hard to develop a definition of the Moravian anthem/duet/aria: "a spiritual vocal piece for use in divine service or other congregational gatherings on feast days. The work expresses sentiments meant to penetrate the hearts of the listeners." Schulz further holds up the example of Graun's *Tod Jesu*, a work that would occupy a uniquely exalted place in the repertoire of German Protestant church music for the next century and a half, as it would also remain a favorite of Moravian congregations.

As described by Howard Smither, the German oratorios of the mid-eighteenth century, and *Der Tod Jesu* in particular, show a number of characteristics that make this music especially well suited to the Moravian aesthetic of the time. In contrast to the Italian oratorio with its emphasis on arias, the German oratorio included a greater number of choruses and often chorales as well, with congregational participation.[20] In Moravian communities, the singing of chorales held a central position that might be described without exaggeration as absolutely essential to the life of the community, since virtually every gathering, whether liturgical or not, included the singing of chorales. The texts of German oratorios also reflected the literary *Empfindsamkeit* of the time as did the hymns of the Moravians with their intensely personal expression.[21] Some common characteristics include use of the present tense, simple, direct language, and an idealized, anonymous narrator. The choruses, chorales, and even arias of contemporary German oratorios thus fit the criteria for inclusion in the Moravians' communal worship and devotional gatherings. Multiple copies of choruses from *Der Tod Jesu* and other oratorios of the period found in Moravian music collections attest to the high esteem in which the Moravians held them and suggest the hypothesis that they served as models for the Moravians who wrote their own music.

Graun used a variety of styles in *Der Tod Jesu*—operatic in the arias and recitatives, including a few measures of coloratura in each aria; chordal and fugal styles in the choruses; and the simple, purely chordal style of the chorales, which comprise six of eleven choruses.[22] There are no purely instrumental movements, not even an instrumental introduction. Instead, the work opens with chorus and basso continuo and the simple, unadorned chorale *O Haupt voll Blut und Wunden* sung to Ramler's text *Du, dessen Augen flossen.*[23] It is perhaps telling that this movement, both with its original text and alternate Moravian texts, appears repeatedly in Moravian collections—for instance, five times in the Salem collection and twice in the Lititz catalogue.[24] Some individual parts carry attributions to Graun, showing that Moravian musicians were well aware of the source of the chorale setting.

Der Tod Jesu was not the only work of Graun's that inspired the Moravians. Other pieces in Moravian collections come from his *Te Deum,* his *Passions-Cantate,* and the anthology of sacred music published in 1758 titled *Geistliche Oden in Melodien gesetzt von einigen Tonkünstlern in Berlin.*[25]

Nor was Graun the only composer whose works the Moravians admired and performed. Oratorios by J. H. Rolle, both in their entirety and in excerpts, are found in Moravian collections. *Der Tod Abels* (1769) was a particular favorite; *Lazarus* is also well represented.[26] Often works of other composers entered the Moravian repertoire by way of parody, that is, with new words substituted for the original text, whether the original words were sacred or secular. Johann Gottlieb Naumann's German opera *Cora und Alonzo* (1780) takes place in a fictional setting in ancient South America, yet a number of excerpts, ranging from aria and duet to chorus, found their way into the Moravian repertoire by way of textual parody. Clearly, Moravian sacred vocal music drew inspiration from a number of sources, not all of them sacred.[27]

How, then, did the Moravian repertoire emerge from the wider context of eighteenth-century sacred music and adapt itself to the specific needs of the Moravians? In the absence of explicit documentation, we can nevertheless make some conjectures about the developmental process.

In the early years of Moravian music composition, the influence of contemporary oratorios and cantatas can perhaps be seen in the multimovement cantatas that Moravian composers wrote for particular occasions. In her study of musical practice among the early Moravians, Anja Wehrend identifies the period of approximately 1739 to 1764 as the time when cantata composition flourished.[28] After about 1770, the trend seems to have turned toward the composition of individual choral pieces, which we have come to call anthems, as well as arias and duets.[29] Cantatas, and later, anthems, were performed on specific occasions, such as birthdays, weddings, funerals, church holidays, dedications, and the customary Moravian lovefeast.[30] Musical works might be called "ode," "psalm," or "cantata," and manuscript and printed texts for them can be found in Moravian music collections.[31] Sometimes, if an occasion called for it, a number of pieces could be linked together in a cantatalike cycle that would also be called a "psalm."[32]

One cantata from this early period can be an example and starting point for looking at some of the characteristics of Moravian sacred vocal music. Johann

Daniel Grimm, the music teacher at the Catharinenhof near Herrnhut, wrote a pair of cantatas for the birthdays of Nicholas Ludwig von Zinzendorf (May 26, 1750) and his son Christian Renatus (September 19, 1750). Both cantatas are for soprano solo and alternate aria, arioso, recitative, and chorales, the latter marked "coro" but presumably meant for congregational participation.[33] Texts of the various movements come from a variety of sources. First, the daily text, or *Losung*, for the days in question—short biblical texts chosen by lot (Los) for each day of the year—provides the first movement.[34] Subsequent movements make use of free poetry and chorale stanzas. Moravian composers would draw on these same textual sources for another hundred years and more. By the third quarter of the eighteenth century, the multimovement cantata was more or less replaced by the single-movement anthem (or less frequently, duet or aria) for chorus and orchestra, on a text coming from the Bible (whether an assigned daily text or not), free verse, or a hymn stanza (or some combination of all three). Our survey will now take a brief look at the sources for these works before examining their melodic, harmonic, rhythmic, and other musical elements in more detail.

Moravian Music Sources

Moravian congregations kept performing libraries of their music manuscripts, which today form the basis for archival collections in various locations. In North America, the Moravian Music Foundation has consolidated various congregational collections under its umbrella. The most important of these are the Bethlehem Congregation Collection, the Salem Congregation Collection, the Lititz Congregation Collection, and the Herbst Collection. Smaller collections from Nazareth, Pennsylvania, and Dover, Ohio, also contain significant works. Published catalogs of the Salem and Lititz collections detail the growth of the collections and re-create, as much as possible, the contemporary catalogues fashioned by the early Moravians as they organized their extensive holdings.[35] In Europe, the Unity Archives in Herrnhut has assembled most of the important European collections under one roof. The holdings include congregational collections, collections of Single Brothers and Single Sisters houses, school collections, and the private music libraries of individuals, including some of the most prominent Moravian composers. In the Netherlands, the collection of the Zeist congregation has been catalogued and now resides at the Rijksarchief, Utrecht.[36] Moravian collections in England and Scandinavia have yet to become generally accessible and more widely known.[37]

From the list of the above archival collections alone it is clear that geography plays a role in the history and analysis of Moravian music sources. As the church built its repertoire of both borrowed and original compositions, the music disseminated to wherever Moravians established their communities. We would find the same core repertoire in comparing the music collections of the European sources with each other, or European collections with American collections. Local differences reveal themselves in the degree to which a particular composer may be represented in his home congregation, but even the Bethlehem composer Johann Christian Till, who never traveled more than a few dozen miles from his birthplace, is represented by several manuscripts in the Herrnhut collection.[38] Recent research shows that during the eighteenth and nineteenth centuries, German Moravian missionaries brought works of European musicians to Labrador in the course of their mission work with the native people.[39] The very locations of Moravian music sources tells us a great deal about the importance of music in Moravian life, and one well-traveled collection in particular offers a starting point for an overview of those sources.

The Moravian Music Foundation administers a uniquely valuable resource known as the Herbst Collection. Comprising over five hundred manuscripts, this was the private library of Bishop Johannes Herbst (1735–1812), a man important not only for the music he composed, but also for the legacy of the collection itself. Begun while Herbst lived in Germany and continued after he emigrated to North America in 1786, Herbst's library is virtually a microcosm of the Moravian sacred vocal repertoire. It is accessible to present-day scholars by means of a microfiche copy and a published catalogue; it is perhaps the best-studied of the major Moravian collections.[40] A look at some of the components of the Herbst collection will help orient the newcomer to the manuscript sources of Moravian music and will show how the sources themselves shed light on the music and its historical context.

First of all, the group of forty-five extended works by non-Moravian composers that make up one part of the Herbst collection makes clear the extent to which the Moravians cultivated large-scale works by contemporary mainstream composers and helps to document the historical background of the Moravian repertoire. Oratorios by Johann Adolph Hasse, Johann Friedrich Agricola, Carl Philipp Emanuel Bach, Nicola Jomelli, Johann Heinrich Rolle, Johann Abraham Peter Schulz, Daniel Gottlob Türk; Passion music by Franz Joseph Haydn and Gottfried August Homilius; liturgical music by Giovanni Battista Pergolesi; Haydn's *Creation*; and Handel's *Messiah* all were part of the Moravians' musical world.[41] Many individual pieces that are in fact excerpts from these larger works appear elsewhere in the Herbst collection as free-standing choruses, again indicating the close relationship of multimovement works and individual anthems.[42] Belonging to the various collections alongside anthems, arias, and duets by Moravian composers, these excerpts from larger works by prominent contemporary composers both inspired the Moravian compositions and remained in the active repertoire with them.

Most of Herbst's collection consists of copies of anthems, arias, and duets by Moravian and non-Moravian composers, including Herbst himself.[43] In its selection of composers and repertoire, the collection is fully representative of other important Moravian collections, allowing, of course, for some variation due to geography. Herbst, after all, used his collection as a traveling reference library, and for that reason alone it can be considered an exemplary collection of Moravian repertoire and a good starting point for the study of Moravian music. In one respect, however, Herbst's copies are exceptional. The great majority of the manuscripts in Herbst's collection are in score format, a far larger proportion than appears in the other collections. Once again, this stems from the collection's function as a traveling library—scores use less paper than sets of parts—but the newcomer approaching the Herbst collection should be aware that manuscripts in score are not typical of the other collections.

Sets of parts are, in fact, the norm in most of the other Moravian collections, which originally functioned as performing libraries. A typical manuscript of a Moravian anthem consists of a set of individual parts for each voice and instrument, together with a keyboard part. Sometimes the organ part doubles as a wrapper, or a separate wrapper may be used, bearing a title such as "Coro" or "Duetto" and the text incipit.

Composer attributions cannot always be taken for granted. Since Moravian composers wrote for the glory of God and not for the promotion of their own reputations, precise attributions were not a high priority. Often a composer attribution is in a hand other than the composer's. The cataloguer Marilyn Gombosi points out that Herbst neglected to identify numerous works, particularly those by Christian Gregor, in the first part of his own collection, but appears to have added more attributions later on.[44] Quite possibly the authorship of many works was simply a matter of general knowledge, particularly in the case of a prominent composer such as Gregor, and written attributions were considered superfluous. The Herrnhut composer Christian David Jaeschke combined personal modesty with some concern for accurate attribution. In a series of organ books compiled for use by the Herrnhut congregation, Jaeschke wrote out other composers' names in full but signed his own pieces with a simple initial *J*.[45] Yet modern cataloguers have worked diligently to cross-reference known works, with the result that relatively few Moravian manuscripts, particularly those in the United States, remain completely anonymous.

Completing the picture of sacred art music sources, the smallest segment of the Herbst collection is a group of volumes that might be described as anthologies, books of keyboard pieces, books of sacred songs with keyboard accompaniment, and a book of chorales.[46] Other Moravian collections include similar books as well, some of them obviously student music books, and others part of the working library of a practicing musician. Herbst's book *Lieder zum singen am Klavier* is an example of the sacred song tradition, with short, strophic songs sung to a keyboard accompaniment, probably intended for school or home use.[47] Bound volumes found in other collections may also contain a selection of anthems in keyboard-vocal score, corresponding to choral-orchestral sets of parts found elsewhere. Keyboard reductions undoubtedly were used in small-scale performances in homes and schools.[48]

Related to these manuscript anthologies are the very few examples of printed Moravian sacred music, nearly all of it in the form of piano-vocal reductions. Probably the best-known of these versions are the collections of the English Moravian Christian Ignatius LaTrobe, one of them specifically designated as music for the Moravian church.[49] Another anthology was published in England by the German-educated Moravian composer Christian Friedrich Hasse.[50] In Germany the musical amateur Gottlob Friedrich Hillmer assembled a selection of Moravian sacred music in two volumes.[51]

The Anthems, Duets, and Arias

Now that we have established a context for the history and documentation of Moravian sacred vocal music, it is time to look closely at the works themselves and examine some of the common characteristics of the individual pieces.[52] Sacred art music of the "golden age" can be described first of all in contrast to Moravian liturgical music of the same period: it is newly composed, unlike liturgical music, which was based almost exclusively on preexisting chorale tunes and chant formulas (although occasionally, as we will see, a chorale might be integrated into the larger structure of an anthem).[53] Art music was also intended for performance by trained choirs, soloists, and instrumentalists, not by congregations, and comprises choral anthems, duets, and arias for voices with orchestral accompaniment.

The majority of Moravian anthems, solos, and duets from this "golden age" share a similar five-part formal structure: orchestral introduction—vocal section—orchestral interlude—vocal section—orchestral coda. In general, the first orchestral section remains in the tonic key; the first vocal section often modulates to a closely related key. The interlude remains in that key or moves to another closely related key, and the second vocal section most often restates musical material from the first vocal section, returning to the tonic for the conclusion of the work. These works vary greatly in length and complexity for both singers and instrumentalists.

Instrumentation

The typical Moravian anthem is written for a four-part mixed choir accompanied by a string orchestra (two violins, viola, cello, and bass) and keyboard (organ or cembalo). Larger works, intended for especially festive occasions, could include wind instruments in various combinations, beginning with flutes and French horns and ranging up to a full wind complement including oboes, clarinets, trumpets, bassoon, and trombone. A few pieces incorporate the complete SATB Moravian trombone choir, in a departure from the more typical three-trombone

orchestration found in the sacred music of contemporary mainstream composers.[54] Instrumentation of a particular piece may differ from one source to
another, undoubtedly due to the differing availability of wind players in different
congregations or at different times in the same congregation. Some of the largest
works call for double choirs, tailored no doubt to the architecture of the grander
Moravian churches, which included balconies for the organ and musicians.[55]

Voicing

Voicing in a Moravian anthem is almost always in four parts, yet the standard SATB
voicing is not the preferred one. Most anthems are scored for SSAB, although
SATB works make up a substantial minority. Reasons for this idiosyncratic voicing
remain in the realm of conjecture. Perhaps the most logical explanation takes into
account the fact that the Moravian orchestra that usually accompanied an anthem
was made up of men exclusively, resulting in a smaller pool of male choral singers.
All Moravian choirs drew their singers from members of the congregation who
were amateur musicians (albeit well-trained amateurs); supplementing the choir
with professionals was not an option. Yet it is also possible that an aesthetic reason
exists for "Moravian" choral voicing. The SSAB texture closely resembles the voicing of parts in Moravian hymn playing as evidenced by those few sources that provide a completely harmonized hymn tune or fragment.[56] The three uppermost
female voices replicate the closely spaced chorale voices played by the right hand
on a keyboard, while the single male voice resembles the bass line of a hymn as
played by the left hand. In the absence of documentary evidence explaining the
Moravian vocal texture, this question remains open to researchers.

Style

A Moravian anthem aims to create a moment of spiritual edification in which
the message of the text is conveyed in part through the emotional and sensual
experience of the music. The words are carried by beautiful melodies and harmonies, but they must be clearly understood. Zinzendorf himself repeatedly
emphasized the importance of text communication in congregational singing
and art music performance.[57] This overriding concern of Moravian composers
resulted in a large body of works, by many individuals and over a long period of
time, that share numerous stylistic features. First and foremost, the choral and
orchestral textures are overwhelmingly homophonic. Homophony was, after all,
one of the major style characteristics of music in the classical era, and it perfectly
suited the aesthetic and spiritual goals of Moravian sacred art music. Even in the
works with the most technically challenging instrumental introductions and
interludes, parts for the instruments during the choral sections are simpler,
allowing the vocal parts to dominate the texture.

A typical homophonic anthem employs that texture exclusively, to the point that all four vocal parts move in the same rhythmic values virtually all the time (see ex. 4.1).

Example 4.1. Johannes Herbst, *Unser Keiner lebt ihm selber* (*None among Us Lives to Self*), mm. 1–11. Edited by Nola Reed Knouse. © 1999 by Hinshaw Music, Inc. Used by permission.

Nothing impedes a clear declamation of the text, and the choral texture resembles a harmonized hymn tune in its simplicity. Even the soprano line often lacks a memorable melody when it is simply derived from the harmony, with all melodic and ornamental interest delegated to the orchestra (see ex. 4.2).

Example 4.2. Christian Gregor, *Ehre sey Gott in der Höhe* (*Glory to God in the Highest*), mm. 29–38. Edited by Nola Reed Knouse. © 2006 Moravian Music Foundation. Used by permission.

In most anthems, the orchestra, particularly the first violin, takes full responsibility for carrying the melodic activity, especially in introductions and interludes.

An examination of a large number of Moravian anthems reveals some distinctions within a mostly homophonic genre and a few exceptions to the generalizations stated above. The anthem repertoire can be divided roughly into four categories: homophonic, combined homophonic-polyphonic, multisectional, and lyrical. Homophonic anthems are by far the largest group and provide a context in which to view the variants of the other anthem types.

The Homophonic Anthem Johannes Herbst's anthem of 1810, *Freuet euch und seyd fröhlich* (*Lift Your Hearts, Rejoicing*) provides a model of the typical homophonic anthem. A fourteen-bar instrumental introduction, seen in example 4.3, has the dual role of foreshadowing the entrance of the choir and expanding that material with decorative passagework.

The voices of the choir proceed mostly in like rhythmic values, declaiming the text simply and without melodic complexity, which might draw attention away from the text. Herbst occasionally lightens the texture by pairing two voices at a time, yet these "duet" passages are always in parallel motion, once again allowing a clear statement of the text (see ex. 4.4).

Four brief instrumental interludes and an eight-bar postlude provide melodic elaboration not found in the choral texture, as in example 4.5.

This descriptive outline could be applied to hundreds of Moravian anthems, yet within the conventions composers occasionally used other techniques. J. G. Gebhard interposed phrases of a chorale between the newly composed segments of *Herr, mein Fels* (*Lord, my rock*).[58] Some Moravian anthems begin, or interrupt the four-part choral texture, with solo passages, usually for soprano as in example 4.6, but sometimes other voice parts as well.

For an especially festive occasion, the fiftieth anniversary of the arrival of the Moravians in North Carolina (1753–1803), Simon Peter composed an anthem in which the choral writing conforms completely to the homophonic style; but he conceived *Siehe, meine Knechte sollen essen* (*Look Ye, How My Servants Shall Be Feasting*) on a grand scale, alternating double choirs with a soprano solo.[59]

In *How Beautiful upon the Mountains,* John Antes creates an echo effect by pairing voices within a strictly homophonic texture (see ex. 4.7).

The American-born composer J. C. Till left us a fine example of homophonic writing in his *Barmherzig und gnädig ist der Herr,* in which the rhythm of the original German text generates the rhythm of the choral parts, as shown in example 4.8.

Clearly, Moravian composers accepted the mission of creating music in which the text takes precedence and worked within the strictures imposed by the community. But other forms of musical expression, including polyphony and melodic lyricism, could be adapted to fit Moravian aesthetic standards. Some Moravian art music makes use of a wider range of compositional techniques while keeping to the ideal of simplicity and directness of expression.

Example 4.3. Johannes Herbst, *Freuet euch und seyd fröhlich* (*Lift Your Hearts, Rejoicing*), mm. 1–16. Edited by Nola Reed Knouse. © 1997 by Hinshaw Music, Inc. Used by permission.

Example 4.4. Herbst, *Freuet euch*, mm. 21–24.

Example 4.5. Herbst, *Freuet euch*, mm. 67–71.

Example 4.6. David Moritz Michael, *Siehe, ich verkündige euch grosse Freude* (*Hearken, For I Bring to You Great Joy*), mm. 1–16. Edited by Andy Moore. © 2004 by Fostco Music Press, A Division of Shawnee Press, Inc.

Example 4.7. John Antes, *How Beautiful upon the Mountains*, mm. 40–48. Edited by Ewald V. Nolte. Boosey & Hawkes 5677. © released to Moravian Music Foundation, 1977. Used by permission.

Example 4.8. Johann Christian Till, *Barmherzig und gnädig ist der Herr* (*Kindhearted and Gracious Is the Lord*), mm. 1–10. Edited by D. Keneth Fowler. © 2000 Moravian Music Foundation. Used by permission.

The Homophonic-Polyphonic Anthem Many pieces depart from strict homophony by incorporating a small amount of polyphony, imitation, or independence of voices. J. F. Peter may even have taken the baroque contrapuntal master George Frideric Handel as his model in choosing the text "Unto us a child is born" ("Uns ist ein Kind geboren"). Handel's *Messiah* was known to the Moravians; Peter was almost certainly familiar with the chorus "For unto us a child is born."[60] Peter's setting, which begins with paired voices in parallel motion, changes to fugal entries for "and the government shall be upon his shoulders," as shown in example 4.9.

Peter, like Handel, then returns to clear-cut homophony for "Wonderful, Counselor."

A more complex contrapuntal section appears in Christian David Jaeschke's extended anthem *Herr, auf dich traue ich* (*Lord, I Trust in You*). The first two-thirds of this 135-measure anthem presents the entire text of the anthem, followed by a twenty-measure fugal section leading to an emphatic homophonic climax. Example 4.10 (a) shows the opening phrase; example 4.10 (b) shows the first eighteen measures of the fugal section.

G. G. Müller's *Ihr seyd theuer erkauft* (*You Are Precious to Him*) opens with paired voices that overlap each other, shown in example 4.11.

The Multisectional Anthem Such limited examples of contrapuntal technique are noteworthy only in the context of the overwhelmingly homophonic style of the Moravian anthem. None of the examples cited above is extensive enough to obscure the text or render the piece inaccessible to an amateur choir. Yet Moravian composers and singers were able to summon the resources for full-scale contrapuntal singing when the occasion called for it. Some of the larger, multisectional works employ fugal writing in their final sections in the manner of earlier baroque choruses ("Worthy is the lamb that was slain" from *Messiah*, for instance), providing an emphatic peroration to a large-scale piece. J. C. Geisler's *Ehre sey dem* (*Glory to Him*) is a multisectional setting of parts of the Moravian Easter Litany text that concludes with a fugue on "forever and ever" ("von Ewigkeit zu Ewigkeit") (see ex. 4.12).

In this example, overlapping repetition of "forever and ever" expresses the meaning of the text rather than obscuring it. Some anthems emphasize a final "Amen" by treating it fugally.[61]

Other multisectional works accommodate long texts, such as an entire psalm.[62] Sometimes the contrasting meanings of two psalm verses inspire contrasting musical sections. Both C. D. Jaeschke and John Gambold set Psalm 126, verses 5 and 6, with contrasting sections of minor/major and slow/fast (see ex. 4.13).[63]

Sometimes a composer combines texts from two different sources, setting each in a different way. J. C. Geisler uses a solo bass voice to declaim the "voice of God" from a Bible verse, "Thus says the Lord" ("*So spricht der Herr*") but changes to a homophonic chorus to set the hymn stanza "We can never describe it" ("*Das ist unbeschreiblich*") (see ex. 4.14).

Example 4.9. Johann Friedrich Peter, *Uns ist ein Kind geboren* (*For unto Us a Child Is Born*), mm. 25–28. Edited by Jeannine Ingram. © 1976, 1977 by Carl Fischer, Inc., New York. Used by permission.

Example 4.10. Christian David Jaeschke, *Herr, auf dich traue ich* (*Lord, I Trust in You*), (a), mm. 15–22; (b) mm. 94–111. Edited by Jayson Snipes. © 2006 Moravian Music Foundation. Used by permission.

Example 4.10 (continued).

Example 4.10 (*continued*).

The Lyrical Anthem The last category of Moravian anthem style reflects the gentler, more introspective side of Moravian composers. A number of Moravian anthems, particularly those with texts of a more personal and inward-looking nature, set those texts with flowing, lyrical melodies in a songlike style. Sometimes these lyrical pieces are in minor keys or in triple meter.[64] Christian Ludwig Brau's choral anthem *O verehrungswürdige Nacht* (*Night of Holy, Highest Worth*) could be mistaken for a soprano aria underlain with a choral accompaniment (see ex. 4.15).

Lyrical anthems, though few in number compared with the more common homophonic pieces, might be considered a bridge to the remaining type of Moravian sacred art music, the duet and solo aria. These pieces are the "chamber music" of Moravian sacred art music, requiring the smaller forces of one or two singers accompanied generally by strings and keyboard only. Duet and aria manuscripts make up perhaps 5 to 10 percent of all Moravian music sources, but they hold their own among the larger choral works as an intimate alternative to large-scale forms of expression.

Virtually all duet and aria manuscripts specify soprano for the vocal parts. In view of the very limited amount of concrete information on contemporary performance practice in Moravian congregations, we can only take the manuscript sources at their face value and assume that solo singing was an art cultivated primarily among women and, perhaps, among young women in the Moravian girls' schools.

Example 4.11. Georg Gottfried Müller, *Ihr seyd theuer erkauft* (*You Are Precious to Him*), mm. 1–10. Edited by Lou Carol Brown and Karl Kroeger. © 1978 by Carl Fischer, Inc., New York. Used by permission.

Duets can be considered in many respects a branch of the anthem repertoire. Little, beyond the reduced voicing, distinguishes duets from anthems. The two voices generally sing either alone or in parallel motion with one another, recalling the way composers also used paired voices in anthems (see ex. 4.16).

Example 4.12. Johann Christian Geisler, *Ehre sey dem* (*Glory to Him*), mm. 73–83. Edited by Karl Kroeger. © 1978 by Carl Fischer, Inc. New York. Used by permission.

Example 4.13. Christian David Jaeschke, *Die mit Tränen säen* (*Those in Sorrow Sowing*), mm. 16–22. Edited by Alice M. Caldwell. © 1990 by Hinshaw Music, Inc. Used by permission.

Example 4.14. Johann Christian Geisler, *So spricht der Herr—Das ist unbeschreiblich* (*Thus Says the Lord—We Can Never Describe It*), mm. 1–59. Edited by Nola Reed Knouse. © 1999 by Hinshaw Music, Inc. Used by permission.

Example 4.14 (*continued*).

Example 4.14 (continued).

Example 4.15. Christian Ludwig Brau, *O verehrungswürdige Nacht* (*Night of Holy, Highest Worth*), mm. 23–33. Edited by Nola Reed Knouse. © 2006 Moravian Music Foundation. Used by permission.

dass dir tau - send Son - nen schie - nen!
more than thou - sand suns all beam - ing!

dass dir tau - send Son - nen schie - nen!
more than thou - sand suns all beam - ing!

dass dir tau - send Son - nen schie - nen!
more than thou - sand suns all beam - ing!

dass dir tau - send Son - nen schie - nen!
more than thou - sand suns all beam - ing!

Example 4.15 (*continued*).

Occasionally a composer takes advantage of his two solo voices by giving them interlocking phrases in imitation, as in Christian Gregor's *Unbeschreiblich schöner* (*Lovelier Beyond All Description*), shown in example 4.17. Note also the internal rhymes in the text, highlighted by the imitation in the voices.[65]

Duet texts lean toward the gentler biblical and hymn verses, avoiding texts of praise and rejoicing more suited to large musical forces.

Solo arias, on the other hand, gave composers an opportunity to express in musical terms the more personal texts in the Moravian canon. Many aria texts are in the first person.[66] *Abide in Me* (*Bleibet in mir*), *I Love to Dwell in Spirit* (*Ich bin in meinem Geiste*), and *My Soul Doth Magnify the Lord* (*Meine Seele erhebet den Herrn*) are some of the "I" texts that Moravian composers set as solo arias.

Herbst's *Einer ist euer Meister* (*One Alone Is Your Master*) shows a solo line not unlike the melody of a lyrical-style anthem, with passing tones, ornamental sixteenths, and appoggiatura figures not generally found in the chordal texture of larger anthems (see ex. 4.18).

We can conclude this survey of style characteristics in Moravian art music with consideration of the question, Is there a specifically "Moravian" style of composition? An answer may come from a Moravian composer himself, if we look at a piece composed for use outside the Moravian Church. Christian Ignatius LaTrobe wrote a number of pieces specifically for the Church of England, and

Example 4.16. Johann Friedrich Peter, *Kindlein, bleibet bey ihm* (*Hearken, Stay Close to Him*), mm. 49–64. Edited by Karl Kroeger. © 1975 by Carl Fischer, Inc., New York. Used by permission.

Example 4.17. Christian Gregor, *Unbeschreiblich schöner* (*Lovelier Beyond All Description*), mm. 6–22. Edited by Nola Reed Knouse. © 2002 Moravian Music Foundation. Used by permission.

his *Jubilate* provides a point of comparison. An excerpt, shown in example 4.19, reveals a complex, polyphonic texture, with an intricate interplay of voices distinctly lacking in LaTrobe's own Moravian works (such as the psalm settings mentioned above) or in the works of other Moravian composers.[67]

Example 4.18. Johannes Herbst, *Einer ist euer Meister* (*One Alone Is Your Master*), mm. 10–27. Edited by Nola Reed Knouse. © 2006 Moravian Music Foundation. Used by permission.

Probably two factors account for the difference in style: first, the previously discussed emphasis on clarity of text communication, and second, a difference of choral performance practice. Church of England choir schools fostered a level of professionalism among choral singers that most likely required more rehearsal time than was judged appropriate in Moravian community life. The simple homophony of Moravian art music fulfilled two functions, not only providing a setting for the clear declamation of religious texts, but also facilitating singing by skilled but nevertheless nonprofessional singers. A look now at other considerations of performance practice will help to round out the picture of Moravian sacred vocal music from its origins to its performance context.

Example 4.19. Christian Ignatius LaTrobe, *Jubilate*, mm. 49–60. Edited by Nola Reed Knouse. © Moravian Music Foundation. Used by permission.

Performance Practice

Moravian anthem sources and contextual documentation offer tantalizingly little information on contemporary performance practice. We know that anthems were performed by mixed choirs of men and women, accompanied by orchestras

Example 4.19 (*continued*).

of men, all under the leadership of the congregation organist, who directed from the keyboard. Beyond these basic facts, we can glean little more specific information from available documents. In some cases, the lack of information in itself provides some clues. We understand, for instance, that choral and orchestral performers were amateurs, presumably all members of the congregation, since church financial records discuss payment only with respect to the congregation organist, not singers or other musicians.[68] In fact, in 1790 a proposed concert by a visiting professional singer, with admission to be charged, caused such a stir in Herrnhut that the Elders decided to cancel it.[69] We should remember, however, that although performance by amateurs was the norm, it was the stylistic ideal rather than the limitations of performers that accounts for the technical simplicity of choral and instrumental parts in Moravian anthems.

The existence of a choir of singers (Sängerchor) in Herrnhaag dates to October 3, 1742, and is noted in the diary as consisting of a group of musically gifted brothers and sisters who would meet regularly for rehearsals.[70] Little additional documentation exists for the Herrnhaag community, and even less for Herrnhut.[71] In the forty-year span from 1786 to 1827, a single reference in the Herrnhut congregation diary to a particular choir member offers us some minimal information on the makeup of the Herrnhut choir:

On May 21, 1800, the single sister Dorothea Wilhelmina Koelbing was called home by our dear Lord after an illness of several days. This home-going was a particular cause of grief not only because we lost a dear, young sister full of hopefulness, but because she was also the first singer in the choir and head teacher in the girls' school. Many tears were shed on her account.[72]

This all too brief passage indicates a hierarchy among choir members and identifies the deceased sister as, most likely, the soprano responsible for solos where they occurred in anthems and for the first solo part in arias and duets.

Little evidence of choir or orchestral personnel at specific performances has been uncovered to date, leaving us to speculate on the numbers involved. Many sources contain only one copy of each part, suggesting at most two to three performers to a part. Some sources contain multiple parts, usually in different handwritings, indicating larger forces at some performances.[73] Often duplicate treble parts are found in the Single Sisters collections of the community as well.[74]

However, lists of musical personnel in Bethlehem during the second decade of the nineteenth century do survive. They reveal that in 1812 the choir had six female singers and seven male singers. Of these, the men, all married, ranged in age from twenty-six to sixty-one. The women ranged in age from eighteen to fifty-four, and all but one were single. The list of instrumentalists included players of violin, viola, *Bass* (cello or contrabass), flute, clarinet, bassoon, horn, trumpet, trombone, and organ, and the list indicates that many men could play more than one instrument.[75]

Keyboard parts also offer us some scraps of information. Most manuscripts include a fully written-out keyboard part on two staves, usually with figured bass symbols below the left-hand staff.[76] These parts are labeled interchangeably "organ" and "cembalo," suggesting that performance on any available keyboard instrument was acceptable. Performances in church would have been accompanied by the organ. A performance in any other location lacking an organ would have been supported by whatever keyboard instrument was available.

Keyboard parts also show us that the director led from the keyboard, as they contain instrumental cues that may or may not have been playable by the organist-conductor. These condensed-score arrangements would also have facilitated the rehearsal of the choir without the orchestra. The actual execution of the keyboard part was probably a matter of improvisation at each performance, with the director outlining the harmonies with the help of both the notes on the page and the figured bass symbols, using one or two hands as they were free while he conducted the choir at the same time.[77]

Moravian continuo performance may have included more than a keyboard, however. Harp parts occur throughout the collections of Moravian manuscripts, more so in European collections than in American. An examination of one particular anthem strongly suggests that the harp may have been considered a necessary partner to the keyboard. Jaeschke scored his *Bleibet in mir und ich in euch* for the usual choir, strings, and keyboard.[78] These parts, as well as a separate harp part, are all in his handwriting. In the harp part, bar 32 is marked "Harpa con cembalo"; bar 53 is marked "Harpa solo." Evidently, the harp was intended not as a substitute for the keyboard but as a partner with it. Continuo use of the harp is one of many questions of performance practice that remain to be answered by today's researchers.

In looking at the history of Moravian sacred vocal music as a whole, we are likely to arrive at the question of why a relatively small church denomination invested so much of its time and effort in developing and maintaining a remarkable musical tradition over many years, and even across continents. The theology of music in the Moravian Church is a complex topic that is best left to the theologians, but even the lay observer can appreciate one of the central motivations behind music and singing in the Moravian Church. With roots in the greater Protestant tradition that preceded it, the Moravian concept regarded music as a mediator between heaven and earth, and the music sung on earth as an image of the music heard in heaven.[79] Seen in such cosmic terms, the Moravians' dedication to the ongoing creation and performance of music in their communities becomes transparent and understandable.

Notes

1. Albert G. Rau and Hans T. David, *A Catalogue of Music by American Moravians, 1742–1842* (Bethlehem: Moravian College and Seminary for Women, 1938; reprint, New York: AMS Press, 1970).

2. Barbara Tagg and Linda Ferreira, "Fourteen Conductors Speak About American Choral Music," *Choral Journal* 48/8 (March 2003), 9–25.

3. See chapter 1, n13.

4. Cited by the editor Marilyn Gombosi in *Catalog of the Johannes Herbst Collection* (Chapel Hill: University of North Carolina Press, 1970), v. Other published catalogues include: Frances Cumnock, ed., *Catalog of the Salem Congregation Music* (Chapel Hill: University of North Carolina Press, 1980), and Robert Steelman, ed., *Catalog of the Lititz Congregation Collection* (Chapel Hill: University of North Carolina Press, 1981). References to specific works in these collections are cited with initials and a catalog number: Herbst Collection—H; Salem Congregation Collection—S; Lititz congregation Collection—L.

5. Paul M. Peucker, "Music in the Moravian Archives, Herrnhut," typescript list assembled by the archivist Paul Peucker, October 2002, filed at the Moravian Music Foundation, Winston-Salem. The Herrnhut collection is further described by Andrea Hartmann in "Musik zu den Festtagen der Brüdergemeine, 1759–1800," *Unitas Fratrum* 47 (2001): 29–40.

6. Randall H. Tollefsen, *Catalogue of the Music Collection of the Moravian Congregation at Zeist* (Utrecht: Rijksarchief, 1985), xv.

7. Material on the historical context of Moravian music is taken from Friedrich Blume, ed., *Geschichte der evangelischen Kirchenmusik* (Kassel: Bärenreiter-Verlag, 1965), 217–49. Georg Feder titles his chapter "Der Verfall" in discussing German

church music as a whole from about 1750–1820, but qualifies that judgment with the note that Saxony and Thuringia, where some of the earliest Moravian communities flourished, maintained a continuously high standard of church music, more so than other regions of Germany (217).

8. Blume, 222–23.

9. Blume, 222. More than a dozen works by Türk are found in American Moravian collections.

10. The high level of music education in German choir schools of the baroque is described by John Butt, *Music Education and the Art of Performance in the German Baroque* (Cambridge: Cambridge University Press, 1994).

11. Blume, 219.

12. Blume, 221–23.

13. Blume, 222: "[D]ie leichte Faßlichkeit und Folge der Rhythmen, die simple und kräftige Harmonie, und die herzschmelzende Melodie."

14. *The New Grove Dictionary of Music and Musicians*, s.v. "Graun, Carl Heinrich." *Der Tod Jesu* is discussed in detail in Howard E. Smither, *A History of the Oratorio*, vol. 3: *The Oratorio in the Classical Era* (Chapel Hill: University of North Carolina Press, 1987), 401–34.

15. Blume, 243; Smither, 349.

16. See chapter 1, pp. 7–8, 14, 16, for observations on Moravian theology.

17. For instance, regular Friday afternoon Passion liturgies. See Alice M. Caldwell, "Music of the Moravian *Liturgische Gesänge* (1791–1823): From Oral to Written Tradition" (PhD diss., New York University, 1987), 158. See also chapter 3, p. 57.

18. Blume, 242–43.

19. From the encyclopedia *Allgemeine Theorie der schönen Künste*, translated in Smither, p. 337.

20. Blume, 369.

21. Blume, 365, 372.

22. Blume, 406–7.

23. The first page of the score, from a 1760 print, is reproduced in Blume, facing p. 225.

24. S 22.2, 22.2a, 260.2, 314.3, 502.1, on tenor part, "Art 151.a.1 nach Graun"; L 62.5, on tenor part "aus Grauns Tod Jesu"; L 307.

25. The *Te Deum* is found in H B VI and L 11.1. Excerpts from the *Passions-Cantate* are found in L 18.2, as well as in the Bethlehem Congregation collection; the entire cantata is in the collections of the Philharmonic Society of Bethlehem and the Salem *Collegium musicum* (see chapter 7). Karl Heinrich Graun, *Geistliche Oden in Melodien gesetzt von einigen Tonkünstlern in Berlin* (Berlin: Christian Friedrich Voss, 1758), is cited in L 21.4.

26. Both oratorios are found in the Herbst collection, and individual choruses throughout the Herbst, Salem, Lititz, and Herrnhut collections. See also Janet Best Pyatt, "Music and Society in Eighteenth-Century Germany: The Music Dramas of Johann Heinrich Rolle (1716–1785)" (PhD diss., Duke University, 1991), and "Johann Heinrich Rolle: A Non-Moravian Composer in the Moravian Music Foundation," *Moravian Music Journal* 38/1 (Spring 1993): 7–13.

27. Naumann's *Cora* is discussed in detail by Pauline Fox in "Parodies for Piety: 'aus Naumanns Cora'" (*Moravian Music Journal* 42/2, Fall 1997, and 43/1, Spring 1998), as well as in her dissertation, "Reflections of Moravian Music: A Study of Two

Collections of Manuscript Books in Pennsylvania ca. 1800" (PhD diss., New York University, 1997), 135–48.

28. Anja Wehrend, *Musikanschauung, Musikpraxis, Kantatenkomposition in der Herrnhuter Brüdergemeine* (Frankfurt am Main: Peter Lang, 1995), chapter 4 and throughout.

29. Marilyn Gombosi also comments on the change from multimovement to individual pieces with respect to her work in reassembling a large-scale work performed in Salem for the communal celebration on July 4, 1783. See Gombosi, *Herbst Collection*, ix.

30. Wehrend, 240–48.

31. Gombosi, *Herbst Collection*, preface; see chapter 2, pp. 35–38, for a description of the lovefeast.

32. For example, the five pieces composed by J. C. Geisler for a congregational gathering in 1766, in H 69.1–5.

33. J. D. Grimm, *Wie soll lich dem Herrn vergelten* and *Alle meine Gebeine müssen sagen,* MS Moravian Archives, Herrnhut, Mus. A7:100; copies of these are also found in the collection of the Salem *Collegium musicum* (see chapter 7). The author is grateful to Jean Sawyer Twombly and Peter Vogt for sharing their research on these cantatas.

34. See chapter 2, pp. 32–33.

35. Cumnock and Steelman; a catalogue of the Bethlehem Congregation collection remains unpublished and is available in card catalogue form at the Moravian Music Foundation offices in Winston-Salem, North Carolina, and Bethlehem, Pennsylvania.

36. See Tollefsen.

37. Karl Kroeger, "An Eighteenth-Century English-Moravian Repertory," *Moravian Music Journal* 27/2 (Fall 1992): 9–22. Sybille Reventlow and Suzanne Summerville, "Die Christiansfelder Musikkataloge—Neues Forschungsunternehmen in Dänemark," *Unitas Fratrum* 3 (1978): 65–69. The author is grateful to Lorraine Parsons and Christina Ekström for recent correspondence concerning these collections.

38. Caldwell, 450.

39. Tom Gordon, "Seal Oil and String Quartets: Moravian Music Among the Labrador Inuit" (lecture, Sixth Bethlehem Conference on Moravian Music, Moravian College, Bethlehem, Pennsylvania, October 23, 2004).

40. *The Johannes Herbst Collection,* microfiche (New York: University Music Editions, ca. 1976). Gombosi, *Herbst Collection,* cited above. Joan O. Falconer, "Bishop Johannes Herbst (1735–1812), an American-Moravian Musician, Collector, and Composer" (PhD diss., Columbia University, 1969).

41. Gombosi, *Herbst Collection,* 233–39.

42. For example, from Homilius's *Passions-Cantate,* H 275.1 or 288.2; from Rolle's *Lazarus,* H 275.2; or from Türk's *Die Hirten bey der Krippe zu Bethlehem,* H 288.1.

43. Each of the approximately five hundred numbered manuscripts in Herbst's collection contains from one to six (or more) individual anthems. There are approximately one thousand distinct works—anthems, solos, or duets—in addition to the extended works discussed above.

44. Gombosi, *Herbst Collection,* xiv.

45. For instance, MS Moravian Archives, Herrnhut, Mus. K100:3, nos. 8, 16, and 31. This is a bound book of organ parts that correspond to sets of parts elsewhere in the collection.

46. Gombosi, *Herbst Collection*, part C, containing four items.

47. In actuality, two such volumes exist: H C.II, in German, consisting of 152 sacred songs, and an English-language volume in the collection of the Moravian Museum of Bethlehem. There is some duplication between the two collections. A selection of the English-language songs has been published in Johannes Herbst, *Hymns to be sung at the Pianoforte*, ed. Monica Schantz (Bethlehem: Moravian College, 1973). See also Joan Falconer, "Birthday Songs for Polly Heckewelder," *Moravian Music Foundation Bulletin* 19/1 (Spring-Summer 1974): 1–3.

48. Two examples are found in Herrnhut, Mus. J190:2 and J190:3. Both books are in two parts, the first a selection of keyboard pieces by various composers, the second containing piano-vocal reductions of anthems in the Moravian repertoire.

49. Christian Ignatius LaTrobe, *Anthems, for one or more Voices, performed in the Church of the United Brethren, Collected and the Instrumental parts adapted for the Organ or Piano Forte, Composed by various Authors* (London: Printed for the Editor, 1811). This volume includes pieces by Gregor, Grimm, Graun, Antes, Naumann, and LaTrobe.

50. Christian Friedrich Hasse, *Sacred Music: partly original; partly selected from the works of the chief of the most modern German composers, by C. F. Hasse, The Vocal parts as in the Original Score, and adapted exclusively to English Words. The Instrumental Parts arranged for the Piano Forte* (Leeds: J. Muff, [1829]). Pieces by John Gambold and C. D. Jaeschke are included with works of non-Moravian composers.

51. Gottlob Friedrich Hillmer, *Sammlung einiger musikalischen Fest-Gesänge der evangelischen Brüdergemeine zum Singen am Klavier eingerichtet*, 2 vols. (Breslau: Grass und Barth, 1803–5). See Caldwell, 331–42.

52. Nola Reed Knouse writes that the Moravians used words such as *Choräle, Arien*, or *Stücken* to identify pieces sung by the choir, and wonders if each of these words might reflect "the place of the choir's music within worship." See Dr. Nola Reed Knouse, "Moravian Music and the Organ," *The Tracker* 48/3 (The Organ Historical Society, Summer 2004): 26, note 6.

53. See Caldwell, parts II and III.

54. J. G. Gebhard's funeral cantata (S 98) or C. D. Jaeschke's *Herr, auf dich traue ich* (S 341.2), both with four trombones (SATB); cf. Mozart's *Requiem* with three trombones (ATB). See chapter 6 for a discussion of the history and role of the Moravian trombone choir.

55. The two balconies of a typical Moravian church are described by August Gottlieb Spangenberg, *Kurzgefasste historische Nachricht von der gegenwärtigen Verfassung der evangelischen Brüderunität* (Berlin: August Mylius, 1796), 56.

56. Caldwell, 480–81, and 537–39.

57. Wehrend, 125, 191–95.

58. Modern edition by Károly Köpe (Chapel Hill: Hinshaw Music, 1988).

59. Ed. Karl Kroeger (New York: Boosey & Hawkes, 1973).

60. Score and parts for the choruses from the *Messiah* are in H VII.

61. For example, Jaeschke's *Gelobet sey Gott der Herr* (MS Unitäts-Archiv Herrnhut, Mus. E46:24).

62. For example, LaTrobe's settings of Psalm 46, ed. K. Kroeger (New York: Boosey & Hawkes, 1983); Psalm 51, ed. Henry B. Ingram, Jr. (New York: Boosey & Hawkes, 1972); Psalm 100, ed. K. Kroeger (New York: Boosey & Hawkes, 1978).

63. Gambold's setting is available in an edition by Ewald V. Nolte (New York: Boosey & Hawkes, 1970).

64. For example, the anonymous *My Saviour Goes to His Suffering* (*Mein Heiland geht ins Leiden*), ed. Károly Köpe (Chapel Hill: Hinshaw Music, 1986) in G minor; J. F. Peter's *Love of God Is Shed Abroad*, ed. Nola Reed Knouse (Chapel Hill: Hinshaw Music, 1997), in 6/8.

65. No singing translation has been made for duet *Unbeschreiblich schöner* because of the dense internal rhymes. The complete German text follows, with a line-by-line literal translation.

> Unbeschreiblich schöner,
> blutiger Versöhner,
> wenn wir kindlich
> herzempfindlich
> und viel tausendmal
>
> deine heil'ge Füsse
> thränend netz'n und küssen
> für die Triebe
> deiner Liebe
> und für unsre Gnadenwahl
> ists doch nicht, doch nicht damit verricht't.
>
> Nimm uns, nimm uns hin
> zum Lohn der Schmerzen
> mit den ganzen Herzen:
> indes bitt' dich,
> nimm mich freundlich
> hin zum Lohn der Schmerzen
> und viel tausend, tausend Herzen.
>
> Indescribably lovely,
> bloody Redeemer,
> when we, in a childlike manner
> and tender-hearted,
> and many thousands of times
>
> your holy feet,
> weeping, moisten and kiss,
> for the impulse
> of your love
> and for our election by grace,
> it is still not, still not for this enough.
>
> Take us, take us
> as recompense for your suffering
> with our whole hearts:
> in the meantime I ask,
> take me, friendly,
> as recompense for suffering,
> and many thousand, thousand hearts.

66. Representative arias are anthologized in: Hans T. David, ed. *Ten Sacred Songs for Soprano, Strings and Organ* (New York: New York Public Library, 1947); Thor Johnson and Donald M. McCorkle, eds., *Three Sacred Songs for Soprano* (New York: Boosey & Hawkes, 1958); Karl Kroeger, ed. *Three Sacred Songs of Johannes Herbst* (New York: Boosey & Hawkes, 1978).

67. This example, along with the existence of the string trios of John Antes and the string quintets of Johann Friedrich Peter (see chapter 7), demonstrates that the Moravian composers' reliance on homophonic textures was a matter of choice rather than the result of a lack of training or accomplishment in more complex compositional techniques.

68. For example, references to the Herrnhut organist C. D. Jaeschke's salary are found throughout the "Protokolle des Aufseher-Collegiums," Moravian Archives, Herrnhut MS R6 Ab No. 49b in the years 1801–21; there are no references to payments to other musicians.

69. Reported in the "Protokolle der Aelt. Confer. In Herrnhut" 1787–92, Moravian Archives, Herrnhut MS R6 Ab No. 41, 10 April 1790: "Bey Gelegenheit, dass sich hier eine Sängerin bey einem öffentl. Concert wolte hören lassen u. dabey von den Zuhörern vor der Entrée 4 gl verlangte, wünschte die Confz., dass die ganze Sache unterbleiben u. einmal eine Resolution gefasst werden könte, dergl. Virtuosen in der Gem. nicht öffentlich mit ihrer Kunst auftreten zu lassen."

70. "Es ist seithero darüber gedacht und gearbeitet worden, ein Sängerchor von denen Brüdern u. Schwestern zu errichten, welche die beste Stimme zum Singen haben. . . . [D]abey sie sich verbanden in der Woche 2mal, nämlich Freitags u. Dienstags nach dem Stundenbegeth eine a parte Singstunde zu halten, biß sie rechat geminmäßig würden singen gelernt haben, damit sie bey allen Versammlungen der Gemeine, den übrigen Geschwistern vorgehen und gleichsam eine Englische Harmonie [gemeint ist die Harmonie des Engelgesangs], so viel bey uns armen Kindern practicable ist, im Gesange unterhalten möchten." Herrnhag Diary 1741–51, Moravian Archives, Herrnhut, MS R8 Nr. 33b, 2c. Quoted in Wehrend, 45.

71. Wehrend, 45–46.

72. Moravian Archives, Herrnhut, MS Herrnhut Gemein-diaria 1797–1800, R6 Ab No. 31. "21 May 1800: wurde die led. Schw. Dor. Wilhelmina Koelbing, nach einer Krankheit von etlichen Tagen, von unserm l. Herrn heimgerufen. Dieser Heimgang verursachte um so viel mehr ein schmerzliches Theilnehmen, da man nicht allein eine liebe, hoffnungsvolle junge Schwester, sondern auch unsere erste Sängerin bey dem Musik-Chor, und die erste Schulhalterin in der Mädchenschule an ihr verlor; dafür wurden ihr manche Liebesthränen nachgeweint."

73. The catalogue of the Herrnhut music collections provides detailed identification of copyists.

74. See Cumnock, 33–39, for a discussion of the Salem Sisters collection and its implications for performance.

75. Vernon H. Nelson, "The Bethlehem Choir and Orchestra, 1812–1816," in *Proceedings of the Seventh Bethlehem Conference on Moravian Music, October 14–16, 2006*, ed. Nola Reed Knouse (Winston-Salem: Moravian Music Foundation, 2007). The lists of musicians are Beth Cong 420 and Beth Cong 421, in the Moravian Archives, Bethlehem, Pennsylvania.

76. Or, in many cases, in between the staves. In a significant number of manuscripts of works by Christian Gregor and Johann Friedrich Peter, there are also some numbers written *below* the right-hand staff which seem to indicate intervals below the

melody—for instance, when the second violin moves in parallel thirds or sixths below the first violin, one often sees a notation such as "3. . . . 6 . . ." See chapter 5, pp. 143–44.

77. See also Timothy Duncan, "The Organ in Moravian Choral Anthems," in *Pleasing for Our Use: David Tannenberg and the Organs of the Moravians*, ed. Carol A. Traupman-Carr (Bethlehem: Lehigh University Press, 2000), 136–51.

78. Moravian Archives, Herrnhut, MS Mus. J117:18; harp part in Mus. K200:3.

79. Wehrend, part III; summarized in English in Peter Vogt's review of Wehrend's work, *Moravian Music Journal* 42/2 (Fall 1997): 3–5.

Chapter Five

The Organ in Moravian Church Music

Lou Carol Fix

Beginning with the renewal of the Moravian Church in the early eighteenth century, organs and organists played an essential role in church and community life, and continue to do so today. In perhaps no other religious community of early America did the organ have such an important and visible presence in the daily life of its members as it did among the Moravians. Moravians were a German-speaking people, and one Episcopal visitor to Lancaster, Pennsylvania, commented on the practice of religion by German ethnic groups: "[T]hey place almost half their devotion in their organs."[1] As William Armstrong observed, the service of dedication for a new organ in a Moravian church was second in importance only to the consecration of a new church building.[2] Although some large urban churches of other denominations obtained organs at an earlier date than did the Moravians, these cases are somewhat isolated and rare.[3] The scope of this study is largely restricted to an examination of how American Moravian communities of the eighteenth and early nineteenth centuries used the organ, as well as the influence Moravian organs had on related activities of early America. The contributions of some prominent Moravian organists of the late nineteenth century mark the transition to modern times.

Moravians wrote extensively about the performance practice for organ in their worship services. A few surviving instruments over two hundred years old allow us to hear the type of sound they preferred. Printed books and manuscript documents contain information on the use of improvisation during hymn singing. A few anthems and hymns provide performance directions relating to dynamics, fingering, and organ registration. The specifications of organ stops included in instruments built for Moravian churches differed from those used in other denominations, such as Lutheran, Reformed and Roman Catholic churches. The presence of organs in various meeting rooms and worship spaces in the eighteenth and nineteenth centuries attested to the instrument's important function in the daily life of the Moravians.

Organs primarily accompanied the singing of hymns and liturgical music in
regular worship services by the congregation. Through the realization of the
continuo line, they supported anthems sung by the choir. The organ's role was
one of servant to the words of faith as expressed in the chorales, the liturgical
responses, and the more elaborate anthems. Especially for the anthems, the
organ functioned as part of an ensemble of instruments including strings, woodwinds, and sometimes brass. It was also used in recreational music making
among the Moravians in the *collegium musicum* ensembles, which performed
sacred and secular music of the classical and early romantic eras.[4]

Very little solo music for the organ has survived from the first two centuries of
the Moravian presence in America. Fortunately, composers from the second half
of the twentieth century on have begun to provide settings of Moravian chorales
that can be used in church or recital.

The eighteenth-century Moravians were also responsible for bringing the central German organ-building tradition, and thus its organ tonal quality, to the
New World. This tradition has been all but lost in Europe, due to the gradual
disappearance of many of the small and mid-sized instruments, but fortunately
the preservation-minded Moravian communities saved a number of old organs
for possible future use. The valuable contribution of the Moravian David
Tannenberg, an expert organ builder whose work was highly praised and well
respected among his contemporaries, cannot be overestimated. In his manufacturing of organ pipes, Tannenberg promoted the use of equal temperament for
tuning by following the intricate mathematical calculations of Georg Andreas
Sorge as described in Sorge's treatise *Die geheime gehaltene Kunst der Mensuration
der Orgel-Pfeiffen*. Sorge sent at least two copies to America for Tannenberg to
study.[5] Tannenberg's work had a major influence on other organ builders, especially those of Pennsylvania German descent, who built organs for mostly small
rural churches and homes.[6] The relative isolation of the rural churches insured
that they would not be so quick to follow the latest fashionable trends in organ
building, and thus would keep their instruments in near-original condition for
a much longer time than their urban counterparts.

Hymns and Liturgies

During the fifteenth and sixteenth centuries, when members of the Unitas
Fratrum gathered, it is likely that their singing consisted of unaccompanied
chorale tunes. Not until the early eighteenth century did the Moravians regularly use the organ for musical support, probably due to the general influence
of the Lutheran church and the specific guidance of Count Nicholas Ludwig
von Zinzendorf.[7]

We can begin an account of the use of the organ in Moravian church music with a description of the types of worship services requiring organ support. Timothy Duncan has described four types of singing services the Moravians held at varying intervals throughout the year: the *Gemeinstunde,* or congregation hour; the *Liturgien,* or liturgy hour; the *Singstunde,* or singing hour; and the *Liebesmahl,* or lovefeast.[8] The congregation hour, which occurred weekly, was open to members of the church and visitors alike, and the organ accompanied the congregational singing of hymns and the liturgy. The vocal choir, orchestra, or trombone choir occasionally participated, presenting anthems or solos, as described in chapter 4. Here the organ provided accompanimental support, yet its primary role was to provide musical support for the singing of hymns.[9] Visitors sometimes compared the differences in singing and organ playing in the German Protestant state churches with the Moravian church services in Herrnhut, as in this account by Christian Gottlieb Frohberger of 1797:

> It would be desirable that the singing in our churches, which is such an important part of public worship and very suitable to evoke good sentiments in the hearts of the singers and to inspire them to pious and godly resolutions, should become more like the singing in the Moravian congregations. In our services at most places, there is more shouting than singing, and the largest part of the singers seems to reveal by their screeching way of singing that they do not believe and feel in their hearts what the mouth sings. In the Moravian Church the soft singing appears to be more the expression of the sensations of the heart. . . .
>
> Similarly charming and worthy of imitation is the playing of the Moravian organists. Whereas an organist among us loses himself in a prelude and seems to forget in his fugues, sinfonias, and other movements that a whole congregation is waiting for him, and in accompanying a hymn strives foremost to display his skills, the playing of the organ in the Moravian congregations is only that what it should be, namely an unaffected, soft accompaniment of the singing, through which the ear of the singer is roused, and the whole congregation is kept in tune.[10]

Frohberger thus describes the organ playing of hymns in Moravian services as being simple ("unaffected"), soft and supportive ("the whole congregation is kept in tune").

In the preface of his 1784 *Choral-Buch,* Christian Gregor (1723–1801) gives advice for the singing and playing of hymns:

> The content of the hymns is also very diverse. One must reasonably see that the singing and playing of these are always the most suitable. Some hymns, for example *Der Tag der ist so freudenreich* etc., require a lively and happy kind of singing, while others, for example, *O Haupt voll Blut und Wunden* etc., need singing that is slow and grave. The singing leader not only has to manage the suitability himself, but also has to motivate the congregation in a proper and undisturbing manner. An attentive organist who knows the hymns by heart can be very helpful to him in this.[11]

Thus Gregor suggests that the organist can best support the singing by ensuring that the tempo and character (perhaps registration and articulation) of his play-ing match the text, and by following the cues of the song leader.

A later, anonymous account from 1805 of visits to five Moravian communities in Saxony also mentions the soft organ playing, and how it differed from that in other churches:

> The festive stillness of the simple moving song accompanied by soft organ playing, which certainly distinguishes itself to great advantage from the overly loud shrieking so com-mon in many churches, is well capable of awakening the heart which is inclined toward religious feeling to an inner devotion and to bring forth therein pious resolutions.[12]

Christian Ignatius LaTrobe wrote of the role of the organ in supporting hymn singing in the preface to his *Anthems for One, Two or more Voices performed in the Church of the United Brethren . . . adapted for the Organ or Piano Forte* of 1811:

> As a great portion of this service [religious worship] consists in the singing of hymns, they endeavoured to make it uniform and harmonious, by encouraging all to join, but checking any disposition to vociferation in individuals, and have thereby, in some of their settlements, acquired a degree of perfection in congregational singing. . . . The organ is directed to accompany the congregation so as not to overpower it, but only to complete and support the harmony of the whole.[13]

Later in the century, Abraham Ritter (1792–1860), organist of the Moravian church in Philadelphia for forty-one years, wrote of the practical benefits of using the organ for hymn singing to maintain the pitch: "[Do not use the organ] . . . as a fancy accompaniment, but as a *support* to the congregational har-mony, which else in singing many verses, is apt to sink, and thus produce dis-cord."[14]

The weekly liturgy hour was exclusively for members of the church. The music for this service included chant, canticles, choral settings of the liturgy, and a hymn liturgy. The chant consisted of a responsorial dialogue between the litur-gist and the congregation, with the organ providing simple harmonic support.[15] Canticles were sung as part of the liturgy; for example, the "Te Deum" was used in the service for July 4, 1783, giving thanks for the end of the conflicts of the Revolutionary War.[16] The texture of the canticles was a simple four-part chordal setting of the words with the organ doubling the vocal parts.

On several occasions other instruments played along with the organ in the singing of hymns or other liturgical responses. Various accounts offer evidence of the use of strings, woodwinds, and brass instruments along with the organ; for instance, the Salem Diary of 1806 gives the following description:

> In the evening the congregation sang the Passion Liturgy No. 27. The service was attended by a number of gentlemen and ladies from Raleigh and other places. As they

wished to hear some rather elaborate music our musicians accompanied the singing of the congregation in the liturgy with violins, flutes, and French horns. After that a number of our chorale tunes were played on the organ, accompanied by the trombones and trumpets.[17]

It is clear that brass instruments could play hymns along with the organ. Duncan also writes that other instruments could also play along with the organ, or, if the service was held outdoors, the brass choir might provide support.[18] A 1799 newspaper account of the dedication of a new organ for the Moravian church in Lancaster, Pennsylvania, described the use of trombones with organ:

Last Sunday . . . was the consecration of the new organ in the church of the United Brethren [Moravians], made by the celebrated artificer David Tanneberg [Tannenberg] in Lititz. The musicians and trombonists from Lititz came the day before. . . . The day of consecration will certainly remain in the memory of everyone who participated. . . . [T]rombonists again played some tunes from the tower of the Reformed Church. They concluded in the evening, in harmony with the organ in the Lutheran Church.[19]

Another organ dedication in 1773 for Hebron Moravian Church in Lebanon, Pennsylvania, included the use of strings: "[T]he organ was accompanied by violinists from the congregation."[20]

Choral settings of the liturgy included accompaniment by the orchestra, with the organ doubling the vocal parts during sung sections and doubling the orchestral parts during the interludes. The congregation would sing whenever a phrase from a chorale occurred. The notated organ part consisted of only a treble and a bass line, with figured bass numbers included for the harmonic realization.[21] The hymn liturgies (*liturgische Gesänge*) featured an alternation of sung hymn verses with spoken verses or readings, and often included the use of antiphonal singing between groups of men and women.[22]

One of the characteristic services conducted by the Moravians was the *Singstunde*, or singing hour. These services were begun by Count Zinzendorf, who himself composed over two thousand hymn texts, most of which were initially sung to German Lutheran chorale tunes.[23] Children in the Moravian community also participated in their own *Singstunde*, and a contemporary account indicated that the children's lovely singing, often with tears of joy, was accompanied by a softly played organ.[24]

The organist thus needed to be very familiar with the vast repertoire of chorale tunes and had to be prepared to play these tunes in any key. In the preface to the *Choral-Buch*, Gregor spoke of the expected role of the organist in the *Singstunde*:

An organist must make it his business to attain the greatest possible skill at playing in all keys, because, in the Brethren's Church, the choice is not up to him. Rather, it depends on the liturgist as to which verse and in which key he wishes to or can begin. Thus the organist must immediately, without first making many false attempts, be capable of falling in with him and without hesitation accompany the singing. Often, in a so-called singing hour, there can be on ten or more melodies in which there is never a whole hymn sung, only single verses concerned mostly with the same subject.

From this it becomes clear that an organist in the Brethren's Church not so much directs the singing after his own discretion as he more often only carefully supports it and aids it, seeing that it proceeds sweetly and appropriately.[25]

What was the organist to do if the song leader began a chorale "between the cracks" of two different keys, or if the organist himself was not skilled enough to play the chorales in keys with many sharps and flats? Christian LaTrobe wrote that if the key selected had too many sharps or flats, "the organist was allowed to 'fall by a half-step' in order to facilitate the accompaniment."[26] A smoother accompaniment would settle into a lower key area, without attempting to force the assembly to a higher pitch.

The organist, along with the congregation, had to be familiar with several, if not all, the verses of the hymns in order to accommodate his playing to the sense of the text as well as to the tune selected by the worship leader. Great flexibility in tune selection was the norm, with a repertoire of many different tunes of the same metrical structure at the leader's disposal. The leader might even combine two shorter verses for use with a longer tune, or choose only half of a longer tune for use with a short verse. The leader might choose to repeat a phrase of text and music, or omit a phrase of text to allow the organist to play the corresponding music alone.[27]

Gregor also advised the organist to play only those notes that the congregation actually sang, including the usual harmonies that people added extemporaneously. The organist normally was not to play a different harmonization for the chorales, even if it was better than the one sung by the people. Gregor did, however, allow for some variety when the organist played alone, or when the choir sang with instrumental accompaniment and each musician had his own written-out part.[28]

With the increase in congregational hymn singing beginning in the sixteenth century, it became the organist's responsibility to provide aural cues for breathing at the end of phrases. To facilitate this process, organists in Germany and Holland began the practice of *Zwischenspielen*, or playing short improvised interludes between the phrases to provide short breaks in the singing. In 1891, Theodor Erxleben identified Johann Pachelbel (1653–1706) as the first organist to include such organ interludes.[29] This improvisational practice came to be regarded as a necessary part of the training of a competent church organist.[30]

These interludes had no thematic connection to the chorale tune itself. Their purpose was simply to provide a smooth melodic, rhythmic, and harmonic transition, and to help the congregation maintain the pitch of a hymn. Gregor allowed some freedom for the song leader and the accompanying organist in the performance of interludes, but cautioned against their too frequent use.[31] Sometimes the song leader might omit the interlude to avoid interrupting a complete thought in the hymn text.

Organists of the eighteenth and nineteenth centuries knew how to improvise interludes according to certain rules that were included in various method books along with continuo realization and rules for ornamentation.[32] Johann Sebastian Bach (1685–1750) wrote out a few examples of rather elaborate interludes for a handful of Lutheran chorales, including *Gelobet seist du, Jesu Christ* (BWV 722), *In dulci jubilo* (BWV 729), *Lobt Gott, ihr Christen allzugleich* (BWV 732), and *Vom Himmel hoch da komm ich her* (BWV 738).[33]

Johann Christian Bechler (1784–1857) provided a Moravian perspective on interludes in an unsigned manuscript on their realization.[34] He supplied many specific examples, both simple and complex, of how to modulate from one chord to the next. Through these rules and examples, it is clear that the interlude favors the *next* chorale phrase, not the *previous* one, and it "provides a sense of forward motion which effectively draws the singers forward to the next phrase."[35]

The use of interludes was not without some controversy among the Moravians. Some thought the brief solo organ passages between the chorale phrases interrupted the singers' pious reflections on the words of the hymn text. Even Gregor cautioned against a careless and cavalier approach in the performance of interludes:

> Everything that sounds strange in the singing of the congregation disturbs not only its agreeable concord, but also the peaceful devotion of the heart. This is especially noticeable in the interludes between lines of the hymn. If these are merely artistic, or quite thoughtless and improper, or if they depart from their real purpose of being simple, agreeable, and proper guides for transition from what precedes to what follows, then they disturb the close connection of the one with the other.[36]

In a letter to his daughter concerning his seminary training, Christian LaTrobe relates the story of how he came to change his mind about the use of interludes after the kind intervention of Augustus Gottlieb Spangenberg (1704–92):

> [O]ur taste at that time was bad. The noble simplicity of our church-music and hymn-tunes was lost in flourishes and ill-placed decorations, and deformed by long straggling interludes. Little attention was paid to that agreement between music and words, by which they are made to speak the same language, and to convey, each in their degree, the same feeling to the mind. Frequent complaints were made by the worthy and venerable fathers of our Church, who . . . felt themselves disturbed by the thoughtless and tasteless manner of playing the organ. But these were not heeded, being rather considered as a proof, that the complainants wanted skill to appreciate the value of the artful and ornamental musical drapery, with which we clothed tunes, otherwise, in our opinion, too dull and monotonous.[37]

LaTrobe goes on to describe the wise and gentle remonstrance offered by Spangenberg, who asked him not to "despise the remarks of an old man, who indeed understands nothing at all of music, and cannot point out the nature of the grievance, but yet thinks that he has a just sense of what is proper and consistent in performing a service in the house of God." Spangenberg then asked LaTrobe to play the next service of Holy Communion simply, without unnecessary flourishes and ornaments. The young LaTrobe was disarmed by the older man's humility, and willingly did as he was asked; and found himself so moved by the simplicity and nobility of the result that he changed his whole manner of playing from that day forward.[38]

In spite of these cautions, however, the use of interludes continued through the nineteenth century. Peter LaTrobe wrote in his 1854 edition of a British Moravian hymnal that Moravian organists adopted the interluding practice from the Lutheran church: "In adopting the German practice, the Brethren have however endeavoured to simplify it. The interlude of a skilful [sic] Lutheran organist, however fine as a composition, is too apt to perplex the hearer by its length and the richness of its combinations."[39]

Abraham Ritter wrote of the interludes as welcome pauses because of the irregular phrase structure and excessive length of some Moravian hymn tunes:

> Many of the verses of the Moravian hymns being very long, some even of *ten* lines, and the peculiar meters being *very* peculiar, interludes between the lines, always befitting the subject, seemed a necessary relief to the voice, as well also to keep up its strength to the pitch. This performance required tact, talent, skill, and practice, for a smooth and congenial connection of the context.[40]

Surviving examples of interludes from nineteenth-century Moravian sources follow various melodic sequential patterns and are usually from two to five beats long. Examples can be found in two personal manuscript copybooks of the Salem Manuscript Books (SMB) collection compiled by Louisa Cornelia Van Vleck (1826–1902) and Arthur Laurence Van Vleck (1824–63).[41] Other Moravian chorale books containing interludes and that were published in the nineteenth century include C. A. Köstner's *Auszug aus dem Choral-Buch der Evangelischen Brüdergemeine* (Niesky, 1841) and A. Nitschke's *Choral-Buch der Evangelischen Brüdergemeine* (Königsfeld, 1868).[42] A recent publication includes organ preludes by Ernst Immanuel Erbe (1854–1927) with accompanying Moravian chorale settings with interludes.[43] In all these books, a number of chorales contain interludes of various patterns that feature parallel thirds (and tenths), parallel sixths, two-note slurs, broken chords, arpeggios, scale passages, chromatic scales, leaping sixths, and sequences of melodic turns.

For the most part it seems clear that the interludes were to be played on the manuals only; where there might be a question, the copyist sometimes gave an indication of "L.H." (left hand) or "Manual" below the bass notes.[44] Thus the entry of the bass notes in the pedals would help to signal the congregation to begin singing the next phrase. A few examples include exact fingering to be used, with a "+" or "t" sign written for the thumb. Fingering numbers of 1, 2, 3, and 4 (beginning with the index finger) correspond with the modern keyboard fingering of 2, 3, 4, and 5. The fingering examples fall comfortably under the hand and permit crossing of the thumb.[45]

Peter LaTrobe set forth six rules for the performance of interludes, stating that they should be short and simple, light rather than heavy, in keeping with the sense of the text, and above all should never disturb the devotion of the congregation. Interludes might also be omitted especially where the first phrase of the chorale is itself repeated or the phrases are quite short.[46]

The practice of playing interludes faded over time as the result of several changes in hymn singing. Tempos became gradually faster, and the final note of each phrase was often held longer to allow for breathing.[47] Printed hymnbooks became more available for congregational use, and the hymnbooks included fermatas at the ends of phrases, so people could see where to breathe.[48] Writing in 1873, Grider described the interludes unfavorably, saying that they "not only tend to obscure the melody, but those features which caused the adoption of choral music by the churches—its grandeur and simplicity. Many object to their use, and they are now frequently omitted by the present organists."[49]

Nevertheless, as late as the 1923 *Hymnal and Liturgies of the Moravian Church*, one example of a written interlude survived, as shown in example 5.1.[50]

Example 5.1. *In This Sepulchral Eden*, text and tune by Christian Gregor. *Hymnal and Liturgies of the Moravian Church* (1923), hymn 212.

Anthems

The organ played a significant and supportive role in the anthems, solos, and duets sung by the choirs and accompanied by the instrumentalists of the *collegium musicum*.[51] Most anthems were composed specifically for use at the Moravian lovefeast.[52]

In only a few instances was the organ used as the sole accompanying instrument in anthems. One major source of this type is Christian LaTrobe's *Original*

Anthems for One, Two, or More Voices . . . Arranged for the Piano Forte or Organ of 1828.[53] In this collection the organ part generally has two or three voices for the right hand to play, and only one or two parts for the left hand, a typical early nineteenth-century accompanimental style.[54] The organ lines may double the vocal parts, or they may include an independent part for the accompaniment. In the majority of these pieces, however, the piano or organ parts are arranged from full orchestrations.

Within the instrumental ensemble, the organ usually played the continuo part, which was often notated with a bass and treble line and figured bass; sometimes this part was completely written out. In most cases the organ part resembles a simplification of the instrumental (primarily string) and vocal parts. A modest proportion of the anthems have two versions of the organ part: one is a reduction of the orchestral and vocal lines, and the other is a continuo part with figured bass. Example 5.2 shows the opening of the two versions of the organ part of *Alles was Othem hat* by Johann Ludwig Freydt (1748–1807), for two horns, two flutes, strings, organ, and SSAB choir. Part (a) shows the simpler organ part, and part (b) shows the more complete part with the figuration as in the first violin part.

Example 5.2. Johann Ludwig Freydt, *Alles was Othem hat* (Salem Congregation Collection 144.2), mm. 1–8. (a) simpler organ part; (b) part adequate for use without orchestra.

Example 5.3 shows the two organ parts of Christian LaTrobe's *Mit deinem verdienstlichen Tod*, for oboe or clarinet, bassoon, strings, organ, and SATB choir. Part (a) shows the simpler part, this one consisting simply of a figured bass, and part (b) shows the completed part, which is adequate without the parts for oboe or clarinet, bassoon, and strings.

The Moravian composers Christian Gregor and Johann Friedrich Peter (1746–1813), among others, included figured bass numbers notated just *above*

Example 5.3. Christian Ignatius LaTrobe, *Mit deinem verdienstlichen Tod* (Salem Congregation Collection 73.1), mm. 1–8. (a) figured bass; (b) realized part.

the bass staff, which seem easier to realize at the keyboard than when placed *below* the staff. Gregor and Peter sometimes added a type of unique "figured treble" tablature notation in which numbers (and dots) appeared below the treble notes. The "figured treble" notation used only the numbers 3 and 6, since it appears only when the music played by the right hand proceeded in parallel thirds or sixths, duplicating the first and second violins or viola. This type of music is structured as a trio texture with two treble lines written against a bass part. Occasionally when Peter wanted to cancel a flat from the key signature he would write a natural sign as part of the "figured treble" tablature notation. In some measures where many successive thirds occurred, the copyist simply wrote a "3" under the first treble note and thereafter just marked a dot under the following notes. In a few instances the figured bass and "figured treble" appear simultaneously, as in figure 5.1.

Examination of the organ parts for a number of Moravian anthems leads to the following general observations concerning the role of the organ.

1. Where there is a "semi-independent" organ section, it lasts only a few measures while the other instruments continued to play the basic harmonies. Here the roles of the organ and the accompaniment of strings and winds were temporarily reversed, as the organ provided decorative figuration and rhythmic intensity coupled with its unique sound color. The solo organ line could include arpeggios, broken chords, Alberti bass patterns, broken thirds, parallel thirds, scale passages, and ornamental trills and melodic turns for the right hand to play. Rhythmic intensity was created by repeated notes and octave leaps in the bass line as well as fast-moving figuration in the right hand.[55]

2. The organ parts were generally written for manuals only and did not require the use of pedals for the bass notes.[56] Often the bass line moved

Figure 5.1. Johann Friedrich Peter, Dem aber, der euch kann behüten (Salem Congregation Collection 101.2), mm. 23–33.

    too quickly or reached into too high a range to be played by the pedals. If the pedals are required, the music was so marked.[57]

3. Dynamic markings for the strings and other instruments were often duplicated in the organ parts, but not consistently. The frequent changes in dynamics (sometimes every half measure) would have required either an organ with two manuals or one with an expression box or a machine stop, and few early Moravian organs had these "extra" accoutrements. Gradual changes in dynamics, marked *crescendo* or *diminuendo*, would be impossible on an organ without an expression box. The implication is clear that the dynamic markings in the organ parts most likely were cues for the organist-conductor as he directed the ensemble from the console.[58]

4. Articulation markings in the strings were usually duplicated in the organ parts, but again, not consistently. Sometimes the articulation was intentionally different, for instance with the strings having staccato marks and the organ a legato slur. In most cases the articulation in the strings and winds was more detached than that of the organ. Also, more articulation marks were written for the other instruments and fewer for the organ. Still, the marked articulation could be played on even the smallest one-manual organ. It seems clear, however, that the other instruments were given a higher priority in the marking of articulation than was the organ.

5. When the word *Solo* appears in the organ part, it was usually, but not always, a cue for another instrument or voice having a solo line.[59] Slight differences in the rhythm and notes between the organ notation and that of the solo instruments suggest that the organ was to double the solo instruments. The word *Tutti* also is written for the organ part when the entire ensemble played together.

6. Specific organ stops for registration were sometimes indicated when the composer identified the organ part as *obligato*. The *Gambe* stop was specified when the organ played the continuo or a reduction of the other instrumental parts. The *Flauto* stop was called for when the organ accompanied a high solo voice with soft strings. Sometimes the organ was asked to play a few notes an octave higher for an added brilliance of sound.[60] This might be due to the fact that the specification of Moravian organs

often did not include much upper work in the 2′ or higher range, and a brighter sound could be achieved only through octave transposition.

7. The word *obligato* in some anthems should not be interpreted to mean that the organ part was optional for other anthems, given the strong emphasis on musical participation by the Moravians, and the likelihood that the organist conducted from the console. A specific direction (*senza organo*) given for the organ not to play in certain sections implies that the organ normally participated in the ensemble of instruments to accompany vocal anthems.

These conclusions regarding organ accompaniment can be used as a guide for the use of the organ during the singing of choral anthems. Additional studies of anthems may shed more light in this particular area of performance practice.

Preludes

Besides accompanying hymns and anthems, the organist was expected to provide prelude music before the service began. Often the simple playing of a chorale or a short improvisation, perhaps based on a familiar tune, would suffice. The fact that so little original organ music composed by Moravians survives from the eighteenth and nineteenth centuries supports Ewald Nolte's thesis that "the Moravian clergymen-musicians attached no significance to composing solo music for the organ."[61]

Both Christian Gregor and Christian Ignatius LaTrobe commented on the playing of organ preludes. Gregor writes in the *Choral-Buch*:

What especially concerns the organist, as has just been noted, is that he should above all things seek to do his duty by heart and especially with devotion and with the intention to create through it blessing and edification in others, just like any other servant of the congregation. His preludes before the beginning of the service must show these qualities, and, through them, serve as agreeable preparation for the singing or liturgy that follows. Thus a good prelude adapted to the place as well as to the circumstances will be suitable for a solemn assembly; on the contrary, those which do not have this quality are unpleasant. Those who lack the necessary skill to play a good prelude would do better and more beautifully, and would better suit the taste of the assembly, if they have appropriate chorale melodies to serve as preludes. This is better than to cause all sorts of inappropriate fantasies to be heard.[62]

Apparently not all Moravian organists took to heart Gregor's advice to play simple chorale melodies for the preludes. The minutes of the Unity Elders' Conference for May 5, 1790 include a plea for organists to follow the recommendations set out in Gregor's preface, noting that the preludes played often conflicted with the spirit of the congregation for worship. The Elders expressed their desire that the organists would simply play chorales. The Elders also noted that this had been a topic of discussion at the recent synod as well.[63]

Writing in England, Christian LaTrobe echoes the preference for a simple prelude, as follows:

> To be able to play a voluntary is by no means an essential part of the qualifications of an organist among the Brethren. The congregation will always prefer hearing Hymn Tunes played in its stead which, besides affording a great variety, have a pleasing and edifying effect. . . . [The organist will] by the whole tenor of his prelude, suited to the solemnity of the occasion, endeavor to prepare the minds of the assembly for the ensuing service, carefully avoiding every strain that might produce a contrary effect.[64]

The fact that LaTrobe felt the need to comment on an organist's ability to play a voluntary implies that this was the usual expectation for church organists in England. Not true, says LaTrobe, for the Moravian churches.

Moravians in America communicated frequently with other Moravians around the world, especially those in the home base of the German-speaking areas of Europe. The American Moravians were able to obtain copies of the latest music composed on the Continent. In an account book from the general store in Nazareth, a Moravian town just north of Bethlehem, is a record of payment on June 30, 1800, for the binding of two organ books originally from Europe. The two books being repaired were *Fugetten*, by Johann Ernst Rembt (1749–1810), and *Orgel Stücke*, by Johann Gottfried Vierling (1750–1813), both of which are assumed to have been owned by Moravians.[65] These two volumes include solo organ music playable on a single manual, and were probably used by organ students and perhaps even utilized as preludes to the worship services.

The nineteenth century brought forth some significant organ works by Moravian composers. Christian LaTrobe's nine brief preludes for organ were published in 1806 in an appendix to L. B. Seeley's English tune book *Devotional Harmony*. The appendix also contained over forty other preludes by non-Moravian composers.[66] LaTrobe's preludes are freely composed works, not based on chorale tunes. There is no evidence that these preludes were played or even meant to be used in a Moravian worship service.[67] The style of the preludes varies from stately homophonic choruses to lyrical character pieces to a quasi-fugue at the end. Although none of the preludes calls for pedals, three require the use of two manuals with their indications of Great Organ and Choir Organ in the score, or quick-changing terraced dynamics. Many levels of dynamic shading occur, ranging from *pp* to *f* and also including *sf*. Prelude III contains four instances of a *forte* chord connected by a slur to a soft *piano* chord, implying the use of Swell shades or an expression box on the organ to accomplish this gradual change in dynamics. Swell shades were commonly used in England (where LaTrobe was born and spent most of the life) by the late eighteenth century. A generous amount of ornamentation occurs throughout the preludes, including grace notes, trills, appoggiaturas, and melodic turns.

The American-born Moravian composer and pastor Francis Florentine Hagen (1815–1907) published two volumes of musical arrangements, transcriptions, and original compositions in his *Church and Home Organist's Companion* of 1880 and 1881.[68] These volumes contain arrangements for the pipe or reed organ of hymns, anthems, marches, popular songs, and excerpts from operas and oratorios, as well as some original organ preludes by Hagen based on popular hymn tunes. Many of the hymn tunes Hagen used were included in Moravian hymnals available in his day, but some were from outside the mainstream of Moravian hymnody, originating in the evangelical and revival movements. These preludes are reminiscent of operatic writing of the mid-nineteenth century, with the hymn tune proper making a grand entrance after a quiet buildup of melodic fragments from the hymn's opening lines. Phrases of the hymn tune are often interrupted with freely composed interludes that form a sort of musical commentary on the phrase just heard. The hymn tune in its entirety is often followed by an extensive developmental section. In some preludes, several chromatic modulations up a half step occur in succession, adding to the intensity of the piece. Hagen uses copious dynamic markings with both gradual and sudden changes, and these markings are the primary clues for organ registration. No specific stops are listed for the registrations, although "Full Organ" appears on occasion. He also included accent marks over strongly articulated beats and called for dramatic changes in tempo to heighten the emotional impact of the music. The preludes may be played on a single manual (and are therefore quite suitable for reed organs) and only very rarely require the use of pedals. Taken as a whole these preludes reflect Hagen's interest in revival and gospel-style music. They form an important link between Moravian organ music of the early nineteenth century and the more recent repertoire of the later twentieth century.

The Moravian composer and organist Ernst Immanuel Erbe (1854–1927) was born in Switzerland and educated at the Moravian schools in Herrnhut. When he was only nine years old, he played as the substitute organist for services, and a woman reportedly spoke of his playing: "When I hear sweet music and see no one, then I know that little Erbe is playing."[69] Later in 1883 a recommendation for an organ job stated that Erbe's "organ playing is secure and quite in the spirit of the church," which perhaps reflects his conservative playing style.[70] He edited a Moravian chorale book called *Auszug aus dem Choralbuch der evangelischen Brüdergemeine* (Ebersdorf, 1885).

After emigrating to America in 1889, Erbe lived primarily in Missouri, where there were no Moravian churches, and played the organ for several congregations of the Evangelical Synod. In 1894 he compiled a chorale book for the evangelical church that received a favorable review.[71] In 1900 he wrote a number of organ preludes based on Lutheran and Moravian chorales, some of which have been published.[72] These preludes may have served as introductions to congregational singing, or he may have played them as preludes to the worship service.

Erbe's seventeen published preludes all require the use of organ pedals, and some call for two manuals. The *cantus firmus* appears variously in the top, middle, or lowest voice, but is clearly stated, though not always heard in its entirety. Several different types of chorale prelude format are used, including the melody chorale, chorale fughetta, and chorale with tenor *cantus firmus*. Erbe frequently uses the technique of *Vorimitation*, with the first notes of a chorale phrase serving as introductory contrapuntal material before the entry of the *cantus firmus* in longer notes in another voice. The harmonic language is conservative for the year 1900. The texture adheres to linear counterpoint throughout, quite unlike the homophonic melody with accompaniment that LaTrobe favored nearly a hundred years earlier. Erbe's preludes are like small trios with independent lines written for both hands and the feet. Overall they seem to follow the Moravian prescription for simple, unobtrusive, yet effective devotional pieces intended to set the proper tone for worship.

Organ Building, Location, and Sound

The Moravian musical ideals of simplicity, clarity, beauty, good craftsmanship, full participation and proper support of congregational singing, and primacy of the word over music were reflected in the physical aspects of organ building, location, and sound. These ideals affected the placement of the organ within a room, the location of the console, the appearance of the organ case, the quality of sound produced, the specification of stops, the pitch for tuning, and the temperament selected for the organ. As mentioned earlier, organs were found in many different places throughout the Moravian community. They were located in the large sanctuaries, in mid-sized chapels and in the common meeting rooms (*Saals*) of most living units. A letter written by a twelve-year-old girl attending the Moravian school in Bethlehem in 1787 details the use and location of organs during her time there:

> Here I am taught music, both vocal and instrumental, I play the guitar twice a day—am taught the spinet and forte-piano; and sometimes I play the organ. . . . [After morning lessons] we go . . . into a large chapel, which also joins this house, where there is an organ. Here we see three gentlemen—the person who delivers a short lecture on divinity and morality—the organist, who plays a hymn, in which we join with our voices—and the boys' schoolmaster. . . . On Sundays divine service is performed in the great chapel, where the whole society, men, women and children meet. . . . They sing enchantingly, in which they are joined with the bass-viols [celli], violins and an organ.[73]

Moravians worshiped together several times throughout the day, and it was important to have an organ located near their daily activities because it provided the primary support for their singing. If a place of worship did not yet have an organ available, often a harpsichord would be used until an organ could be built.[74] Likewise, in more modern times, when the 1800 Tannenberg organ was removed from the Home Moravian Church of Salem, North Carolina in 1910, a piano and the church orchestra provided the musical accompaniment for three years until a new organ was installed.[75]

Organs in Moravian worship spaces were not centered in the front, where they would remain in plain view throughout the service. Usually they were placed at the side of the room, or sometimes in the rear, where they provided aural support for the singing without being a visual distraction. If a church had a balcony, the organ was usually located there, either in the back or, again, off to the side. This architecture reflected the Moravian concept that the music of choir, ensemble, and organ should reflect the song of "*die obere Gemeine*"—the heavenly congregation.[76]

To facilitate direct communication between the organist and the leader of the service, other musicians, and the congregation, Moravian organ builders developed a unique design of detached, reversed consoles. Organs of this design have the keyboard console located a few feet in front of the case with the organist facing *away* from the organ and *toward* the congregation. The trackers connecting the keys and pedals to the pipework run under the feet and bench where the organist sits and make their connections inside the case behind him. The detached, reversed console allowed the organist to participate fully in the worship service, with a clear and direct view of the proceedings in front of him (see fig. 5.2).

A clear sight line for the organist was so important that one instrument had a window cut out through the center of the organ because the organist sat behind the case. This unique organ was built in 1773 by the Moravian Joseph Ferdinand Bulitschek (d. 1801) for the Bethania congregation in North Carolina.

The materials used in the construction of organ cases included durable hardwoods that were meant to last for generations. The design of the organ cases followed the clean, classic lines popular in eighteenth-century furniture styles, but also incorporated decorative details in the pipe shades and moldings. The eye appreciated the classic simplicity and elegance of the organ case, just as the ear enjoyed the straightforward, heartfelt singing of the text in hymns and anthems. The cases were often painted pure white, to match the customary color of the walls of the *Saal*, and included touches of gold leaf applied to the pipes or molding. Again, neither the organ nor the organist was to stand out in the presentation of the music and would best serve the needs of the people in a supportive, though beautiful, role.

The quality of sound desirable in organs built for the Moravians has been described in various writings. Gregor mentioned "a lovely harmony of voices and musical instruments, especially the organ," and later declared, "All voices should seek to unite with one another so that the generally softened tones appear to lose themselves in a sweetly flowing and yet powerful harmony."[77] Gregor also advised the organist to support the singing carefully and to make sure it "proceeds sweetly and appropriately."[78]

Figure 5.2. David Tannenberg's 1800 organ for the Salem church, restored in 2003 by Taylor and Boody Organbuilders, Staunton, Virginia. Collection of Old Salem Museum and Gardens. Used by permission.

In 1746, members of the Moravian community were admonished to temper the volume of their singing: "Brothers and Sisters were reminded in the future to listen to the organ when singing, and not to sing [so] loudly."[79] Later, in 1811, LaTrobe spoke of the volume of the organ sound and what constituted beauty in music: "The organ is directed to accompany the congregation so as not to overpower it, but only to complete and support the harmony of the whole," and further cited "Correctness and *Simplicity* [LaTrobe's italics], the two grand sources of beauty in the performance of Music, producing a sweet confluence of harmony."[80]

Moravian organ builders gave careful consideration to the tonal quality of the organ-pipe sound. David Tannenberg (1728–1804) was the preeminent organ builder in eighteenth-century America. In the specifications for an organ proposed for the large church in Bethlehem, Tannenberg wrote of the flute and string stops of 8′ and 4′ pitch: "these are lovely stops, and pleasing for our use." Specifically of the Gamba 8′, Gedeckt 8′, and Flute 4′ stops, he said: "these are lovely voices."[81] From the writings of Gregor, LaTrobe, and Tannenberg, we see that for Moravians the organ sound must be lovely; it must blend well with the sound quality of the human voice and with chamber instruments of strings and woodwinds; it should be soft and not dominate the instrumental ensemble or the voice of the congregation, but must be firm enough to provide adequate support; and it must be sweet and gentle.

The specifications of organs built for Moravian churches included an abundance of 8′ and 4′ stops for accompanying singing and playing along with instruments. Eight-foot stops provide the basic layer of fundamental pitch, and the 4′ stops highlight the first level of the harmonic series by adding the octave above for a touch of brightness. These stops allow the organ to produce the basic foundation tones, along with a middle layer of sound, without dominating the music ensemble. Most Moravian organs included very little upper work in the 2′ or higher range, and they did not generally have mutation stops or solo reeds. The higher-range stops and brilliant colors of reeds and mutations were not needed either for congregational singing or for the continuo part in the instrumental ensemble. When other instruments from the string, woodwind, and sometimes brass families played along with the organ, their unique timbres provided tonal color and brilliance.

The organ specifications of instruments built for Moravian churches (including proposals for organs never built) reveal that string and flute stops were the most numerous, with principal stops coming next. String stop names included various spellings of *Violon Baß, Violon, Violonalto, Viola de Gamba, Gambe, Viola, Salicional, Salicet, Stille Gambe,* and *Gems Horn.* Flute stop names are *Subbass, Flaut Baß, Gross Gedackt, Lieblich Gedackt, Gedackt, Flöte Grave, Stopped Diapason, Bourdon, Quintadena, Dolce Flöte, Flauto amabile, Flaute, Floeth, Rohr Floethe, Flauta douce, Holzflöte, Piccolo,* and *Flageolet.* Principal stops included *Principal Baß, Octav Baß, Principal Discant, Principal dulcis, Principal, Prestant, Open Diapason, Principal octav,*

Octave, Quinte, Twelfth, Sub [sic] Octave (Super Octave), *Fifteenth, Sedecima, Cornet (treble) IV* ranks, and *Sesquialtera (bass) III* ranks. The few reed stops were *Posaunen Baß, Oboe,* and *Hautboix.*[82] It is interesting to note the frequent use of qualifying adjectives describing a soft and quiet stop, such as *Stille Gambe, Lieblich Gedackt, Flöte Grave, Dolce Flöte, Flauto amabile, Flauta douce,* and *Principal dulcis.* The soft stops suited the requirements of Moravian music making to be sweet and gentle. The only 8′ reed listed was the gentle oboe, whereas the trombone bass in the pedals (which was to have been made of wood, not metal, thus producing a somewhat muted sound) perhaps was chosen because of the important role trombones played in Moravian music. In one case of a 1748 proposal for an organ for the Moravian church in Fulneck, England, the builder John Snetzler suggested the addition of a Trumpet stop to the Swell division. A representative from the Fulneck church asked him not to include the Trumpet stop "because it would require higher wind pressure than is needed 'for a *pleasant* effect in the *subtle* stops.' "[83] A higher wind pressure would make the string and flute stops sound too loud and bright, thus producing a too-dominant sound in the organ for the overall balance of the ensemble.

We can find further evidence for the role of the organ as a supportive ensemble instrument in an examination of the pitch standard used by Moravian organ builders. Organs in seventeenth- and eighteenth-century Germany could be pitched at two different levels according to their primary function. If their main role was to accompany singing, the *Chorton* (choir pitch), which is slightly sharper than the modern A = 440, was used. If instead the organ was used to accompany instruments, the *Kammerton* (chamber pitch), almost a whole tone below modern pitch, was chosen for tuning the organ.[84] Barbara Owen reports that Gregor emphasized the need for *Kammerton* in letters he wrote to organ builders in Germany, and that all nine of Tannenberg's extant organs are built at the lower pitch.[85] Moravian organs were thus well suited to accompany instrumental music during the singing of anthems; instruments could also be used with the organ during congregational singing.

However, Moravian church organs were not all tuned to the same pitch level. Moravians often shared music with other congregations in nearly communities, but adjustments had to be made. Frances Cumnock writes that some music used in the lovefeast psalms appears in two different keys for the instrumental parts to accommodate a different pitch level of the organ in another church.[86]

The temperament used in organ tuning affects the availability of suitable keys in which music can be played on the instrument. No standardized temperaments were used in Europe or America during the eighteenth century. The flexibility of key described in the discussion of the *Singstunde* above could be effective only if the accompanying organ was tuned in equal temperament.[87]

In 1764 David Tannenberg received a copy of a treatise on organ building written by the organist and music theorist Georg Andreas Sorge (1703–78). Sorge's treatise, *Die geheime gehaltene Kunst der Mensuration der Orgel-Pfeiffen*

("The Secretly Kept Art of the Scaling of Organ Pipes"), gives detailed information on the use of logarithms to determine the scaling of organ pipes, producing equal temperament. Tannenberg used Sorge's treatise to approximate equal temperament in his organs.[88]

Moravian Organ Builders and Organists

The contributions of Moravian organ builders affected the organ building profession in various regions of the United States, especially in Pennsylvania. Johannes Gottlob Klemm (1690–1762) was the first known organ builder whom the Moravians engaged to repair and build organs for them.[89] He received his training in his native Germany, near Dresden, and worked for seven years in the Moravian community of Herrnhut before emigrating to America in 1733. His two most important organs were the 1738 instrument for Gloria Dei Church (Swedish Lutheran) in Philadelphia, and his largest organ, built in 1741, for Trinity Church in New York City. The Trinity organ followed English models and had a Swell division (a Choir division was added later), but no pedals. In 1742, the Moravian church in Philadelphia had two organs, possibly built by Klemm. In 1746 he installed an organ, most likely his own, in the Moravian Church in Bethlehem.[90]

By 1757, the aging Klemm asked the Moravians if he might live out his final days with them in Bethlehem. Although because of his tumultuous relationship with the Moravians he was viewed as a "lapsed brother," the Moravians considered him a friend and could not "turn away from him in his necessity."[91] Klemm then moved to Bethlehem, began repairing organs, and took on as an apprentice the bright young David Tannenberg, who was just beginning his organ-building career. Klemm was then able to pass along his knowledge of the central German style of organ building as the two men built five organs for the Moravians.[92] One instrument was even transported south to the Moravian settlement in Bethabara, North Carolina.

In 1758, a committee including the two organ builders met "to decide whether to build our organ for Nazareth Hall so that the organist sits facing the organ or so that he sits with the organ behind him."[93] This is the first mention of a possible detached, reversed console, which came to be a hallmark of organs built for Moravian churches. Klemm died in 1762 in Bethlehem and is buried in the Moravian cemetery there.[94]

David Tannenberg (1728–1804) was born in Berthelsdorf, Saxony, near Herrnhut, to Moravian parents.[95] Zinzendorf himself saw Tannenberg's potential and arranged schooling for him at age ten in the Hesse region of central Germany. At about age fourteen, at his own request, Tannenberg returned to live with his parents, but chose to return to the congregation in 1746. By age twenty (1748) Tannenberg was sent to live with the Moravians in Holland, and departed the next year with a group of them sailing for America to the new community in Bethlehem, Pennsylvania. He was married shortly after his arrival in America. Tannenberg worked as a joiner and business manager in Bethlehem and nearby Nazareth until Klemm arrived in 1757. Soon thereafter Tannenberg began his apprenticeship with the old organ builder.

The Moravian Elders expressed concern about Tannenberg's continuing in the profession of organ building, and wanted him to "give up his organ building shop and go into cabinet making, for the former is tied up with much disorder."[96] Tannenberg convinced them otherwise and continued his work, even building other types of keyboard instruments. In 1764 he received a copy of Sorge's treatise on pipe scaling and temperament and began applying the complex mathematical calculations in the making of organ pipes. Tannenberg's experience as a joiner, his apprenticeship with Klemm, and his study of Sorge's treatise in the making of pipes all contributed to his future success as the premier organ builder in eighteenth-century America.

In 1765 Tannenberg and his family moved to the Moravian town of Lititz, Pennsylvania, where he set up his workshop and participated in the musical life of the community as a vocalist and violinist. He began building organs at the rapid rate of about one a year for Moravian, Lutheran, and Reformed churches, as well as instruments for a Catholic church in Lancaster and for various individuals. His organs were installed in German-speaking congregations in six states: Pennsylvania, New Jersey, New York, Maryland, Virginia, and North Carolina. In all Tannenberg produced nearly fifty organs during his lifetime, of which nine are extant.[97]

Tannenberg's reputation for building excellent, well-crafted, and beautiful organs spread throughout the mid-Atlantic region, and received rave reviews in the newspapers. One Philadelphia account from the *Pennsylvania Gazette* edition of January 10, 1771, wrote of his 1770 organ for a Reformed church in Lancaster:

> The organ was made by David Tanneberger [*sic*] of Lititz—A Moravian town nearby—and I dare venture to assert, is much superior in workmanship and sweetness of sound to any made by the late celebrated Mr. Feyering, who was so generally taken notice of for his ingenuity. It does great honor to the maker and is worth the attention and notice of the curious who may happen to pass this way.[98]

A later report praised the organ Tannenberg built in 1790 for Zion Lutheran Church in Philadelphia as "unquestionably the largest and finest organ built in America during the eighteenth century . . . and comparable in size and tonal development to those built for large city churches in Europe."[99] This organ had three manuals and thirty-four stops:

> This great and beautiful creation is the work of Mr. David Tanneberg [*sic*], of Lititz in Lancaster County, who began to build organs here in America by his own instincts, but

through reading, reflection and unwearied industry has raised himself to such a height that if the most skilled European builder should come here and examine this work, in the judgment of experts, he could only bestow praise and be won to him.[100]

Soon thereafter Tannenberg, now in his sixties, began to think of the future and sought a skilled associate for his business. He asked that Philip Bachman (1762–1837), a Moravian living in Herrnhut and trained in building musical instruments, be sent to Lititz. Bachman arrived in 1793 and subsequently married one of Tannenberg's daughters. With an assistant by his side and with help from the Lititz community, Tannenberg was able to increase his rate of production and completed fourteen more organs before his death in 1804. He died while installing his last organ in the Lutheran church in York, Pennsylvania. That organ was played for the first time at Tannenberg's funeral.

The specifications of the organs that Tannenberg built differed according to the church denomination for which they were intended.[101] In general the organs installed in Lutheran and Reformed churches had stops from the flute, string, and principal families, including mutations. Mid-sized organs also had mixtures, and larger ones included reeds. The largest organ that Tannenberg built for a non-Moravian church was for Zion Lutheran in Philadelphia in 1790, and included three manuals of thirty-four stops. According to the dedication program, the stop list contained a variety of principals, flutes, and strings in the 8' and 4' ranges, as well as a 16' flute on the Great manual, two 2' stops, one 6' (5 1/3') and two 3' (2 2/3') mutation stops, two mixture stops, and three 8' reeds on the manuals, plus a 16' reed in the pedals. In addition, a glockenspiel was installed two years later. The organist was expected to play solo voluntaries with a loud and full sound as well as chorale preludes that required a variety of colorful solo stops to sound the tune. Even the small non-Moravian churches routinely had a 3' mutation and a 2' stop for the upperwork.

Moravian churches, on the other hand, had different organ-specification requirements. The organ's primary function was to accompany the voices of the congregation and provide continuo support for the instrumental ensemble during the singing of anthems. It needed only a variety of fundamental 8' and 4' stops, with an abundance of soft strings and flutes, to provide sufficient support for the music, and perhaps a bit of upperwork in the largest instruments to help fill the space of a large sanctuary. The largest organ that Tannenberg built for the Moravian Church was completed in 1800 for the new church in Salem, North Carolina. It had thirteen stops on two manuals and two stops in the pedal. The specifications included ten fundamental 8' and 4' stops in the manuals, plus a small upper work of two 2' stops and one 3' mutation. Tannenberg knew full well the musical requirements of his own church.

Tannenberg's influence spread throughout the state of Pennsylvania, especially in the communities of the Pennsylvania Germans. Their organ builders often adopted the style and methods of Tannenberg's organ designs. Some—including two Schwenkfelder brothers, John (1770–1819) and Andrew (1771–1841) Krauss—used Sorge's mathematical principles in the making of pipes and followed his recommendations for pitch and temperament.[102] It is significant that previous generations of the Krauss, Klemm, and Tannenberg families lived together in Herrnhut on Zinzendorf's estate around the year 1726 before some of their members emigrated to America.[103] Organs by other Pennsylvania German builders, including John Jacob (1744–1803) and Christian (1769–1829) Dieffenbach, have a similar construction to those built by Tannenberg, although there is no evidence that the builders ever met.[104]

Other Moravian organ builders included Tannenberg's former associate Philip Bachman, David Tannenberg, Jr. (1760–ca. 1802), Joseph Ferdinand Bulitschek (1729–1801), and Robert Hartaffel (1717–82). Bachman established his business independent of Tannenberg in 1800, and built ten organs for Moravian, Reformed, and Lutheran churches until 1821.[105] One organ for a Lutheran church had a detached console.

David Tannenberg, Jr., learned organ building from his father but was a wayward son, often at odds with the Moravian community. Fortunately he spent nearly a year and a half helping the Krauss brothers build organs in Lehigh County, Pennsylvania. The younger Tannenberg brought the knowledge passed on to him by his gifted father as well as a copy of the Sorge treatise to the Krauss homestead, and in this way provided a link between the Moravian organ-building tradition and that of the Pennsylvania Germans.[106] Brunner writes, "In matters of pipe scaling and temperament the German organ builders in Pennsylvania were at the forefront of organ development and were ahead of many of their European counterparts."[107]

J. F. Bulitschek of Bohemia apprenticed with the elder Tannenberg after his arrival in America. Bulitschek moved to North Carolina and built two small organs for the Moravians in Bethabara and Bethania.[108] Finally, Robert Hartaffel, a Moravian, worked as an organ repairman and visited Bethlehem in 1751 to fix the Klemm organ in the chapel. Although we know of no organs he built, his visit may have inspired Tannenberg to consider building organs.[109]

The Moravians in Europe sent not only skilled music instrument builders to America but also music teachers. The composer and organist Johann Christian Bechler was sent to America in 1806 to teach at the *Paedagogium* in Nazareth and later at the newly formed Moravian theological seminary. In his prior assignment as instructor at the seminary in Barby, Germany, Bechler had the responsibility of "train[ing] a considerable number of efficient organists for the service of the Church," and he continued to teach music along with other subjects in Nazareth.[110] Among Bechler's organ students was the fourteen-year-old Moravian student Peter Wolle (1792–1871).[111] Thus began a long association of the Wolle family with organs and Moravian church music.

The Wolle family of Bethlehem produced three organists, each of whom contributed substantially to the musical life of the Moravian community and beyond. The first generation included Peter Wolle, who studied organ with Bechler and compiled an important hymn-tune book in 1836.[112]

Peter Wolle taught his son Theodore F. Wolle (1832–85) to play the organ. By age ten, Theodore "could play from memory nearly every chorale or hymn tune in his father's tune book."[113] Theodore headed south in 1853 to teach music at a women's school in Greensboro, North Carolina, and later played in a Confederate military band. By 1865 he returned to Bethlehem to work as the organist at the Moravian Chapel, and in 1871 was appointed organist and choir-master at Central Moravian Church. During his tenure there the 1806 John Geib organ was replaced by a three-manual organ with forty stops built by the New York City firm of Jardine & Sons in 1873. Theodore Wolle himself helped design the instrument, maintaining the previous century's legacy of the Moravian organ designers John Klemm and David Tannenberg. The organist played the new Jardine organ from a detached, reversed console, facing the pulpit.

To commemorate the new organ and to nudge the Moravians into a more prominent role of music leadership in Bethlehem, Theodore Wolle organized a benefit public organ concert for the "good causes of the Congregation."[114] Three aspects of this concert, which took place on January 15, 1874, reflected a shift in attitude from earlier Moravian ideals. First, tickets were sold to an event inside the church; second, reserved seating was provided for the clergy, their families, and other dignitaries in a denomination known for avoiding outward displays of rank or status; and third, fees were paid to outside professional musicians.[115]

Wolle family biographer Paul S. Larson observes that Theodore Wolle was instrumental in changing the role of the Moravian organist and the Moravian organ tradition.[116] With the installation of the Jardine organ, three elements of organ design and appearance affected the traditionally conservative view of the instrument's role of supporting music in the church and of creating an unob-trusive presence in the worship space. One change included the addition of expression pedals to accommodate the gradual dynamic changes required in romantic-style music. Second, the organ featured a large stop list containing many color stops of reeds, mixtures, and mutations to support the performance of popular transcriptions of orchestral and operatic works. Finally, some exposed pipes were painted a lilac color, complete with gilt ornamentation, all of which drew attention to the organ as a work of art in itself and suitable for decoration. The organ's appearance no longer blended into the background of the church interior, and it no longer functioned primarily as the continuo instrument in the *collegium musicum*. The Moravian church in Bethlehem took a giant leap into the Victorian age of industrial America with its emphasis on heightened musical expression, decoration, and technological aids. Because of the new organ and Theodore Wolle's support of public concerts featuring con-temporary music both sacred and secular, Central Moravian Church once again assumed a prominent position in music making in Bethlehem. Wolle's production of a public concert for the Jardine organ dedication inspired other organists in town to play recitals. Wolle himself also dedicated other new organs in town. Larson credits him with being the first Moravian organist to play organ recitals.[117]

The third member of the Wolle family to become an organist was J. Frederick Wolle (1863–1933), the grandson of Peter Wolle's younger brother. "J. Fred." (as he preferred to sign his name) achieved great fame as a performer and conductor outside the boundaries of Pennsylvania; most important, he advanced the music of J. S. Bach and founded the Bach Choir of Bethlehem. He was also one of the founders of the American Guild of Organists in 1896. He studied organ with Theodore Wolle as well as with David Wood of Philadelphia. J. Fred. Wolle seems to have favored the music of Bach, even to the point of obsession, early in his life. An unidentified manuscript relates the following personal quote:

> I began to study organ. My first lesson was on a little fugue of Bach's. For some reason or other this piece took hold of me, and I asked my teacher to give me Bach compositions entirely. . . . I seemed to feel that I was coming back to something that I had known or heard before.[118]

In 1884 Wolle was accepted as one of only four students to study in Europe with the organist Josef Rheinberger (1839–1901), known for his interpretations of Bach's organ music. J. Fred., however, had different ideas about how Bach should be played on the organ than his illustrious teacher. Rheinberger preferred a dry and straightforward approach to playing Bach, whereas J. Fred. believed that Bach's music, and indeed "all music—would express human feeling."[119] J. Fred. became acquainted with the music of Richard Wagner (1813–83) during his stay in Munich while studying with Rheinberger. He soon set about transcribing Wagner's operas for the organ, as it was quite fashionable for organists to play excerpts from popular operas at their organ recitals.

In 1885, on the death of Theodore Wolle, the position of organist at Central Moravian in Bethlehem was offered to the young J. Fred. He accepted the offer and left Europe after only one year of study. Two years later he accepted the position of organist-choirmaster at Packer Memorial Church on the campus of Lehigh University in Bethlehem. Thus, his Sunday duties included a first church service at Central Moravian in the downtown area, followed by a quick walk across the river to play a second service at the Episcopal church on the college campus. Wolle's repertoire at Packer Chapel included his own transcriptions of Wagner's operas, whereas his offerings at the Moravian church were undoubtedly more subdued. Larson also reports that J. Fred. rarely attended meetings concerning church music at Central Moravian.[120] He did, however, receive national recognition for his organ playing when he performed recitals at two major events: the 1893 World's Columbia Exposition in Chicago and the 1904 St. Louis Exposition.

By the early twentieth century, in the southern Moravian community of Salem, North Carolina, the Tannenberg organ installed in Home Moravian Church in 1800 was having mechanical problems after over a hundred years of service. In 1910 the organ was removed and placed in storage, but the three heavy bellows situated in the attic of the church remained in place. For three years, while the sanctuary was renovated and expanded, the church continued to hold services using a piano and the church orchestra for musical accompaniment. A new two-manual and pedal organ of twenty-two stops built by the Kimball firm of Chicago was installed in 1913 with the latest technology of full pneumatic action. A church member wrote that "the console was large because of the many lead tubes and bellows required to operate."[121] The front of the case included wooden columns and panels that were made in nearby Hickory, North Carolina.[122] The Moravians continued their concern for the proper use and suitability of an organ, as expressed by B. J. Pfohl: "There are in Winston-Salem a number of fine and costly organs but, none we venture to state, *fulfils its purpose better* [italics mine] than the Home Church Kimball organ . . . with tonal qualities and effect unsurpassed by any other."[123]

The original Tannenberg organ remained in storage until near the end of the twentieth century, when it was restored by Taylor & Boody Organbuilders of Staunton, Virginia.[124] A symposium and rededication of the organ took place in March of 2004 after it was installed in the newly built James A. Gray, Jr. Auditorium of the new Old Salem Visitors' Center. In 2006 the smaller organ Tannenberg built for the Salem *Gemeinhaus* was also restored and replaced in the Single Brothers' House, where it had resided since its earlier restoration during the mid-1960s.

Conclusions

The organ has functioned as an important part of Moravian music for over 250 years. When Count Zinzendorf offered refuge to the European Moravians on his estate in Saxony in the eighteenth century and assumed a strong leadership and advisory role, he encouraged them to learn how to play musical instruments and to include music in all their daily activities, whether religious worship, work, or leisurely pursuits.

From the eighteenth century forward, the organ's primary role was to enhance the worship life of the congregation. The organ was intended to support congregational hymn singing and to serve as the continuo instrument within the instrumental ensemble accompanying choral and solo singing. This clear definition of the instrument's purpose influenced all aspects of organ playing, music composition, organ building, and even placement of the instrument within the worship space itself.

The *Singstunde* required that the organist possess a thorough familiarity with the hymn tunes and the ability to accompany hymn singing immediately in any key. The organist was expected to match the style of his playing to the sense of the text as well as of the hymn tune, and thus had to be familiar with the hymn texts. Although in the eighteenth century (and through part of the nineteenth) the organist played interludes between lines of the hymns, this practice was discontinued, not because the organists lost that skill but rather because the practice was judged to be detrimental to worship.

Music for organ other than hymns was limited in scope and complexity. Sacred anthems, solos, and duets sung during the festival services were accompanied by the musicians of the *collegium musicum* along with the organ. The very existence and use of stringed and wind instruments in Moravian music influenced the character of the organ parts written: very few works have truly independent organ parts, and even within those the independent organ writing is sporadic. Moreover, very little music was written specifically for organ solo, as the expectation was clear that a simple hymn tune for a prelude served the needs of the worshipers far more effectively than a complex voluntary.

Organ building itself was also influenced by the Moravians' ideals and values. The detached, reversed console was a practical innovation designed to allow the organist to see the worship leader. Organs built for Moravian churches had a much more limited selection of solo stops and mixtures, because the organ was not seen as a solo instrument but rather as a support for singing and a part of the ensemble. Moreover, the placement of the organ (and choir) within the worship space reflects Moravian theology. The musicians were seen as part of the worshiping congregation, but not as performers in the front; and they were often elevated in a balcony or on a platform to symbolize the music of the heavenly congregation above.

The nineteenth and twentieth centuries saw significant changes in these ideals, with the dissolution of the *collegia musica* and the increase in solo organ playing. By the late nineteenth century, Moravian composers were writing organ preludes and playing solo organ recitals, and many Moravian churches (either newly constructed or renovated) placed the organ (and choir) in the front of the sanctuary. Recent years have seen a resurgence of interest in earlier Moravian worship practices, accompanied by the restoration of several historic organs built by David Tannenberg.

Notes

1. Quoted in William H. Armstrong, *Organs for America: The Life and Work of David Tannenberg* (Philadelphia: University of Pennsylvania Press, 1967), 73.

2. Armstrong, 76.

3. Donald M. McCorkle, "The Moravian Contribution to American Music," *Moravian Music Foundation Publications* No. 1 (Winston-Salem: The Moravian Music Foundation, Inc., 1956), 7. Reprinted from *Notes*, Music Library Association, September 1956. Organs already existed in Anglican churches such as King's

Chapel, Boston (1713); Bruton Parish Church, Williamsburg; and St. Philip's, Charleston (1728). Other early organs were present in Pennsylvania among the Wissahickon Mystics (ca. 1703), the Ephrata Cloister, the Swedish Lutherans in Philadelphia, and some Roman Catholic churches.

4. See chapter 7.

5. Georg Andreas Sorge, *The Secret Art of the Mensuration of Organ Pipes, described by Georg Andreas Sorge, Court and Town Organist at Lobenstein, 1764*, trans. and ed. Carl O. Bleyle (Buren: Frits Knuf, 1978). See also Carl Otto Bleyle, "Georg Andreas Sorge's Influence on David Tannenberg and Organ Building in America During the Eighteenth Century" (PhD diss., University of Minnesota, 1969).

6. Raymond Brunner's excellent study of Pennsylvania German organ builders details the many connections between Tannenberg and others in his field. Raymond J. Brunner, *That Ingenious Business: Pennsylvania German Organ Builders* (Birdsboro: Pennsylvania German Society, 1990).

7. Karl Kroeger, "The Moravian Tradition in Song," *Moravian Music Foundation Bulletin* 20/2 (Fall–Winter, 1975): 8. See chapter 1, pp. 10–17, for Zinzendorf's influence on the Moravian Church.

8. Timothy P. Duncan, "The Role of the Organ in Moravian Sacred Music between 1740 and 1840" (DMA diss., University of North Carolina at Greensboro, 1989), 128. See also chapter 2 for a discussion of Moravian worship.

9. Duncan, i, 19, 38–39.

10. "Besonders wäre zu wünschen, daß der Gesang in unsern Kirchen, der ein so vorzügliches Stück der öffentlichen Gottesverehrung, und so recht eigentlich geschickt ist, in den Herzen der Singenden gute Gesinnungen zu erwecken, und zu frommen und Gottwohlgefälligen Entschliessungen zu ermuntern, dem Gesange in den Brüdergemeinen mehr ähnlich werden möchte! In unsern Versamlungen wird an den mehresten Orten mehr geschrieen als gesungen, und der größte Theil der Singenden scheint durch seinen Schreyenden Gesang zu verrathen, daß er im Herzen nicht glaube und fühle, was der Mund singt. In den Brüdergemeinen scheint der sanfte Gesang mehr Ausdruck der Empfindungen im Herzen zu seyn. . . .

"Eben so reizend und nachahmungswürdig ist das Spielen des Organisten in den Brüdergemeinen. Wenn sich bey uns der Organist in einem Vorspiele ganz vergißt, in Fugen, Sinfonien und andern Gängen zu verlieren scheint, eine ganze Gemeine auf sich warten läßt, und bey der Begleitung des Gesangs seine ganze Organistenkunst anzubringen sucht: so ist das Spielen der Orgel in den Brüdergemeinen nur das, was es eigentlich seyn soll, nämlich ungekünstelte, sanfte Begleitung des Gesangs, wodurch das Herz der Singenden ermuntert, und eine ganze Gemeine im Tone erhalten werden soll." Christian Gottlieb Frohberger, *Briefe über Herrnhut und die evangelische Brüdergemeine; nebst einem Anhange* (Budissin: George Gotthold Monse, 1796), 346–48. Trans. Peter Vogt in "Listening to 'Festive Stillness': The Sound of Moravian Music According to Descriptions of Non-Moravian Visitors," *Moravian Music Journal* 44/1 (Spring 1999): 18.

11. "Der Innhalt der Lieder ist hiernächst auch sehr verschieden. Man hat daher billig darauf zu sehen, dass Singen und Spielen demselben immer möglichst gemäß sey. Das eine Lied, z. B. Der Tag der ist so freudenreich u. erfordert eine lebhafte und fröhliche, hingegen ein andres, z. B. O Haupt voll Blut und Wunden u. eine langsame und gravitätische Art des Gesangs. Dem gemäß hat der Vorsänger sowol selbst zu handeln, als auch die Gemeine auf eine schickliche und unvermerkte Weise dazu zu veranlassen. Ein aufmerksamer und dem Gesange von Herzen dienender

Organist kan ihm dabey sehr behülflich seyn." Christian Gregor, *Choral-Buch, enthaltend alle zu dem Gesangbuche der Evangelischen Brüder-Gemeinen vom Jahre 1778 gehörige Melodien* (Leipzig: Breitkopf, 1784; facsimile edition, ed. James Boeringer, Winston-Salem: Moravian Music Foundation, 1984), 49. Preface trans. Karl Kroeger.

12. "Die feierliche Stille, der einfache, rührende Gesang, mit sanftem Orgelspiele begleitet, der sich gewiß von dem in manchen Kirchen so gewöhnlichen überlauten Geschrei sehr vortheilhaft unterscheidet, vermag wohl ein zu religiösen Gefühlen geneigtes Gemüuth zur innigen Andacht zu erwecken, und fromme Entschließungen in ihm hervorzubringen." [Anon.] *Reise durch Kursachsen in die Oberlausitz nach den Evangelischen Brüdergemeinorten Barby, Gnadau, Herrnhut, Niesky und Kleinwelka* (Leipzig: N.p., 1805), 81–82. Trans. James D. Nelson in "Herrnhut: Friedrich Schleiermacher's Spiritual Homeland" (PhD diss., University of Chicago, 1963), 181. Quoted in Vogt, 19.

13. Christian Ignatius LaTrobe, ed., *Anthems for One, Two or more Voices performed in the Church of the United Brethren, Collected, and the Instrumental parts adapted for the Organ or Piano Forte* (London: Printed for the Editor, 1811), 2.

14. Abraham Ritter, *History of the Moravian Church in Philadelphia, from Its Foundation in 1742 to the Present Time* (Philadelphia: Hayes and Zell, 1857), 150. A brief obituary of Ritter, describing him as "one of the fathers of the Moravian Church in Philadelphia," is given in the *Moravian*, November 8, 1860, 358–59.

15. For an example see Christian Ignatius LaTrobe, *Original Anthems for One, Two, or More Voices Adapted for Private Devotion or Public Worship Composed and the Accompaniments Arranged for the Piano Forte or Organ* (London: Printed for the Author, 1828), 185.

16. Marilyn Gombosi, *A Day of Solemn Thanksgiving: Moravian Music for the Fourth of July, 1783, in Salem, North Carolina* (Chapel Hill: University of North Carolina Press, 1977), 43–49 See also chapter 2, p. 39.

17. "Br. Benzien sang Abends mit der Gem. die Passions Lit. No. 27. Es wohnten derselben mehrere Herrn u. Ladies von Raleigh u. andern Orten, die hier besuchten, mit vielem Wohlgefallen bey. Da dieselben gewunscht hatten, eine etwas vollständige Musick zu hören, so begleiteten unsre Musici den Gesang der Gem. in dieser Lit. mit Violinen Flöten u. Waldhörnern. Nach derselben spielten sie ihnen noch mehrer unsrer Choralmelodien mit voller Orgel, unter Begleitung von Posaunen u. Trompeten." *Salem Diary* of August 8, 1806. Manuscript in Moravian Archives, Winston-Salem. Adelaide L. Fries, ed., *Records of the Moravians in North Carolina* (Raleigh: Department. of Archives and History, 1943), 6:2852.

18. Duncan, 27–31.

19. Quoted in Armstrong, 76.

20. Armstrong, 94.

21. Duncan, 31–34. The Moravians' use of figured bass numbers and variations on this shorthand form of notation will be discussed later in the chapter.

22. Duncan, 36–37. Moravians typically separated the men from the women on different sides of the room during the worship services, and this arrangement was ideal for antiphonal singing between them. See Alice M. Caldwell, "Music of the Moravian 'Liturgische Gesange' (1791–1823): From Oral to Written Tradition" (PhD diss., New York University, 1987).

23. John R. Weinlick, "Zinzendorf, Nikolaus Ludwig von (1700–1750)," *The New Grove Dictionary of Music and Musicians*, 2nd ed., ed. Stanley Sadie (London: Macmillan, 2001), 27:849. See chapter 2, pp. 33–34, for a description of the *Singstunde*.

24. Nelson, 180.

25. "Ein Organist muß sichs ferner angelegen seyn lassen, die möglichste Fertigkeit zu erlangen, aus allen Tönen spielen zu können. Weil es in den Brüder-Gemeinen nicht auf ihn, sondern auf den Liturgum ankommt, was für einen Vers und aus welchem Tone dieser denselben anfangen will oder kan, so muß der Organist sogleich, ohne erst viele Tangenten probiren zu müssen, mit einzufallen und ohne Anstoß den Gesang zu begleiten, im Stande seyn, welches oft in einer sogenannten Singestunde auf zehn und mehrerley Weise erforderlich seyn kan, indem darinnen nie ganze Lieder sondern lauter einzelne Verse, die jedoch meistens von einerley Materie handeln, gesungen werden.

"Daraus erhellet, daß ein Organist in den Brüder-Gemeinen, den Gesang nicht sowohl nach eigener Willkühr zu dirigiren, als vielmehr denselben nur sorgfältig zu unterstützen und zu helfen habe, daß er lieblich und zweckmäßig fortgehe." Gregor, 49.

26. Christian Ignatius LaTrobe, ed., *Hymn Tunes sung in the Church of the United Brethren* (London: J. Bland, for the author, ca. 1790), vi.

27. Gregor, 47–48.

28. Gregor, 49–50.

29. Theodor Erxleben, *Hilfsbuch für Liturgen und Organisten in der Brüdergemeinen*, 2nd ed. (Gnadau: Verlag der Unitäts-Buchhandlung, 1891), 6.

30. For instance, the German organist and composer George Friedrich Kauffmann (1679–1735) wrote in his *Harmonische Seelenlust* (1733) that "for such inexpert amateurs as have been described here are not in a position to do anything suitable at these points; yet to remain silent would be too bad." Quoted in Thomas Spacht, "Toward an Understanding of Some Hymn Accompaniment Practices in Germany and Pennsylvania around 1850," *The Tracker—The Organ Historical Society* 42/1 (1998): 14–17.

31. Gregor, 47–49.

32. Duncan, 131, and Karl Kroeger, "On the Early Performance of Moravian Chorales," *Moravian Music Foundation Bulletin* 24 (Fall–Winter, 1979): 5.

33. Johann Sebastian Bach, *Neue Ausgabe Sämtlicher Werke*, Serie IV: Orgelwerke, Band 3: Die einzeln überlieferten Orgelchoräle, ed. Hans Klotz (Basel: Bärenreiter, 1961), 30–31, 50–53, 63–64, 94–95.

34. [Johann Christian Bechler], "Rules for Interludes," unpublished ms. (Lititz: Historical Society Museum, n.d.). See also Kroeger, "On the Early Performance," 5–8, and Duncan, 94, 99.

35. Duncan, 91.

36. "Alles, was bey dem Gesange der Gemeine fremde klingt, stört sowol dessen angenehme Uebereinstimmung, als die ruhige Andacht der Herzen. Diß ist sonderlich auch bey den Zwischen-Spielen von einer Gesangs-Zeile zur andern, zu merken. Wenn diese mehr etwas blos gekünsteltes, oder gar unbedachtes und unschickliches sind, als daß sie nach ihrem eigentlichen Zweck einen simplen, angenehmen und bestimmten Wegweiser zum Uebergange aus dem Vorherigen ins Folgende, abgeben: so stören sie den nahen Zusammenhang des einen mit dem andern." Gregor, 49.

37. Christian Ignatius LaTrobe, *Letters to My Children; Written at Sea During a Voyage to the Cape of Good Hope, in 1815*, ed. and with intro. by the Rev. J. A. LaTrobe (London: Seeley's, 1851), 36.

38. LaTrobe, *Letters*, 36–41.

39. Peter LaTrobe, *Hymn-tunes Sung in the Church of the United Brethren* (London: William Mallilieu, ca. 1854), 22.

40. Ritter, 154.

41. Salem Manuscript Books Collection, SMB 96 and 97, Moravian Music Foundation, Winston-Salem, NC. This collection includes more than one hundred music copybooks used primarily by young students (mostly girls) in the Moravian community. They contain hundreds of popular songs of the day, solo piano works, a few chorales, marches, rudiments of music and other musical items the students wished to preserve for their own private use.

42. Kroeger, "On the Early Performance," 7.

43. Ernst Immanuel Erbe, *Seventeen Organ Chorales*, ed. James Boeringer (Charlotte: Brodt Music Co., 1983).

44. SMB 96, pp. 19, 21.

45. SMB 97, pp. 4, 5, 9.

46. As quoted in Duncan, 87–89.

47. Erxleben, 120.

48. Spacht, 15.

49. Grider, 12.

50. *Hymnal and Liturgies of the Moravian Church* (Bethlehem: Globe Times Printery, 1923), no. 212.

51. See chapter 4 for a discussion of the sacred vocal music (anthems, solos, arias) of the Moravians.

52. See chapter 2, pp. 35–38.

53. LaTrobe, *Original Anthems for One, Two, or More Voices.*

54. Duncan, 55–57.

55. For example, August Heinrich Gehra, *Man singet mit Freuden*, Herbst Collection H 298.1, Moravian Music Foundation, Winston-Salem.

56. Duncan, 63–65, notes that the anthem *Freuen und fröhlich* by Johannes Herbst (Herbst H 401a), is "marked manual and pedal in the appropriate places." Here there are two musical lines written in the bass staff, with the left-hand notes written with stems up, and the pedal notes with stems down. This specification of the pedal is a rare marking in anthem scores.

57. For example, Johann Ludwig Freydt, *Das Wort ward Fleisch*, Herbst Collection H 296.1, Moravian Music Foundation, Winston-Salem.

58. For example, Freydt, *Das Wort ward Fleisch.*

59. Duncan, 62–63, reports the anthem *Lob sey Christo*, by Johann Gebhard (Herbst H 428b), is marked "*Solo*" for the organ in measures 5–8, in which the organ is the only instrument playing. This is a very rare instance of solo organ playing within a Moravian anthem. The organ solo here consists of a tuneful, sequential melody in parallel thirds with a simple bass-line support.

60. For example, Johann Ludwig Freydt, *Alles was Othem hat—Ach wär ein jeder Puls*, Herbst Collection H 317.2, Moravian Music Foundation, Winston-Salem; August Heinrich Gehra, *Man singet mit Freuden*, Herbst Collection H 298.1, Moravian Music Foundation, Winston-Salem.

61. Ewald V. Nolte, "Publications: The New Grove Dictionary and Moravian Music," *Moravian Music Journal* 26/2 (Summer 1981): 30.

62. "Was den Organisten insonderheit betrifft, so ist, wie eben bemerkt worden, vor allen Dingen nöthig, daß derselbe diesen seinen Dienst so von Herzen, und mit eben der Andacht und Intention, Segen und Erbauung bey andern damit zu schaffen,

als irgend ein andrer Diener der Gemeine zu thun suche. Davon müssen auch seine Präludia vor dem Anfange einer Versammlung zeugen, und dadurch auf den vorsehenden Gesang oder Liturgie eine angenehme Vorbereitung gemacht werden. So gern ein gutes, und dem Orte wie den Umständen gemäßes Präludium, vor einer feyerlichen Versammlung gehöret wird; so unangenehm sind hingegen solche, die diese Eigenschaft nicht haben. Derjenige, dem die nöthige Geschicklichkeit zu guten Vorspielen mangelt, thut besser, sich schöner und zu der Art der Versammlung passender Choral-Melodien zu Vorspielen zu bedienen, als allerhand daher sich nicht schickende Phantasien hören zu lassen." Gregor, 49.

63. C. Daniel Crews and Nola Reed Knouse, "Questions of Music in the Church: As Seen by the Unity Elders' Conference, May 1790," *Moravian Music Journal* 44/2 (Fall 1999): 6.

64. La Trobe, *Hymn Tunes* (ca. 1790), vi.

65. Laurence Libin, "Music-Related Commerce in Some Moravian Accounts," in *Pleasing for Our Use: David Tannenberg and the Organs of the Moravians*, ed. Carol A. Traupman-Carr (Bethlehem: Lehigh University Press, 2000), 90–91.

66. Christian Ignatius LaTrobe, *Nine Preludes for Organ*, ed. Karl Kroeger (Charlotte: Brodt Music Company, 1978), [2].

67. Knouse, "Moravian Music and the Organ," 25.

68. Francis Florentine Hagen, ed., *Church and Home Organist's Companion: A Choice selection of Voluntaries Consisting of Anthems, Reveries, Transcriptions of well-known Hymn Tunes, Prayers Marches, etc., etc. arranged for the Pipe or Reed Organ*, 2 vols. (Philadelphia, Fred. Williams, 1880, 1881). Modern editions of twenty-four of Hagen's organ preludes have recently been published by the Moravian Music Foundation: vol. 1, ed. Nola Reed Knouse and Andy Moore (2002); vol. 2, ed. Jayson Snipes (2004); vol. 3, ed. Jayson Snipes (2006).

69. Quoted in and translated by Karl Kroeger, "Ernst Immanuel Erbe: A Forgotten Moravian Composer," *Moravian Music Foundation Bulletin* 24 (Spring–Summer 1979): 10. Much of the information about Erbe is derived from this article.

70. Kroeger, "Ernst Immanuel Erbe," 10.

71. Kroeger, "Ernst Immanuel Erbe," 10. The Evangelical Synod was an association of congregations formed in the mid-nineteenth century by groups of German-speaking immigrants of Lutheran and Reformed backgrounds. In 1934 this body united with the German Reformed church to become the Evangelical and Reformed Church, which in 1957 united with the Congregational and Christian churches to form the United Church of Christ. A review of Erbe's book for the Evangelical Church reported that the music had "smoothly-flowing harmonization . . . All that is too elaborate has been kept out, thus preserving the noble simplicity of the chorale." Erbe seems to have followed the advice of Gregor and LaTrobe for accompanying hymns.

72. Erbe, *Seventeen Organ Chorales.*

73. Quoted in McCorkle, "The Moravian Contribution to American Music," 4–5.

74. Armstrong, p. 97, writes that according to the 1768 diary of the Lititz Moravian Single Brethren's Choir, a harpsichord was used for services in the chapel until a Tannenberg organ was installed in 1777.

75. Bernard J. Pfohl, "The Home Moravian Church Organ," Bernard J. Pfohl Collection, #11: b) Paper of 1947 (Winston-Salem: Moravian Music Foundation).

76. Anja Wehrend, *Musikanschauung, Musikpraxis, Kantatenkomposition in der Herrnhuter Brüdergemeine* (Frankfurt am Main: Peter Lang, 1995), 176–77. See also

3

Anja Wehrend, "Gottesdienstliches Musizieren als Vorspiel zur himmlischen Harmonie: Der Einfluß der barocken Musikanschauung auf Zinzendorfs Abbild- und Harmoniebegriff," *Unitas Fratrum* 47 (2000): 89–106.

77. "[E]ine liebliche Harmonie der Stimmen und musikalischen Instrumente, sonderlich der Orgel" and "[S]ich alle Stimmen so ein einander zu fügen suchen, daß sich die durchgängig-gemilderten Töne in eine sanft zusammen geflossene und doch kraftvolle Harmonie zu verlieren scheinen." Gregor, 46, 48.

78. "[D]aß [der Gesang] lieblich und zweckmäßig fortgehe." Gregor, 49.

79. Quoted in Barbara Owen, "'Pleasing for Our Use': David Tannenberg's Moravian Organs," 63 (minutes of the Bethlahem Helfer Conferenz, June 9–20, 1746).

80. LaTrobe, *Anthems for One, Two or more Voices* (1811), preface, 2–3.

81. Proposal dated March 6, 1803. Moravian Archives, Bethlehem.

82. Stop names taken from Brunner, *That Ingenious Business*, 74–95, and Owen, "Pleasing for Our Use," 52–60.

83. Quoted in Owen, "Pleasing for Our Use," 59; italics mine.

84. Owen, "Pleasing for Our Use," 61.

85. Owen, "Pleasing for Our Use," 61.

86. Frances Cumnock, "The Lovefeast Psalm: Questions and a Few Answers," *Moravian Music Foundation Bulletin* 23/1 (Spring–Summer 1978): 5.

87. In equal temperament, the distance between the chromatic notes of the scale is exactly the same throughout the compass of an octave. Our modern ears are used to equal temperament, in which music played in any key sounds equally good, even though each key area is slightly out of tune. Equal temperament allows music to be heard in any key equally well without the harsh dissonances of tuning that appear in other temperaments of the day, such as mean tone. In mean-tone tuning, harmonic intervals of thirds and fifths sound pure in the commonly used keys. Temperaments such as mean tone, in which the distance between the half steps of the scale varies, work extremely well for pieces set in keys with no more than three sharps or two flats. However, music in keys with many sharps or flats in the key signature sounds very dissonant, harsh, and out of tune, and those keys must be avoided.

88. Brunner, 31–37. See also Carl Otto Bleyle, *Georg Andreas Sorge's Influence*.

89. See appendix 1, p. 276, for Klemm's biography.

90. Owen, "Pleasing for Our Use," 31.

91. Quoted in Owen, "Pleasing for Our Use," 33.

92. Laurence Libin, "New Facts and Speculations on John Clemm," *The Tracker* 31/2 (1987): 22.

93. Quoted in Owen, "Pleasing for Our Use," 34.

94. Information on Klemm's life is found in Armstrong, 12–15, Brunner, 60–63, and Owen, "Pleasing for Our Use," 24–37.

95. The following account of Tannenberg's life comes variously from Armstrong; Brunner, pp. 68–74; Gary J. Albert, ed., *Splendid Service: The Restoration of David Tannenberg's Home Moravian Church Organ* (Winston-Salem: Old Salem, Inc., 2004), 1–11; and papers delivered at the symposium held March 19–21, 2004, in the Old Salem Visitor Center's James A. Gray Jr. Auditorium for the rededication of Tannenberg's 1800 Home Moravian Church organ. See also Laurence Libin, "The Memoirs of David Tannenberg," *Journal of Moravian History* 2 (2007).

96. Quoted in Brunner, 70. The construction of organs required much travel and contact with the outside world to receive exotic materials and supplies. The Elders,

perhaps recalling Tannenberg's wayward actions during his teen years, thought it best that he give it up.

97. Organs for English-speaking churches were usually imported from Britain or made by lesser-known builders in the English style, and sent to the large urban centers of Boston, New York, Philadelphia and Charleston, South Carolina. Information on the Tannenberg organs comes from Albert, *Splendid Service*, 14–18. The nine extant Tannenberg organs are:

1. 1770 organ for Zion Lutheran Church, Moselem Springs, Pennsylvania;
2. 1776 organ for Single Brethren's House, Bethlehem, located today at the Moravian Historical Society, Nazareth, Pennsylvania;
3. 1787 organ for Lititz Moravian Church, Lititz, Pennsylvania;
4. 1791 organ for Zion Lutheran Church, Spring City, Pennsylvania;
5. 1793 organ for the Moravian Church, Graceham, Maryland, located today at Lititz Moravian Church, Lititz, Pennsylvania;
6. 1798 organ for the *Gemeinhaus* in Salem (now Winston-Salem), North Carolina, located today in the chapel of the Single Brethren's House in Old Salem, North Carolina;
7. 1800 organ for Home Moravian Church, Salem (now Winston-Salem), located today in the James A. Gray Auditorium, the Old Salem Visitor's Center;
8. 1802 organ for Hebron Lutheran Church, Madison, Virginia;
9. 1804 organ for Christ Lutheran Church, York, Pennsylvania, located today in York County Historical Society Museum.

98. Quoted by Armstrong in *Splendid Service*, 7. Philip Feyring was a German Lutheran organ builder in Philadelphia.

99. Brunner, 73.

100. Quoted by Armstrong in *Splendid Service*, 9.

101. See Owen, "Pleasing for Our Use," 49–67.

102. The Schwenkfelders were a Protestant sect arising from followers of the Silesian Reformed theologian Caspar Schwenkfeld (1490–1561), who could not accept the Lutheran doctrine of Holy Communion or of salvation by grace. Following persecution in the seventeenth and early eighteenth centuries, several hundred of the Schwenkfelders found temporary refuge in Saxony, aided by Zinzendorf, and then migrated to Pennsylvania in 1734. See Howard Wiegner Kriebel, *The Schwenkfelders in Pennsylvania* (Lancaster, PA: Pennsylvania German Society, 1904), and Brunner, 33, 35, 110. Information on the connections between Tannenberg and various Pennsylvania German organ builders comes from various pages in Ray Brunner's excellent book.

103. Brunner, 128.

104. Brunner, 109.

105. Brunner, 99–103, and Armstrong, 49–52, 115–16.

106. Brunner, 104–5, 130, 224.

107. Brunner, 37.

108. Armstrong, 69, 126; Duncan, 17; Brunner, 16, 105–6.

109. Armstrong, 14–15; Brunner, 107.

110. [John Christian Bechler,] "Memoir of the Rt. Rev. John C. Bechler, translated by Samuel Reinke, one of his former pupils," *The Moravian* (June 26, 1857): 1.

111. Paul S. Larson, *An American Musical Dynasty: A Biography of the Wolle Family of Bethlehem, Pennsylvania* (Bethlehem: Lehigh University Press, 2002), 39.

112. Peter Wolle, *Hymn tunes used in the Church of the United Brethren, arranged for four voices and the organ or piano-forte* (Boston: N.p., 1836).

113. Walser H. Allan, "Three Musical Moravians Named Wolle," *Moravian Music Foundation Bulletin* 18/2 (Fall–Winter, 1973): 4.

114. Larson, 148.

115. See chapter 4, p. 124, for earlier Moravian reaction to the use of outside "professionals."

116. Larson, 146, 151.

117. Larson, 152.

118. Larson, 185.

119. Larson, 186.

120. Larson, 294, 298.

121. Pfohl. Information about the Kimball organ in Home Moravian Church was gathered from this collection.

122. Likewise, the casework of the old Tannenberg organ was made by local craftsmen, whereas the rest of the organ was constructed at Tannenberg's workshop in Lititz, Pennsylvania.

123. Pfohl.

124. See the excellent account of the restoration in *Splendid Service.*

Chapter Six

The Role and Development of Brass Music in the Moravian Church

Paul Peucker

One Saturday evening in 1760, a young German man named Johann Heinrich Danke was working in the fields on a farm located a mile or so south of the Moravian community of Zeist in the Netherlands. In the distance, Danke heard music; trombones were playing a familiar German tune. When he asked the farmer about the music, the farmer responded, "That is in Zeist with the Herrnhuters." Danke had never heard about the "Herrnhuters," and the farmer did not have a high opinion of them. But when he had the chance, Danke visited Zeist. The worship service he attended there made such an impression that he left his job and joined the Moravians. In 1768 Danke was sent as a Moravian missionary to Egypt.[1] His experience of Moravian music was enough to draw him into the Moravian community.

The Beginnings of Moravian Brass Music

The earliest reference to the use of brass instruments in Moravian worship dates from 1729. In his written account of Herrnhut from about 1729, Christian David describes in the chapter about the celebration of Sunday that, at the end of the day, the congregation assembled in the meeting hall in the Herrnhut *Gemeinhaus*:

> Then the congregation comes together, and the brothers from Berthelsdorf join us. First about three hymns are sung, accompanied by the organ, and the French horns are played. Then the Count [Zinzendorf] takes a verse from the Bible and gives a sermon about it. Finally this meeting, which is over around 7 o'clock, is closed with a prayer.[2]

The next known reference to horn players in the early Herrnhut records dates from April 1, 1731, when the congregational council discussed if the horn players should be paid for their services. Hans Raschke, who was one of those musicians, protested and said they would play for free. Apparently, by that time music in Herrnhut was becoming more organized. During this same meeting, the congregational council considered the formation of a *collegium musicum*. It was proposed that the *collegium musicum* should be held in the local inn every day. With 52 yeas and no nays, the proposal was approved, and it was noted that "the whole congregation is pleased."[3] Two weeks later, the Herrnhut diary records that "the *Collegia musica* during the night are uncommonly uplifting."[4] From this entry, we can conclude that music was played "during the night" or in the late evening for the residents of Herrnhut; presumably the musicians were outdoors. It was at this time that the trombones made their first appearance in Herrnhut, and it seems very plausible that they were connected to the activities of the *collegium musicum*.

On April 15, 1731, two weeks after the formation of the *collegium musicum*, the congregational council discussed how to spend a large donation of 233 Reichstaler. Hans Heinrich Schulthess, a Swiss merchant from Zurich, gave this money to the Herrnhut community. Schulthess had corresponded with Zinzendorf; recently, two Herrnhuters had visited him, telling him about the "hardships" in Herrnhut. Therefore Schulthess sent Zinzendorf a large check to be spent at his discretion.[5] After the check was cashed, the congregational council finalized on April 29 how the money was to be spent: one-third went to the orphanage, a large amount was given to Pastor Rothe (see below), 50 Reichstaler were used to pay off debts, and, among other things, 12 Reichstaler were to be used "zu Posaunen" (for trombones). The Herrnhuters did not wait long before purchasing the trombones.[6]

The first public performance using the newly acquired trombones was on May 12, 1731, at the birthday celebration of Johann Andreas Rothe, pastor of the Lutheran parish at Berthelsdorf, to which the Herrnhut community formally belonged. Zinzendorf's secretary, Tobias Friedrich, who himself was the first organist in Herrnhut and also an active violinist, reported to the count, who was away in Denmark:[7]

> Mr. Rothe is most cordial and in good spirits. His birthday was last Saturday. I requested the people in Herrnhut to write down hymn verses for him hoping he would gain more trust in us and that it would cheer him up for the upcoming holidays [Pentecost]; thank God this succeeded. I sent him the verses in the evening, for which he wrote the enclosed letter to the congregation. After the singing service Dober and I invited the brethren to come with us to Berthelsdorf and to play Mr. Rothe some music with trombones to end his birthday. More than 50 came together with lanterns and went to the parsonage and stirred the whole village. He did not indicate that he heard us, but on Pentecost Monday when he was especially uplifted, he publicly thanked us for it.[8]

The Herrnhut diary entry describing the same event is more specific about the instruments: "[W]e had the trombones and French horns."[9]

The next two recorded public trombone performances took place outdoors as well. In June 1731, a group of Moravian refugees arrived in Herrnhut. David Hans, who was among them, later described their arrival in his memoir as follows:

> On June 1, 1731, we went to Herrnhut, where we arrived in the evening after the *Singstunde*. . . . As the congregation had received its first trombones in these days, they welcomed us with these instruments and the Brethren sang the hymn "*Wie schön ist unsers Königs Braut*, etc." It impressed me so much that I believed I was no longer in this world and I could not stop weeping.[10]

Three days later the trombones played at the funeral of Rosina Schindler in the newly laid-out God's Acre, or cemetery, for the Herrnhut community.[11]

Traditionally, brass music in the Herrnhut community has been linked with musical customs in Moravia, the country of origin of about half of the residents of Herrnhut. A 1755 manual, written for traveling Moravians to assist them in answering questions that they could be confronted with, has two paragraphs about music:

> 174. Do they [the Moravians] have organs?
> In many places yes, but not everywhere.
> 175. Do they [the Moravians] have violins, French horns and other music?
> The Bohemians are musicians by birth and therefore there is no shortage of a fairly complete music [group] here and there. If combined, they would be one of the largest and finest orchestras.[12]

It is true that the earliest horn players in Herrnhut came from Moravia. A 1728 list identifies two musicians in Herrnhut. The first, Hans Raschke, one of the horn players, was born in Lichtenau (Lichkov) in Bohemia; he also played the organ. The other musician was his countryman, August Leupold, born in Wigstadtl (Vitkov).[13] That the refugees actually brought instruments with them to Herrnhut, as is sometimes argued, is possible but uncertain.[14] We know for sure that the trombones were not brought from Moravia or Bohemia, but that they were purchased by the Herrnhut community in early May of 1731.

The Herrnhut trombones were acquired as an important addition to the recently organized *collegium musicum*. Within a period of only a few weeks, we see the trombones (sometimes combined with the horns) used on occasions that have ever since been the traditional domain of the brass choir: funerals, birthdays, and general outdoor occasions. In later years, other functions were added. Brass music was not limited to Herrnhut alone; as the activities of the Unitas Fratrum became more widespread, Moravian brass music was instituted in other parts of Europe and overseas as well. Before we look at the spread of Moravian brass music to other communities, we need to focus on the role this music played in the Moravian liturgical tradition.

The Meaning of Brass Music

Eighteenth-century Moravians expressed their faith and ideas in their hymns. An excellent source for understanding Moravian theology, symbolism, and ideas lies in the hymnal. The Moravian hymnbook used during the creative years of the 1740s contained 2,357 hymns, published in several appendices and additions during the period 1735–48.[15]

The German word for "trombone" is *Posaune*. It can also be made into the verb *posaunen*, meaning *to trumpet*. Where Luther's German translation of the Bible uses the word *Posaune*, the English language King James Version has *trumpet*. A word search for *trombone* will turn up entries in the German hymnal and Bible but does not work with an eighteenth-century English text. We can therefore conclude that playing trombones had a deeper biblical connotation for the Moravians, who were principally German-speakers than it might have had for English-speaking religious groups. We must bear in mind that the ancient instruments referred to in the Bible were in fact quite different from the musical instruments we today call either trumpets or trombones.

In Luther's translation of the Old Testament, the trombone is an instrument with which the people of God are called together, important news is announced, and the call to battle is made; the sound of trombones accompanies the righteous fight for God. The trombone is the instrument of the priests when they announce a new king and when they march ahead of the Ark of the Covenant. It is the sound that accompanies the voice of God and symbolizes the power of God and his judgment. Furthermore, the trombone is played to please and praise God, together with a wide array of other musical instruments. In Luther's translation of the New Testament, the trombone is the instrument that God's companions, the angels, use to gather his elect to announce the Resurrection, the end of times, Judgment Day, and the Second Coming of Christ. When God speaks, his voice sounds like a trombone.[16]

In many Moravian hymns, *Posaunen* proclaim the Gospel. "[W]ollt ihr Posaunen der Gnade sein?" ([D]o you want to be trombones/trumpets of grace?), asks Zinzendorf in one of his hymns (HG 1360). Every Moravian is called on to trumpet out loud the grace and salvation obtained through Jesus' blood (HG 1254, 1687, 1851), so that they themselves become *Blutposaunen*, or trumpets of blood (HG 1721, 1851, 2196). Not only Christians trumpet the Gospel, the Gospel itself trumpets out loud and gathers people (HG 1529, 1561). "Souls" are being trumpeted to new life in Jesus, sang Anna Nitschmann in the year 1740 (HG 1401). The trombone signaling the resurrection of the dead appears in (surprisingly) only two hymns; one is a hymn from the Ancient Unity by Michael Weisse (HG 49); the other was written in 1748 (HG 2345). Rather, the Moravians sing of the trombone as a signal to rise to battle, to follow the Lord in the fight and to conquer the world for him (HG 1043, 1316, 1485, 1509, 1815, 2155). The trombone signals the end of time (HG 652, 854), but this subject seems to be of minor importance, since it appears only in hymns by eighteenth-century non-Moravians that were included in the Moravian hymnal during a relatively early period.

When examining the origins of the use of brass music in the Moravian Church, we should consider the *Stadtpfeifer* or *Stadtmusiker*, a parallel tradition of town musicians that existed in many German cities in early modern times.[17] It is even frequently claimed that the Moravian brass choirs were direct descendants of the German *Stadtpfeifer*.[18] These musicians were employed by the town councils and the churches and were responsible for all public instrumental music in the town. They were to play at certain hours of the day from a tower or from the town hall and at important communal and religious events. The town musicians could also be hired for weddings and funerals. Because they were organized as a guild, they enjoyed certain privileges and were protected from competition by other musicians. Although they played many different instruments, town musicians were mostly associated with brass music. The townspeople considered the music of brass instruments as representing the power and splendor of their town. Both the town musicians and the Moravian trombone players served their communities. Some of their tasks were similar (playing at religious events, to welcome guests, in processions), but other traditional responsibilities of the *Stadtpfeifer* were performed by different people within the Moravian communities (watches, weddings). The overall role and function of the Moravian brass choirs, as well as their position within the community, especially compared with the privileged position and highly regulated organization of the town musicians, seem to have been different, as we will see below.

The Role of Brass Music in Early Bethlehem

As was noted above, trombone music had a biblical connotation for eighteenth-century Moravians. By analyzing the use of the word *Posaune* in Moravian hymns, we have found that trombones were used in proclaiming God's word and motivating people to preach the Gospel. We will now examine how brass music was used in the liturgical life of a Moravian congregation by looking at Bethlehem, one of the centers of Moravian activity in the New World.[19]

Before the Moravians in Bethlehem possessed trombones, a *collegium musicum* existed that served functions similar to those in Europe. The Bethlehem *collegium musicum* is mentioned as early as December 1744 at a lovefeast for missionaries.[20] That year, the Single Brethren began incorporating "music" into their daily meditation services; in the following summer they started to go around Bethlehem regularly, singing songs accompanied by "music."[21] We know they had horns (1744), trumpets (1745), and a harp and violins (1752).[22] By January of 1748, fourteen musicians are mentioned, all single brothers or older boys. During a lovefeast on January 14, these musicians decided to reorganize:

Johann Westmann was to become their new leader, replacing Christoph Pyrlaeus, who was away from Bethlehem at the time. Westmann was to make sure that the musicians practiced one hour every evening so that "their playing would become even more harmonious than before." A fund was established for purchasing needed instruments. All their music making was to be focused on the Lamb.[23]

The *collegium musicum* played indoors, but many outside performances are also mentioned in the diaries. Unlike most other musical instruments, brass instruments are ideal for outdoor use. Their sound carries over long distances; they can be used for accompanying outdoor congregational singing; and they can be played in the rain and even—as long as they still function—at below-freezing temperatures. The Moravian definition of liturgical space was not confined to meeting rooms but extended throughout the whole settlement.

In Bethlehem, trombones were played for the first time during the celebration of the Single Brothers' Festival on August 31, 1754.[24] The set of four trombones—a soprano, an alto, a tenor, and a bass—must have arrived from Europe shortly before.[25]

Shortly after their appearance in Herrnhut, trombones were being played at funerals; it was no different in Bethlehem. Here trombones played at a funeral service for the first time on November 6, 1754. Because of heavy rains, however, they did not lead the congregation to God's Acre but remained behind at the *Saal* (now the Old Chapel) while the congregation proceeded to the graveyard.[26] In his description of Moravian burial practices in 1735, Christian David mentioned the singing of hymns during the procession to the cemetery as well as at the grave, all with the accompaniment of instruments.[27] Because most significant liturgical acts in the Moravian Church are accompanied by congregational singing, the coffin was also lowered into the grave while the congregation sang the appropriate hymns, accompanied by the brass choir.

The role of the brass choir during funeral services is more than simply that of a transportable organ. When playing at the graveside, the trombones also symbolize the *Posaune* (the English Bible translation uses "trumpets") in 1 Corinthians 15: "[F]or the trumpet shall sound, and the dead shall be raised incorruptible, and we shall be changed."

Trombone music was discussed during the General Synod of 1764, the synod that reorganized the church following Zinzendorf's death. That synod recommended the use of trombone choirs during funerals because they expressed the "joyful way of going home," which supposedly made a good impression, especially on guests.[28]

Related to funerals are the death announcements made by the Moravian brass choirs. This practice must have started in the 1740s either in Herrnhut or in Herrnhaag and spread rapidly to most of the other congregations. The introduction of a specific tune indicating the choir of the deceased happened in 1754. At a lovefeast following a funeral in Herrnhut on January 6, it was resolved "that from now on, when music is played after the departure of one of the brothers or sisters, following the usual tune 'Schon wieder eins erblasset' the choir verse will be played."[29] Every choir was assigned its own tune or "choir verse"; the members of each choir were supposed to recognize the tune when it was played by the trombones to come together for a liturgical choir meeting. Thus, the use of the choir verses was extended to the death announcements. The 1757 liturgy book states that trombones should play the tune "O Sacred Head Now Wounded" twice, and between the repetitions a tune by which listeners could recognize "what particular choir hath been thus graciously visited," without giving the particular tune numbers.[30] The 1791 liturgy book gives the tune numbers for each choir together with the hymn texts.

In Bethlehem, the announcement of a death with music happened for the first time on November 20, 1751, with trumpets playing from the roof gallery of the Single Brothers' House. As soon as the Bethlehem congregation acquired trombones, death announcements began to be made with these instruments (November 5, 1754). The practice of the threefold death announcement was established in Bethlehem on April 4, 1757, similar in manner to that in Herrnhut three years prior. That day it was decided what the particular tunes for each choir were to be, "so that one can gather the choirs for their liturgy, without having to make known beforehand in which order [the liturgies were to be held]." The same tunes were then also to be used for the death announcements.[31]

Brass instruments were played in order to make other announcements as well. Special congregational holidays and festivals were announced by making music and awaking the congregation. A day that began with music was no ordinary day, and the music of the brass choir marked the significance of the occasion.[32] Birthdays of important church leaders were also announced with the sound of trumpets and trombones. In Bethlehem trumpets were played on the birthdays of Anna Nitschmann, Johannes von Watteville, and his wife, Benigna von Watteville, for example. The music made clear to the congregation that these individuals (even while far away in Europe) were of high standing and great importance.

Guests were greeted with trumpets and trombones. Brothers and sisters arriving after a long and tedious journey from Europe were welcomed with music as they entered the community.[33] The governor of Pennsylvania was entertained with chorale music when he visited Bethlehem on July 13, 1752. One week later a large group of Nanticoke and Shawnee arrived in Bethlehem from Gnadenhutten. As the trumpets were playing from the roof of the Single Brothers' House, the people of Bethlehem watched as the Native Americans walked up the streets.[34] Greeting guests with music could be interpreted as a mere expression of joy, but in these instances, the meaning went deeper. The arrival of the brothers and sisters from overseas or of the Native Americans from Gnadenhutten were made into liturgical events. When a group of men left

Bethlehem to start the new Wachovia settlement in North Carolina in 1753, they walked out of the Single Brothers' House while trumpets were being played. This was not an ordinary goodbye; their departure was considered a sanctified act.[35] The brothers were leaving to work for the church, and the music gave expression to this concept. An entry in the diary of Anna Johanna Piesch, Chief Eldress of the Single Sisters, depicting her arrival to Bethlehem after the long journey at sea, described how impressive the music of the welcoming trumpets was: it was as if the entire atmosphere reverberated and resounded.[36] Indeed, brass music permeates the air; those within its presence cannot evade it. This was the exact intent of the Moravians.

Trombones were not only used outdoors; they were also played indoors during the liturgical services in order to enhance the effect. One example is during the New Year's Eve celebrations, when midnight was greeted with trumpets or, beginning in 1754, with trombones. Brass music not only marked the importance of the moment but was also meant to surprise and impress the worshipers. This effect of interruption was not restricted to New Year's Eve but was also utilized on other occasions. During the Christmas wake of 1751, two brothers alternately sang stanzas from the *Te Jehovah* from the gallery of the recently constructed chapel. Zinzendorf wrote this version of the "Te Deum" in 1744, and it may have been familiar to the congregation. In order to introduce a new element into this piece, while the congregation was on their knees adoring the Christ Child in the manger, trumpets were suddenly blown. Note the wording in the diary—"the sound penetrated the ears to the bottom of our hearts, and with such an effect, that we could have sunk into the earth out of deference." All the participants were caught by surprise by the penetrating noise of the trumpets. The intended shock and deafening, vibrating effect were transformed into a strong religious experience. Joshua, one of the Native Americans present, described this experience the following day when he told Spangenberg he had been absolutely certain that "the Saviour was coming and he had to turn around to see if He was not there already."[37]

Brass music had more than just an aesthetic function among eighteenth-century Moravians. The music of the brass instruments had biblical connotations that resonated in the minds of the listeners when the brothers played their instruments on the rooftops or in the streets of the settlement. Brass music had a liturgical purpose: when it was played on certain occasions, these events were sanctified and became an integral part of the liturgical life of the community. Brass instruments could be played outdoors much more effectively than any other instruments. When they were played outdoors, these instruments extended the liturgical space beyond interior rooms such as the *Saal* and other meeting places. For example, on September 30, 1754, the choir house for the married men (an institution unique to Bethlehem) was dedicated. The celebration started in the *Gemeinhaus* and was to be continued in the new house nearby. As the married brothers stepped outside the *Gemeinhaus*, "trumpets and other music" broke forth, making the walk from one house to the other an integral part of the celebration and showing that the liturgical space did not end at the door of the *Gemeinhaus* but continued outside and beyond.[38]

Since Moravians believed that life itself was a liturgy and that no separation should exist among worship, work, and leisure (all activities served the Savior and the congregation), the brass choir helped to create this extended liturgical space. When the Bethlehem brothers and sisters walked to Gnadental or Nazareth to help with the harvest, music accompanied them.[39] This was done not so much to keep them in good spirits and motivate them for the hard work ahead of them, but rather to emphasize that this activity served the common good and was also part of the liturgy of the congregation. By playing their music outdoors, the Moravian brethren successfully extended their liturgical space— apparently over great distances, as we saw at the beginning of this chapter. When outsiders were drawn into this liturgical space, the trombones truly became preachers of the Gospel.

The Spread of Brass Music Throughout the Moravian Church

At the same time the Herrnhut community was purchasing its first set of trombones in 1731, the Moravian brothers and sisters were also preparing to spread their activities beyond the immediate surroundings of Herrnhut. Herrnhuters went out as messengers to seek kindred spirits in Europe, to start missionary work on other continents, and to begin new Moravian colonies elsewhere. They brought their liturgical and musical traditions with them, and Moravian brass music developed in many places.

Moravian brass music does not consist only of the use of individual brass instruments during church services. No one would characterize the use of trumpets, trombones, or horns as something exclusively Moravian. An essential element defining brass music as *Moravian* is the choir setting.[40] A typical Moravian band plays in four parts: soprano, alto, tenor, and bass, imitating the harmonious setting of a vocal choir.

The choice of instruments, specifically the exclusive use of the trombone, can also be defined as characteristically Moravian. Trombones were conveniently available in soprano, alto, tenor, and bass. Their slide mechanism made it possible to play a chromatic scale and therefore fairly easy to play a melody or any accompanying part. Playing a tune on any other brass instrument of the time was much more complicated, since valves had not yet been invented. Nevertheless, on many occasions, the trombones were joined by additional horns and trumpets. After valve instruments became available in the nineteenth century, many Moravian trombone choirs welcomed them in their midst, although some remained exclusively trombone choirs.

It is important to note that the use of the word *Posaune* ("trombone") in the archival sources is not always consistent. For example, when a group of Single Sisters arrived in Bethlehem from Europe in 1752, their diary records that "die Posaunen" were played to welcome them. A private diary describing the same event writes that the sisters were welcomed "mit Trompeten," which was correct, since the first trombones did not arrive in Bethlehem until 1754.[41] Even the (modern) German word *Posaunenchor* does not exclusively designate a group of trombone players but can refer to any ecclesiastical brass ensemble. The more appropriate word *Bläserchor* is also commonly used in German. Whereas in most English-speaking branches of the Moravian Church the brass ensemble is called a "band," the terms *trombone choir* or *brass choir* are still commonly used in the American Northern Province.

A third characteristic of Moravian brass music is the use of the music within the liturgical life of the community. Even after the Moravian communities of the eighteenth century opened up and Moravian church life adjusted to the circumstances of the subsequent centuries, brass instruments were still used for some of the traditional purposes that originated in the years around 1750. In this part of the chapter we will consider the spread of Moravian brass music to other Moravian communities and the further development of its use and repertoire.

The first Moravian brass ensemble (the word "group" might be more appropriate) outside of Herrnhut existed among the Moravians in Savannah, Georgia. Moravians came to Savannah in 1735, and it seems likely that the instruments (trumpets and French horns) arrived the following year. We learn about the instruments from a letter written by Peter Böhler and sent to Herrnhut in December of 1739, when the Moravian community in Savannah was being dissolved. Böhler reported: "General Oglethorpe bought the brethren's trumpets and horns and gave them ten shillings more than they requested." From the same letter we learn that the Moravians used their brass instruments at funerals (they were asked to play at the funeral of Tomochichi, chief of the local Yamacraw Indians), and that Oglethorpe intended to hire Johann Böhner, one of the Moravians, as his trumpeter.[42] Born in 1710 in Grumberg (now Podlesi) in Moravia, Böhner arrived in Savannah in February 1736. Later he was involved with the founding of both Nazareth and Bethlehem; he died as a missionary on the island of St. Thomas now in the U.S. Virgin Islands in 1785. Böhner tried to set up a musical ensemble on St. Thomas in 1742, consisting of horns and violins, but he did not succeed.[43] For a few years the plantation on St. Thomas that was owned by the Moravians was even called *Posaunenberg* (meaning "Trombone Hill," now New Herrnhut).[44] Today there is a trombone choir at the New Herrnhut Moravian Church, and there are brass choirs in some of the church congregations on the islands.

In Europe the earliest mention of Moravian brass music outside of Herrnhut can be found in the Wetterau, the region north of Frankfurt am Main, where beginning in 1738 Marienborn and Herrnhaag developed as important

Moravian centers. Brass instruments (trumpets and horns) were played there as part of the *collegia musica* as early as 1739.[45] In most of the Moravian communities founded in the eighteenth century, brass instruments were played and, if possible, a trombone choir was established. Even in Königsfeld in the Black Forest, the most recently founded traditional Moravian community (*Ortsgemeine*) in Europe, a trombone choir was organized in 1812.[46]

Similar developments can be found in the New World. Although the Moravians in Savannah sold their instruments before moving to Pennsylvania, other Moravian immigrants soon brought brass instruments with them, as we have seen. The first set of trombones was played on August 31, 1754; from the relevant diary entry it is clear that this practice followd the custom in the European churches.[47] By December of 1792 there were two sets of trombones in Bethlehem.[48] By then many of the Moravian churches in America had trombone choirs: Christiansbrunn, Pennsylvania (1762); Bethabara, North Carolina (1768); Lititz, Pennsylvania (1771); Salem (now Winston-Salem), North Carolina (1772); Nazareth, Pennsylvania (1785); Hope, New Jersey (1789); Bethania, North Carolina (1790). When the Moravian community of Hope, New Jersey, was dissolved in 1808, its trombones were sent to Bethlehem. In many congregations, as in Lititz or Bethabara, other brass instruments, such as horns and trumpets, were used before there was a full set of trombones.[49] Nineteenth-century trombone choirs include Gnadenhutten, Ohio (1820); Emmaus, Pennsylvania (1820); and Dover, Ohio (1843). In more recent years new trombone choirs were formed: the Moravian Trombone Choir of Downey, California (1965); the Glenwood Moravian Trombone Choir in Madison, Wisconsin (1983); and the Salem Trombone Choir in Winston-Salem, North Carolina (1984).

There is much more uncertainty regarding Moravian brass music in Great Britain and Northern Ireland. It is certain that there were brass musicians and possibly even trombone choirs in the eighteenth-century Moravian Church in England.[50] There are also references to "musical groups" in nineteenth-century texts, but this subject requires further research in order to establish how long brass choirs actually existed in the British Province. The tradition ended, and no brass choirs are now known to exist within the British Province of the Moravian Church.

Moravian missionaries sometimes brought musical instruments with them and started brass choirs in their mission stations. Around 1760 trumpets and French horns were played by the Inuit in the mission stations in Greenland "as a signal, instead of the bell, to call the baptized or communicants to their meetings."[51] During the nineteenth, century brass choirs were begun in Labrador, South Africa, and Australia.[52] In Suriname there were various short-lived attempts to organize brass choirs throughout the twentieth century; in Labrador and in South Africa, brass choirs still exist. In South Africa, where the first choir was formed in Genadendal in 1838, Moravian brass music has greatly expanded. In 1951, the Moravian Brass Band Union (Moraviese Blasersbond) was formed to coordinate, organize, and promote brass music in the various congregations.[53] The first Unity-wide Moravian brass festival was hosted by South Africa in 2007 for the five hundred fiftieth anniversary of the founding of the Unitas Fratrum.

A similar organization developed in the European Continental Province. In 1924 the Brüderische Bläserbund (Moravian Brass Union) was formed in Gnadenberg (Silesia). The main function of the Bläserbund was to organize the biennial brass festivals. The loosely organized Bläserbund was replaced by the more regulated Verband der Posaunenchöre der Brüdergemeine (Union of Brass Choirs of the Moravian Church) in 1934, when the Moravian Union had to adapt to the new national-socialist government requirements in Germany and join the Reichsmusikkammer (National Bureau of Music). The Union was able to continue its work until the Second World War interrupted most brass music activities. The brass festival that was to be held in Niesky in May of 1940 had to be "postponed," and most of the choirs had to cease their activities as the men were conscripted to fight in the war.[54]

Following the Second World War, the brass festivals resumed, taking place in Western Europe every two years, and on a more irregular basis in East Germany. The first joint brass festival after the fall of the Berlin wall was held in Niesky in 1991—notably, the place where the last pre–World War II festival was supposed to take place. However, the prewar Brass Union, with its bylaws and regulations, was not revived after 1945.

The influence of the Moravian brass tradition reaches even beyond the Moravian Church by means of the *Posaunenchöre* that exist throughout the German Evangelical church. Many local churches in Germany have their own brass ensembles (the designation *Posaunenchor* or "trombone choir" is not to be taken literally) to accompany congregational singing and to make instrumental music for evangelizing purposes. The first (non-Moravian) ecclesiastical brass ensemble started in 1823 in Düsselthal near Düsseldorf among circles closely connected to Moravian diaspora preachers. During the nineteenth century, numerous other ensembles were established throughout Germany and its colonies. Today there are brass organizations in every regional church under the directive of a coordinating national Posaunendienst; the Moravian Church in the European Continental Province is a member of this organization. It is commonly accepted that the German brass movement was inspired by the Moravian tradition.[55] Brass music has gained importance far beyond the Moravian Church.

Instruments, Service, and Repertoire

Although the diverse activities of all these Moravian brass ensembles cannot be generalized, they do exhibit some common characteristics. As mentioned above, many brass choirs incorporated other brass instruments in addition to trombones during the nineteenth century. The invention of valves made it possible to play the full chromatic scale and harmonies on these instruments. The integration of horns, euphoniums, and tubas changed the sound of the Moravian brass choirs. In the American Southern Province, not only brass instruments are played in church bands; woodwind instruments are also allowed. The Bethlehem Trombone Choir continues to adhere strictly to the tradition of being an exclusively trombone choir.

Most of the traditional responsibilities of Moravian brass choirs are performed outdoors. When a member of a congregation passes away, the brass choir announces the death to the congregation. Playing death announcements was meaningful during times when the congregation lived near the church and the brass players could gather quickly to make the announcement. In some places, the custom of playing death announcements is still observed; in other places, it is done in connection with the Sunday morning church service, or else the custom has been abandoned altogether.

Wherever possible, brass choirs play at funerals (see above). The brass choir precedes the funeral procession to the graveyard (God's Acre), plays at the graveside and accompanies the hymns sung during the committal. This tradition started in Herrnhut in 1731 and still is a responsibility of many of the Moravian brass choirs.

Another brass choir tradition is playing before and during the Easter morning sunrise service. An Easter sunrise service was held for the first time in Herrnhut in 1732. Traditionally, the liturgy begins inside the church, approximately fifteen to thirty minutes before sunrise. During the service, the congregation follows the brass choir to the graveyard, where the service continues while the sun rises over the horizon. The rising sun symbolizes the Resurrection, and the brass instruments sounding over the graves recall 1 Corinthians 15 (see above). The brass musicians begin long before the sun comes up, walking through the community and playing Easter chorales. In Winston-Salem, North Carolina, up to several hundred musicians from various Moravian churches join together for the Easter morning service.

At other holidays the brass players would also go around early in the morning to awaken church members with their music. The German term for this practice is *aufblasen*, which literally means "to blow up."[56]

Since brass music can easily be played outside, brass choirs often play before special services to welcome the worshipers, or afterward to play while they are leaving. Instead of (or in addition to) the ringing of the church bells, the brass choirs also often play before a communion service or lovefeast. Nowadays Moravian brass choirs also play during church picnics, at special birthdays, and for wedding anniversaries.

Indoor playing has become more common than previously. In the past, brass music was perhaps considered too loud to be played inside the church for Moravian ears, which were attuned to the usually soft accompaniment of the organ. The exception to the rule is the New Year's Eve Vigil, when the brass choir interrupts the meditation of the minister at exactly midnight by playing *Nun danket alle Gott* (*Now Thank We All Our God*) or *Wachet auf, ruft uns die Stimme* (*Wake, Awake, for Night Is Flying*). During the twentieth century, more and more choirs started to play inside the church sanctuary, accompanying congregational singing or playing music composed specifically for brass instruments.

Because of the widespread development of this type of ecclesiastical ensemble in Germany, a wide range of music is available for brass choirs. In order to make it easier to play with the church organ, German (non-Moravian) church bands started to play in the key of C instead of playing from the transposed parts traditionally used for brass instruments. Most Moravian choirs within the European Continental Province adopted this practice and started to play in C, so that they can play organ or church choir settings without needing to transpose the written music. Moravian brass choirs are using music that has become available for church brass ensembles through the German Posaunendienst. Much of this music can be used as preludes or as interludes during church services.

A rediscovery of eighteenth-century trombone music has also taken place in recent years. The collection of the Salem *collegium musicum* contains are eight sonatas for two trumpets and two trombones, most likely composed by Johann Gottfried Weber (1739–97), who sent the music over from Herrnhut to Salem in 1785. Possibly at the same time, the Salem music collection was enriched with a collection of six sonatas for trombone written by "Cruse."[57] A set of twenty-three sonatas for four trombones was found in the music collection of the Zeist Moravian congregation. The sonatas are attributed to Christian Gottfried Geisler (1730–1810), the music director at Zeist. In the Unity Archives in Herrnhut, a similar collection of twelve sonatas was found for *tromba* 1 and 2 and alto, tenor, and bass trombone. These sonatas, composed by Daniel Johann Grimm (1719–60), were probably written during Grimm's years in Herrnhaag and Marienborn (1748–50).[58] Ben van den Bosch, brass music director of the European Continental Province, adapted them for modern use and published the sonatas.[59]

Apart from these sonatas and the Moravian chorales, not much else is known about the eighteenth-century repertoire of the brass choirs. During the nineteenth century, brass choirs started including "worldly" compositions in their repertoire. An example of this development occurred in Salem, where instrumentalists from the church and the *collegium musicum* organized the Salem Band as a secular ensemble, which became well known throughout North Carolina.[60] Moravian musicians in Europe also enjoyed the more typical orchestral music for wind instruments. The Unity Archives has some late nineteenth-century arrangements from the Niesky brass choir collection. The members of the Zeist brass choir founded a wind orchestra in 1882 that soon took over the responsibilities of the brass choir in the Moravian congregation. In 1949 a new Zeist brass choir was founded.

By the end of the nineteenth century, Moravian composers such as Heinrich Theodor Lonas (1838–1903) and Georg Friedrich Hellström (1825–1912) included brass music in some of their compositions. Lonas did so in his *Heilig, heilig, heilig ist Gott der Herr*, composed for the three hundredth anniversary of Comenius's birthday in 1892. Hellström included a brass quartet in his adaptation of the popular Moravian Christmas hymn *Morning Star*.

Conclusion

Since its origins in Herrnhut around 1730, brass music has become an important institution within the Moravian Church. Although in many places early brass music included various instruments, exclusive trombone choirs were started in many congregations throughout the eighteenth century. With the invention of valve instruments in the nineteenth century, most choirs opened their ranks to other brass instruments or even to woodwind instruments. The main task of the brass choir was to extend the liturgical space beyond traditional worship places such as chapels and churches. The playing of music outdoors and even during what seemed to be worldly activities underscored the Moravian notion that every activity serving the community is a liturgical act. Playing in the choirs gave members of the congregation an important task that some performed over long periods of time. The brass choirs gave the Moravians a sense of belonging to a community within the larger church congregation. During the twentieth century, North American Moravian Music Festivals, the European Bläsertage (brass festivals), and the South African Brass Band Festivals became important events in the life of the church. Especially in these regions of the worldwide Moravian Unity, the tradition of brass music has remained alive and seems to be more important than ever.

Notes

1. See his *Lebenslauf* in *Nachrichten aus der Brüdergemeine* (1822), 840–41. W. Lütjeharms, *Het philadelphisch-oecumenisch streven der hernhutters* (Zeist, 1935), 74–75.
2. "Denn kommt in Herrnhut die gantze Gemeinde zusammen, da denn die Brüder aus Bertholdsdorff mit dazukommen. Erst werden etwa 3 Lieder gesungen, da wird die Orgel dazu gespielet und die Waldhörner geblasen, denn nimmt der Herr Graff einen Spruch aus der Bibel und hält eine Rede darüber. Endlich wird diese Versammlung mit einem Gebete geschloßen, welches um 7 Uhr aus ist." Christian David, description of Herrnhut, older version, drafted in Livonia, ca. 1729, R.6.A.a.22.2, Moravian Archives, Herrnhut. David left out the information about the horns from the printed version of this manuscript ([Christian David], *Beschreibung und Zuverläßige Nachricht von Herrnhut in der Ober-Lausitz . . .* [Leipzig, 1735]).

3. "Es ward vorgebracht, ob und was man den Waldhornbläsern geben solle, da protestirte gleich Hans Raschke, sie wolten durchaus nichts nehmen. Ob nicht täglich solle ein Collegium musicum im Gasthof gehalten werden. Ja [52 votes]. Nein [no votes]. Die gantze Gemeine ist zufrieden." Minutes of the Herrnhut *Gemeinrat*, Apr. 1, 1731, R.6.A.a.25, Moravian Archives, Herrnhut.

4. "Die Collegia musica des Nachts sind ungemein erwecklich." Zinzendorf's diary of Herrnhut, April 17, 1731, R.6.A.b.10, Moravian Archives, Herrnhut.

5. Correspondence with Hans Heinrich Schulthess ("bein gwundnen Schwerdt"), 1730–36, letter 7, March 23, 1731, R.19.C.5.3.a, Moravian Archives, Herrnhut.

6. No information was found on where the trombones were bought. Tobias Friedrich kept an account book, but the earliest surviving volume dates from 1733 to 1746. UVC, I.A.5, Moravian Archives, Herrnhut.

7. Anja Wehrend, *Musikanschauung, Musikpraxis, Kantatenkompositionen in der Herrnhuter Brudergemeine* (Frankfurt am Main: Peter Lang, 1995), 48.

8. "Herr Rothe ist noch ungemein herzlich und aufgeweckt. Am Sonnabend war sein Geburtstag. Da schickt ich in Herrnhut rum, und ließ Versgen vor ihn aufschreiben in Hofnung, es werde ihn solches ein mehrers Vertrauen gegen uns und eine große Aufmunterung auf die Feyertage machen, welches Gottlob gelung. Abends schickte ihn solche zu, da er denn beygehendes Briefgen an die Gemeine schrieb, und nach der Singstunde invitirten Tober und ich die Brüder mit uns nach Berthelsdorf zu gehen und Herrn Rothen zu seinem Geburtstags Beschluß eine Music mit Posaunen bringen zu helfen. Da kamen gleich etliche und 50 mit vielen Laternen zusammen und giengen miteinander hinein in den Pfarrhof und machten das ganze Dorff davon rege. Er aber ließ sich nichts mercken, als hörte ers. Am 2ten Feyertag aber als an welchen Tag er ganz besonders erweckt war, danckte er öffentlich sehr herzlich davor." Tobias Friedrich to Zinzendorf, Herrnhut, May 16, 1731, R.6.A.a.27, Moravian Archives, Herrnhut.

9. "Wir hatten die Posaunen und Walthhörner." Herrnhut diary, May 12, 1731, R.6.A.b.10, Moravian Archives, Herrnhut.

10. "Den 1ten Juni 1731 gingen wir nach Herrnhut, wo wir abends nach der Singstunde ankamen. . . . Da eben in diesen Tagen die Gemeine die ersten Posaunen bekommen hatte, so bewillkommten sie uns mit denselben, und die Brüder sungen das Lied dazu: Wie schön ist unsers Königs Braut p., welches mich so einnahm, daß ich glaubte, ich wäre nicht mehr in der Welt und mich vor Weinen nicht zu laßen wußte." *Lebenslauf* of David Hans (Zauchtental 1707–Herrnhut 1799), R.22.31.32.b, Moravian Archives, Herrnhut. The *Lebenslauf* is published (with slight alterations) in *Nachrichten aus der Brüdergemeine* (1842), 1049–57. The Herrnhut diary mentions the arrival of a group of Moravians that day, but does not record the playing of trombones.

11. Herrnhut diary, June 4, 1731. R.6.A.b.10, Moravian Archives, Herrnhut. The entry for the burial of Rosina Schindler in Herrnhut on June 4, 1731—the first burial with trombone accompaniment—describes the hymns that were sung: "Am 4ten also wurde die Schwester [Schindler] begraben. . . . Etliche 100 Brüder und Schwestern giengen mit, in der schönsten Ordnung zugleich, zuerst ihre Bande, hernach alle Schwestern, dann die Brüder, je 3 und 3. Erstlich wurde gesungen: Mein edler Geist p., Hernach: Wie schön ist unsers Königs Braut p., bei der Einsenckung: Die Seele Christi heilge mich p.; alles mit Beynehmung der Posaunen."

12. "1. Hat man Violinen, Waldhörner und andre Music?

THE ROLE AND DEVELOPMENT OF BRASS MUSIC ❧ 185

"Die Böhmen sind Musici von Haus aus, und also ist an einer ziemlich completen Music hier und da kein Mangel. Wären sie beysammen, so wäre es eines der grösten und schönsten Orchestren." N. L. von Zinzendorf, *Summarischer Unterricht in Anno 1753 für reisende Brüder* (London, 1755), 40.

13. Wehrend, 48.

14. For example, Ben van den Bosch, *The Origin and Development of the Trombone-Work of the Moravian Churches in Germany and All the World*, trans. C. Daniel Crews (Winston-Salem: Moravian Music Foundation, 1990), 3.

15. *Das Gesang-Buch der Gemeine in Herrn-Huth.* Daselbst zu finden im Waysenhaus. 12 Anhänge + 4 Zugaben 1735[-48]. Recently, Erika and Hans Schneider in Bad Bentheim, Germany, converted the texts of these hymns as a text file on a CD-ROM that offers many interesting tools for analysis. The hymns in all of the appendices and additions are numbered consecutively following the first (1735) volume. References to hymns in this series are noted as HG, followed by the hymn number.

16. For an eighteenth-century interpretation of the use of the trombone in biblical times, see Johann Heinrich Zedler, *Grosses vollständiges Universal-Lexicon aller Wissenschaften und Künste*, vol. 28 (Leipzig–Halle, 1741). Available on line at: http://mdz.bib-bvb.de/digbib/lexika/zedler (accessed 2/27/07).

17. *Die Musik in Geschichte und Gegenwart*, 2nd ed. (Kassel, 1994), s.v. "Stadtpfeifer," 8:1719–32.

18. Ruth Holmes Bird, "Music Among the Moravians: Bethlehem, Pennsylvania, 1741–1816" (master's thesis, University of Rochester, 1938), 70. See also David P. Keehn, "The Trombone Choir of the Moravian Church in North America" (master's thesis, West Chester State College, 1978), 188–90.

19. A well-documented study of Moravian brass music is Harry H. Hall, "The Moravian Wind Ensemble: Distinctive Chapter in America's Music" (PhD diss., George Peabody College, 1967).

20. Single Brothers (BethSB) diary, Dec. 19, 1744 (temp. no. 1), Moravian Archives, Bethlehem.

21. BethSB diary, Dec. 12, 1744, April 10, 1745, Moravian Archives, Bethlehem.

22. Bethlehem diary resp. Aug. 8, 1744; May 28, 1745; and July 13, 1752, Moravian Archives, Bethlehem.

23. "Diesen Abend hatten die Musici, derer 14 waren, und meist alle aus ledigen Brüder und großen Knaben bestunden, ein niedliches und vergnügtes Liebesmahl. Br. Westmann wurde die Aufsicht in Abwesenheit des Pyrlaei übertragen, der wird drauf sehen, daß sie alle Abend eine Stunde bekommen möchten zur Übung, damit ihr Spielen noch harmonischer gehen möge als es bißher geschehen. Die Brüder wurden mit ihrer Music zum Lämmlein gewiesen, daß sie bey ihm möchten das rechte spielen lernen. Es wurde auch eine Casse aufgerichtet, da die nöthigsten Instrumente könten draus angeschafft werden." BethSB no. 1 diary, Jan. 14, 1748 (ns), Moravian Archives, Bethlehem.

24. Not on August 13, which appears as the date in some publications.

25. "Nachmittags gegen 5 Uhr wurde zu unserer Chorviertelstunde vom Gemeinsaal geblasen und zwar mit einem Chor Posaunen, zum erstenmal hier in Bethlehem, welches zugleich von der ganzen Gemeine mit großem Vergnügen angehört wurde." BethSB 1 diary, Moravian Archives, Bethlehem.

26. Bethlehem diary, November 6, 1754, Moravian Archives, Bethlehem.

27. [Christian David], *Beschreibung und Zuverläßige Nachricht von Herrnhut in der Ober-Lausitz . . .* (Leipzig, 1735), 96.

28. "Sodann wurde in Gefolge der Materie von den Heimgängen, von der Music bey den Begräbnissen gesprochen. Wo ein Posaunen-Chor ist, kann man sich dessen gerne bedienen. Es macht, auch in den Herzen fremder Leute, einen lieblichen Eindruck von unserm freudigen Heimfahren zum Herrn." Minutes of the General Synod 1764, R.2.B.44.1.c, 1406–7, Moravian Archives, Herrnhut.

29. "Bey dem Liebesmahl, das der hinterlassene Wittwer für die Krancken-Wärter gab, wurde resolvirt, daß künftig, wenn zum Heimgang der Geschwister geblasen wird, nach dem gewöhnlichen Vers: Schon wieder eines erblaßet, etc., sogleich der Vers des Chors, aus dem eins heimgegangen, wie schon beym Blasen zu den Chorliturgien gewöhnlich ist, angestimt werden soll." Diary of Herrnhut, *Jüngerhausdiarium* (ms.) 1754, supplement 9.

30. *Das Litaneyen-Büchlein nach der bey den Brüdern dermalen hauptsächlich gewöhnlichen Singe-Weise . . .* (Barby, 1757). English ed.: *The Litany-Book according to the Manner of Singing at present mostly in Use among the Brethren . . .* (London, 1759), 203. The previous German edition of 1755 mentions only repeating the tune *O Haupt* several times, without a specific tune for a choir.

31. "Wenn diese Chormelodien einmal bekannt sind, so kan man die Chöre zur Liturgie zusammen kriegen, ohne vorher bekannt zu machen, in welcher Ordnung sie seyn werden." Minutes of the Jünger Conference, April 4, 1757, Bethlehem congregation, 95, Moravian Archives, Bethlehem.

32. "Das gemeinschafftliche Aufstehen des morgens vor der Viertelstunde und auf den Saal kommen soll wiederum seinen Anfang nehmen. Die Musici können es mit Music anfangen, *damit es den Brüdern wichtig wird.*" BethSB no. 1, diary September 14 (o.s.), 1746, Moravian Archives, Bethlehem. See chapter 1, p. 27, n76, for an explanation of "old system" and "new system" dates.

33. The diary uses the word *reinblasen* or *hereinblasen*: "Diese Brüder [who had just arrived from Europe] wurden mit Music in Bethlehem bewillkommet und rein geblasen. Es wurde gleich ein Liebesmaal vor sie auf unserem ledigen Brüder Saale zurechte gemacht." BethSB 1, diary June 25, 1748 (n.s.), Moravian Archives, Bethlehem.

34. Bethlehem diary, July 20 (n.s.), 1752, Moravian Archives, Bethlehem.

35. BethSB no. 1, diary October 8, 1753 (n.s.), Moravian Archives, Bethlehem.

36. "Den 25ten Nov. sind wir eine Stunde nacheinander alle in Bethlehem angekommen zu aller Geschwister Freude. Man empfing uns mit Trompeten, daß die Lufft davon erthönte, und was das seligste und beste war, wir kamen zum Abendmahl zurecht." Travel report by Anna Johanna Pietsch to Anna Nitschmann about her journey to America on board the *Irene*, September 28–November 25, 1752, Bethlehem diary, supplement, 1355–1410, Moravian Archives, Bethlehem.

37. "Darnach wurde mit Choralen die Geburt unsers lieben Herrn im Stall zu Bethlehem von der Gemeine besungen. Zuletzt das Te Jehova von 2 Brüdern auf der Gallerie chorweise gesungen, bis auf die Worte 'Und da lag in Praesepio.' Da fiel die gantze Gemeine auf die Knie nieder, das Kind in seiner Krippe anzubeten, und als bey denen Worten 'Abiad, El gibbor, Schilo' unversehens die Trompeten angestoßen worden, so durchgieng es die Ohren bis auf des Hertzens Grunde mit einem solchen allgemeinen Eindruck, daß wir hätten vor Beugung in die Erde hinein sincken. Der Indianer Josua erzehlte Tags darauf dem Br. Joseph, er hätte nicht anderst gedacht, als der Heiland käme jetzt und er hätte sich müßen umsehen, ob er nicht schon da wäre." Bethlehem diary, December 24, 1751 (n.s.), Moravian Archives, Bethlehem. The *Te Jehovah* is number 1897 in the 1735–48 Herrnhut hymnal.

38. Bethlehem diary, September 30, 1754, Moravian Archives, Bethlehem.

39. E.g., Single Brothers' diary, July 16 (o.s.), 1746, or July 25 (n.s.), 1748, Moravian Archives, Bethlehem.

40. Unlike the "choir system" discussed in chapter 1, here the term *choir* does refer to a musical ensemble.

41. Bethlehem Single Sisters, diary Nov. 25, 1752 (n.s.), temp. no. 1, Moravian Archives, Bethlehem. Travel diary of Anna Johanna Piesch, Nov. 25, 1752 (n.s.), temp. no. 20, Moravian Archives, Bethlehem.

42. "Nachhero kaufte er [Oglethorpe] den Brüdern ihre Trompeten und Waldhörner ab und gab ihnen 10 Schilling mehr als sie begehrten. . . . Den Bruder Böhner hat er durchaus bereden wollen, sein Trompeter zu werden und ihm 110 Schilling des Monats versprochen. Als toma Chachi begraben worden, hat er auch die Brüder bezahlen wollen, wenn sie Music machen wollten, allein sie schlugens ihm ab." Quoted by Richard Träger (Moravian Archives, Trägermappe "Posaunen," Herrnhut) from R.14.A.6.e.710–13, Moravian Archives, Herrnhut. See also Adelaide L. Fries, *The Moravians in Georgia, 1735–1740* (Raleigh: Edwards & Broughton, 1905), 216.

43. C. G. A. Oldendorp, *Historie der caribischen Inseln St. Thomas, St. Crux und St. Jan*, unabridged ed. (Berlin: Verlag für Wissenschaft und Bildung, 2002), vol. 2/1, 529.

44. This was Zinzendorf's translation of the toponym *Heerentoetoe*, in which *Heeren-* is the Dutch-Creole equivalent for the German prefix *Herrn-* (the Lord's) and *toetoe* is the conch shell, blown to call the slaves to church.

45. Wehrend, 57, n151.

46. The years in the list of choirs in the Continental Province in van den Bosch, 24, are in need of correction.

47. In the hymn composed for the occasion (Single Brothers' Festival) a footnote at the word "Posaunenklang" (sound of trombones) says: "Today for the first time in America." Beth SB no. 1, Single Brothers diary, Moravian Archives, Bethlehem.

48. William C. Reichel, *Something About Trombones, and the Old Mill at Bethlehem*, ed. John W. Jordan (Bethlehem: Moravian Publication Office, 1884), 7.

49. David C. Runner, "Music in the Moravian Community of Lititz" (DMA diss., Eastman School of Music, 1976), 46–47. The Lititz Moravian Archives Museum has some of the original instruments.

50. See Karl Kroeger, "A Preliminary Survey of Musical Life in the English Moravian Settlements of Fulneck, Fairfield, and Ockbrook During the 18th and 19th Centuries," *Moravian Music Journal* 29/1 (Spring 1984): 20–25, for an overview of surviving early music and some mention of instruments in these English congregations.

51. David Cranz, *The History of Greenland* . . . (London, 1767), II:423.

52. A. Schulze, *200 Jahre Brüdermission* (Herrnhut, 1932) II, see index.

53. Available on line at http://www.moravianbrass.co.za/index.php (accessed 2/28/07).

54. For the Brass Union in Germany, see the biennial reports in the *Jahrbuch der Brüdergemeine* (until 1941/42). The records of the Brass Union are held in the congregational archives in Königsfeld.

55. *Die Musik in Geschichte und Gegenwart*, 2nd ed. (Kassel, 1994), s.v. "Posaunenchor," 7:1751–56.

56. This specifically Moravian term can cause some confusion among non-Moravians. A young German Moravian, who was a prisoner of war in Russia after

1945, experienced this when he received a letter from his family mentioning the *aufblasen* his father had done on his mother's birthday. He had to explain to a startled camp guard who had read the letter what exactly his father had done to the poor mother. Helmut Hickel, *Lebenserinnerungen* (Herrnhut, 1992), 69.

57. See Hall, *The Moravian Wind Ensemble*, 191–97. Hall suggests the identification of "Cruse" with G. D. Cruse, Director of Music at the Rostock theater in 1787. The Unity Archives holds some music by "Kruse." Further research is needed.

58. Grimm's name is sometimes listed as Johann Daniel, sometimes as Daniel Johann.

59. [Christian Gottfried Geisler], *Dreiundzwanzig Herrnhuter Sonaten für 2 Trompeten und 2 Posaunen*, ed. Ben van den Bosch (München: Strube Verlag, 1988); Daniel Johann Grimm, *12 Sonaten für Blechbläser (2 Trompeten und 3 Posaunen)* ed. Ben van den Bosch (München: Strube Verlag, 1987).

60. Donna K. Rothrock, "The Perpetuation of the Moravian Instrumental Music Tradition: Bernard Jacob Pfohl and the Salem, North Carolina, Bands" (1879–1960) (EdD diss., University of North Carolina at Greensboro, 1991), 199, 29ff.

Chapter Seven

The Collegia Musica

Music of the Community

Nola Reed Knouse

Although sacred vocal music and hymns have been the central focus of the musical life of the Moravians from their earliest years, at no time in their history have they eschewed the use of musical instruments. With no dividing line between "sacred" and "secular" aspects of life, the Moravians could adopt (and adapt) many positive features of their surrounding culture for their life of personal and communal piety and evangelism. Even their emphasis on the primacy of the text did not lead them to avoid the use of stringed and wind instruments in addition to the organ for their anthems; from the middle of the eighteenth century, Moravian composers wrote very few sacred vocal works *without* such accompaniment. Moreover, although the Moravian composers were careful to avoid obscuring the text through contrapuntal writing, their instrumental parts were not simplistic; they require accomplished players.

The festival services at which these anthems were to be sung, therefore, necessitated the presence of a competent instrumental and vocal ensemble. Not only did the individual musicians themselves need adequate training, but the ensemble as a whole could only benefit from playing together.

The Moravian composer, editor, and administrator Christian Ignatius LaTrobe wrote of music in Moravian life and worship:

> In most of the Brethren's settlements, there is likewise a small band of vocal and instrumental performers, composed of persons voluntarily engaging their services. They sometimes meet for practice, and on particular occasions, enliven the service by the performance of the following, or similar Anthems, suited to the subjects under contemplation.
>
> The practice of Instrumental Music is recommended by the Brethren, as a most useful substitute for all those idle pursuits, in which young people too often consume their leisure hours; and since its application as an accompaniment and support to the voice

is calculated to produce the most pleasing effect, its use in the Church has been retained.[1]

These two needs—of accomplished musicians for worship and of appropriate recreational activities—combined to give rise to one of the most fascinating and significant aspects of the Moravian musical culture: their instrumental and vocal music in the community, apart from formal worship.

The *Collegium Musicum*

The term *collegium musicum* denotes a varied and rich tradition of music making, largely by amateur musicians for the entertainment of themselves and their friends, which ranged through German-speaking regions of Europe from the sixteenth through the early eighteenth centuries. These groups were associated with the rising educated middle class, occupying a "position between institutionalized church music and the music of the princely courts."[2] The term was not precisely defined. *Collegia musica* differed in size, in social status, in level of musical training and accomplishment, in choice of music, and in the degree of privacy or public appeal of their performances. In general, they met regularly to rehearse and/or perform, and guests were welcome. The music lexicographer Heinrich Christoph Koch, writing in 1802, described the *collegium musicum* as follows:

> By this name heretofore was held, in various royal chapels, a weekly music gathering on a specified day. This was neither an ordinary rehearsal in which new pieces were practiced or already familiar ones prepared for public performance, nor a public concert. Rather it was intended to keep the orchestra "in practice" on already familiar pieces.
> It should be noted here that Johann Friedrich, Prince of Schwarzb. Rudolstadt, one of the greatest art connoisseurs of his time, had such a *collegium musicum* at his court chapel around the year 1756, under the direction of the *Kapellmeister* Scheinpflug, which also had the purpose of disseminating theoretical knowledge among the members of the chapel. The *Kapellmeister* gave instruction between the different pieces as well as at the end of the performance, with friendly conversation about the pieces as well as generally about theoretical and practical subjects of the art. This was to encourage the chapel members to reflect about their own art, and to read about it in the writings already on hand as well as those still being published, which were held in the court reference library, and to put them to their proper use.[3]

By the second half of the eighteenth century, an increased emphasis on "professionalism" led to a shift in terminology, so that public performances came to be called "concerts" and the performing groups "academies," rather than simply *collegia*.[4]

As described by Koch, the *collegium musicum*'s dual purpose, encompassing both entertainment and instruction, was certainly compatible with the Moravians' view of music as expressed by LaTrobe. Since all of life was "liturgical," activities with no direct spiritual meaning, such as the practice and performance of secular instrumental music, could be viewed as an endeavor undertaken in the spirit of devotion that ideally marked all aspects of Moravian life. Because labor, leisure, and the sacred were all seen as elements of devotion, instrumental music and song were encouraged and used in all activities and segments of society.[5]

An Overview of *Collegia Musica* in Moravian Settlements

The congregation diary at Herrnhut notes the existence of a *collegium musicum* as early as January of 1731. It is possible that this ensemble began with brass instruments, only later adding strings and woodwinds under the direction of the Herrnhut music director Tobias Friedrich (1706–36), himself a violinist as well as an organist.

The diary from Herrnhaag and Marienborn mentions the "renewal" of a *collegium musicum* there by early 1741; the prior existence of at least three cantatas with instrumental accompaniment indicates that such a group was active in Herrnhaag before that time.[6]

These groups were noted for the quality of their music making, and it was noted that in Herrnhut there was no lack of "*einer ziemlich vollständigen Musik*"— that is, an ensemble equivalent to a baroque orchestra.[7] Even a critic of the Moravians, Alexander Oda, found words of praise for their music:

> The Herrnhuters have among themselves musicians on all instruments, some of whom could be counted as virtuosos; and in many royal chapels one finds no better music; there they play concertos, cantatas, and all sorts of artistic works.[8]

By the 1750s the Moravians themselves attributed the founding of their *collegia musica* to the musical accomplishments of emigrants from Bohemia and Moravia. Another strong factor in the founding of these groups, as well as their high quality, was the musical education at the theological school at Jena, which had a *collegium musicum* led by Johann Nikolaus Bach (1669–1753), a cousin of Johann Sebastian Bach. Many of the "Herrnhuters" attended this institution, including the brethren Philipp Heinrich Molther (1714–80), Ludolph Ernst Schlicht (1714–69), and Johann Michael Graff (1714–82), among others. Each of these men later composed music and directed or otherwise encouraged the *collegium musicum* in his future assignment. Although their participation in the Jena *collegium musicum* has not been verified, it seems likely that these gifted musicians would not have missed such an opportunity.[9]

In their settlement congregations throughout the European continent and beyond, the Moravians took with them their choir system, their schedule of daily and weekly worship, and the need for a *collegium musicum*. Generally, within a very few years of the establishment of a new congregation town, its diary makes mention of the *collegium musicum*, often associated with the Single Brethren's Choir. The following examples, although not exhaustive, are illustrative:

The congregation at Zeist in Holland was founded in 1746; the *collegium musicum* of the Single Brethren's house was first mentioned in 1748. It lasted until well into the nineteenth century. The Zeist music collection includes more than nine hundred sacred vocal pieces with instrumental accompaniments, as well as nearly two hundred purely instrumental works (mainly orchestral), dating mostly from the last quarter of the eighteenth century and the first quarter of the nineteenth.[10]

The Moravian congregations in England also had active musical groups. Although the documentation is not as complete as we might wish, Karl Kroeger notes that

> one receives an impressionn . . . of an extensive and well-regulated musical life. . . . In the church, hymns, sacred songs, and anthems were sung, frequently accompanied by organ and orchestra. In the school, vocal and instrumental music was taught to Moravian and non-Moravian students alike. Skilled instrumentalists in the community got together to play symphonies by Haydn, overtures by Handel, concertos by Avison, and chamber music by other composers.[11]

Kroeger observes that the printed music remaining in the English Moravian collections includes symphonies and overtures; a music inventory from Ockbrook, dated 6 January 1776, lists sonatas, concertos, overtures, and symphonies.[12] The Fulneck congregation diary for April 11, 1752 cites music being played from the battlements of the Congregation House—a practice also documented in other Moravian communities.[13]

The eighteenth- and nineteenth-century music of the congregation at Neuwied in Germany (founded 1749) was discovered in 1995 in a box behind the organ. This collection was taken to the congregation archives and catalogued; it contains between five and six hundred sacred vocal works dating from 1759 to 1900. Most of these have instrumental parts, and "*Collegium musicum Neuwied*" is noted on a significant number of manuscripts dating from the 1780s through the mid-1840s. Although little has been found regarding strictly instrumental music at Neuwied, it is not difficult to imagine an active instrumental musical group there as well.[14]

The situation is similar at the Christiansfeld congregation in Denmark (founded in 1773). Its music catalog shows similarities to those of other Moravian communities in its sacred vocal music with accompaniment by instrumental ensemble, but little is known about purely instrumental music at Christiansfeld.[15]

Extensive research has been conducted regarding the *collegium musicum* in the American Moravian settlements. August Gottlieb Spangenberg (1704–92), a wise and beloved administrator and a close friend of Count Zinzendorf, was present at the "renewal" of the Herrnhaag *collegium musicum*, and he is credited with establishing the *collegium musicum* in Bethlehem, Pennsylvania. The first meeting took place on December 13, 1744, with John Christopher Pyrlaeus being chosen to lead.[16] In its early years, the Bethlehem *collegium musicum* focused on the improvement of musical skills for the purpose of raising the quality of music in worship. The group's progress was enhanced by the arrival in 1761 of Immanuel Nitschmann, who, although not a composer himself, added to the music library through his extensive copying of music, including string quartets and symphonies by Haydn. The arrival in 1773 of Johann Friedrich Peter gave the group an even more significant boost. During his seven years in Bethlehem, Peter led the *collegium musicum* in weekly rehearsals and made the group a part of regular worship services. By 1780 this group consisted of about fifteen performers, including strings and winds.[17] On Peter's move to Salem, North Carolina, it seems that Immanuel Nitschmann again assumed his leadership. After his death in 1790, he was succeeded by his son-in-law Jacob Van Vleck.

David Moritz Michael (1751–1827) assumed leadership of the Bethlehem *collegium musicum* on his move to Bethlehem in 1808. The Moravian musician and historian Rufus Alexander Grider (see below) reports that this organization soon showed a dramatic increase in the number of concerts and rehearsals:

> About the year 1806, an effort was made to revive the then flagging musical spirit. A benefit concert was given in 1807, after which, $19.15 was collected, which at that time, was deemed a large amount. No tickets were sold, no admission fee charged, persons deposited their gifts at the door, in a tin box, placed on the right hand, or west side of the door, for that purpose. The box was painted green, and marked, "For the Support of Music."
>
> The treasurer's accounts, which are preserved, and which have been placed in the church archives, show the number and date of concerts given during a number of years, and also the amount received after each concert. From them we gather the following information, viz:

Date.	Concerts.	Amount rec'd.
1807,	17,	$31.47.
1808,	28,	32.00.
1809,	36,	42.86.
1810,	24,	32.00.
1811,	24,	32.00.
1812,	16,	25.28.
1813,	24,	42.00.
1814,	14,	16.41.
1815,	12,	7.28.
1816,	10,	12.50.
1817,	12,	10.63.
1818,	11,	10.50.
1819,	13,	8.20.
In 13 years,	241 concerts,	$301.73.[18]

Grider also relates anecdotes regarding Michael's accomplishments and sense of humor:

> Among the accessions to the colony, was a professor of music, a member of the church, named David Moritz Michael, he was a *virtuoso* on the violin, performed well on the French horn, clarinet and other instruments. I remember hearing my father relate, that he saw him take two French horns, place one under each arm, place one mouth-piece on each side of his mouth, and play a duet on the two instruments. This is attested by persons still living in Bethlehem. . . . His violin performance excelled all that had been heard here up to that time. The young players all took lessons of him, and were greatly benefited, they acquired more proficiency, a better style, more neatness, and greater brilliancy of tone, and more spirit in executing. He was a composer also, noted more particularly for compositions for wind instruments, then in vogue, called "PARTHIEN," or *Harmony Music*, composed for five or six instruments, generally two clarinets, two French horns and two bassoons.[19]

The Bethlehem *collegium musicum* was reorganized and renamed the Philharmonic Society of Bethlehem on December 20, 1820. Throughout the middle of the nineteenth century, the records show that musicians from Bethlehem were called on from time to time to assist with orchestral concerts in Philadelphia.[20] After some years, however, the number of concerts decreased, indicating that interest in this society was declining. It was reorganized again in 1858 and 1869 and continued to give two or three concerts per year, as well as participating in the musical "Entertainments" sponsored by the Young Ladies' Seminary.[21] It seems to have ceased its activities in the late 1870s or early 1880s.

The preservation of the repertoire of the Philharmonic Society of Bethlehem is due in large part to the diligence of its historian and librarian, Rufus A. Grider, who lived in Bethlehem from 1843 to 1879. He organized its music and prepared a catalog in 1873, which includes an inventory of all the property owned by the Philharmonic Society at that time.

The Nazareth, Pennsylvania, *collegium musicum* was founded around 1780. While serving in Nazareth (1795–1808), David Moritz Michael began a record book entitled *Verzeichniß derer Musicalien welche in Concert sind gemacht worden* (Register of Music Performed in Concert). This manuscript book documents concerts from October 14, 1796 until January 30, 1845, and contains 1,093 entries.[22] The performing group was the "Paedogogium Collegium musicum Nazareth"—the *collegium musicum* of the very institute that Michael served. Much of the success of the *collegium musicum* in Nazareth can therefore be attributed directly to the staff at the school, which included the following musically gifted teachers, with their years of service at the school:

Georg G. Müller (1785–88)
John F. Früeauff (1788–91)
Henry Christian Müller (1794–95)

David Moritz Michael (1795–1804; he then served as leader of the Single
   Brethren's Choir from 1804 until his move to Bethlehem in 1808)
Jacob Van Vleck (principal, 1802–9)
Johann Christian Bechler (1806–12; principal, 1817–22)
Samuel Reinke (1810–16)
Peter Wolle (1810–14)
Peter Ricksecker (1811–21)
Francis F. Hagen (1837–41)[23]

Although the Nazareth *collegium musicum* probably shared some music and musicians with Bethlehem, it had its own identity and function and thus certainly merits further investigation. The *collegium musicum* was reorganized in 1837 as the Musical Society of Nazareth.

Unfortunately, although the "congregation music" (sacred vocal music collection) from Nazareth survives as a separate collection, the music of the Nazareth *collegium musicum* was dispersed, probably folded into the collections of the Bethlehem and Lititz groups. Reconstruction of the specific repertoire of Nazareth, then, relies almost exclusively on the *Verzeichniß*. It lists works by ninety-nine composers, of whom eleven received significantly more attention. These include, in descending order, Rolle, Haydn, Pleyel, Graun, Gyrowetz, Stamitz, Vanhal, Handel, Pichl, Michael, and Mozart. A concert generally included at least one symphony, part of a large vocal work or several individual motets, a chamber piece, and some selections for wind ensemble.[24]

A *collegium musicum* in Lititz is documented in the Lititz congregation diary entry of November 17, 1765. The diary noted that the musicians were directed by Bernard Adam Grube, who arrived as pastor in Lititz in May of that year. However, this reference is vague; as in most other Moravian settlements, the term *collegium musicum* may have been used simply to denote the musicians of the Lititz Congregation.[25] As elsewhere, the congregation music—sacred vocal music— includes instrumental parts, indicating the presence of a group of capable instrumentalists. Purely instrumental works were acquired for Lititz beginning with some Haydn symphonies, annotated "Lititz Collegium musicum 1791."

As in Bethlehem, the Lititz *collegium musicum* was renamed the Lititz Philharmonic Society during the nineteenth century, perhaps as early as 1815, although this date is uncertain. This "daughter" organization (whose name, like that of the Bethlehem group, indicates the move to more public concerts) continued to exist and present concerts at least as late as 1897.[26] The history of the Lititz *collegium musicum* and Philharmonic Society has yet to be studied in depth.

The earliest reference to the *collegium musicum* in Salem, North Carolina is contained in the Elders' Conference diary entry for December 19, 1781, in which the elders refer to a collection to be made by Johann Friedrich Peter for the expenses of the *Musicanten-Collegium*.[27] However, as in Bethlehem, instrumental music seems already to have been a part of the community's life; the

Elders Conference on 31 October 1781 directed the musicians of the community not to perform in private homes for the members of the North Carolina Assembly scheduled to meet in Salem. To ensure that this directive was carried out, the elders ordered that the violins and the mouthpieces of the wind instruments be locked up.[28] Over the following few years, instruments and music were added, and by 1788 the Salem *collegium musicum* had at least three violins, two violas, three cellos, a flute, two horns, and two clarini.

After Peter's 1790 departure from Salem, the musical directorship was less centralized; his musical responsibilities were divided among five people.[29] The *collegium musicum* in Salem thrived in the first quarter of the nineteenth century. With a greater number of string and woodwind players living in Salem, the group could play more orchestral works, as well as the newer woodwind suites (the two "water music" suites and *Parthien*) written by David Moritz Michael, of which seven were copied and sent to Salem. The *collegium musicum* remained in existence "until the 19th-century upsurge of interest in public concerts forced its gradual disintegration—most probably in the late 1830s or early 1840s."[30] During these years the records show a gradual replacement of the term *collegium musicum* with *Musik Gesellschaft* or "Musical Society."[31]

The Salem *collegium musicum* collection consists of more than 580 compositions, of which about 150 are in manuscript form. The Salem collection is heavily weighted toward chamber music; even those works which appear to be orchestral music are intended for a small chamber orchestra, providing internal evidence that the group was small (in number of players and instruments) for most of its existence. Included are at least thirty-three manuscripts copied by Peter during his time at the Moravian seminary in Barby (1765–69), among them works by Johann Christoph Friedrich Bach, Johann Ernst Bach, Franz Bech, Nathanael G. Gruner, Leopold Hofmann, Franz Joseph Haydn, Joseph Riepel, and Johann Stamitz. From his arrival in America in 1770 through the conclusion of his service at Salem in 1790, Peter copied and added to the Salem collection works by Carl Friedrich Abel, Johann Daniel Grimm, Karl Heinrich Graun, Michael Haydn, Ignaz Pleyel, and others. Much later additions to the collection were Peter's copies of works by Adalbert Gyrowetz and Johann Meder, made in 1797 or later.[32] During the last decade of the eighteenth century and the first decade of the nineteenth, both early classical and romantic printed music began to be imported to Salem in significant amounts.

Still to be researched is the existence of *collegia musica* in other Moravian settlements around the globe. Extensive research and cataloging of Moravian musical collections in Labrador is now in progress. The extent of musical activities in the Moravian settlements in South Africa and other places is still unknown, although the long-term use of selections of Ernst Wilhelm Wolf's *Oster Cantate* in South Africa raises at least the distinct possibility of a lively musical life there in the late eighteenth and nineteenth centuries.

The Repertoire of the American Moravian *Collegia Musica*

Although some cataloging work has been done on the instrumental music and larger vocal works contained in the European Moravian collections, more extensive cataloging has been completed for the American Moravian holdings. These collections present a cross section of European musical life in the late eighteenth and early nineteenth centuries, with a few contributions by Moravian composers in America. An overview of the three American *collegium musicum* collections provides insight into not only the musical life of the Moravians in America, but also that of the European Moravians as the primary source of this rich musical culture.[33]

Larger Works: Instrumental Music

Among the composers whose orchestral works are represented in the three collections are Abel, J. C. F. Bach, Beethoven, Benda, Boccherini, Eichner, Gyrowetz, Haydn, Hofmann, Mozart, Pichl, Pleyel, Carl Stamitz, Johann Stamitz, and Wanhal. There is also a wide variety of overtures from operas and oratorios, representing such composers as Auber, Boieldieu, Cherubini, Donizetti, Gyrowetz, Rossini, and Suppé. The collection of the Philharmonic Society of Bethlehem contains the only known copies of two *sinfonien* by J. C. F. Bach, copied by J. F. Peter; the Salem *collegium musicum* collection holds two others, also the only known copies.[34] The Bethlehem collection also holds a viola concerto by the Moravian composer August Heinrich Gehra.

Notable large-ensemble works in the holdings of the Philharmonic Society of Bethlehem include overtures by two nineteenth-century composers, one Moravian and one not. The Overture in F Major by Francis Florentine Hagen (1815–1907) is the only orchestral work known to have been written by a nineteenth-century American Moravian composer. This work, in one movement with three sections, reflects both Hagen's classical roots and the influence of romanticism.

Also in the Philharmonic Society collection are an overture and a symphony by the Philadelphia composer Charles Hommann (1803?–72). A violinist and violist, he was a friend of the Bethlehem clock builder and trombonist Jedediah Weiss, one of the trombonists "borrowed" by the Musical Fund Society of Philadelphia for its performances in 1821 and 1822. His Overture in D Major was dedicated to Weiss, and his Symphony in E-flat Major was written specifically for the Philharmonic Society of Bethlehem.[35]

Larger Works: Vocal Music

Each of the three American *collegium musicum* collections contains a surprising number of large-scale works for voices and orchestra. There is a good deal of overlap among the three collections, including such works as Franz Joseph Haydn's *Die Schöpfung* and *Die Jahreszeiten*; selections from Karl Heinrich Graun's *Tod Jesu* and *Ein Lämmlein geht und trägt die Schuld*; Ernst Wilhelm Wolf's *Oster Cantate*; the *Passions-Cantate* of Gottfried August Homilius; *Die sieben Schläfer* of Karl Gottfried Löwe; and selections from music dramas by Johann Heinrich Rolle.[36]

Each collection also has some works not in either of the others; for example, J. S. Bach's *Ein feste Burg* (BWV 80), copied by Johann Christian Till in 1823–24, is in the Philharmonic Society of Bethlehem collection, as are both the *Fairfield Cantata* and selections from *The Dawn of Glory* by Christian Ignatius LaTrobe. A mass by Pergolesi is in the Salem *collegium musicum* library, along with two cantatas by the Moravian composer Johann Daniel Grimm. The existence of such an extensive range of vocal works in all of these collections makes clear that the very term "*collegium musicum*" refers not strictly to the *instrumental* musicians in each settlement, but rather to the community's musicians as a whole.

David Moritz Michael's eleven-movement setting of Psalm 103 survives in the collections of both the Salem *collegium musicum* and the Philharmonic Society of Bethlehem. Scored for SATB voices, 2 flutes, 2 clarinets, bassoon, 2 clarini, strings, and organ, the work had its premiere in Nazareth on November 8, 1805. According to Karl Kroeger, this is "the first extended, cantata-like work written by an American Moravian composer, and quite possibly the earliest work for these performing forces written in America."[37] Not intended or used for worship, but rather for concert performance, this work truly shows the extent of Michael's compositional gifts. Kroeger asserts that Psalm 103 alone

> shows Michael to have been a capable composer of considerable craftsmanship, and perhaps the only Moravian composer in America during his time who could have successfully handled a large-scale, lyrico-dramatic choral form. On the basis of *Psalm 103* alone one must rank Michael as a major figure in American Moravian music.[38]

Chamber Music for Strings

Similarly, each collection contains a wide variety of chamber works. As noted above, the Salem *collegium musicum* collection is more heavily weighted than the others toward pieces useful for smaller forces, but this should not be interpreted as implying any dearth of small-ensemble works in the other two American collections. All three contain string quartets by Devienne, Haydn, Hoffmeister, Pleyel, and many others. All contain trio sonatas and string trios by a variety of composers.

The Philharmonic Society of Bethlehem collection contains the six string quintets of Johann Friedrich Peter (1746–1813). The Lititz *collegium musicum* collection contains an unusual work by Johann Christian Bechler, *Der Nachtwächter*, a set of variations on a chorale tune for two violins and violoncello. The Salem *collegium musicum* collection contains a set of thirteen string trios by

Johann Daniel Grimm (1719–60), as well as the three string trios of John Antes (1740–1811).

John Antes may have written his three string trios, identified as op. 3, and at least one set of string quartets (which are missing) during his service as a missionary in Egypt.[39] He is known to have sent a copy of the quartets to Benjamin Franklin. As C. Daniel Crews observes in his biography of Antes,

> The global sweep of this little episode is amazing: here we have an American-born missionary in Egypt sending copies of his quartets to an American diplomat in France, quartets which he had written for an English nobleman and his associates in India! This makes his dedication of the *Three Trios* to the Swedish ambassador in Constantinople almost an anti-climax.[40]

The trios were published in London by John Bland in the early 1790s, with the following notations on the title page:

> *Tre Trii, per due* Violini *and* Violoncello, *Obligato Dedicati a Sua Excellenza il Sigre G. J. de Heidenstam, Ambassatore de Sa Maj il Ri de Suede a Constantinople, Composti a Grand Cairo del* Sigre Giovanni A-T-S. *Dillettante Americano. Op. 3. London, Printed & Sold by J. Bland at his Music Warehouse No. 45 Holborn.*

They found their way to America, with a nearly complete copy (lacking the first page of the cello part) surviving in the Salem *collegium musicum* collection.[41] One other partial copy (lacking the first violin part) was purchased in 1941 by the Eastman School of Music. No other copies are known to exist.

Each of the trios has three movements. The formal structures are marked by classical balance, with sections delineated not by sharp thematic contrast but rather by key area. Most of the movements have a rounded binary or sonatalike form, but quite often in his recapitulation Antes omits the opening melodic material entirely, or just alludes to it, rather than making a literal restatement. Later themes are clearly restated in the tonic in the recapitulation. In Antes's practice, the form is based on harmonic balance, articulated by the fact that all of the primary themes are eventually stated in the tonic key, whether in the exposition or in the recapitulation.

Antes gives the three instruments equal importance and shows a mastery of texture, register, and instrumental timbre. For instance, the Allegro of Trio no. 2 in D Minor opens with the three instruments in close proximity. Within the first sixteen measures we see not only an increasing range, but also a brief passage of imitative writing within a dense texture, building the intensity and drama of this movement (see ex. 7.1).

Karl Kroeger rightly points out the density and consistency of texture in the trios; rarely do we find a full measure of rest. Kroeger speculates that the trios may be self-made arrangements of the lost quartets, omitting a viola part and distributing

Example 7.1. John Antes, Trio no. 2 in D Minor, 1st mvt., Allegro, mm. 1–16.

its motivic material among the remaining three instruments.[42] Although Kroeger's theory is plausible, we can hope for the rediscovery of more chamber music by this gifted composer.

With the exception of six string quintets, all of the nearly one hundred known compositions of Johann Friedrich Peter are sacred concerted vocal works. These compositions have earned him the reputation of being the most gifted among the Moravian composers in America.[43] The full score of his string quintets is dated January 9, 1789, and the parts are dated February 28, 1789, indicating the probability that these works were composed during his later years in Salem. Peter kept no personal diary as such; we have no evidence as to *why* he wrote these works or over how long a period of time he worked on them. The very existence of these, his only purely instrumental works, is thus a mystery, because they would not have been necessary to the life of the church. Did Peter write them simply out of the compulsion to compose, the need to use his gift for instrumental writing without the restrictions of text and occasion? Was he experimenting? These questions are made more intriguing by the fact that when Peter left Salem in 1790, he took the only known copy of both the score and the parts of the quintets with him—hence their survival in the collection of the Philharmonic Society of Bethlehem rather than the Salem *collegium musicum*.[44]

Not surprisingly, the string writing in the quintets is more virtuosic than in his vocal works. The formal structures adhere to classic principles of statement, digression, and return, often within a clear sonatalike structure. In Quintet no. 4, however, he expands the norms by introducing a foreign key (major submediant) and new thematic material in the development of the first movement. In the third movement of the same quintet, he builds a first key area of sixteen measures not by phrases in multiples of two measures, but rather by the use of two three-measure phrases followed by two two-measure phrases and an additional pair of three-measure phrases (see ex. 7.2).

Peter's quintets are lovely and compelling examples of the genre in their own right, worthy of careful attention and rewarding to performer and listener alike. They also provide a foil to his sacred vocal works, showing a facet of his musical gift that is not always readily apparent in the vocal works: a gift for sustaining a larger-scale form with variety and interest, while maintaining coherence and unity.

Chamber Music for Winds: Harmoniemusik

The last quarter of the eighteenth century and first quarter of the nineteenth saw increased interest in woodwind chamber music in the Moravian *collegia musica*, evidenced by a wide variety of pieces of early classical and classical-era music, ranging from duets and trios to eight- and ten-part works. Among the various combinations of woodwinds, the favorite among the Moravians seems to have been a basic combination of clarinets, horns, and bassoons, with an occasional flute or oboe.[45] This music was very popular, both indoors and outdoors, from about 1800 to about 1830. Over one hundred wind chamber works by thirty different composers survive in American Moravian collections.[46]

Chamber music for woodwinds, as it came to fruition in the later eighteenth and early nineteenth centuries, includes a developmental line not only from the amateur, voluntary associations of the *collegia musica*, but also from the professional, hired European court and military bands. Dating from the early eighteenth century, wind bands were employed at the courts of central Europe. By the middle of the century, "every European aristocrat who could afford to retain an ensemble of wind players did so. These players were referred to as the *Harmonie*. Their duties were largely undefined but as a general rule they provided background music whenever needed."[47] Army officers, drawn primarily

Example 7.2. Johann Friedrich Peter, String Quintet no. 4 in C Major, 3rd mvt.,
Allegro non tanto, mm. 1–16.

from the nobility, were accustomed to musical entertainments and often hired professional musicians to accompany their regiments, paying their wages and providing uniforms. These professional musicians most often did not lose civilian status and entertained the officers by providing dinner music, dance music, and serenades.[48]

Heinrich Christoph Koch's 1802 encyclopedia includes this definition:

> *Harmoniemusik*, one calls those [pieces] which consist of loud wind instruments, and especially two oboes, two clarinets, two horns and bassoon. The term is used either for pieces especially set for this combination, which are called Parthien, and which consist of movements of different motion and meter, each taking on its [different] character, but which follow one another in no particular order; or one arranges operas and other pieces for these instruments, which originally are for another use, because until now there has been a lack of good pieces originally written for this type of music.[49]

The term *Harmoniemusik* has been applied in recent scholarship to the music of the Moravians in America as follows:

> Of particular notice is the *Harmoniemusik* of the Moravian settlement congregations in the USA [*sic*]. In the first third of the nineteenth century, the centers were Bethlehem, Lititz, and Nazareth, Pennsylvania, and Salem, North Carolina. The repertoire and instrumentation resembled European *Harmoniemusik* (extended for a long time), but not the function. As part of a religious community, the performers had the same social status as the listeners, and played as much for themselves as for the community, as a contribution to the religiously ordered life of the society. They imported *Harmoniemusik* from Europe, from composers such as A. Gyrowetz, Hoffmeister, Pleyel, Righini, Rosetti, Stamitz, Devienne, Ahl and Stumpf. *Harmoniemusik* composed by the Moravians themselves, mostly called *Parthia*, is generally for two clarinets, two horns, and one or two bassoons, with the occasional flute, trumpet, oboe or piccolo. The largest group of pieces (14) were written by David Moritz Michael (1751–1827), previously an oboist with a German military group, as well as among them *Parthia bestimmt zu einer Wasserfahrt* and a *Suite: bey einer Quelle zu blasen.*[50]

David Moritz Michael's music for wind ensemble consists of fourteen *Parthien* and two "water music" suites; some of these pieces are contained in each of the three American *collegium musicum* collections.[51] Each of the *Parthien* consists of three to five movements, with formal structures similar to those of early classical symphonies: an extended binary or sonata-form first movement, a slow movement, a minuet and trio, and an extended final movement (either a sonata form, rondo, or large ternary form). The dates of composition of the *Parthien* have not been determined; there is speculation that the numbers may have been added by a copyist. However, examination of the fourteen *Parthien* as a set shows a growing mastery of instrumental timbres and compositional technique, so that these numbers may well reflect the order in which the *Parthien* were composed.

In Bethlehem in the early nineteenth century, Whitmonday (the Monday following Pentecost) came to be celebrated as a general music festival and informal anniversary of the Philharmonic Society of Bethlehem. The inhabitants of the town would gather on the banks of the Lehigh River and enjoy the spring weather, conversation, and music. David Moritz Michael, who initiated the use of the wind ensemble for the Whitmonday celebration, wrote two suites specifically for this day: the *Wasserfahrt*, or "Water Journey," in 1809, and *Suiten Bey einer Quelle zu blasen*, or "Suites to Play by a Spring," presumably in 1810. The *Wasserfahrt* has fifteen movements plus two unnumbered sections. The piece was meant to be played outdoors, and, in fact, was played on a boat piloted along the Lehigh River near Bethlehem, with the musicians on board. Mirroring the various "experiences" the boat passes through, each movement depicts a condition of the river, from the quiet, still stream at the beginning, to a whirlpool in the middle, to the safe journey home. According to Grider's account,

> [T]he inhabitants assembled on the river bank. . . . A large flat-bottomed boat . . . propelled by long poles and provided with seats and music stands, received the musicians. A procession was formed by those who intended to participate. . . . [W]hen all was in readiness, the boat started, the music began; the party moved up the Lehigh, accompanied by hundreds of listeners, enjoying the music, social intercourse, and delightful prospect. . . . Eventually the poles no longer touched bottom [and] the composer, poet-like, supposed a case of great peril, caused the music to convey the idea of fear and terror; the boat was kept in the whirlpool [evidently a very gentle one] long enough for the musicians to act out their part, when it emerged . . . the sounds changed into lively airs and graceful melodies. The boat meanwhile glided with the current, and the party wended their way homeward.[52]

Many considered *Die Wasserfahrt* to be Michael's masterpiece. Three copies of the suite survive: two sets in the Bethlehem Archives and one in Winston-Salem. Michael's second "water music" suite, *Bey einer Quelle zu blasen*, consists of an introduction and three sections (*Pars*), each roughly equivalent to a *Parthia* in length and design—fourteen movements altogether.

When we listen to any of his wind works, Michael's mastery of the instrumental capabilities and timbres is immediately apparent. His use of tone color—sometimes in contrasts, sometimes skillfully blended—is an integral part of the success of these compositions. Although the tunes are facile and pleasing, the harmonies effective, and the formal structures well crafted and balanced, it is Michael's skill as an orchestrator that really makes these pieces "work." In the recapitulations of his sonata-form or rondo movements, quite often the second theme is orchestrated differently—providing a balance of unity and variety within the movement. Moreover, Michael's mastery of the instruments is not limited to idiomatic writing for each instrument; he uses them in diverse combinations to add a striking variety of color to the *Parthien*. For instance, the opening theme of the Allegro of *Parthia X* is presented in a passage whose texture is light and thin (see ex. 7.3).

Example 7.3. David Moritz Michael, *Parthia X*, 2nd mvt., Allegro, mm. 1–4.

Example 7.4. Michael, *Parthia X*, 2nd mvt., Allegro, mm. 13–19.

The transition to the dominant key begins with the same theme, but it turns quickly into a sequential passage featuring a dense, "busy" texture (see ex. 7.4).

The second theme, in the dominant, begins with a contrapuntal passage for the two clarinets and one bassoon (see ex. 7.5).

Example 7.5. Michael, *Parthia X*, 2nd mvt., Allegro, mm. 28–33.

The American Moravian music collections contain a total of fifty-three distinct pieces of *Harmoniemusik*.[53] By far the majority of these works are found in only one, or at most two, of the three surviving *collegium musicum* collections (those of Lititz and Bethlehem in Pennsylvania, and Salem in North Carolina). Copies of Michael's works, in contrast, are found in all three, indicating that they filled a need and leading to speculation as to the development of the taste for *Harmoniemusik* among the American Moravians.

Also of particular interest in the wind music in the American Moravian collections is the woodwind *Parthia* by Johann Christian Bechler, contained in the Lititz collection, and the five *Parthien* by the unidentified composer "Collauf"; all five of these are in the Lititz collection, and a copy of one is also in the Salem collection.[54] In addition, the Bethlehem collection contains a printed copy of a *Divertimento* by the European Moravian composer Johan Hermann Mankell (1763–1835).

A number of the *Harmoniemusik* works in the Bethlehem collections are bound together into partbooks, each containing works by multiple composers. Michael's own *Parthien* are in these books, which may indicate that they were obtained in Bethlehem at about the same time as the other *Harmoniemusik*. It may indeed be that Michael's experience prior to joining the Moravians was the catalyst that led to the popularity of this genre among the American Moravians. More extensive study is needed to determine when these various works were acquired, and from where.

Conclusions

The legacy of the *collegium musicum* tradition in Europe is far reaching, with its emphasis on music making by amateur musicians for entertainment and for growth in skill and understanding. These groups created a voracious demand for new music in many forms, from duets to oratorios. In turn the demands of this music raised the level of the amateur's achievements.

In each of their settlements, the Moravians took full advantage of this societal institution, adapting it to fit the needs of their communal life. As the most visible expression of the community's musical life outside of specific services of worship, the *collegium musicum* among the Moravians was "the point of departure for a tradition of musical performance that still subsists."[55] By means of the *collegium musicum*, the musicians honed their skills, making it feasible for composers to write anthems with instrumental and vocal parts requiring accomplished musicians (and for those anthems to be well played and sung). Visitors to Moravian settlements were consistently impressed by the musical ability of the Moravians. Often quoted is the experience of the Marquis de Chastellux, who around 1780 wrote that he "was astonished with the delicious sounds of an Italian Concerto, but my surprise was still greater on entering a room where the performers turned out to be common workmen of different trades, playing for their amusement."[56]

These skills were passed down to succeeding generations, preserving a culture of amateur music making long after the societal trend to formal concerts by "professionals." In America, these accomplished amateurs were the necessary raw materials out of which community orchestras and bands could arise in the mid-nineteenth century. They made possible the founding in 1898 of the Bach Choir of Bethlehem, the first of its type in America and a model for many other groups around the country.[57]

In turn, the development of skills among the musicians in the *collegium musicum* gave rise to greater demand for new music, resulting in the acquisition and preservation of extensive collections far beyond what the Moravians would have used in worship services. The *collegium musicum* collections preserve a rich cross section of the musical culture of Europe in the eighteenth and nineteenth centuries, including many works not known to be extant anywhere else.

Thus the legacy of the *collegia musica* among the Moravians is really the legacy of the entire Moravian musical culture—a heritage of music making by dedicated amateur musicians, playing and singing for the dual purposes of their own enjoyment and that of their community, and the development of their skills for the enhancement of worship.

Notes

1. Christian I. LaTrobe, *Anthems for One, Two, or more Voices performed in the Church of the United Brethren, Collected and the Instrumental parts adapted for the Organ or Piano Forte, Composed by various Authors* (London: Printed for the Editor, 1811), 2.

2. *The New Grove Dictionary of Music and Musicians*, 2nd ed., ed. Stanley Sadie (London: Macmillan, 2001), s.v. "Collegium musicum," 6:116.

3. Heinrich Christoph Koch, *Musikalisches Lexikon* (1802; reprint ed., Hildesheim: Georg Olms Verlagsbuchhandlung, 1964), 346–47. "Unter diesem Namen war ehedem bey verschiedenen Hofkapellen eine wöchentlich an einem

bestimmten Tage veranstaltete Musik gebräuchlich, die weder eine gewöhnliche Probe, in welcher neue Tonstücke einstudieret, oder schon bekannte zum Behufe einer öffentlichen Musik wiederholt wurden, noch ein öffentliches Concert, vorstellte, sondern bloß die Absicht hatte, das Orchester im Vortrage der schon bekannten Tonstücke in Uebung zu erhalten.

"Es verdient hier bemerkt zu werden, dass Johann Friedrich, Fürst zu Schwarzb. Rudolstadt, einer der größten Kunstkenner seiner Zeit, gegen das Jahr 1756 ein solches Collegium musicum bey seiner Hofkapelle unter der Direktion des Kapellmeisters Scheinpflug veranstaltete, welches zur Absicht hatte, auch theoretische Kenntnisse unter den Mitgliedern der Kapelle zu verbreiten. Der Kapellmeister bekam die Instruktion, sowohl zwischen den vorgetragenen Tonstücken, als nach der Beendigung der Musik, freundschaftliche Gespräche sowohl über die ausgeführten Tonstücke, als auch überhaput über theoretische und praktische Gegenstande der Kunst, zu veranlassen, um die Mitglieder der Kapelle unvermerkt zu eigenem Nachdenken über ihre Kunst, und zur Lektüre der über dieselbe vorhandenen und herauskommenden Schriften zu ermuntern, die in die Fürstl. Handbibliothek angeschafft, und jedem zu beliebigem Gebrauche überlassen wurden." Schwarzburg-Rudolstadt was an independent principality of Germany, consisting of several separate regions between the territories of Prussian Saxony, the Saxon duchies, and the principality of Reuss. J. Thomas and T. Baldwin, eds., *Complete Pronouncing Gazetteer, or Geographical Dictionary, of the World* (Philadelphia: J. B. Lippincott & Co., 1855), 1734-35.

4. *The New Grove,* s.v. "Collegium musicum," 6:116.

5. Michael Johns, "Collauf and His Contribution to Moravian Music" (DMA diss., Temple University, 1996), 19.

6. Anja Wehrend, *Musikanschauung, Musikpraxis, Kantatenkomposition in der Herrnhuter Brüdergemeine* (Frankfurt am Main: Peter Lang, 1995), 47.

7. Wehrend, 48.

8. Alexander Oda, *Das Entdeckte Geheimnis der Bosheit der Herrnhuter Secte* (Frankfurt, 1748), quoted in Wehrend, 47. "Die Herrnhuter haben Musicos von allen Instrumenten unter sich, die theils für Virtuosen passieren können, und wird man in mancher Fürstl. Capelle keine so solide Music antreffen; da werden Concerten, Cantaten und allerhand künstliche Stücke gespielet. . ."

9. Wehrend, 48-50.

10. Randall H. Tollefsen, *Catalogue of the Music Collection of the Moravian Congregation at Zeist* (Utrecht: Rijksarchief, 1985), xiv.

11. Karl Kroeger, "A Preliminary Survey of Musical Life in the English Moravian Settlements of Fulneck, Fairfield, and Ockbrook During the 18th and 19th Centuries," *Moravian Music Journal* 29/1 (Spring 1984): 25.

12. Kroeger, "A Preliminary Survey," 23.

13. Cited in Colin Podmore, *The Moravian Church in England 1728-1760* (Oxford: Clarendon Press, 1998), 150.

14. Neuwied music collection, typescript catalog, July 1995, photocopy in Moravian Music Foundation Collections File.

15. Sybille Reventlow and Suzanne Summerville, "Die Christiansfelder Musikkataloge—Neues Forschungsunternehmen in Dänemark," *Unitas Fratrum* 3 (1978): 65-69.

16. The use of musical instruments had been a part of the Moravians' life in Bethlehem even before this time, for instance accompanying the singing of the

Litany on December 28, 1743. See Kenneth Hamilton, trans., *The Bethlehem Diary, Volume I: 1742–1744* (Bethlehem: Archives of the Moravian Church, 1971), 181, and Thomas Jerome Anderson, "The Collegium Musicum Salem, 1780–1790: Origins and Repertoire" (PhD diss., Florida State University, 1976), 65–66.

17. Rufus A. Grider, *Historical Notes on Music in Bethlehem, Pennsylvania (from 1741–1871)*. Reprinted from the original edition of 1873 as Moravian Music Foundation Publications No. 4 (Winston-Salem: Moravian Music Foundation, 1957), 6.

18. Grider, 27. Note the decline in number of concerts following Michael's return to Europe in 1815.

19. Grider, 8–9. See appendix 1 for further information about Michael's other compositions.

20. See, for instance, Grider, 34.

21. See chapter 9.

22. See Barbara Jo Strauss, "A Register of Music Performed in Concert, Nazareth, Pennsylvania, from 1796–1845: An Annotated Edition of an American Moravian Document" (master's thesis, University of Arizona, 1976).

23. Strauss, 262.

24. Strauss, 255.

25. Richard D. Claypool, "Catalog of the Lititz Collegium Musicum Collection" (unpublished typescript, Moravian Music Foundation, Winston-Salem, 1980), vi.

26. Claypool, vii.

27. Minutes of the Salem Aeltesten Conferenz, December 19, 1781 (Moravian Archives, Winston-Salem): "Das Musicanten-Collegium hat um einen Beytrag zu ihren Expences ersuchet, welchen Br. Fr. Peter am 27ten Dec. einsammeln wird. Dies Collecte wird am Weynachtstage in der Gemeine bekannt gemacht werden."

28. Minutes of the Salem Aeltesten Conferenz, October 31, 1781 (Moravian Archives, Winston-Salem): "Die Musici sind zu instruiren, dass sie während der Zeit der Assembly nicht in der Privat-Hausern den Herren Music zu machen annehmen, sondern denjenigen, die es begehren, gerade zu sagen, dass wir dieses nicht thun; in unsrer Gemein-Music aber lassen wir uns nicht stören. Jedoch sind die Violinen zur Vermeidung unschicklichen Gebrauchs unter Verschluss zu halten, so wie auch die Setzstücke zu den blasenden Instrumenten."

29. C. Daniel Crews, *Johann Friedrich Peter and His Times* (Winston-Salem: Moravian Music Foundation, 1990), 21.

30. Jeannine Ingram, "Reflections on the Salem *Collegium Musicum*," *Moravian Music Foundation Bulletin* 20/1 (Spring–Summer 1975): 8.

31. Ingram, 9.

32. Donald M. McCorkle, "The Collegium Musicum Salem: Its Music, Musicians, and Importance" (reprinted from *North Carolina Historical Review* [October 1956], rev. ed. [Winston-Salem: Moravian Music Foundation, 1979]), 22–23.

33. The Philharmonic Society of Bethlehem, the successor to the Bethlehem *collegium musicum*; the Lititz *collegium musicum*; and the Salem *collegium musicum*.

34. See Johann Christoph Friedrich Bach, *Four Early Sinfonias*, ed. Ewald V. Nolte, *Recent Researches in the Music of the Classical Era* 15 (Madison: A-R Editions, 1982).

35. These works, with Hommann's additional surviving overture, make up the forthcoming Volume 17 in the American Musicological Society's "Music in the United States of America" (MUSA) series, edited by Joanne Swenson-Eldridge.

36. Selections from Wolf's *Oster Cantate* are also a part of the Moravian music collections in South Africa.

37. Karl Kroeger, "David Moritz Michael's Psalm 103: An Early American Sacred Cantata," *Moravian Music Foundation Bulletin* 21/2 (Fall–Winter 1976): 10.

38. Kroeger, "Psalm 103," 10.

39. See K Marie Stolba, "Evidence for Quartets by John Antes," *Journal of the American Musicological Society* 33/3 (Fall 1980): 565–74, and "From John Antes to Benjamin Franklin—A Musical Connection," *Moravian Music Foundation Bulletin* 25/2 (Fall–Winter 1980): 5–9.

40. C. Daniel Crews, *John Antes* (Winston-Salem: Moravian Music Foundation, 1997), 13.

41. SCM 240, *collegium musicum* collection, Salem.

42. Karl Kroeger, "What Happened to the Antes String Quartets?" *Moravian Music Journal* 41/1 (Spring 1996): 23–26.

43. See chapter 2, p. 58, for a discussion of Peter's personal struggles with his musical gifts.

44. Bethlehem catalog number PSB 1327.

45. The oboe was more prevalent in Zeist, probably due to the fact that Georg Melchior Hörr, the music director from 1803 to 1840, was himself an oboist.

46. Katherine Ann Hahn, "The Wind Ensemble Music of David Moritz Michael" (master's thesis, University of Missouri—Columbia, 1979), 45–46.

47. Johns, "Collauf and His Contribution," 41.

48. Raoul F. Camus, *Military Music of the American Revolution* (Chapel Hill: University of North Carolina Press, 1976), 21.

49. Koch, 738. "Harmoniemusik, nennet man diejenige, die aus lauter Blasinstrumenten, und zwar gewöhnlich aus zwey Oboen, zwey Clarinetten, zwey Hörnern und Fagotts bestehet. Man bedient sich dabey entweder besonders dazu gesetzter Tonstücke, die den Namen Parthien führen, und die aus Sätzen von verschiedener Bewegung und Taktart bestehen, und jeden Charakter annehmen können, aber im keiner bestimmten Ordnung auf einander folgen, oder man arrangirt für diese Instrumente Opern und andere Tonstücke, die eigentlich zu einem andern Gebrauche bestimmt sind, weil es bis jetzt noch an einer hinlänglichen Anzahl guter Tonstücke fehlet, die ursprünglich für diese Art der Musik gesetzt wären."

50. *Die Musik in Geschichte und Gegenwart* (1994), s.v. "Harmoniemusik," 164. "Besonders hingewiesen sei auf die Harmoniemusik der Brüdergemeine in den mährischen Siedlungsgebieten der USA, der Moravians. Zentren waren im ersten Drittel des 19. Jh. Bethlehem, Lititz, und Nazareth in Pennsylvania und Salem in North Carolina. Repertoire und Besetzung ähnelten der europäischen Harmoniemusik (wenn auch mit großer zeitlicher Verzögerung), nicht aber die Funktionen. Die Spieler hatten als Teil der religiösen Gemeinschaft den gleichen sozialen Status wie die Zuhörer und musizierten gleichermaßen für sich wie für die Gemeinde, also als Beitrag zum religiös ausgerichteten Gemeinschaftsleben. Aus Europa importierte Harmoniemusik stammt u.a. von A. Gyrowetz, Hoffmeister, Pleyel, Righini, Rosetti, Stamitz, Fr. Devienne, Ahl und Stumpf. Von den Moravians selbst komponierte Harmoniemusik (zumeist Parthia genannat) ist in der Regel für 2 Klar., 2 Hr. und 1–2 Fg. Gesetzt; gelegentlich finden sich Fl., Trp., Ob. oder Piccoloflöte. Die meisten Stücke (14) stamen von David Moritz Michael (1751–1827), zuvor Oboist in einer deutschen Militärkapelle, darunter Parthia bestimmt zu einer Wasserfahrt und eine Suite: bey einer Quelle zu blasen."

51. *David Moritz Michael: Complete Wind Chamber Music*, ed. Nola Reed Knouse. Recent Researches in American Music 59; Music of the United States of America 16. (Middleton, VT: A-R Editions, 2006).

52. Grider, 9.

53. Johns, "Collauf and His Contribution," 46.

54. See Michael Johns, "A Second Look at Collauf," *Moravian Music Journal* 41/2 (Fall 1996): 7–15, for a discussion of these works and Johns's attempt to identify this capable composer.

55. *The New Grove*, s.v. "Collegium musicum," 6:116.

56. Quoted in Donald M. McCorkle, "The Moravian Contribution to American Music" (reprinted from *Notes* [Music Library Association, September 1956] as Moravian Music Foundation Publications No. 1) (Winston-Salem: Moravian Music Foundation, 1956), 4.

57. The Bach Choir of Bethlehem gave the first American performance of Bach's Mass in B Minor on March 27, 1900.

Chapter Eight

Music in Moravian Boarding Schools through the Early Nineteenth Century

Pauline M. Fox

Early Factors in Founding of Schools

A number of factors in the history of the Moravian Church contributed to the success of music education in the schools. From its inception, leaders of the ancient Unitas Fratrum valued education. By 1495, Bishop Lukáš of Prague had led the church to establish a school in each of its two hundred congregations and to open several institutions of higher learning.[1] Although a 1508 mandate prohibited Moravian religious practices, before 1510 fifty or more printed works appeared from the press of the Unity.[2] Bishop Jan Amos Comenius (1592–1670), the author of historical and theological treatments of his church, also expounded on the necessity of early childhood training that included music.[3]

At Herrnhut, music flourished in the 1730s as an instrumental ensemble was introduced to accompany sacred choral and solo works. Documentation of a *collegium musicum* there dates from 1731. Communal housing for Single Sisters and Single Brothers provided not only lodging and apprenticeships in trades, but also units for day-to-day social camaraderie, spiritual discussions, the instruction of youth, and group singing.[4]

Two schools established by the Brethren in Saxony became the primary institutions of training for Moravian clergy and teachers: the *Paedagogium* (boarding school for boys) at Niesky, established in 1742, and the theological seminary at Barby, established in 1754. Although these educational divisions were subsequently moved on occasion between Niesky and Barby, those two centers remained the major sources of training in theology and music for the European teachers of the Moravian men discussed in this study. A publishing house was also started at Barby.

Bethlehem, Pennsylvania, was founded in 1741 as the administrative head-quarters of the Brethren's missionary enterprises in the New World. Although it remained the focal point of Moravian activity in America, Nazareth, Lititz, and Salem all gained fine reputations as centers of education. The excellent progressive education offered at these Moravian schools may be credited in large part to the heritage of Hus, Comenius, Zinzendorf, and other university-trained leaders. While parents traveled on missionary assignments, boarding schools were a natural outgrowth of the Single Sisters' and Single Brothers' houses for nurturing children left in care of the home congregation. Children of local residents attended the "day" or "town" school.

Each boarding school was subsidized by the larger church and managed by a board of trustees, who appointed a principal (often the local head pastor) to be responsible for day-to-day administration. The principal and his wife were to be further regarded *in loco parentis*. Because church workers were assigned to rotate among the settlements, transmission of the same core values and materials—including music repertoire—was the same in every school. Spouses of principals and teachers also served in a variety of roles.

There was no difference between "sacred" and "secular," for the work in the field, the tailor shop, or the classroom was just as essential to the continuation of missionary efforts as were the actual journeys over the mountains or sea. Manual occupations were valued equally with intellectual and evangelistic assignments, for Zinzendorf himself had written:

> Each one should be faithful in his own share of the responsibility, whether to sweep the meetingroom, to pave the street, . . . to teach children the alphabet or to teach Greek, Latin, and French, to convert the heathen, . . . to drive the donkeys. . . . Everything has the same amount of merit. . . . The basis for this is the trustworthy handicraft of the Savior.
>
> He was a carpenter. Was that a suitable occupation for . . . the creator and architect of the whole world?[5]

The Moravian historian James Henry states that the purpose of schooling was to lay a foundation so that the "heart [could be] awakened into sympathetic action with the brain." Programs were designed not to provide data but to teach youth *how* to learn, according to the principle that "all heads are not adapted to all studies[. Education] should . . . train the mind for the task of grasping the aims of its own individuality . . . [and] mould the character into forms of correctness."[6]

The American Moravian Boarding Schools

The Seminary at Bethlehem

Within the year following the settlement of Bethlehem, a school for girls was opened on May 4, 1742, when Zinzendorf's daughter Benigna, assisted by two other women and three men, enrolled twenty-five girls in Germantown (just north of Philadelphia). By June the group had been transferred to Bethlehem, and in July of that same year a school for boys was opened there by George Neisser, one of Benigna's assistants. Although the locations of both schools were shifted several times during the next few years, the school for girls has existed in Bethlehem since 1748.

At the Herrnhut Synod of 1782, it was suggested that the boarding schools in America follow the lead of the European schools, which had begun to enroll non-Moravian students. One of the immediate results of the occupation of Bethlehem buildings by the Continental army for use as hospital facilities during the War of Independence had been the spreading of news about the school for girls, which offered instruction in academic subjects and fine arts as well as in domestic arts.[7] Partly in response to eager inquiries from families prominent in American political circles concerning the admission of their daughters to this unusual school, the church announced in 1784 that the brethren felt "obliged to all useful services for our fellow men, and were induced by [this] desire to establish such an institution for small and big girls of such parents and guardians who have a special confidence in the education of children in the Brethren's congregation here in Bethlehem."[8]

Thus the Moravian Boarding School for Young Ladies at Bethlehem opened in October of 1785 under Principal Johann Andreas Hübner, pastor of the congregation, with six boarders, fifteen day students, and three resident female tutors. Girls between the ages of eight and twelve were admitted and could remain until age sixteen. The fee of 5 pounds (Pennsylvania currency) per quarter covered board and tuition for the ordinary classes in reading and writing, grammar, arithmetic, geography, history (and Bible history), astronomy, spinning and plain sewing, singing, and instruction in the German language. Extra fees were charged for tambour (decorative embroidery) and lessons on the pianoforte or guitar. Although the familiar tongue was still German, the influx of non-Moravian students necessitated instruction in English also; therefore, on Wednesdays the entire school spoke only English.

Enrollment rose quickly, requiring the construction of a new building in 1790 to accommodate the seventy-five students and six resident teachers. School financial records of 1788–94 indicate payments for the tuning of seven pianofortes and clavichords, for the services of music copyists and book binders, and for music imported or printed by American publishers.[9] Instruction was now given in English only, and lessons in French and in new methods of ornamental needlework became available. Certainly this academic program including the arts and exposure to three languages was an unusual option for girls in the eighteenth century!

In the years 1800 to 1813 Principal Andrew Benade devoted his attention to the instruction of the faculty in methods of pedagogy, rather than to the expansion of curricular offerings. In 1815 the school, now with 108 boarders and 24 day students, moved into the former Single Brothers House and became known as the "Seminary for Young Ladies," or the "Female Seminary."[10]

Between 1816 and 1818, Principal Henry Steinhauer taught French, drawing, and botany; bought apparatus for natural sciences; purchased new musical instruments; expanded the library; introduced more branches of art; scheduled evening cultural events; invited guest lecturers on languages and science; and hired three Moravian female tutors from England. Undoubtedly, it was such innovations that earned the Seminary a reputation as "the most fashionable school in the United States."[11]

Offerings in the arts were expanded in 1822–36. Under the principalship of Charles Seidel, programs at Christmas and in May occasionally included performances by mixed voices, and cultural events continued to be held on winter evenings. Seidel also commissioned paintings by Gustavus Grunewald and hired more non-Moravian female tutors. The excellent reputation of the seminary continued only to grow throughout ensuing years.

Changes were occurring at this time within other branches of the educational system of Bethlehem—first when the day schools were reorganized in response to an 1834 statewide mandate from the Pennsylvania legislature requiring the formation of public schools, and necessarily again in 1845 on the incorporation of Bethlehem as a borough, whereby the church relinquished control of public education. By 1850 the former day schools had either split into the public system or had joined boys' and girls groups' together into what would at first be called the Moravian Parochial School, renamed the Moravian Preparatory School in 1917. In 1971 this school merged with the Seminary for Girls, the direct descendant of Benigna's school, to form the present coeducational Moravian Academy.

Nazareth Hall

The early history of this boys' school is inextricably woven with that of the girls' school, narrated above. When 111 boys and 19 staff members were moved in June of 1759 from Bethlehem to Nazareth, the school was named Nazareth Hall Academy. Because of financial troubles after the war years, the school was temporarily closed, and the eleven remaining students returned to Bethlehem. In 1785 it reopened at Nazareth, accepting boys aged seven to twelve and offering instruction in reading, writing, arithmetic, history, geography, mathematics, music and drawing, as well as English, German, Latin, French, and Greek, with daily speech in both English and German.

In his discussion of the daily routine at Nazareth Hall, James Henry outlines the division of the students and faculty into "Rooms" (noting that the same system was applied to the "female character" in other schools):

In each [Room] we find two colleagues, or companion teachers, who live constantly with the pupils, taking watch over their charge by turn, and each serving his day in rotation. It is the duty of the Room-teacher to rise with his fifteen or eighteen boys, the largest number a Room should reach, to take them to meals, to morning prayer, and to remain with them, while pursuing their preparatory studies, until the eight o'clock bell announces the commencement of the school day. From that time the teacher is engaged in different departments, he himself teaching; the boys, who constitute his Room, are distributed throughout the different classes, higher or lower, according to their grade of merit and proficiency, without reference to their ages or the Room in which they live. . . .

   At four, [on] the play-ground there are many amusements . . . and these are participated in together.[12]

Nearly all of the Moravian men who figure in this chapter either attended or taught at Nazareth Hall for at least a short period.[13] The Hall held a reputation for excellence until it closed in 1929. As an outgrowth of the Hall, the Moravian Theological Seminary had been started in 1807 to fulfill a need for training Moravian ministers in the United States. This school closed from 1813 to 1820, but was revived and moved to Bethlehem in 1838, becoming a forerunner of the present Moravian College and Theological Seminary in Bethlehem.

Linden Hall

Linden Hall traces its history to a school begun in 1746 and held in the first *Gemeinhaus* in Lititz. In 1763 the students were divided, the girls being sent to the Sisters' House for instruction and the boys remaining in the *Gemeinhaus*. In 1766 several girls from Lancaster enrolled, and in 1769 a larger building was erected for the sixteen students and two teachers. The first non-Moravian boarder arrived from Baltimore in 1794. The school then grew so that in 1804 the twenty-four pupils and six teachers moved into another new building. Throughout its fine history, however, this school was always smaller than its counterpart in Bethlehem.

   For many years the school was known as the Boarding School for Girls, but in the 1850s it became known as Linden Hall, for the trees planted by Brother and Sister Eugene and Agnes Früauf during Brother Früauf's long principalship. Today it offers girls a college-preparatory curriculum.

The Boarding School for Young Ladies at Salem

In 1772 Salem, North Carolina, was only a tiny settlement, but it provided schooling for both girls and boys. Even before the founding of Salem in 1766, visitors had asked to send their children to be taught by the Moravians. The boys' school, begun in 1771 shortly after the formal organization of the Salem Congregation, lasted until 1910, after village schools were established. The girls' school began humbly in 1772, with Single Sister Elisabeth Oesterlein caring for the very young daughters of two families. In 1792, the Salem church leaders again noted requests from visitors for education for their children, and within ten years a boarding school for girls was planned. The first "outside" students were received in May of 1804, and the school grew over time into Salem Academy and College.[14]

The first boarding program at Salem was headed by Single Sister Sophia Dorothea Reichel, an alumna of the Bethlehem school and newly arrived with her father, Bishop Carl Gotthold Reichel, who had been called to be the pastor of the Salem Congregation. In 1809 the widower Bishop Reichel married the leader of the Single Sisters from Lititz, Catherine Fetter, whose two unmarried sisters elected to move to North Carolina with her and join the staff of the Salem school—an excellent example of circulation of personnel among the schools.[15] In those days, when the education of girls was neglected in the South, non-Moravian families begged that their daughters be admitted to the Salem school, modeled after the one in Bethlehem.

Eventually the primary grades of the girls school were dropped and the school was divided into a high school academy and a college, both flourishing today.

Music in the Boarding Schools

The value placed on music instruction within the curriculum of the Moravian schools may well have been rooted in the Comenian philosophy that education should include the introduction of musical activities during the earliest years of childhood. The Moravian minister-composer Christian LaTrobe (1758–1836) wrote that students in Moravian schools were "taught to consider the practice of [music], whether vocal or instrumental[,] as leading to the same grand point, namely . . . the service of the Lord, and the promotion of His glory on earth."[16] He reminded his daughter Agnes that the effect of music "upon the mind and heart may, under the guidance of God and his Spirit, be truly profitable in advancing our best interests."[17] A recent writer concluded that the "Moravians readily perceived music as an effective force for stimulating, developing, and refining . . . aesthetic sensibilities." This conclusion is entirely consistent with the perspective that Reichel stated many years earlier that music was "regarded not merely as an elegant accomplishment, but as a refiner of the mind and a handmaid to devotion."[18]

The following features were part of the music curriculum in each of the Moravian boarding schools:

- All students were required to attend frequent, if not daily, singing classes, in which both tunes and texts of chorales and hymns were memorized.

  The exercises in choral singing by whole classes is a feature of our system which cannot be too highly recommended. . . . It is the primary step to an emotional education, which, in connection with the intellectual department, should form the highest aim of the instructor of youth. By imbibing the first principles of harmony, such as the old Lutheran chorale exhibits, the foundation is laid for a good super-structure of musical thought, on which much of the refinement of human life is built.[19]

- The Moravian educators considered the practice of copying music to be a legitimate and most worthwhile method of instruction (and if well done, perhaps a source of cash income). Eliza Jacobs Haldeman, a student at Linden Hall in 1800–1802, recalled that printed music, "being very expensive," was "unknown, the notes being all written with the pen."[20] In this time period, American copyright laws were neither detailed nor enforced. Because "music was expensive at this early time and available to only a few," it was accepted practice that people borrowed "printed music which they could copy out in manuscript form and retain for permanent use."[21]
- Individual lessons on keyboard and sometimes on other instruments were offered at an extra fee.
- Public examinations were held each spring, growing from simple closing programs into a week-long series of speeches, exhibits, and musical performances.[22]

Examples of School Musicians and Their Repertoire

Because very few written or printed programs survive from the earliest years of these schools, and because most of the published music in American Moravian collections is of later origin, manuscript books belonging to students and teachers at the boarding schools provide invaluable documentation of the pedagogical repertoire. A portion of the contents of such books sheds light on such functions as concerted performance within church services, the accompaniment of hymns sung in nonliturgical settings, and music for civic holidays. This indeed affirms the German cultural roots that the Moravians preserved as they settled in the New World. Many more vocal and keyboard entries, however, reveal the blossoming of relationships between musical life within Moravian society and that of mainstream American culture. The proximity of Bethlehem and Lititz to Philadelphia, an urban seaport only 50 miles away, had political, cultural, and economic implications that contributed significantly to social changes that affected the Moravian academic and musical circles.

The following sketches of people and repertoire associated with the Moravian boarding schools offer a sense of growth from the early days of the schools into the mid-1830s. These illustrative examples have been chosen mainly from forty-four manuscript books held by the Archives of the Moravian Church in Bethlehem and known to have been used by teachers and students at the Bethlehem, Nazareth, Lititz, and Salem schools.[23] The abbreviation BMB stands for Bethlehem Manuscript Book, LMB for Lititz Manuscript Book. Biographical information was drawn from church archival records.

Of course, many other well-known Moravian musicians (including Johannes Herbst and David Moritz Michael) influenced musical activities at these same institutions during the late eighteenth and early nineteenth centuries; information on their influence is readily available in other studies as well as elsewhere in this volume.

1785–90: Johann Andreas Hübner

Johann Andreas Hübner trained at the University of Halle and at Barby. After being principal at the Herrnhut *Knäbchenanstalt* (boys' school) and pastor at Niesky, he came to Bethlehem in 1780 as principal preacher. Still with general pastoral oversight, he became principal of the Boarding School for Young Ladies in 1785, moving to become pastor at Lititz in 1790.

Entirely in tablature and unique among the holdings of the Moravian Music Foundation, book BMB 4 bears the inscription "J. A. Hübner" and was probably prepared in Europe a few years before Hübner's arrival in Bethlehem. The music is written in French tablature, for a six-course stringed instrument. Sixty-six chorales, beyond a beginner's skill, are followed by fifteen short pieces in menuet and polonaise dance form, with progressive levels of technical difficulty indicating a pedagogical function. Occasional amateurisms in composition suggest the practical efforts of a local teacher.

No record of Hübner's personal involvement in musical performance has been found. Records of the school, however, list fees for lessons on guitar, and other archival papers mention the playing of guitar, cithern, and lute to accompany singing.

1790–1810: Johann Friedrich Peter and His Students

The name of Johann Friedrich Peter (1746–1813) commands respect among Moravian circles as "the consummate writer of fine anthems."[24] In July of 1770 Johann Friedrich and his older brother Simon arrived in America for employment as teachers at Nazareth Hall, bringing along a large quantity of manuscripts copied at Niesky from chamber music and symphonies by such contemporary composers as C. F. Abel, J. C. F. Bach, Haydn, Boccherini, and both Johann and Karl Stamitz. Following subsequent appointments in Bethlehem, Lititz, Salem, Graceham in Maryland, Hope in New Jersey, and Donegal near Lancaster, Pennsylvania, J. F. Peter was reassigned to Bethlehem.[25] There he remained as a clerk, organist, teacher, music copyist, and composer until his death. Musical events during his time in Bethlehem included the communitywide mourning of the death of George Washington on February 22,

1800; the dedication of the newly built (and present) Central Moravian Church edifice in 1806; and an early American performance of excerpts from Haydn's *Creation* in 1811.

Peter's own repertoire was demonstrably broad, for his book BMB 15 contains classical works such as C. P. E Bach's *Melodien zu Zwölf Oden u. Lieder von Gellert* (Wotquenne 195). Excerpts from J. G. Naumann's 1780 opera *Cora* appear with parodied texts in BMB 15 and in Peter's hand in BMB 16. The *Peter Codex*, his sketchbook of 278 selections, prepared in Bethlehem in the few years around 1800, is a "forceful indicator of Moravian preferences in music . . . since Peter's apparent purpose in the preparation of his book was to copy music which might later either be requested by others in the community or be used in music classes."[26]

Among Peter's students were Christian Schropp and George Hartman. Schropp (1756–1826), a nailsmith, schoolmaster, and musician, directed the Lititz town school for local young boys for fourteen years, served the Lititz church as organist for forty years, and provided music-copying services. Schropp's LMB 15, dated 1799 and largely in Peter's hand, begins with contemporary American patriotic songs that were published in Philadelphia, Boston, or New York in or soon after 1798, indicating a rapid transmission into the circle of musical Moravians.

George Adolphe Hartman (1781–1839), the son of a blacksmith and mason assigned to the newly planted (and short-lived) Moravian settlement at Hope, New Jersey, studied under Peter there in 1791–93 and taught at the Hope boys' school in 1803–4. Hartman then taught at Nazareth Hall from 1807 until 1817, when he became the pastor of the Staten Island congregation. His BMB 5 from 1804 contains excerpts from J. A. P. Schulz's *Lieder im Volkston*, English songs listed in the Sonneck and Wolfe bibliographies with pre-1798 publication dates, and keyboard pieces such as "The White Cockade" and "Washingtons [*sic*] March Resignation," apparently for pedagogical use.

A further sampling of Peter's repertoire as music copyist, and of the repertoire presented in musical education of the period, is seen in books BMB 1–2, owned in 1805–6 by the twelve-year-old Bethlehem student Maria Elizabeth ("Betsy") Bischoff: contemporaneous secular songs by Hiller, Kospoth, Schulz, Shield, and Storace, in addition to sacred songs in German; keyboard *Duettos* by the European composer Theodore Smith; other keyboard works by Hässler, Abel, Haydn, Just, and Boccherini; and Viguerie's *Battle of Maringo* [*sic*] in that favorite genre of the period. Two features seen in these and numerous other student copybooks suggest that their purpose was pedagogical. First, the variety in media, language, and character of the selections and the lack of clustering of any of those traits—indeed, a perceptible progression from Christmas to Trinity—may indicate that entries were gradually added in the order in which they were assigned during keyboard and voice lessons throughout the school year. Second, BMB 1 bears a page of examples of notation and of the execution of ornaments.[27]

If we survey a range of entries in books owned or copied by Peter and others in Bethlehem, Nazareth, Lititz, and Salem during the decades surrounding 1800, it is evident that although the traditional German song was still thriving and keyboard work was valued, interest in a new vocal repertoire was developing, with an obvious correlation between a more secular content and the use of English. The presence of this light music, sometimes with downright frivolous texts, in the repertoires of clergy and teachers at this early period invites us to speculate that such diversification contributed to the excellent reputations enjoyed by the Moravian schools.

Lesser-Known Men from Lititz

Just as J. F. Peter influenced repertoire in both Bethlehem and Lititz, similar associations between Lititz and Nazareth can be seen in the following few decades. Music in books owned by men about whom we have only sketchy biographical information, yet who are known to have been musically active, may accurately portray the inclinations of numerous other by now obscure aficionados of music.

John William Rauch (1790–1863), a confectioner remembered as the first pretzel maker in Lititz, was skilled as a tenor singer, soprano trombonist, and first violinist, quite likely having been a student of Christian Schropp. His wife, Lisetta Wolle, taught at Linden Hall for eighteen years. Rauch's collection of duets and trios for unspecified treble instruments (LMB 8), dated 1813 when he was teaching boys in Lititz, may have been a reference manual. The fifty-three titles seem to be drawn from popular contemporary tunes. They are strikingly international in flavor, with references to German, Hungarian, Russian, Tyrolese, Venetian, Sicilian, Greek, French, Scotch, Irish, English, and New York elements. Examples include "Ballade: Ich träumt ich wär ein Vögelein," "The Village Maid," "Le Petit Tambour," "A Favorite Duett in the Magic Flute" [Mozart], and "The Duke of York's Quick Step." Because the ranges lie far above a normal vocal tessitura, no text is present, and articulation markings as for bowing commonly appear, we may suppose that the arrangements were Rauch's own, perhaps for his violin students.

William Henry Hall (1809–68) taught briefly at Nazareth Hall (1827–29) and then at Lititz Academy. He took up the trade of clockmaker, also serving many years as organist for the Lititz congregation.[28] His book (LMB 7) contains typical keyboard solos and duets plus both German and English vocal pieces popular at this period. The bulk of the entries appear to be in Schropp's hand. Most of the titles also appear in other books from Lititz and Bethlehem; several are also in the *Peter Codex*. Particular favorites among Lititz owners seem to be the Vanhal waltzes, "The Deathsong of the Cherokee Indians," and Kotzwara's four-hand *Battle of Prague*.

1820s: The Kluge Sisters at Linden Hall

Seven copybooks owned by the three daughters of John Peter Kluge yield rewarding information about the Moravian educational community. Following missionary service in Suriname and then on the frontier of what is now the state of Indiana, Kluge served as a pastor in North Carolina, Maryland, and Pennsylvania. His daughter Henrietta attended the boarding school at Salem (where her book, LMB 6, was begun in 1814) and then taught at Linden Hall. Later, as the widowed Mrs. Moore and living in Lebanon, Pennsylvania, she taught in a non-Moravian school for girls and in 1852 was in charge of new programs instituted by the public school system. The second daughter, Caroline Amelia, studied at Linden Hall; a history of her father's church in nearby York claims that she was "a most competent master" of the organ.[29] The younger daughter Clementina also studied at Linden Hall, then taught there for a number of years. Upper intermediate-level pieces in her books LMB 3, 4, 5, and 21 are seen in books also used by Nazareth Hall students. The sisters were in Lititz during the years 1822–27, as the books were inscribed. The hand of the copyist Christian Schropp is evident in five of the books.

Because the seven books may be representative of a new direction in the repertoire chosen as appropriate for the education of youth in the 1820s, we can make several observations about them. First, the high percentage of songs of a lighthearted nature certainly indicates open-mindedness to a diversity of cultural, social, and religious expressions during the formative years of the student owners. Groupings of excerpts from James Hook's Drury Lane stage entertainment *Tekeli* and from John Braham's *Kais* and *The Devil's Bridge* seem to have been treated as individual songs of intrinsic merit, isolated from their original dramatic settings. Such variety must have been acceptable within the bounds of propriety held not only by John Peter Kluge, who would have provided the financial support for his daughters, but also by the Moravian clergy-principals, representing the approval of the higher authorities.

Second, the contents of the books indicate that the music faculty at Linden Hall had access to, and perhaps even preferred, a contemporary repertoire of English-language songs available from American publishers after 1800. Third, concordances in books associated with persons at each of the boarding schools indicate that a single standard of performance skill was upheld for both female and male students.

1820s: Men at Nazareth Hall

The historian James Henry had himself studied at Nazareth Hall and in 1830–31 taught languages and music there, probably using his book (BMB 10) with its collection of keyboard works by European composers, largely in variation and sonata forms. He had studied pianoforte under Charles Frederick Kluge, brother of the Kluge sisters discussed above. Kluge was a career educator who served assignments at the boarding schools in Nazareth, Salem, and Lititz.

Julius Theodore Bechler was son of the pastor-organist-composer Johann Christian Bechler, who had also served as principal at the Nazareth and Lititz boarding schools. On inscriptions in his books (LMB 9, 10, and 22) we see "Julius T. Beckler's/Piano Book./Nazareth Hall," with dates from 1824 to 1829. School records show he "distinguished himself" as a pianoforte student of C. A. Bleck. After teaching at the Hall from 1832 until 1838, J. T. Bechler served pastorates in North Carolina and Pennsylvania, followed by the principalship at Linden Hall. Bechler's second wife, Theodora Elizabeth Früauff, was skilled in music, art, and languages and became known as an outstanding educator.

In Bechler's books, the copyist occasionally recorded internal dates signifying November, January, and April, perhaps points at which new material was assigned. Although the total of thirty-one entries are mostly in variation form, apparently Bechler's teacher considered the ten selections in sonata or rondo form to be pedagogically healthful, perhaps reflecting the perspective later articulated by James Henry, a schoolmate and colleague of Bechler.

> To . . . exercises in singing I must add the very essential portion of a Moravian cause of instruction, music on the piano, as conducive to [culture]. Whether the pupil . . . becomes proficient in the art, is not the sole inquiry; the aim being more a general refinement of thought and introduction to musical feeling, produced by an acquaintance with the choicest airs and sonatas of Mozart, Haydn, and Beethoven.[30]

1820s and 30s: Mary Sautter Henry

In 1833 James Henry married Mary Sautter, a student at the Bethlehem Seminary from 1818 until 1827 and then a resident teacher from 1830 to 1833. From her years at the Seminary, Mary's books (BMB 7, 8, and 11) contain nine sets of keyboard variations, that ubiquitous favorite form of those decades. Books 7 and 11 display a wide spectrum of vocal solos and ensembles, ranging from older German texts to English songs freshly published in America. Book 8, dated 1832, is a collection of thirty-seven works largely for ensembles of two to five voices, usually written in open score; six of the works specify male singers, who were invited from the church choir by Charles F. Seidel, the principal, to supplement performances at the Seminary. After her marriage, Mary provided service as a music copyist.

More than twenty of the Bethlehem and Lititz Manuscript Books are almost completely devoted to secular pieces such as American patriotic songs, arrangements of British folk material, and airs from the English theater. The increasing presence, in other books dating from the 1790s to the 1830s, of this sort of light music, often arranged for vocal solo or two- or four-hand keyboard, affirms that Moravian instructors accepted it as suitable for pedagogy and social pleasure.[31]

A high percentage of correlation exists between entries in student copybooks and the contents of the early nineteenth-century American publications *The Orphean Lyre*, vol. 1 (1816); *Twelve Little Ballads and a Favorite Lesson*, book 2 (1810–14); *The Musical Journal for the Piano Forte*, vols. 3 and 5 (1803–4); and William M'Culloch's *Selected Music* (1807).[32] This gradual diversification of content is incontrovertible evidence that Moravian clergy-educators of the early nineteenth century deliberately assimilated selected material consistent with the tastes of mainstream American society into their pedagogical curricula without sacrificing the spiritual import of music found in strictly Moravian sources.

Conclusions

We can substantiate that during the early decades of the nineteenth century, the musical repertoire of many pastors, teachers, and students associated with the American Moravian boarding schools was drawn both from the base of their Germanic heritage and from the wealth of materials—including patriotic songs and popular excerpts from the London stage—increasingly available from American publishers. Considering the sources of Moravian culture, we should expect the continued use of German materials in pedagogy. Considering the Zinzendorfian principle of investing all available resources toward a greater purpose, we should also expect the Moravians' appropriation of readily accessible Anglo-American materials.

As stated above, Moravian educators sought to "lay a foundation." They regarded the study of music to be a valuable tool in the task, for its effect "upon the mind and heart may, under the guidance of God and his Spirit, be truly profitable in advancing our best interests."[33] Moravian goals for education and the respect for music are brought together well by Karl Kroeger: "The music used in these schools varied widely from hymns and sacred songs to popular and patriotic airs, but all had one basic characteristic: they taught moral precepts."[34]

The core of Moravian identity, as we have seen, was to regard all activities as service to God. The extension of this principle to cover the selection of music that could be utilized constructively in pedagogy may have been not merely an option but rather an obligation that the Moravian clergy-educators cheerfully assumed, unencumbered as they were by constraints imposed by the artificial and mutually exclusive categories of "sacred" and "secular." Thus it appears that they held an extraordinarily flexible aesthetic perspective in which disparities such as abstract music and nonscriptural texts could be compatible with, and even contribute to, growth in piety. To an admirable degree, these early Moravians succeeded in laying a firm foundation for the future of their educational institutions by both adopting benefits of the host culture and retaining values of their own heritage.

Notes

1. Edmund deSchweinitz, *The History of the Church Known as the Unitas Fratrum, or The Unity of the Brethren*, 2nd ed. (Bethlehem: Moravian Publication Concern, 1901), 225–26.

2. Thomas Sovík, "Music of the American Moravians: The First Tradition," *Czechoslovak and Central European Journal* (now *Kosmas*) 9, nos. 1/2 (Summer/Winter 1990): 35.

3. John Amos Comenius, *The School of Infancy*, ed. and intro. by Ernest M. Eller (Chapel Hill: University of North Carolina Press, 1956), 74, 94–96. See also Donna K. Rothrock, "Moravian Music Education: Forerunner to Public School Music," *Bulletin of Historical Research in Music Education* 8/2 (July 1987): 64–66.

4. See chapter 1, p. 16, for a description of the Moravians' "choir system."

5. Excerpt from a 1747 homily, in Hans-Christoph Hahn and Hellmut Reichel, *Zinzendorf und die Herrnhuter Brüder: Quellen zur Geschichte der Brüder-Unität von 1722 bis 1760* (Hamburg: Friedrich Wittig Verlag, 1977), 211–12. I thank Peter Vogt for bringing this resource to my attention through personal correspondence, February 11, 1997.

"[E]in jeder in seinem Teil treu sein soll, warum den Saal kehren, den Platz pflastern, . . . Kinder im A-B-C-Buch informieren, oder Griechisch, Lateinisch, Französisch lehren, die Heiden bekehren, . . . Esel treiben. . . . [A]lles einerlei ist in Ansehung der Merite. . . . Die Ursache davon ist des Heilands seine Handwerkstreue.

"Er war ein Zimmermann. Was ist das für eine Okkupation für . . . den Schöpfer und Architekt der ganzen Welt?"

6. James Henry, *Sketches of Moravian Life and Character* (Philadelphia, J. B. Lippincott & Co., 1859), 184; 188–89. See Mabel Haller, "Early Moravian Education in Pennsylvania" (PhD diss., University of Pennsylvania, 1953), reprinted in *Transactions of the Moravian Historical Society* 15 (1953), chapter 7 for discussion of the aims and curricula of schools, and chapter 8 for discussion of instructional principles and practices.

7. "[I]n December of 1776, the general hospital of the Continental army was moved to Bethlehem, and the town was ordered to provide a large building to accommodate it. The Single Brothers' House was turned over to the authorities. A few of the Brethren remained to help with the wounded, but the rest . . . had to live scattered throughout the surrounding area wherever they could find shelter. . . . In addition, large parties of soldiers also bivouacked in the fields around the town, and from time to time the stores of General Washington's army were headquartered there." C. Daniel Crews, *Johann Friedrich Peter and His Times* (Winston-Salem: Moravian Music Foundation, 1990), 17. The Single Brothers' House was returned to the brethren on June 1, 1778.

8. Susan M. Swasta and Richard D. Krohn, *Mind, Body & Spirit: Moravian Academy, 1742–1992* (Bethlehem: Moravian Academy, 1991), 20, quoted from the Bethlehem Diary, appendix to September, 1785. Soon the school roster would "list the daughters of General Nathanael Greene and of John Jay, and the nieces of Ethan Allen, of George Washington, and of Thomas Jefferson" (Swasta and Krohn, 28). Much of the information in this section concerning the Bethlehem school is drawn from this source and from William C. Reichel, *Bethlehem Seminary Souvenir: A History of the Rise, Progress, and Present Condition of the Moravian Seminary for Young Ladies, at Bethlehem, Pa., with a Catalogue of its Pupils, 1785–1858*, 4th ed., rev. and enlarged by William H. Bigler (Bethlehem: Published for the Seminary, 1901).

9. Reichel, 155–56. For example, in 1792 a charge is recorded for music imported from Holland: seven sonatas by Haydn, fourteen variations by Vanhal, six sonatas and a concerto by Hoffmeister, a concerto for four hands by Giordani, and Haydn's sonatas for four hands. Seminary Ledgers A–B and *Haupt Buch* in the Moravian Archives at Bethlehem record transactions in the 1780s and 1790s.

10. In this chapter it will be referred to simply as the Seminary.

11. Cited in Haller, "Early Moravian Education," 364, from "MS. in the Archives of the Moravian Seminary and College for Women, copied from an old [1817] newspaper which stated in a subtitle: 'Harriet Gould Drake takes a trip . . . to Bethlehem, where she enters . . . the most fashionable school in the United States.' " Miss Drake, from Oswego, New York, was the daughter of a United States Congressman.

12. Henry, 174–77.

13. See chapter 7, pp. 194–95, for a listing of musically accomplished instructors at Nazareth Hall from 1785 to 1841.

14. C. Daniel Crews and Richard W. Starbuck, *With Courage for the Future: The Story of the Moravian Church, Southern Province* (Winston-Salem: Moravian Church in America, Southern Province, 2002), 85, 178.

15. Frances Griffin, *Less Time for Meddling: A History of Salem Academy and College 1772–1866* (Winston-Salem: John F. Blair, 1979), 34, 118. See also Crews and Starbuck for a great deal of information about the history of Salem Academy and College.

16. See chapter 5, p. 142, and chapter 9, pp. 232–33, for discussion of LaTrobe's music.

17. Christian I. LaTrobe, ed., *Hymn-tunes sung in the Church of the United Brethren* (London: ca. 1790), quoted in Harry H. Hall, "Moravian Music Education in America ca. 1750 to ca. 1830," *Journal of Research in Music Education*, nos. 29/3 (Fall 1981): 226; Christian I. LaTrobe, *Letters to My Children; Written at Sea During a Voyage to the Cape of Good Hope, in 1815*, ed. and intro. by the Rev. J. A. LaTrobe (London: Seeley's, 1851), 27. See also Ewald V. Nolte, "Christian Ignatius LaTrobe's Letter to His Daughter Agnes," *Moravian Music Foundation Bulletin* 10/1 (Fall 1965), 2–4.

18. Hall, "Moravian Music Education in America," 226; Reichel, 155.

19. Henry, 184.

20. The school newspaper *Linden Hall Echo* printed Haldeman's reminiscences in September 1877.

21. Richard J. Wolfe, *Early American Music Engraving and Printing* (Urbana: University of Illinois Press, 1980), 229.

22. When writing of Bethlehem's "very justly celebrated female seminary," the Philadelphia correspondent of *Dwight's Journal of Music*, "Manrico," continued, "Their public entertainments . . . are almost invariably graced with compositions of a very high order of merit" (August 7, 1858), cited in Irving Sablosky, *What They Heard: Music in America, 1852–1881* (Baton Rouge: Louisiana State University Press, 1986), 179. I thank Paul Larson of Moravian College for bringing this book to my attention.

Donald Graham Hoople states, "At their extreme, the public examinations would be one of the few matters in which the Moravians would be accused of indulging in vanity or self-congratulation. Of course, they had good reason for their pride. Their schools were the envy of nearly everyone and their methods . . . were studied, assimilated, and initiated in countless schools, both public and private, throughout the country. The public examinations were simply a way of proving themselves accountable." "Moravian Music Education and the American Moravian Music Tradition" (EdD diss., Columbia University Teachers College, 1976), 56.

See Jewel A. Smith, "Music, Women, and Pianos: The Case of the Moravian Young Ladies' Seminary in Bethlehem, Pennsylvania (1815–1860)" (PhD diss., Cincinnati College–Conservatory of Music, 2003), appendix 3, for charts dating Seminary Entertainment Performances.

23. Many of the titles of early entries are listed in Richard J. Wolfe, *Secular Music in America 1801–1825: A Bibliography*, 3 vols. (New York: New York Public Library, 1964), a source providing details that help identify the original exemplars, often published in Philadelphia or Baltimore, that the Moravian copyists used.

The information in this section is drawn primarily from my dissertation, "Reflections on Moravian Music: A Study of Two Collections of Manuscript Books in Pennsylvania ca. 1800" (New York University, 1997). For continuing details concerning the Bethlehem Seminary, see Smith, "Music, Women, and Pianos," which focuses on the subsequent decades of the mid-1800s. Some research into music materials at Salem has also been done recently by Lou Carol Fix of Moravian College.

24. Crews, *Johann Friedrich Peter*, 7. See appendix 1, p. 280, for Peter's biography.

25. At Salem in 1789 Peter composed his only known nonliturgical work—the set of six string quintets thought to be the earliest chamber music composed in America (see chapter 7, pp. 200–201). See also chapter 2, p. 39, for a description of Peter's responsibilities during his service in Salem, as well as a glimpse at his personal life and faith.

26. Jeannine Ingram, "A Musical Potpourri: The Commonplace Book of Johann Friedrich Peter," *Moravian Music Foundation Bulletin* 24/1 (Spring–Summer 1979): 2.

27. It also appears that a line can be traced from Peter's pupils Johann Christian Till and Peter Wolle through their student Theodore F. Wolle to John Frederick Wolle, the founder of the present-day Bach Choir of Bethlehem. See Albert G. Rau, "John Frederick Peter," *The Musical Quarterly* 23 (1937): 313.

28. Hall's sister Ida Cecelia (1815–84) studied at both Linden Hall and the Bethlehem Seminary, then began a forty-year career of teaching at Linden Hall.

29. S. C. Albright, *The Story of the Moravian Congregation at York, Pennsylvania* (York: Maples Press, [1927]), 66–67.

30. Henry, 185.

31. It seems that very few examples of early primers are extant, perhaps because such materials were passed along to newer beginners until no longer in usable condition, whereas intermediate or more advanced repertoire was preserved in more protective binding for future use. Of the examples cited in this study, BMB 6 includes pieces from G. Willig's *Juvenile Instructor* [ca. 1835] and C. Meineke's *A New Instruction for the Piano Forte Containing the Rudiments of Music explained in a concise manner, and a Sett of Lessons Calculated to establish the True Method of Fingering And afford an agreeable Study for Pupils*, 2nd ed. (Philadelphia: Willig, 1823). For information concerning primers and the teaching of music theory in the mid-1800s, see Smith, chapter 4.

32. *The Orphean Lyre* (Boston: S. H. Parker, [1816]), vol. 1; *Twelve Little Ballads and a Favorite Lesson* (Philadelphia: G. E. Blake, 1810–14), book 2; *The Musical Journal for the Piano Forte* (Philadelphia: B. Carr, 1803–4), vols. 3 and 5; William M'Culloch, *Selected Music* (Philadelphia: N.p., 1807).

33. LaTrobe, *Letters*, 27.

34. Karl Kroeger, "The Moravian Tradition in Song," *Moravian Music Foundation Bulletin* 20/2 (Fall–Winter 1975): 9.

Chapter Nine

The Piano among the Moravians in the Eighteenth and Nineteenth Centuries

Music, Instruction, and Construction

Jewel A. Smith

One of the first instruments transported to the New World by the Moravians was a spinet, which arrived on January 25, 1744. The instrument suffered considerable damage during the voyage, but was quickly repaired and used in the following day's service.[1] The Moravian scholar William Reichel documents that in 1792 the Moravian Young Ladies' Seminary in Bethlehem, Pennsylvania, owned seven pianos and clavichords, and in 1805 an invoice for tuning harpsichords suggests that it might have owned at least as many of these instruments.[2] In Maximilian Wied's diary, which chronicles his travels in North America from 1832 through 1834, he recalls visiting the Moravian Young Ladies' Seminary in Bethlehem and seeing ten rooms, each with a piano.[3] It appears that this instrument was popular at the Seminary, which by 1866 owned nearly forty pianos.[4]

I am grateful to Tim Hamilton, piano restorer, Boston, Massachusetts; Richard Hester, fortepiano builder and restorer, Coeymans Hollow, New York; Jack Krefting, piano proprietor and restorer, Krefting Pianos, Ludlow, Kentucky; Laurence Libin, research curator, the Metropolitan Museum of Art, New York, New York; John Koster, conservator and professor of Museum Science at the Shrine to Music Museum (National Music Museum), Vermillion, South Dakota; and Eric Wolfley, head piano technician, University of Cincinnati, for answering technical questions regarding nineteenth-century American square pianos.

Although Moravians have a long history of composing and making music, by and large they did not devote their creative efforts to composing music for stringed keyboard instruments. Given the limited number of keyboard compositions written by a small group of composers, we might conclude that the harpsichord, clavichord, and piano were not among the instruments favored by the Moravians. On the contrary, the Moravians placed considerable emphasis on teaching and learning to play, on building instruments of quality, and (to a lesser extent) composing music for keyboard instruments.

Moravian Composers of Piano Music

Although Moravians played spinets, harpsichords, and clavichords, their known stringed keyboard compositions are limited to music for the piano. Johann Gottfried Gebhard (1755–after 1799), John Gambold, Jr. (1760–95), and Christian Ignatius LaTrobe (1758–1836), living in the late eighteenth and early nineteenth centuries, composed sonatas for the piano. Even though their primary life's work and commitment was to the church as ministers and/or educators, their sonatas reveal their unusual compositional skill. Although Gebhard, Gambold, and LaTrobe received their training in Germany, their piano sonatas exhibit some style characteristics unlike those of other classical-era composers.

Johann Gottfried Gebhard's three-movement Sonata in C Minor[5] shows stylistic traits of the *empfindsamer Stil*, including broken chords in the right and left hands, improvisatory style, and melodic and harmonic chromaticism. The first movement (Allegro) is in sonata form and includes a dramatic transition to the relative major key, as shown in example 9.1.

The development section begins with a lyrical melody and Alberti bass accompaniment, not appearing earlier in the movement, and leads to a false recapitulation in the minor dominant before finally returning to the tonic for an abbreviated recapitulation. The entire movement is full of drama and intensity, only briefly relieved in the lyrical beginning of the development.

The second movement, an Adagio in the relative major key, is in a binary form with less complex harmonic structure than the first movement. This lyrical movement is rhythmically complex, with duple-against-triple cross-rhythms and frequent written-out ornaments to the *cantabile* melody, as shown in example 9.2.

The third movement, a Presto in sonata form, shows the same harmonic daring as the first movement, especially in the retransition to the recapitulation, with sequential brief tonicizations of C-sharp minor, E major, G major, and B-flat major (see ex. 9.3).

The development is also marked by broken chords in both hands reminiscent of the figuration in the first movement. This entire sonata shows a mastery of classical form and keyboard facility, along with harmonic and motivic patterns of the *empfindsamer Stil*.

Example 9.1. Johann Gottfried Gebhard, Sonata in C Minor, 1st mvt., Allegro, mm. 26–36.

Example 9.2. Gebhard, Sonata in C Minor, 2nd mvt., Adagio, mm. 72–80.

John Gambold's *Sechs kleine Klavier-Sonaten*, dedicated to Lady Schönberg, share some characteristics of the mature classical style.[6] Most of the movements of Gambold's sonatas have a straightforward melody and accompaniment. Other common classical-period techniques include broken chords, Alberti bass, and repeated notes in the accompaniment; sighing figures; embellished

Example 9.3. Gebhard, Sonata in C Minor, 3rd mvt., Presto, mm. 116–24.

melodic lines; and scale figurations. According to Ewald Nolte, who prepared an edition of Sonata IV in C minor and Sonata III in F major, the use of the signs *sf* and *dimin.* suggest that Gambold intended these works for the pianoforte rather than the harpsichord.[7]

The first movement of Sonata III (three movements: Allegro; Andante; Presto) is in the classical style, with periodic phrase structure and melody in the right hand, supported by a repetitive accompaniment of thirds, fifths, and octaves in the left hand, and finally an Alberti bass (see ex. 9.4).

Example 9.4. John Gambold, Jr., Sonata III, 1st mvt., Allegro, mm. 1–8.

The second movement of Gambold's Sonata II in G major (three movements: Allegro con spirito; Larghetto; Presto) has a long, ornamented melody and incorporates sighing figures characteristic of the *empfindsamer Stil* (see ex. 9.5).

Example 9.5. John Gambold, Jr., Sonata II, 2nd mvt., Larghetto, mm. 1–10.

Gambold's structure of movements shows some variation from the classical norm. It is not unusual for all the movements in his sonatas to be in the same key. Several movements are considerably shorter (often only one page) than those in the high classical style and are in ABA′ form rather than sonata form. Finally, in three of Gambold's six sonatas, the first movement is a slow movement—a Largo or Adagio.

Christian Ignatius LaTrobe's three piano sonatas are representative of the High Classical style.[8] Since LaTrobe was a friend of Franz Joseph Haydn and dedicated his three sonatas to him, it is not surprising to find similarities between their works. The variation in the number of movements in LaTrobe's three sonatas (four, three, and two movements, respectively), is also evident in Haydn's works. Haydn often used monothematic sonata form, as LaTrobe does in the first movement of Sonata I. In the piano sonatas, LaTrobe's writing, like that of Haydn, is based on motivic development rather than the use of long, melodic themes. For example, the first movement of LaTrobe's first sonata opens with a rhythmic motive of dotted eighth, sixteenth, and quarter notes. LaTrobe repeatedly brings this motive back, including in the left hand crossing over the right hand (see ex. 9.6).

Example 9.6. Christian Ignatius LaTrobe, Sonata I, op. 3, 1st mvt., Allegro. (a) mm. 1–2; (b) mm. 35–37.

Both LaTrobe and Haydn use the fermata to delineate sections, Alberti bass and broken octaves in the accompaniment, treble and bass in octaves, and modal mixture. Haydn often varies the texture by having both hands play in octaves, which LaTrobe also does occasionally. Haydn creates interest by moving between the major and minor mode, frequently several times within the same movement. LaTrobe begins the first movement of Sonata III with an Adagio molto introduction in B-flat minor. This section closes with a fermata and is followed by an Andante pastorale in B-flat major (see ex. 9.7).

Example 9.7. Christian Ignatius LaTrobe, Sonata III, op. 3, 1st mvt., Adagio molto—Andante pastorale, mm. 17–27.

The sonatas by these three Moravians are idiomatic for the eighteenth-century fortepiano. The range extends from four and one-half octaves in Gambold's sonatas (BB-flat to f^3) to five octaves in Gebhard's and LaTrobe's sonatas (FF to f^3). In addition, the dynamic indications are those commonly used for eighteenth-century instruments (e.g., *pp, p, f, mf, ff, sf*).

Piano works of the nineteenth-century Moravian composers (even those who lived into the twentieth century) are generally characteristic of the romantic period. Moravian composers such as Francis Florentine Hagen (1815–1907), Ernst Immanuel Erbe (1854–1927), Carl Anton Van Vleck (1794–1845) and his daughters Lisette Van Vleck Meinung (1830–1914) and Amelia Adelaide Van Vleck (1835–1929) typically composed in smaller forms, such as waltzes, rondos, polkas, marches, transcriptions, and variations.[9] Like their predecessors in the eighteenth century, these composers were familiar with the works of their European counterparts and trends in musical composition.

Carl Anton Van Vleck's Rondo is more accurately described as being in ternary form, with an eight-measure repeated A section in F major, a B section based on similar thematic material and moving from the relative minor to the dominant, and an A′ section with coda. The engaging theme is shown in example 9.8.

Example 9.8. Carl Anton Van Vleck, Rondo (Salem Manuscript Book 80.14), mm. 1–8.

Francis Florentine Hagen's *Remembrance Rondoletto* is a more expansive work, suitable for the intermediate player. This work is in seven-part rondo form (ABA'CA″B'A‴ and coda), with both B sections being quite short and the C section rather long. The theme, shown in example 9.9a, is varied in its third iteration by crossing the hands, as in example 9.9b.

Example 9.9. Francis Florentine Hagen, *Remembrance Rondoletto* (Salem Manuscript Book 21.4), (a) mm. 1–16 and (b) mm. 75–82.

Hagen's *Scherzo Capriccioso* was dedicated to Carl Anton Van Vleck. The scherzo section is marked by homophonic texture and a lilting rhythm (see ex. 9.10a) and the contrasting trio by extended scale passages alternating between the two hands (see ex. 9.10b).

Example 9.10. Francis Florentine Hagen, *Scherzo Capriccioso,* (a) mm. 1–8 and (b) mm. 81–88.

Some of Hagen's most interesting piano writing is found not in his own fully independent compositions, but rather in his transcriptions and arrangements of sacred melodies, including *Am I a Soldier of the Cross, I'm a Pilgrim,* and *There'll Be No Sorrow There,* published by W. F. Shaw in 1882. Although we might classify each of these pieces as a paraphrase or a set of variations, the word *transcription* is part of the title (e.g., *Transcription for the Piano of the Beautiful Sacred Melody I'm a Pilgrim*). *Am I a Soldier of the Cross* displays Hagen's employment of classical traits in a nineteenth-century composition, for example, his use of the broken chord accompaniment (see ex. 9.11).

After an eight-measure introduction, Hagen varies the hymn tune three times. He includes five measures of the introduction between the second and third verses, followed by a *cadenza ad lib.* These piano works were probably intended for home use; many of his other transcriptions were published in the *Church and Home Organists' Companion.*[10] Given that the Moravians themselves composed many hymns and anthems for the church, it might be surprising that Hagen made transcriptions of hymns not by Moravians; however, these hymns were well known in America at the time, and Hagen was an advocate of using popular music for worship rather than German chorales.[11]

Ernst Immanuel Erbe's piano compositions are the most extensive of any Moravian composer prior to the end of the twentieth century. In his character piece *Der Bach,* op. 11, his explicit instructions regarding the tempo (*Allegretto* [*Nicht zu rasch*]), the rhythmic interest in the melody line, and the running sixteenth and eighth notes in the bass suggest a rippling stream (see ex. 9.12).

Erbe's *Humoreske,* op. 18, no. 3, conveys a fanciful character. Written in F major and 2/4 meter, it is based on a short motive consisting of two sixteenths

Example 9.11. Francis Florentine Hagen, *Am I a Soldier of the Cross*, mm. 17–30.

Example 9.12. Ernst Immanuel Erbe, *Der Bach*, op. 11, mm. 1–11.

and three staccato eighth notes that immediately imply a playful character (see ex. 9.13). The eight-measure melody that opens the *Humoreske* returns periodically to give the piece continuity. Erbe's ingenuity in combining harmonic variety with this rhythmic motive creates a charming work.

Example 9.13. Ernst Immanuel Erbe, *Humoreske*, op. 18, no. 3, mm. 1–26.

Erbe's sonata for piano, op. 14, is one of his more complex works in any genre. Whereas Gambold's sonatas reflect some characteristics of Mozart's writing and LaTrobe's of Haydn's, Erbe's sonata suggests his familiarity with Beethoven's style. The first movement opens with a forceful motive, followed by a driving, repeated eighth-note chord accompaniment with a fast harmonic rhythm (see ex. 9.14). A similar intensity also appears in the second and fourth movements, but the Menuett and Trio reflects a lighter character and is the easiest to play.[12]

Some of Erbe's compositions, such as his five etudes, were teaching pieces. Although all of these are relatively short, they present challenges. The first one focuses on several technical difficulties: repeated thirds, trills (written out), balance between the hands, and playing two parts in the same hand. Unlike the first, the second etude contains various expression marks, for example, *dolce* and *cresc.* This etude was intended to teach balance between melody and accompaniment, along with smooth figuration in the right hand.

Erbe also composed two marches for piano duet and an untitled movement for duo piano.[13] The marches are straightforward, each with a trio in the subdominant. The duo piano parts are of equal difficulty and require the skills

Example 9.14. Ernst Immanuel Erbe, Sonata, op. 14, mm. 1–19.

of advanced players. Figurations, repeated notes, and passages of thirds performed *allegro* make these works technically demanding.

Although the Moravians offered men and women an equal education, there are few known compositions by Moravian women until at least the middle of the nineteenth century. Amelia Adelaide Van Vleck (known as "Miss Amy") and her sister Lisette Van Vleck Meinung displayed compositional ability and accomplishment. Several of "Miss Amy"s waltzes and marches were published during her lifetime. *Irma Waltz*, published by Louis H. Ross & Co. in 1897, is a delightful piece. The composer adds variety in the left hand with grace notes, leaps of an octave or more, and clef changes, rather than the typical waltz-bass accompaniment. The waltz is to be performed at a *molto vivace* tempo (see ex. 9.15). A codetta brings the work to a dramatic close with sixteenth-note arpeggios played in unison, followed by full chords covering the range of the keyboard.

Hatch Music Company in Philadelphia published Amy Van Vleck's *Centennial March*, probably in the mid-1870s. It is suitable for concert performance.

Example 9.15. Amelia Van Vleck, *Irma Waltz*, mm. 147–70.

Although she dedicated it to the "Faculty and Pupils of the Salem F. Academy and College, N.C.," it may have been intended to commemorate the one-hundredth anniversary of the founding of the Salem Congregation (1771).[14] There is no tempo marking; however, the composer did include various accents, dynamics, and *ritardandos* to produce a stately march.

Lisette Van Vleck Meinung was equally gifted as a composer in the smaller forms. Through her piano study and performance in Musical Entertainment Programs at the Moravian Young Ladies' Seminary in Bethlehem, she would have been exposed to a variety of nineteenth-century piano literature, including the popular dance forms such as the waltz, polka, mazurka, and galop.[15] Her *Nettie Galop*, published in 1868 by S. Brainard & Son in Cleveland, begins with a five-measure introduction. This piece spans the entire range of the keyboard and abounds with sixteenth-note octaves and chords (see ex. 9.16).

Meinung's manuscript *Mollie March* opens with a four-measure introduction. The dotted eighth and sixteenth notes in the right hand, accompanied by steady quarter and eighth notes in the left hand, create a march style. This march includes a contrasting trio (not labeled as such) in the subdominant.

Arrangements of some of the sisters' piano compositions—such as Van Vleck's *Carolina March* and *Serenade Waltz*, and Meinung's *Military Parade March* (arranged from the *Mollie March* mentioned above)—were included in the band books of the Twenty-Sixth North Carolina Regimental Band. These arrangements were for brass instruments and drum.[16]

Example 9.16. Lisette M. Van Vleck, *Nettie Galop*, mm. 53–62.

The piano repertoire by Moravian composers attests to their creative ability and knowledge of contemporary European composers and compositional style. During the eighteenth and nineteenth centuries, more piano music by Moravians was published than any other type of music by Moravians.[17]

Piano Music at the Moravian Young Ladies' Seminary: A Case Study in Moravian Instruction

Music study was the most popular "ornamental branch" of instruction offered during the nineteenth century at the Young Ladies' Seminary in Bethlehem, Pennsylvania. In addition to singing, playing the piano was the foremost musical art regularly taught at the Seminary, and parents and guardians regarded it as one of the few public accomplishments appropriate for young women. Founded in 1742, the Seminary is believed to be the oldest girls' school of importance in the New World and probably the second church-related boarding school for girls to be established in what became the United States.[18] In 1785 it began accepting applications from non-Moravian students and was often filled to capacity with a waiting list. This institution is an excellent example for an investigation of music studied and performed by non-Moravians within a larger Moravian setting. However, it was not the sole Moravian school where music was emphasized—other Moravian schools offered comparable musical educations and could boast of similar musical performances.[19]

    The inventory records, invoices, and programs from the Bethlehem Seminary testify that its teachers and students kept abreast of the latest compositions published in Europe and America. Piano students learned to play music written by contemporary composers and performed on concert stages by artists such as Henri Herz, Sigismond Thalberg, Clara Wieck, and Franz Liszt. Their repertoire included compositions by nearly one hundred fifty composers, such as Beethoven, Chopin, Haydn, Mozart, and those listed above. Composers named in invoices, expense journals, inventory lists, and programs represent a variety of nationalities, mostly European. The majority were of German, French, Bohemian, and Austrian descent, with the largest number being from Germany.[20] Other nationalities represented include Dutch, Polish, Irish, Italian, Czech, Belgian, British, and Hungarian, as well as a few Americans, such as Louis Moreau Gottschalk and Charles Grobe.

The students' repertoire encompassed various types of solo and ensemble music. Contemporary nineteenth-century piano literature was the principal repertoire, including sets of variations, dances, transcriptions, marches, rondos, fantasies, etudes, and character pieces (for example, capriccios, polonaises, nocturnes, and impromptus), in addition to sonatinas, sonatas, and battle pieces.[21] Pieces from the classical era were less well represented, and apparently no compositions from the baroque era were among their studies.

Although solo literature made up the majority of works studied and performed at the Seminary, programs frequently included chamber pieces such as duets on one or two pianos, music for six hands, and music for piano with other instruments (guitar, flute, violin, or cello). Occasionally, students performed concertos with an orchestra consisting of citizens of Bethlehem. Of the ensemble music, piano duets were the most popular, including arrangements of operatic airs, songs, incidental music, overtures, string chamber works, and symphonies.[22] As with the solo repertoire, the wide range of ensemble literature purchased and performed illustrates the Seminary's concern for staying current with contemporary compositions. A review of the Musical Entertainment Program held on December 17, 1863, printed in the weekly journal, *The Moravian*, confirms the high quality of chamber music performances:

> We especially admired two grand trios for the piano-forte, violin, and violoncello, the first an Andante from Marschner, in which Miss Ziegler performed the leading part and the other entitled "Molto Allegro Agitato," by Mendelssohn, in which Miss Ziegler played the piano, Prof. Agthe and Prof. Black taking the violin parts. But all the music was excellent. The pupils of Professors Hering and Agthe and of Madame Dressler had been evidently carefully trained.[23]

Moravian Builders of Stringed Keyboard Instruments

As builders of stringed keyboard instruments, Moravians are mostly known for building pianos from the mid-nineteenth century forward. There is, however, indication of some such activity by at least two earlier Moravian musicians well known today. John Antes (1740–1811) described himself in a letter to Benjamin Franklin as "a young Man wich [*sic*] in the year 1763 amused himself with making Musicall Instruments such as harpsichords, violins etc."[24] David Tannenberg has long been regarded as an organ builder, but he also built stringed keyboard instruments. In fact, in 1762 he lodged a complaint with the congregation elders in Bethlehem that Antes's work as an instrument builder might infringe on his own trade. The Elders Conference responded by instructing Antes to build stringed instruments, not keyboards, from that time on.[25]

Although it has been assumed that Tannenberg built a harpsichord, the instrument is not known to exist.[26] In addition, the assumption that he built virginals cannot be documented. However, a clavichord, dating from 1761 and known as his oldest instrument, came to light only as late as 2004.[27] Tradition has held that this clavichord, a gift of William Peter Knowlton (a Moravian fan maker in London), was the first keyboard instrument to arrive in Bethlehem in 1743. This date, however, appears to be incorrect. A label reading "*David Tanneberger/Im Junii 1761 bey Bethlehem*" is glued inside the soundboard box. The clavichord's range is C to d³, a span of twenty-nine notes.

In 1789 Jeremy Elrod brought a "*clavicembalo*" to Salem. Tannenberg built this instrument for the Single Sisters' use, but it is not clear whether it was a spinet or a harpsichord.[28] Tannenberg is also credited with building two pianos: the first one sometime between 1795 and 1799 for a Brother Lembke, and the other between 1799 and 1804 for the *Kinderhaus* (now Linden Hall) in Lititz, Pennsylvania.[29]

The success of piano manufacturing firms in Bethlehem, as well as numerous advertisements in *The Moravian* for pianos built by other manufacturers in the surrounding areas (including Wilhelm & Schuler in Philadelphia and Grovesteen & Co. in New York), testify to the piano's popularity among Moravians in the middle of the nineteenth century.[30] John Christian Till and his son, Jacob, and John Christian Malthaner were successful in the piano business, operating as self-employed craftsmen in Bethlehem. The Tills received contracts for pianos for the parlors of the Sun and Eagle hotels in Bethlehem, where Moravians entertained dignitaries.[31] Only two known Till pianos survive. Both are wood-frame instruments in rectangular cases with 1.5-inch-thick bottoms and no metal parts. Since Jacob's name is on the nameplates of the pianos, it seems likely that he constructed the mechanism, whereas John built the cabinets. The Moravian Museum of Bethlehem houses a Till piano built in 1825 (see fig. 9.1).[32] This piano design resembles that of the early nineteenth-century English piano that was widely imitated by major piano manufactures in New York and Boston.

The compass is FF to c⁴ (sixty-eight notes), and the action is the English double or "grasshopper" type that John Geib patented in 1786.[33] It is double strung, as was common at that time, and straight strung.[34] The dampers follow the English form, that is, over the hammers. However, the instrument has some

Figure 9.1. Jacob Till piano, ca. 1825. Photo by the author.

characteristics that resemble those of German or Austrian pianos of the period, such as a lyre that holds the two pedals and a moderator that can be brought between hammers and strings. The piano's case and four legs are of pine with a mahogany veneer.[35] The horizontal panel of bird's-eye maple over the keyboard provides decoration. The hefty turned legs and the lyre are in the Sheraton style, as crafted by famous New York cabinetmakers of the early 1800s (for example, Duncan Phyfe).[36] The case measures 67 inches (170.1 cm) by 26½ inches (67.3 cm) by 22½ inches (56.1 cm).

The Moravian College in Bethlehem owns the other extant Till piano, from about 1830 (see fig. 9.2).[37] Additional keys in the treble, which expand the compass from FF to f⁴ (seventy-three notes), and the rounded corners of the case also suggest a later date than the 1825 Till piano.

The circa 1830 piano is constructed in much the same manner as the earlier instrument: English double action, double stringing, and straight stringing with overdampers. The legs and pedals are missing; however, the lyre and the mechanism survive. The Tills constructed the case of pine and employed oak and/or maple on the top one-third of the pin block. They used mahogany cross-banded with rosewood for decorative trim, such as that surrounding the keyboard.[38] The case dimensions are 69 inches (175.2 cm) by 26½ inches (67.3 cm) by (without legs) 10¼ inches (26 cm).

Figure 9.2. Jacob Till piano, ca. 1830. Photo by the author.

The cost of a Till piano varied depending on the materials used, fluctuations of the economy, and type of instrument. In August 1818 the Young Ladies' Seminary in Bethlehem purchased a Till piano for $200, which was well within the average range of piano prices at that time. This instrument was a new piano, since it carried a one-year warranty.[39]

John Christian Malthaner's pianos were more in the mainstream than those of the Tills. The Moravian Museum of Bethlehem houses a Malthaner piano built in 1838 (see fig. 9.3).[40]

The number 12 is written on the inside, possibly indicating that this was the twelfth piano Malthaner produced. The compass is FF to f⁴ (seventy-three notes). The ¾ plate constructed of cast iron and the large heavy case represent a level of technology that went beyond that represented by the Tills' pianos (see fig. 9.4).[41]

The partial cast-iron plate could accommodate the increased tension of slightly larger-diameter wire and produced increased acoustical resonance. The action is of the English double type; the materials and placement of the hammers, strings, and dampers, and the number of pedals are standard for an 1830s American square piano. The inner and outer layers of the hammers are buckskin and possibly calfskin, respectively. Unlike later instruments that used overstringing, this piano is straight strung. The use of double-strung iron strings with soft-iron-wrapped

Figure 9.3. John C. Malthaner piano, 1838. Photo by the author.

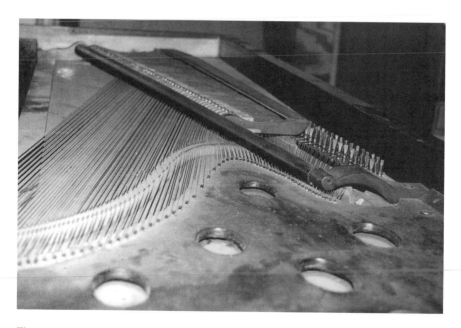

Figure 9.4. Cast-iron plate, John C. Malthaner piano, 1838. Photo by the author.

Figure 9.5. John C. Malthaner piano, ca. 1848. Photo by the author.

cores in the bass helped to produce a round, bell-like sound. Usually square pianos of this period have two pedals, but the *una corda* pedal has been lost.[42] The lid is made of solid mahogany, and the sides of the case are veneered with crotch-figured mahogany over pine and oak. This piano is in the late Sheraton style typical of the 1830s with heavy, squatly turned legs.[43] The case measures 69 inches (175.2 cm) by 28 inches (71.1 cm) by 22⅝ inches (56.2 cm).

Another Malthaner piano is currently on display at the Goundie House in Bethlehem (see fig. 9.5).[44] The number 62 is written on the soundboard, indicating a much later piano—possibly by ten years, since it is estimated that Malthaner was building three to five pianos a year.[45] The case design also suggests a later date. The legs are no longer rounded; rather, on either side of the case above each front leg is an indentation with a pointed arch, a trademark of the neo-Gothic style.[46] Finally, the massive block at the front edge of the sound-board also implies a date later than that of the 1838 piano. The size of the legs and the changes in furniture styles reflect the weight of the piano, since those with cast-iron frames weighed considerably more than those with wooden frames. Although enormous legs provided more support for the heavier pianos, this was also the style of American parlor furniture of the same era.

A comparison of the 1838 instrument with this later one reveals many similarities. They have the same compass and partial cast-iron plates, are double and straight strung, and possess overdampers and two pedals. Significant changes from the earlier piano include an action modeled on the Petzold type and the larger, thicker hammers, which are graduated in size.[47] The top treble octave hammers have four layers, two hard and two soft; the next three descending are constructed with six layers, four soft and two hard; and the rest of the hammers have five layers, four soft and one hard.[48] The case measurements of the later piano are 71.25 inches (180.9 cm) by 34.25 inches (86.9 cm) by height 35 inches (88.9 cm).

Malthaner pianos were capable of producing a pleasing tone and were highly prized. In May 1862 Peter Wolle, a bishop, executive official, and musician in the Moravian Church, wrote in his diary that he had played his son James's new Malthaner piano and found it to have a remarkably sweet tone.[49] In 1866 James Wolle purchased another piano for $500. His father described it as a first-rate instrument.[50] Malthaner kept pace with current advancements in piano building. By 1865 his overstrung, seven-octave pianos carried five-year warranties. Francis Wolle, principal of the Seminary from 1861 to 1881, gave the following testimonial, which Malthaner reprinted for advertising copy:

> This certifies that we have in use in the Moravian Seminary for Young Ladies, at Bethlehem, Pa., upward of twenty pianos from the manufactory of Mr. John C. Malthaner of our place, and nearly as many more from other noted establishments. That we find his pianos equal to the best of others in point of finish and excellency of tone. For service and durability we find NONE EQUAL to those of Mr. Malthaner's.[51]

Conclusions

As with the music of the *collegium musicum*, the Moravians studied and appreciated music for piano from a wide variety of sources and in various genres. Secular repertoire by popular composers beyond Moravian circles, including transcribed string quartets and symphonic music, became part of their standard literature. Given the importance of music to the Moravians, it is not surprising that piano instruction and performance were a vital part of the curriculum and lifestyle at Moravian schools, such as the Young Ladies' Seminary in Bethlehem.

That the Tills and Malthaner were able to establish successful piano manufacturing businesses in Bethlehem, at a time when only Moravians lived in the community, is additional evidence of the importance of the piano to the Moravians. Further, the Young Ladies' Seminary continually upgraded its instruments and consistently purchased Till and Malthaner pianos. Although Moravians were not professional musicians, being engaged in other vocations, these amateurs left their industrial labors at the close of the day to fill their evening hours with music making. The value that Moravians placed on musical performance, composing piano music, and successful piano-manufacturing businesses testifies to the importance of the piano in their lives.

Notes

1. Joseph Mortimer Levering. *A History of Bethlehem, Pennsylvania: 1741–1842 with Some Account of Its Founders and Their Early Activity in America* (Bethlehem: Times Publishing Co., 1903), 171.
2. William C. Reichel, *Bethlehem Seminary Souvenir: A History of the Rise, Progress, and Present Condition of the Moravian Seminary for Young Ladies, at Bethlehem, Pennsylvania, with a Catalogue of its Pupils 1785–1858*, 4th ed., rev. and enl. by William H. Bigler (Philadelphia: J. B. Lippincott & Co., 1901), 141; folder FemSem187.4, Moravian Archives, Bethlehem. The invoice for tuning harpsichords, dated September 30, 1805, lists seven tunings by John Frederick Peter from June 17 to 24 and July 30 to August 9.
3. Maximilian Wied, *Travels in the Interior of North America*, trans. H. Evans Lloyd (London: Ackerman & Co., ca. 1843), 99.
4. Francis Wolle, the principal of the Seminary from 1861 to 1881, gave a testimonial in the *Moravian* applauding the Moravian builder John C. Malthaner's pianos and spoke of the Seminary's owning nearly forty pianos. *The Moravian* (Bethlehem), February 1, 1866 (testimonial dated November 6, 1865).
5. Johann Gottfried Gebhard, *Eine Sonate für das Klavier* (Barby: For the composer, 1784); Moravian Music Foundation, Winston-Salem.
6. John Gambold, *Sechs kleine Klavier-Sonaten* (Leipzig: For the author, 1788), ed. James Boeringer, *Six Little Keyboard Sonatas Dedicated to Lady Schönberg by John Gambold, Schoolteacher and Organist at Niesky* (Winston-Salem: Moravian Music Foundation, n.d.).
7. Boeringer, ed., *Six Little Keyboard Sonatas*, preface, 6.
8. Christian Ignatius LaTrobe, *Three Sonatas for the Pianoforte, Composed & Dedicated, by Permission, to Mr. Haydn, Op. III* (London: J. Bland, for the Author), ed. Charles E. Stevens (New York: Boosey & Hawkes, 1970).
9. See appendix 1 for biographical sketches of these composers.
10. *Church and Home Organists Companion*, vols. I (1880) and II (1881), ed. and arr. by Francis Florentine Hagen (Philadelphia: Fred Williams).
11. See especially Francis Florentine Hagen, *Unitas Fratrum in Extremis; or, thoughts on the past and present condition of the Moravian Church in America, Respectfully Submitted to the Provincial Synod of 1893 at Bethlehem, Pennsylvania* (Bethlehem: Moravian Publication Office, 1893), 10–11. See chapter 3, p. 73.
12. Erbe also transcribed this sonata for string quartet.
13. One of these marches (catalogued as "Erbe 32 a" in the "Ernst Immanuel Erbe Collection" at the Moravian Music Foundation) also exists in a version for solo piano.
14. Although Salem Academy and College now considers 1772 its founding date, there is no evidence that such was the thinking in 1872. The centennial of the school was celebrated in 1902, one hundred years after the calling of the Girls Boarding School's first head. See C. Daniel Crews and Richard W. Starbuck, *With Courage for the Future: The Story of the Moravian Church, Southern Province* (Winston-Salem: Moravian Church in America, Southern Province, 2002), 467.

15. For example, for the Musical Entertainment program dated November 9, 1840, Lisette performed a "Duetto on the Piano" with Agnes Kummer. Folder, "Musical Entertainments and Public Examinations 1838–1846," box, "Musical Entertainment," Moravian Archives, Bethlehem.

16. For example, the bandmaster William Henry Hartwell arranged *Military Parade March* for E-flat cornet 1, 2; E-flat alto 1, 2; B-flat tenor 1, 2; B-flat baritone; E-flat bass; and drum. Hartwell, assigned to the 16th Mississippi Volunteer Infantry Regimental Band, was possibly the best known of all the Confederate bandmasters. Members of the 26th North Carolina band described Hartwell's band as the finest one in the Confederate army. He gave band members some lessons in 1863. See Harry H. Hall, *A Johnny Reb Band from Salem*, rev. ed. (Raleigh: Office of Archives and History, North Carolina Department of Cultural Resources, 2006), 112, 129, 146, 184–85.

17. See chapter 10.

18. The first such institution was founded in 1727 by Ursuline nuns in New Orleans. See James Mulhern, *A History of Secondary Education in Pennsylvania* (Philadelphia: Printed for the author, 1933), 15; cited in Jewel A. Smith, "Music, Women, and Pianos: The Moravian Young Ladies' Seminary in Antebellum Bethlehem, Pennsylvania (1815–1860)" (PhD diss., University of Cincinnati, 2003), 67.

19. See chapter 8 for a more comprehensive overview of Moravian musical education.

20. Well-known German composers are included within the text. Lesser-known German and Swiss composers include Jacob Blumenthal, Christian Brunner, Karl Curschman, Johann Gottfried Eckard, Heinrich Esser, Adolf Henselt, Diederich Krug, Theodor Kullack, Charles Lysberg, Charles Mayer, August Eberhard Müller, Johann Peter Pixis, Karl Gottlieb Reissiger, Jacob Rosenhain, Joseph Schad, Fritz Spindler, Daniel Steibelt, the German-born American publisher George Willig, and Hermann Adolf Wollenhaupt. French composers include Alexander Croisez, Charles Delioux, Henri-Louis-Charles Duvernoy, Eugène Ketterer, Louis James Léfebure-Wély, Emile Prudent, and Henri Rosellen. Bohemian, Hungarian, and Austrian composers include Théodor Döhler, Alexander Dreyschock, Stephen Heller, Franz Kotzwara, Leopold Kozeluch, Joseph Labitzky, Ignaz Jospeh Pleyel, Julius Schulhoff, Ludwig Stasny, Maurice Strakosch, Ignaz Amadeus Tedesco, Sigismond Thalberg, Johann Baptist Vanhall, and Joseph Wölfl.

21. For a detailed discussion of the repertoire studied and performed at the Seminary, see chapters 6 and 7 of Smith, "Music, Women, and Pianos."

22. For more information on arrangements for piano duets, see Thomas Christianson, "Four-Hand Piano Transcription and Geographies of Nineteenth-Century Musical Reception," *Journal of the American Musicological Society* 52/2 (1999): 255–98.

23. "Bethlehem Female Seminary," *Moravian* (Bethlehem), December 24, 1863.

24. Quoted in K Marie Stolba, "From John Antes to Benjamin Franklin—A Musical Connection," *Moravian Music Foundation Bulletin* 25/2 (Fall–Winter 1980): 5.

25. C. Daniel Crews, *John Antes* (Winston-Salem, Moravian Music Foundation, 1997), 3. See also Richard D. Claypool, "Mr. John Antes: Instrumentmaker," *Moravian Music Foundation Bulletin* 23/2 (Fall–Winter 1978): 10–13.

26. Edward L. Kottick, *A History of the Harpsichord* (Bloomington: Indiana University Press, 2003), 384; Donald H. Boalch, *Makers of the Harpsichord and Clavichord 1440–1840*, 3rd ed., ed. Charles Mould (Oxford: Clarendon Press, 1995), 650.

27. I am grateful to Laurence Libin for information concerning the stringed keyboard instruments of David Tannenberg (e-mail to author, April 4, 2005). More information about this clavichord is in Libin's forthcoming article "New Insights to Tannenberg's Clavichords." The clavichord (accession number 760) is housed in the Moravian Historical Society, Nazareth.

28. Adelaide L. Fries, *Records of the Moravians in North Carolina* (Raleigh: State Department of Archives and History, 1922), 5:2268.

29. W. U. Hensel, "A Famous Organ Builder," Historical Papers and Addresses of the Lancaster County Historical Society 11 (1907), 352; William H. Armstrong, *Organs for America: The Life and Work of David Tannenberg* (Philadelphia: University of Pennsylvania Press, 1967), 113, 133, n.115.

30. Advertisements for Wilhelm & Schuler and Grovesteen & Co., *Moravian* (Bethlehem), January 8, 1858, and October 6, 1864.

31. Levering, 716.

32. Photograph by author. Both Hamilton and Koster agree that this piano was built in 1825.

33. See chapter 3 ("The Pianos at the Young Ladies' Seminary: Documenting the Development of the American Square Piano") of Smith, "Music, Women, and Pianos" for a detailed discussion of the construction of the mid-eighteenth-century piano.

34. The following details of piano construction may be helpful: Double stringing indicates the use of two strings per note. Straight stringing indicates that all the strings run parallel and are all on the same plane, on one continuous bridge. "Overstrung" applies to a piano in which the strings are arranged in two planes, with the bass strings passing diagonally over those of the middle range. A hammer is the part of the piano action that strikes the strings of a particular note. Dampers cover the individual strings to stop them from sounding when the key is released. When the key is depressed the dampers lift off the strings to allow them to sound. Overdampers rest on top of the strings rather than underneath them. My appreciation to Eric Wolfley, head piano technician at the University of Cincinnati, for his assistance. See also Edwin M. Ripin, et al., *New Grove Piano* (New York: W. W. Norton & Co., 1988).

35. Mahogany was obtained from the Caribbean. It was commonly used for good furniture and supplied by merchants in large cities.

36. Koster, e-mail to author, July 13, 1999; Hamilton, telephone interview by author, Boston, November 30, 1999; Hester, letter to author, December 12, 1999; Frank Farmer Loomis, appraiser, Cincinnati, letter to author, January 4, 2000.

37. Photograph by author.

38. Rosewood, which had to be shipped from Brazil, was more expensive than mahogany and had come into use in the eighteenth century. The later nineteenth-century economy made rosewood increasingly available and affordable.

39. Entry dated August 6, 1818, "Music School" account in the Bethlehem Female Seminary Expense Journal, January 1, 1814–March 31, 1819, FemSem 20, Moravian Archives, Bethlehem, Pennsylvania. The actual bill, labeled no. 395, is in FemSem 187.6.1.

40. Photograph by author. The date is written on the underside of the soundboard in pencil.

41. Photograph by author.

42. Hamilton, interview by author, August 24, 1999; Hester, letter to author, July 17, 2000; Wolfely, interview by author, October 3, 2000.

43. Hamilton, telephone conversation with author, October 19, 1999; Loomis, letter to author, January 4, 2000. This piano was restored by Hamilton in 1999.

44. Photograph by author. The Goundie House is under the jurisdiction of the Bethlehem Historic Partnership, Bethlehem.

45. In 2002, the Moravian Historical Society, Nazareth, acquired a Malthaner piano, no. 75. According to Mark Turdo, the curator, the piano dates from ca. 1850 (telephone conversation with author, January 30, 2003).

46. Loomis, letter to author, January 4, 2000.

47. See chapter 3 of Smith, "Music, Women, and Pianos" for a discussion of the Petzold action.

48. Hester, letter to author, December 12, 1999; Libin, telephone conversation with author, May 4, 1999, and letter to author, December 6, 1999.

49. Levering, 587.

50. Peter Wolle, diary, Lititz Moravian Museum, Lititz.

51. Francis Wolle, "Advertisement," *Moravian* (Bethlehem), February 1, 1866 (testimonial dated November 6, 1865).

Chapter Ten

Moravian Music

Questions of Identity and Purpose

Nola Reed Knouse

Before the founding of the Unitas Fratrum, Jan Hus advocated congregational song in the vernacular. Music has been an integral part of the life of the Moravian Church since its very beginnings. Tradition holds that the ordination of the first ministers of the Unitas Fratrum in 1467 was marked by the singing of a new hymn. The Unitas Fratrum published an astonishing array of hymnals, providing an abundance of texts for its members to use in sharing their faith, strengthening their community, and steeling their souls in the face of turmoil and persecution. These hymnals were published in Czech, German, and Polish, reinforcing the young church's insistence on worship in the language of the people.

Hymnals produced by the Unity included texts by members of the Unity and by others, reflecting the Unity's ecumenical openness. When successive hymnals were printed, the texts that were retained were often revised to reflect current theological needs and understandings. This practice has continued to the present day, causing some discomfort as people must become accustomed to the new wording, but also allowing the hymnals to reflect and express the enduring beliefs of the church in contemporary language and interpretation.

Most of the Unity's hymnals of the sixteenth and seventeenth centuries included tunes as well—a laborious and costly enhancement, especially in light of the tender age of the art of printing. Education was a vital part of the Unity's ministry as well, but even Comenius, himself highly educated and renowned for his educational reforms, urged that the hymns be kept simple so that those without formal education would be able to profit from them.[1]

The renewal of the Moravian Church in the eighteenth century saw the flowering of many sorts of music, instrumental and vocal. With their emphasis on community and deemphasis on individualism, very few of these works are for solo performer, or even for two performers; most of the works by Moravian composers are for voices with chamber orchestra. With few exceptions, instrumental works written by Moravians during the eighteenth century are for three or more players.[2]

For the Moravians, music helped to create and confirm an international consistency and conformity of life and culture across several continents. The use of the Daily Text, the celebrations of festival occasions, the constant flow of correspondence and reports, and a consistency of worship style and format—all these factors strengthened connections that provided a sense of community and stability for Moravians wherever they traveled, whether for a brief visit or a new, long-term assignment.

All of this music had its roots in worship. With the Moravian Church's sense that singing was the rightful language of worship, hymns were an essential part of every gathering. The report of the Synod of November 18, 1750, identified the singing of a congregation as a measure of its spiritual well-being and stated that a congregation without song can have no joy on the earth.[3] Many hymns from the ancient Unity were preserved, and a great many more were written. The memorization of hymns was a very high priority, allowing for smooth progression between hymns in the *Singstunden* and allowing Moravians to reflect on the hymns throughout their daily activities.

We have Christian Gregor's own words describing how he was moved to begin writing special music for use in festival lovefeasts, thus giving rise to the practice of incorporating anthems into *Singstunden* for special occasions.[4] The organ was intended to support congregational singing and to be part of the ensemble accompanying anthems. Brass ensembles played outdoors, expanding the liturgical space to reach far beyond the walls of the church.

Even the *collegium musicum*, that most "secular" of musical organizations, had its roots in the need for well-trained musicians for worship, as well as in the community's need for appropriate recreational activities. In the schools, music education was intended to lay the foundation for living all of life as a liturgy in worship of the Savior. Any and all music could be used for training, and the Moravian schools were well known for the quality of the musical education they offered.

Music in the eighteenth-century Moravian communities was composed by amateurs—people with other primary occupations—for performers who were accomplished amateur musicians and who had limited time for rehearsals. Although Moravian clergy were trained in music and were expected to identify and assist young people with musical gifts, few indeed had music as their primary responsibility. Music was in the service of worship, and worship and educational responsibilities took priority.[5] Music was present throughout life, but few Moravian composers mentioned music in their *Lebensläufe*. Those who did mention it noted that it was something important to them but always to be kept in its proper place. Johann Friedrich Peter questioned his own motivation for composing music; Johann Christian Bechler acknowledged that he could devote to music only such time as was left from his other duties. Music, though essential, was an ordinary, expected, almost taken for granted part of life.

Written for and performed by people with other important skills and duties, musical works of the eighteenth-century Moravian Church shared significant characteristics. Hymn settings by Christian Gregor were generally much simpler than harmonizations of the same tunes by Johann Sebastian Bach. Anthems were largely homophonic; although the primary reason for this was the desire for ease of understanding the text, an additional benefit was the ease with which choirs could learn them. Instrumental parts were well crafted and interesting, especially during interludes when the choir or soloist was not singing, but they were never virtuosic. The music was intended to enhance the worship experience for the congregation, never to display the accomplishments of the musicians.

Because of its intimate connection with worship, music received a great deal of attention. In keeping with the Moravians' consistent choices for quality—good education, sturdy construction, careful town planning and architecture, high standards of craftsmanship—music was not to be taken lightly. Minutes show that music was a frequent topic of discussion at meetings of the Unity Elders. Christian Gregor's instructions for the organist in the preface to his 1784 *Choralbuch* show a remarkable attention to detail. Christian LaTrobe's experience with Bishop Spangenberg regarding his organ playing for worship is particularly telling: all was to be done in order with proper humility and care to omit anything that interfered with worship.

Moreover, however important it was that the music be performed well, it was not to be allowed a more important place in worship than was proper. The Moravians sang and played together in praise and glory of the Savior and for the edification of their community, not for the enjoyment or entertainment of visitors. Never was the music to be allowed to steal the worshipers' attention away from the proper object of worship, the Savior. If the elders suspected that this was the case, the music was to be removed from the services. If events in London were indicative of normal practice, we should not assume that all music was dispensed with, but rather only music that might be seen as attracting visitors unduly. The Pilgrim House Diary for April 10, 1747 states, "In the Church Meeting we had no other music but the organ, and Br. Boehler sang a long hymn, in order that those who might have come only for the music might go away again, but no one went."[6]

Even outside of organized services of worship, the musicians were not to play for private entertainment of visitors. In Salem in 1781, when the musicians were instructed not to perform in private homes for the entertainment of the visiting North Carolina General Assembly, the implication was that the instruments and the music were to be kept for the service of the church and the well-being of the community, not for personal gain or pride.[7]

Visitors to Moravian communities, however, certainly did hear their music and were affected by it. The Moravian theologian and historian Peter Vogt has examined a large number of travel diaries of the eighteenth and nineteenth centuries, excerpting accounts of visits to Moravian worship services. These accounts agree that the music in Moravian worship had a particular beauty and appeal, being lovely, gentle, noble, and solemn. The writers noted that the Moravians sang well together, as if with one voice. The singing was simple and natural, slow and quiet. The organ was noted as supporting the singing and the devotion of the worshiping congregation. These visitors to Moravian worship were deeply moved, some to tears. Some even identified the music as a foretaste of heaven. Finally, they saw this lovely singing as expressive of the Moravians' deep devotion and faith; several noted that the Protestant state churches could benefit from observing and adopting Moravian practices.[8]

This "golden age" of Moravian music could not endure through the social and cultural changes of the nineteenth century. Throughout Europe and North America in particular, consciousness of national identity supplanted the Moravians' earlier focus on their international unity. Moravians in America made conscious choices to conform to the culture of their neighbors.[9] By the middle of the nineteenth century in America, English became the language of worship. As we saw in chapter 3, many of the late-eighteenth-century English translations of hymns lacked the vigor and passion of the German originals. The effects of these translations on the nineteenth- and twentieth-century Moravian Church in England and America, in theology as well as in church and community life, remain to be analyzed.

As the Moravian communities became more receptive to non-Moravian residents, attitudes toward worship changed as well. Whereas during the eighteenth century church authorities resisted music's appeal to visitors, fearing that they would come for the music and not to worship the Savior, by the end of the nineteenth century some members were calling for the use of music for the very purpose of attracting people. Francis Florentine Hagen was especially concerned about the continuing use of German chorale tunes in nineteenth-century America, writing, "By forcing upon English-speaking American Churches foreign tunes, which but few are able to sing properly, we estrange from our services the very people among whom God has placed us to work. Need we wonder at our stunted growth?"[10]

Moravian composers in America wrote fewer sacred vocal works from the second quarter of the nineteenth century on. Alongside the shift from German to English as the common tongue, more published music in English and in the current musical styles became readily available. Also, composers may well have discovered that it is generally easier to compose a new anthem than it is to create an effective English translation of one originally in German.

Moreover, musical tastes were changing, reflecting the trend away from classical ideals and expressions and toward romanticism. Jillian Boand has examined the characteristics of romantic music and their incompatibility with the values of Moravian worship and life. Romanticism's emphasis on individual expression was incompatible with the Moravians' communal ideals. Extended melodies, experimentation with harmony and rhythm, and the extremes of length and musical forces of romantic compositions (from the miniature to the gargantuan) certainly placed a strain on the Moravians' preference for balance and symmetry.[11] Some nineteenth-century Moravian composers were able to live with a foot in both worlds; Francis Florentine Hagen's anthems show his classical training and "Moravian" musical heritage, while his solo songs, piano works, and organ works show the influence of romanticism. It appears, however, that most simply adopted the musical preferences of the surrounding culture, packing the old manuscripts away, while they composed fewer works of their own.

In nineteenth-century Germany, similar changes were occurring with regard to Moravian church music (although, of course, the question of English translation is irrelevant). In 1865 the church published the *Hilfsbüchlein für Liturgen und Organisten in den Brüdergemeinen*, an official manual for organists and worship leaders listing choral pieces considered suitable for use in Moravian worship throughout the church year. The purpose of this publication was to make it easier for those in charge to select appropriate music for worship, or, as Peter Vogt writes, "to safeguard the integrity and uniformity of the Moravian music tradition by putting into writing what had been handed down from the past."[12] The repertoire was deliberately conservative, limited to music composed from the 1750s to the 1840s and including no works by living composers. This in itself is a very significant contrast to the earlier period, when by far most music sung was contemporary.

By the publication in 1891 of a new edition of the *Hilfsbuch*, the attitude and intention of the editors had made a dramatic shift in the other direction. More than 70 percent of the pieces listed in the 1865 edition were omitted, and some three hundred new pieces, most by contemporary composers, were added, resulting in a repertoire that Vogt describes as "strikingly broad, up-to-date, and forward-looking."[13] This edition brought Moravian church music into closer connection with the wider range of Protestant church music in Germany, as well as highlighting the creativity of Moravian composers of the later nineteenth century. On the basis of his study of these two editions, Vogt observes that "the Moravian music tradition was very much alive in Germany well into the Twentieth Century, although it obviously took a different turn than the development of Moravian music in North America."[14]

Outside of formal worship, attitudes shifted in the community's musical life as well. The *collegium musicum* became the "Philharmonic Society," the emphasis moving from music made by members of the community for their own enjoyment and for musical training for worship, to music performed by professionals in public concerts. Although the number of participants—both performers and listeners—grew, the musical presentations were no longer subject to the ideals of the Moravian Church. Musical accomplishments became more important than membership in the community of faith. No longer was all of life to be lived as a liturgy.

In America, community bands and orchestras certainly benefited from the Moravians' musical accomplishments and those of graduates from Moravian schools. However, these organizations were not connected to the Moravian Church, and again, were not subject to Moravian Church governance. For instance, the end of the nineteenth century saw the formation of the Bach Choir of Bethlehem, whose founder, J. Fred Wolle, was Moravian and the descendant of Moravian musicians. His original concept was that Bach was for everyone, and no auditions were required to sing in the Bach Choir. The move toward professionalism in the membership of the Bach Choir in the twentieth century resulted in a separation of the Bach Choir from the Moravian Church.[15]

The increase during the nineteenth century in the number of published works written by Moravians is evidence of this changing focus. Whereas very few compositions by eighteenth-century Moravian composers were published or known beyond the Moravian communities, during the nineteenth century Moravian composers were no longer writing solely for their own congregations at worship. Works by American Moravian composers for voice and piano, piano solo, organ, and (to a lesser extent) choir were published in such cities as New York and Philadelphia. By the late nineteenth century, Moravian composers in America were no longer content to write just for themselves and their near neighbors, but were competing with mainstream American composers.[16]

The twentieth century was marked by the rediscovery of the richness and breadth of the musical life of the Moravians in America. This rediscovery, however, was accomplished largely by musical scholars who were not associated with the Moravian Church. "Moravian music" was extolled as previously unknown evidence of a highly sophisticated musical culture even in the backwoods of early America. The music of the Moravians was made known not according to the Moravians' own objectives and standards, but in accord with the standards of modern culture, with emphasis on professional performance—a standard that the eighteenth-century Moravians themselves rejected.[17] "Moravian music" was placed not within its natural context of worship and liturgy, in a community united by faith, life, and mission, but on the concert stage. Audiences were deliberately sought not within the membership of the Moravian Church, but among concertgoers and music critics. Performers were not Moravians leading their brothers and sisters in worship or even playing "just for fun," but professionals engaged to ensure a high-quality performance. The music selected for these concerts was not always the best that Moravians had written, but rather works that matched the perceived expectations of concertgoers and critics.[18]

Some commercial music publications of Moravian music in the mid-twentieth century also failed to present a true picture of the music of the Moravians. As noted in chapter 1, some editors "corrected" aspects of the music and the texts to make them more "acceptable" (and therefore more marketable). Fortunately, some very fine editions of Moravian music were published by the New York Public Library, and these brought significant credibility to the Moravians and their music within the academic community. Throughout the end of the twentieth century, then, one's opinion of "Moravian music" depended on what editions one had encountered.

Here, at the beginning of the twenty-first century, many scholars in America are coming to a new appreciation of the true merits of the music of the Moravians by seeking to understand this music within its intended context. Within the past ten years there has been a resurgence of interest in Moravian music among scholars on the European Continent as well. With such fine works as Anja Wehrend's *Musikanschauung, Musikpraxis, Kantatenkomposition in der Herrnhuter Brüdergemeine* (1995) at the forefront, this new interest may well move directly into the proper consideration of the music of the Moravians in its proper context of "*liturgisch leben*"—living liturgically.[19]

In recent years many members of the Moravian Church have also shown a new interest in their own heritage of music and worship. The rediscovery of the music preserved by the eighteenth-century Moravians in America was the impetus for the first Early American Moravian Music Festival and Seminar, which was held in Bethlehem, Pennsylvania, in 1950. Over the past fifty-six years there have been twenty-two such festivals. More recent festivals have broadened their focus to include music of the Moravians in Europe and other regions. Moreover, the seminars and workshops held at these festivals are geared toward music in today's Moravian Church rather than primarily toward topics in historical musicology. Other conferences sponsored by the Moravian Church in America have begun to explore how the Moravian heritage of music and worship can enrich the worship and outreach of today, as deep roots can enable new growth. Research into such divergent areas as Moravian missions, women's memoirs, industry, theology, horticulture, and relationships with Native Americans and African Americans; new translations of diaries, correspondence, discourses and hymns; and new relationships among Moravian musicians from America, Europe, and South Africa all have become resources not only for scholars but also for "persons in the pew" to rediscover their own heritage.

The student of the music of the Moravians is an explorer in largely uncharted territory. Research in Moravian archives leads down fascinating paths to finds of great importance in the musical and cultural history of many locales. Many trails have not yet been traveled. This book has begun to draw the broad outlines of the worldwide map of Moravian music and to fill in the details in a few spots, but most of the map remains blank.

For instance, music in the eighteenth-century choir houses (Single Brethren, Single Sisters) has yet to be fully explored. Because of the eighteenth-century Moravian recognition that people in different stages of life have different spiritual needs and understandings, each choir had separate liturgies and hymns, and each had its own festival day and festival services. What might these resources reveal about the eighteenth-century Moravians' understanding of religious experience, and what of this might be helpful today? Since liturgies were intended to be sung as well as spoken, both textual and musical analysis is needed.

We have noted that as Moravians traveled, they took with them copies of both instrumental and vocal music. Johann Friedrich Peter copied many works prior to coming to America, and we presume others did likewise before traveling to the farther outposts. What sources did these composer-copyists have at hand? The cataloging of Moravian music holdings in Labrador, Great Britain, and South Africa broadens the discussion to include areas far beyond the passage between Germany and North America. The "flow" of the music used by the Moravians worldwide has yet to be traced.

We have seen the beginnings of exploration into the interaction between the music of the Moravians and that of their neighbors in some locations, in the use of sacred vocal music by other composers in Moravian worship, in the use of popular tunes in music education, in the adaptation of hymns by Charles Wesley for use with Moravian tunes, in the use of hymns by James Montgomery in the hymnals of many denominations, and in the employment of musicians from Bethlehem for concerts with the Musical Fund Society of Philadelphia in the 1820s. For the most part, however, these studies have looked more at what the Moravians brought into their own community than at what they exported to others. Hymnologists and theologians in particular will find much fertile ground for study in examining Moravian hymnals (of different centuries and in different languages) alongside those of other denominations for possible overlap and mutual influence.

Some of the trails leading from Moravian points of origin intersect with other paths and lead in wonderful new directions. Such is the case with the nineteenth-century Moravian brass tradition in America. The Moravians' strong heritage of brass playing intersected with the rising popularity of community brass bands in America (itself fueled by the invention of the rotary valve), and the result was the band of the 26th North Carolina Regiment of the Confederate States of America—one of the finest of the Confederate bands. This group of Moravian musicians collected a repertoire of nearly three hundred tunes, including four-part chorales (such as those they played at home for Easter dawn), popular ballads, arrangements of operatic arias and choruses, patriotic tunes, and pieces composed by Moravians in Salem specifically for this band. The study of this repertoire, when completed, will provide rich new insights into the musical life not only of the Moravians from Salem, but of the entire country during a time of great upheaval.

Music in the home is also largely unexplored terrain. Moravian music collections in America include many bound volumes containing published sheet music of the early nineteenth century; these were the personal property of individuals and families, used for enjoyment at home. These have been cata-loged—and one was found to contain one of nine known surviving copies of the first printing of "The Star-Spangled Banner."[20] But the repertoire itself has not been studied for what it will reveal about what music was popular at home, as well as the level of musical accomplishment of the owners.

The success of the Bach Choir of Bethlehem following its founding in 1898 led to the establishment of other such groups around the country. Where else did Moravian-rooted musical activity wield influence far beyond Moravian com-munities? A study of other musical organizations that arose in Moravian com-munities and their evolving relationships with the Moravian Church would certainly prove fruitful and fascinating. This path branches into many trails in many different countries.

Much of the discussion of the music of the Moravians in the chapters of this book has been in the past tense. Nevertheless, significant aspects of this rich musical culture continue today in parts of the worldwide Moravian Unity. Many of the features of the early Moravian Church have retained their importance, including the emphasis on the church as a worldwide unity.[21]

Although the multitude of daily and weekly worship services of the eighteenth-century Moravian settlement congregations has not survived the transition to modern social and community life, many aspects of Moravian worship and devo-tional life, as described in chapter 2, do continue to this day. Some 1.5 million copies of the 2007 *Daily Texts* were printed in fifty-one languages and dialects. The popularity of the *Daily Texts* beyond the Moravian Church is evident in that membership of the Moravian Church worldwide is seven hundred thousand in its nineteen provinces. More than one million copies of the 2007 German-lan-guage *Daily Text* alone were printed.[22]

The Moravian lovefeast and services of Holy Communion continue to reflect their roots in the *Singstunde*. Moreover, the *Singstunde* itself continues in many Moravian congregations, especially in Germany, where the Saturday evening *Singstunde* is a weekly event. Hymn stanzas for the *Singstunde* are still selected to communicate the theme, often the Daily Text for the day, but where the eighteenth-century Moravians would have sung mostly from memory, today worshipers are handed a card listing the selected hymn numbers and stanzas. The organist plays an interlude or introduction as the worshipers search their hymnals for the next stanza on the list. The *Singstunde* as a service independent of the lovefeast or Holy Communion is also enjoying a renaissance in the American Moravian church.

As discussed in chapter 3, the hymnody of the Moravian Church continues to thrive, with its preservation of hymns of the past, new translations of old hymns, and the addition of new expressions of faith. With regard to hymn tunes, the Moravian Church in Germany has adopted versions of tunes (and the tune num-bering system) compatible with those used in the Evangelical Church in Germany. The 1975 British hymnal committee chose to use tune settings known in the ecumenical community and to try to use a different tune with every text. The American Moravian Church and the Moravians in South Africa continue to use mostly Gregor's settings of tunes, using the same tune numbers.

Approximately five hundred Moravian anthems from the eighteenth and early nineteenth centuries have been published in the United States within the past fifty years. These are more widely used in churches of other denominations than in Moravian congregations in America.[23] Moravian congregations tend to be fairly small (fewer than three hundred members), with small choirs; and the decline in music literacy and vocal training among church members, along with the high tessitura of many Moravian anthems, has resulted in many Moravian church choirs' lacking confidence in their ability to sing these pieces well. A few Moravian anthems, however, have retained their place of honor within special services. With this in mind, the Moravian Music Foundation has initiated a series of simplified arrangements of Moravian anthems, in lower keys, for use with organ or piano alone rather than with the original chamber-orchestra instrumentation. In addition to the recovery of anthems from the past, many Moravian congregations are encouraging church members to compose new anthems, especially for anniversary celebrations; many of these also make use of the Daily Text for the day.

The organist in Moravian worship retains a position of significant worship leadership. Although very few American Moravian congregations employ full-time church musicians (director of music, organist, choir director), most maintain high expectations of the organist, not as a solo recitalist, but rather as a sensitive hymn player and leader of congregational singing. Many Moravians still sing in four-part harmony, whether or not they read music; many improvise alto and tenor parts based on lifelong familiarity with the hymn tunes. The organist is expected to accompany and support the hymn-singing congregation, not to display his or her improvisatory ability.

In many American Moravian congregations, the trombone choir has given way to the church band. In some locations the band is solely brass, whereas in others the band includes all wind instruments. The emphasis remains on ensemble playing of chorales, and those instruments which lend themselves to solo sounds (piccolo, E-flat clarinet, piccolo trumpet, and the like) are best left at home or in the community band. In many congregations, the church band plays at the graveside for funerals; it plays (outdoors or inside) before special festival services. The band accompanies the procession to God's Acre for Easter dawn services. The role of the band varies from congregation to congregation. Moreover, wherever Moravians gather, for conferences, provincial synods, and festival occasions, a band is usually assembled from among the participants.

Ensembles consisting solely of trombones have not disappeared from Moravian life, however. The Bethlehem Area Moravians Trombone Choir celebrated its two-hundred-fiftieth anniversary in 2004 with an international trombone and brass festival. The Moravian congregation in Downey, California, has an active trombone choir, as does the Glenwood Moravian Church in Madison, Wisconsin. The Salem Trombone Choir was reestablished in 1984 and performs at Moravian Church and civic occasions. These ensembles play chorales, music from the eighteenth century originally written for trombone choir, and new music composed and arranged for trombone choir.

With these as examples of the continuation of the Moravian musical heritage, it becomes clear that throughout most of its history, the Moravian Church has maintained an admirable consistency of purpose for music.[24] From the very beginning of the Unitas Fratrum in the fifteenth century, congregational participation was an essential part of Moravian worship, and hymn singing by the congregation was carefully nurtured. Over the next several centuries, musical training was an essential part of education. Those with special musical gifts were given the opportunity to use them for the benefit of the *Gemeine*, but music as a career was rare among the Moravians. In retrospect, it seems that not all musically gifted Moravians were given full scope for the expression of their talents.[25] In all cases, the musical gift took second place to the more important work of spreading the Gospel.

Two anecdotes serve to illuminate the essence of Moravian music. Around 1780, the marquis de Chastellux wrote of his visit to Bethlehem that he "was astonished with the delicious sounds of an Italian Concerto, but my surprise was still greater on entering a room where the performers turned out to be common workmen of different trades, playing for their amusement."[26] Two aspects of this experience are notable: the fine quality of the music, and the identity and purpose of the performers. Some two and a quarter centuries later, in July 2004, during a presentation at the International Trombone and Brass Festival celebrating the two-hundred-fiftieth anniversary of the Bethlehem Trombone Choir, the members of the choir introduced themselves. Although some of their members were absent, those present included a computer consultant who is also an official scorer for Major League Baseball, a retired pastor, a church sexton, a chemical technician, a small-business owner, a software developer, and a retired accountant—none with music as his or her primary occupation. This venerable Moravian musical institution depends on amateurs, not hired professionals, for its continuation.

This, then, is the core of the Moravian musical heritage throughout its five hundred fifty years. Moravians believe that as a gift of God, music is the language of the heart and the mind in worship. As the people's expression of faith, music is worthy of great care and effort, including proper education, training, preparation, and leadership. However, music is the purview not of a few specially gifted professionals who are hired to perform, but rather of the entire community of faith. Educated musicians are welcomed, but all are invited (and expected) to participate, and the focus is on the music of the people at worship, not on the musical accomplishments of the few. I would submit that if the Moravian musical heritage ever depends on hired professionals for its continuation, then it is already dead; and, given the centrality of music to the expression of the faith of the community, the Moravian Church itself would not be far behind.

Dr. Bill J. Leonard, dean of the School of Divinity at Wake Forest University, has written convincingly of the history of the Baptist church around the world as a struggle for identity.[27] Dr. Leonard recognizes that at the beginning of the twenty-first century, churches are facing major "transitions in culture, economics, globalism, pluralism, and other aspects of national and international life."[28] In the face of the upheavals of contemporary life, he believes that one of the greatest challenges for the church in the twenty-first century is the creation of "intentional identity with integrity."[29] This is indeed the challenge facing the Moravian Church, and if its past is any indication, music will remain one of the most effective means of addressing this need.

The transitions and uncertainties in life at the beginning of this new century call to mind the troubled state of central Europe following the Thirty Years' War and into the eighteenth century. In the face of the challenges of that time, refugees of the Unitas Fratrum found a new home, renewed their church, and began a worldwide mission endeavor. At the same time they created a musical culture that both helped to form their identity and to carry that identity and mission to new lands.

Moravian musicians today (whether "amateur" or "professional") would be well advised to know their heritage, study their traditions, and seek new expressions of faith both within and beyond those traditions. Musicians and scholars seeking to learn more about the music of the Moravians would be well advised to get to know the history, theology, and life of the Moravians in community and thus study this musical culture within its own natural habitat. For both, it is crucial to recognize that for the Moravians music is only part of living all of life as a liturgy.[30] All of the people are the musicians. And the audience is God.

Notes

1. See Olga Settari, "The Sacred Song of Johann Amos Comenius," in Jan Amos Comenius, ed., *Kancionál* (1659); reprint, ed. and intro. by Olga Settari (Kalich: Kultur Kontakt, 1992), 27–29.

2. The exceptions are the keyboard sonatas composed by Moravians J. G. Gebhard, J. Gambold, Jr., and C. I. LaTrobe discussed in chapter 9. It is well to recall that Gebhard and Gambold were music teachers in Moravian schools, and LaTrobe, a friend of Franz Joseph Haydn, worked and wrote in London and dedicated his piano sonatas to Haydn.

3. "Die Lieder sind eine incomparable Sache. Eine Gemeine Jesu ohne Lieder kann keine Freude auf der Welt haben. Der Vorwurf: Die Leute haben lauter Verse ist ein halber Beweis von der Göttlichkeit einer Gemeine, wenn sie die Schriftwahrheiten durch singen und sie dadurch lebhaft machen kann." Cited in Hans-Christoph Hahn and Hellmut Reichel, *Zinzendorf und die Herrnhuter Brüder:*

Quellen zur Geschichte der Brüder-Unität von 1722 bis 1760 (Hamburg: Friedrich Wittig Verlag, 1977), 222.

4. See chapter 2, p. 37.

5. For instance, both Johann Friedrich Peter and Johannes Herbst, two of the most prolific Moravian composers in America, had very heavy responsibilities besides their musical ones. See Adelaide Fries, ed., *Records of the Moravians in North Carolina* (Raleigh: North Carolina Historical Commission, 1941), 5:2131, 2138, for excerpts from board minutes in Salem, North Carolina, describing Johann Friedrich Peter's instruction of young keyboard players. See also C. Daniel Crews, *Johann Friedrich Peter and His Times* (Winston-Salem: Moravian Music Foundation, 1990), 18–19, for an account of Peter's many and varied responsibilities during his ten years' service in Salem (1780–90).

6. AB41.A2, Moravian Church House, London; cited in Colin Podmore, *The Moravian Church in England 1728–1760* (Oxford: Clarendon Press, 1998), 151.

7. See chapter 7, p. 196.

8. Peter Vogt, "Listening to 'Festive Stillness': The Sound of Moravian Music According to Descriptions of Non-Moravian Visitors," *Moravian Music Journal* 39/1 (Spring 1999): 15–23.

9. See C. Daniel Crews and Richard W. Starbuck. *With Courage for the Future: The Story of the Moravian Church, Southern Province* (Winston-Salem: Moravian Church in America, Southern Province, 2002), especially 134–39 and 186–87, for descriptions of the changes in Moravian life in the Southern Province of the United States in the early nineteenth century. Some of the more unfortunate results of these attempts to conform were the removal of women from positions of church leadership and the increasing acceptance of slavery.

10. Francis Florentine Hagen, *Unitas Fratrum in Extremis; or, Thoughts on the Past and Present Condition of the Moravian Church in America, Respectfully Submitted to the Provincial Synod of 1893, at Bethlehem, Pennsylvania* (Bethlehem: Moravian Publications Office, 1893), 10, n.1.

11. Jillian Boand, "The Road Not Taken: A Discourse on Moravian Deviation from Romanticism in the Nineteenth Century" (unpublished paper presented at the Sixth Bethlehem Conference on Moravian Music, October 23, 2004, filed at the Moravian Music Foundation).

12. Peter Vogt, "A Codified Repertoire? The Scope and Character of Moravian Music According to the *Hilfsbuch* of 1865, 1891 and 1907" (unpublished paper presented at the Sixth Bethlehem Conference on Moravian Music, October 7, 2004, filed at the Moravian Music Foundation; publication forthcoming), 6.

13. Vogt, "A Codified Repertoire," 8.

14. Vogt, "A Codified Repertoire," 10–11.

15. My thanks to Dr. Paul Larson, professor emeritus of Moravian College, for this insight.

16. Nineteenth-century Moravian composers have thus far been largely overlooked in studies of American music. For instance, the noted American composer Edward MacDowell was still in school during the years that Moravian composer Francis Florentine Hagen was publishing his *Church and Home Organist's Companion* (1880 and 1881). MacDowell was one of the earliest American composers to receive international recognition, partly through the contacts he made during his study at the Hoch Conservatory in Frankfurt am Main (1879–80) and afterward, including a meeting with Franz Liszt in 1882. Hagen, on the other hand, studied only at

Moravian schools in America and never sought such recognition, and he has indeed received none outside of the Moravian Church.

17. See chapter 4, p. 124, for an account of the Moravians' reaction to hiring a "professional" to perform in Herrnhut in 1790.

18. One of the concerts at the opening of the John F. Kennedy Center for the Performing Arts in Washington, D.C., was a concert of Moravian music presented on September 12, 1971. The music selected for this concert included one of the Peter string quintets, selections from Michael's *Die Wasserfahrt*, and the multimovement cantata *The Dawn of Glory* by Christian Ignatius LaTrobe, an oratorio written not for Moravian church worship but for British audiences and in the style of Haydn. None of these works are the most characteristic of the music of the Moravians, nor are they arguably the best of the compositions of the composers represented, and the reaction of the critics was predictable. Paul Hume, writing for the *Washington Post* (September 13, 1971), characterized the afternoon as a "succession of works by unsophisticated practitioners of an art whose masters they constantly call to mind." Even Irving Lowens (certainly a friend of Moravian music and a consultant to the Moravian Music Foundation) wrote in the *Washington Evening Star* (September 13, 1971) that the LaTrobe oratorio was "a 45-minute-long tissue of clichés which sounds twice that lengthy." Thus, because of a less than felicitous selection of music, this event, which should have brought national renown to and interest in the music of the Moravians, perpetuated the view that Moravian music is interesting as a historical curiosity but not as well-written music on its own merits.

19. The study of Moravian music in Germany, in particular, is unhampered by questions of translations of texts into English (although archaic spellings and meanings abound, creating the distinct possibility of confusion!). Moreover, early studies of "American music" were at risk of being tainted by the same sort of inferiority complex that prevented American audiences from accepting American-born composers and conductors as truly educated without the obligatory European studies. Scholars in Germany, it seems to me, are already so secure in well-justified pride in their own musical heritage that they may well be able to evaluate the music of the Moravians with a clearer view of its own merits as another part of that musical heritage.

20. Identified by a typographical error in the subtitle: the first printing subtitles the work "A PARIOTIC SONG." The error was corrected in subsequent printings.

21. The Moravian Church today is governed not by a board of elders residing in Herrnhut, but by the Unity Synod, which consists of representatives from all provinces of the Unity and meets every seven years. During intersynodal periods, the Unity is governed by the Unity Board, which consists of a representative from the Provincial Elders' Conference of each province.

22. *Moravian Daily Text* (Bethlehem and Winston-Salem, Moravian Church in North America, 2006), v.

23. Based on usage of Moravian anthems in the Music Lending Library managed by the Moravian Music Foundation and on sales figures over the past ten years.

24. There were some notable digressions during the nineteenth century, especially in North America, but it seems that the church and its musicians have regained their perspective and focus.

25. For instance, Simon Peter's few compositions are of a very high quality, but for most of his life he served in the "country congregations," which had no instrumental ensembles and small (if any) choirs. Had he been assigned to a settlement

congregation (such as Salem, North Carolina, or Lititz or Bethlehem, Pennsylvania) he may well have written a great many more fine pieces.

26. Cited in Donald M. McCorkle, *The Moravian Contribution to American Music,* reprinted from *Notes* of the Music Library Association (September 1956; reprint, Winston-Salem: Moravian Music Foundation, 1956), 4.

27. For instance, see Bill J. Leonard, *Baptist Ways: A History* (Valley Forge: Judson Press, 2003); Leonard, *God's Last and Only Hope: The Fragmentation of the Southern Baptist Convention* (Grand Rapids: W. B. Eerdmans, ca. 1990); Leonard, "Perspectives on Baptist Denominationalism: Anticipating the Future," in *Findings: A Report of the Special Study Commission to Study the Question: "Should the Cooperative Baptist Fellowship Become a Separate Convention?"* ed. Randall C. Lolley (Atlanta: Cooperative Baptist Fellowship, 1996), 102–11.

28. Leonard, *Baptist Ways,* 423.

29. I am grateful to the Rev. Dr. Gerald R. Harris, who first brought this concept to my attention in a sermon at Home Moravian Church in Winston-Salem, North Carolina, on August 19, 2001, having himself heard Dr. Leonard discuss it in a presentation to clergy.

30. The Greek origin of the word is *leitourgia,* a combination of the adjective *laós* (public, people) and the noun *ergon* (work), therefore literally "the work of the people."

Appendix One

Biographical Sketches

John Antes (1740–1811) was born and raised in Pennsylvania. His father, Henry Antes, was a member of the Reformed church and shared Zinzendorf's interest in bringing about unity among the various Christian denominations in Pennsylvania. After Henry Antes became disillusioned with the Reformed church and joined the Moravians, John was baptized in 1746 by Augustus Gottlieb Spangenberg. After working for a few years as an instrument maker in Bethlehem, he was invited to come to Europe, where he undertook several kinds of business with little success. Called to serve the church as a missionary in Egypt beginning in 1769, he survived many adventures both in travel and in his work there. He was tortured and nearly killed by followers of Osman Bey, a local official of the Ottoman empire. After undergoing the bastinado (beating of the soles of the feet), he was finally released. It was sometime during this Egyptian period of his life that Antes wrote the Three Trios, identified as op. 3, and a set of string quartets that are missing; in fact, a letter to Benjamin Franklin with which he sent a copy of the quartets is dated some four months before his torture. This same letter to Franklin also illuminates anther side of Antes: he interceded for the American Moravians in their hardships during the American Revolution. Antes was recalled to Germany in 1782, and beginning in 1785, he worked as a business manager in Fulneck, England. His composition of sacred concerted vocal works (some three dozen in all) began during the 1780s, and he retired to Bristol, England, in 1808, where he died on December 17, 1811. His Three Trios, though they were written abroad, are the earliest known chamber music composed by an American.

Much of the information in these biographies is taken from the *Dienerblätter*, a multivolume compilation of basic biographical information about prominent Moravian church members in the eighteenth and nineteenth centuries. Copies of the *Dienerblätter* are housed in the Moravian Archives in Herrnhut, Bethlehem, and Winston-Salem. My thanks also to C. Daniel Crews, whose 1990 compilation *Moravian Composers: Paragraph Biographies* (Winston-Salem: Moravian Music Foundation, 1990) provided not only the model but also much of the material for this appendix.

Jan Augusta (1500–1572) was born in Prague and joined the Unitas Fratrum in 1524. He was known as a man of boundless energy and strong will and became a very well-known preacher. He was acquainted with Martin Luther. He was chosen a bishop in 1532 at the synod at which he and four of his young friends were elected to the Inner Council. Along with Jan Roh, he prepared Czech and Latin versions of a confession of faith for the Unity. These confessions of faith, and Luther's obvious respect and support, won for the Unity wider interest and regard. He was imprisoned from 1548 to 1564, during which time he maintained correspondence with other leaders of the Unity. He was reluctant to relinquish his leadership role to others, but was reconciled to them following his release from prison. In addition to the confessions of faith and correspondence noted above, his writings included hymns and a schedule of scripture lessons to be used throughout the church year.

Johann Philip Bachmann (1762–1837) was born in Thuringia and learned carpentry from his father (who may have been a maker of pianos). After leaving home at age sixteen to work with a master carpenter, he became acquainted with the Moravians, and eventually moved to Herrnhut, where he learned the craft of making musical instruments. At the request of Moravian organ builder David Tannenberg, Bachmann moved to Lititz, Pennsylvania, in February of 1793 to assist Tannenberg and learn the art of organ building. He married Tannenberg's youngest daughter, Anna Maria, in April of 1793. With Tannenberg's advancing age, Bachmann assumed the responsibility of traveling to install the master's organs, including two trips to Salem, North Carolina (in 1798 and 1800). Relationships between the two men deteriorated, and Bachmann separated from Tannenberg in 1803, but the two were able to continue some collaboration. Bachmann is known to have built at least seven organs between 1803 and 1819, and after that time he may have focused his energies on fine cabinetmaking and piano building. For more than the last twenty years of his life he suffered from rheumatism. He died on November 15, 1837, after several months as a complete invalid.[1]

Johann Christian Bechler (1784–1857) was born on the Baltic island of Oesel (modern Saaremaa), where his father was a Moravian minister. He was educated at Moravian schools in Niesky and Barby, Germany. Music was his favorite subject, and he says that he "devoted every moment of time left by other duties, to the acquisition of the various branches of this charming art with the greatest delight, learning to sing, to play various stringed instruments, but more particularly the piano and the organ."[2] At the completion of his studies he taught organ at Barby. In 1806 accepted a call to America, where he became one of the first professors at Moravian Theological Seminary. His interest in music continued, and he composed many choral and liturgical pieces. He served as minister to the Moravian congregations of Philadelphia, Staten Island, Lititz, Pennsylvania, and

Salem, North Carolina. In 1836, shortly after his consecration as bishop, he went to serve the congregation in Sarepta, Russia. In 1849 he retired to Herrnhut, the center of the Moravian Church in Germany, and died there on April 18, 1857.

Jan Blahoslav (1523–71) was educated in the schools of the Unitas Fratrum and at the universities of Wittenberg, Königsberg, and Basel. He was ordained in 1553 and became one of the most prominent and effective leaders and writers of the Unity. He was chosen as bishop in 1557 while Jan Augusta was in prison. He was the editor of the Czech-language hymnal of the Unity, printed in 1561; this hymnal was reprinted and revised some ten times over the next fifty years. In addition, he was the author of *Musica* (1558), a theoretical instruction book for the singing of hymns, noted as "the first book in Czech presenting the theory of music and singing."[3] He worked for many years on a new translation of the New Testament into Czech and was also responsible for the Unity's archives.

Christian Ludwig Brau (1746–77) was born in Drammen, Norway, but was educated in Moravian schools in the Netherlands and Germany. He wanted to become a missionary to the West Indies, but his health was poor and could not stand up to the rigors of that calling. Instead, he was able to put his musical gifts to good use working with children in Moravian schools in Gnadau, Zeist, and elsewhere. In 1776, ill health forced him to give up teaching, and he was called to Barby to recuperate. He died there on February 17, 1777, at only thirty-one years of age.

John Cennick (1718–55) was a British Methodist evangelist who joined the Moravians in 1745. He worked largely in the west of England and Ireland and wrote some two hundred hymns. In leading his congregations to join the Moravian Church as well, he was influential in strengthening and broadening the base of Moravian work in the British Isles.

Theodor Liley Clemens (1858–1933) was born on December 8, 1858, in Baildon, Yorkshire, and was the son of a Moravian minister. He was ordained in 1886 and was sent to Spring Gardens on Antigua. Shortly after his marriage to Mary Mercer in 1888, he was called to the Moriah Congregation on Tobago, where he served until 1917. During his twenty-eight years on Tobago, he gained the respect and affection of his people and had a significant positive effect on the moral tone of the community. Clemens had a great love and talent for music and trained a fine choir. Since his church could not afford to buy music from England, he wrote many hymns, anthems, and organ pieces for his congregation. In his spare time he also composed nearly one hundred secular pieces. Several of his compositions were printed in England during his lifetime. His health forced him to take a disability leave from 1917 to 1919, but he returned to serve in Trinidad. He retired in 1921 and returned to England, where he died at Eydon on July 23, 1933.

Jan Amos Comenius (1592–1670) was the most significant figure for the preservation of the Unity's history, church order, and hymnody during and following the persecutions of the seventeenth century. A bishop of the Unity, he traveled throughout Europe, and was twice exiled by persecutions. His writings in Czech focused on pastoral care, comfort, and encouragement for the members of the Unity following the defeat at the battle of White Mountain. His Latin writings on education brought him renown throughout Europe. He also published a history of the Unity, a reprint of the Unity's large catechism and its confession of faith, and edited the Unity's hymnal of 1659, including a preface discussing the role of music in worship. Before his death he made provision for the preservation of the Unity's episcopate, seeing that two priests were consecrated as bishops. Many of his writings were known to later Pietist leaders at Halle, as well as to Zinzendorf.

Jeremias Dencke (1725–95) was born in Silesia. He joined the Moravian congregation at Gnadenfrei and was called to the Moravian center in Herrnhut in 1748, where he became an organist. He came to America in 1761 on the same ship with the father of Johann and Simon Peter. Dencke wrote a simple piece for chorus, strings, and organ for the Provincial Synod in Bethlehem in 1766; it is believed to be the earliest example of Moravian concerted church music composed in America. Other significant works are three sets of sacred songs for soprano, strings, and organ, which are preserved in copies by Johann Friedrich Peter. Dencke died in Bethlehem in 1795.

Karl Otto Eberhardt (1711–57) was the son of a Lutheran organist and teacher. His earliest music instruction was at home. He became a teacher of Latin and music and was received into the Moravian Church in 1740. He died in Herrnhut, where he had been serving as a teacher and organist since 1756.

Ernst Immanuel Erbe (1854–1927) was born in Bern, Switzerland, where his father was a Moravian minister. He was educated in Herrnhut and was a regular church organist when he was fourteen. He was such an accomplished musician that at age seventeen his entry in a musical contest was returned because the judges thought it must have been written by a teacher. He came to America when he was thirty-five and spent most of the rest of his life in St. Louis, serving as organist in several congregations of the Evangelical and Reformed church, and supplementing his income by working as a bookkeeper. His works include organ and piano pieces, string quartets, solos for men, a cantata, and numerous anthems.

Gottfried Theodor Erxleben (1849–1931) was a German Moravian clergyman who served congregations in Silesia and Russia and as director of the teacher-training school at Niesky. His manuscript *Kleine Choralkunde*, produced in retirement, is a 153-page work with notes on texts and tunes and includes some citation of opening measures of the tunes.

Johann Ludwig Freydt (1748–1807) was born in Aschersleben, Germany. His father was a Prussian army officer, but Johann preferred music to a military career. He taught himself to play the violin and flute and later received formal musical training at Stassfurt. In 1767 he became a bassoonist in the band of the Royal Footguards in Hannover. He joined the Moravian Church in 1777 after a long period of soul searching. His talents were quickly put to work in the Moravian school at Niesky, where his coworker Christian I. LaTrobe praised his musical talent. He continued to serve in Moravian schools until illness forced his retirement in 1805. He spent his remaining years in Niesky, revising earlier compositions and giving private music lessons to children. He died on January 4, 1807. He was a prolific composer whose works were very popular in Moravian musical collections in America and Europe at the close of the eighteenth century.

Tobias Friedrich (1706–36) was the first organist of Herrnhut, commended by Zinzendorf for his great musical gifts in accompanying congregational song. He was largely responsible for establishing the firm foundation for Moravian hymnody in the Renewed Church, and is identified as the probable composer of some twenty tunes in the *Choralbuch* of 1784.[4]

John Gambold, Jr. (1760–95), not to be confused with his father (who was the first British Moravian bishop and a writer of hymn texts), was born in London on November 15, 1760. In 1774 he was sent to Germany for schooling at Niesky and Barby. He intended to make a name for himself through scholarly research, but the church assigned him to teach in its schools for young people instead, and he spent the remainder of his life in that calling. Gambold composed twenty-six vocal pieces and six keyboard sonatas, the latter of which were published in Leipzig in 1788. His health was never good, and he died in Barby on June 21, 1795.

Carl Bernhard Garve (1763–1841) was a Moravian pastor who served in Holland, Germany, and Silesia. He was educated in the Moravian schools in Zeist and Niesky, and was received into the Moravian Church in 1770. He then attended the theological seminary in Barby. He served as a professor at the theological seminary at Niesky and archivist at Zeist. After his ordination in 1799, he served congregations in Amsterdam, Ebersdorf, and Berlin. He edited a new edition of the liturgical hymns in 1823 and produced two collections of sacred songs in 1825 and 1827. He retired in 1836 and died in Herrnhut in 1841.

Johann Gottfried Gebhard (1755–after 1799): Little is known of this talented composer. In 1777 we find him at the Moravian Theological Seminary in Barby, Germany, where he became music instructor in 1784. In 1790, he left the seminary, and Moravian records make no mention of him after 1799; the date and place of his death remain unknown. His music includes piano sonatas and over forty anthems.

Christian Gottfried Geisler (1730–1810) has been largely overshadowed by his more famous brother, Johann Christian (and the fact that both have the name "Christian" further confuses matters). He was born on October 10, 1730, in Töppliwoda, Silesia, and came into the Moravian Church through the influence of his parents and brother. His early interest in music was so great that he neglected to learn a "useful" trade to support himself. He served the church through music and in other ways at Neusalz and Herrnhaag and worked three years in the Single Brethren's kitchen in Zeist in the Netherlands. After a brief stint as organist in London, where the climate disagreed with him, he returned in 1757 to Zeist, where he was a school and church organist for more than fifty years. During this period he wrote at least ten anthems and copied many others. He married Catharina Brandenburg in 1765; they had no children. He died at Zeist on June 3, 1810, at the age of seventy-nine.

Johann Christian Geisler (1729–1815) was born in Töppliwoda, Silesia, and learned to play the organ and harp at an early age. At sixteen he was instrumental in starting a trombone choir for the Gnadenfrei congregation in Silesia. He knew Christian Gregor and other leading Moravian musicians of the period and may have been a teacher of Johannes Herbst. His first wife was a harpist, and it is perhaps no accident that thirteen of his anthems utilize that instrument. Geisler served as minister to several congregations in Europe and became a member of the Unity Elders Conference, the Moravian Church's chief governing board. He began to compose in 1760 and by 1805 had written approximately three hundred musical works. Although he never visited America, most of his pieces found their way into Moravian collections here. He died in Berthelsdorf, near Herrnhut, on April 14, 1815.

Christian Gregor (1723–1801), "the first outstanding musical personality in the Renewed Moravian Church,"[5] has also been called the "father of Moravian music."[6] He was born in Silesia and joined the Moravian Church when he was seventeen. He served the church as organist and minister and held important positions as a church administrator, visiting Pennsylvania and North Carolina in that capacity in 1770–72. He was consecrated a bishop in 1789. Gregor was instrumental in Moravian liturgical development and introduced the use of concerted anthems and arias into the services. In addition to editing the hymnal of 1778 and the chorale book of 1784, he composed several hundred other musical works—over eleven hundred manuscripts of Gregor's music are preserved in the American collections. He died in Berthelsdorf, near Herrnhut, on November 6, 1801.

Rufus A. Grider (1817–1900) was born in Lititz, Pennsylvania, and lived in Bethlehem for many years. An artist, businessman, and musician, he also wrote *Historical Notes on Music in Bethlehem, Pa. (From 1741–1871),* the source for many of the colorful anecdotes regarding music in early Bethlehem. He sang tenor in the church choir and played flute in the church orchestra, and served as librarian of the Bethlehem Philharmonic Society. He later taught art in Philadelphia, and in 1883 moved to Canajoharie, New York, where he taught until his retirement in 1898. He created watercolors and pencil, pen and ink sketches of scenes and buildings in Bethlehem as well as in Mohawk County, New York, and various sites in New England.

Johann Daniel Grimm (1719–60) (sometimes Daniel Johann) was born in Stralsund on the northern coast of Germany and was an accomplished musician before joining the Moravian Church at the age of twenty-eight in 1747. He served as musician in Herrnhut and Marienborn and taught in the school at Gross Hennersdorf. One of his students there was Johann Friedrich Peter, who was later to become the leading Moravian composer in America. In addition to numerous anthems, Grimm also wrote at least thirteen short string trios (*Terzetti*) and a similar number of cantatas, which form the earliest known examples of art music in the Moravian Church. He was instrumental in compiling the 1755 chorale book of almost one thousand tunes and established a system (modified by Gregor) of numbering the chorales according to meter. He died at Gross Hennersdorf on April 27, 1760.

Bernard Adam Grube (1715–1808) was born in Walschleben, and had a lifelong interest in music. When he was seventeen he not only started teaching children but also secured a position as a choir singer.[7] He came to Bethlehem in 1748 as a missionary to the Native Americans. He learned the Delaware language and traveled widely in New England, North Carolina, and Pennsylvania. He was called to Lititz, Pennsylvania, as pastor in 1765 and had an immediate influence on the congregation's music. In November 1765, he became the congregation's music director, organizing both the choir and the *collegium musicum*. He was the composer of a number of sacred vocal works. His later service included assignments in Hope, New Jersey, and Bethlehem and Emmaus, Pennsylvania.

Heinrich Gottlob Gütter (1797–1847) was born in Germany and came to Bethlehem in 1817 to live with his uncle, the instrument maker Christian Gottlob Paulus. He joined the Moravian Church in 1819 and most likely opened his own instrument shop in that year. He was primarily a musical instrument dealer and repairman rather than an instrument maker himself. He played clarinet in the Columbian Band, a local ensemble that supported the 97th Regiment of the Pennsylvania militia. In addition to his musical instrument business, he operated a lumber business.

Francis Florentine Hagen (1815–1907) was born and grew up in Salem, North Carolina, and received theological training at the Moravian Theological Seminary in Pennsylvania. Though he was always devoted to music, he, like so many other Moravian composers, spent his professional life first as a teacher and then as the pastor of several congregations. His musical style reflects eighteenth-century Moravian roots blended with influences of later romanticism. His compositions include anthems, an orchestral overture, solo songs, solo piano works, and both original compositions and arrangements for organ, many of which were published during his lifetime. He died at Lititz, Pennsylvania, on July 7, 1907.

Christian Friedrich Hasse (1771–1831) was born in the Moravian outpost in Sarepta, Russia, and was educated at Niesky and Barby, where Gregor was one of his teachers. Having completed his studies, he himself taught at those schools and at Gross Hennersdorf until he was called to the boys' school at Fulneck, Yorkshire, in 1804. There he taught music and foreign languages and also served as organist and music director for the congregation. He wrote anthems for church use and published a two-volume collection of some of his own works and those of German composers entitled *Sacred Music* (1829–32), parts of which came out after his death. He married Ann Cossart in 1808, and they had six children, founding a family that rendered valuable service to the British Province for many years. Hasse died suddenly on May 1, 1831, while in his sixty-first year.

Georg Friedrich Hellström (1825–1912) was born in Zeist to a Swedish father and a Danish mother. He was educated in Niesky, where he played viola in the orchestra, sang in the choir, and was trained as an organist. After serving as a teacher in Niesky, Kleinwelka, and Ebersdorf, he was called to Christiansfeld, Denmark, in 1852. During his forty-two years of service there, he witnessed the transition of the congregation's music towards a more romantic style. He was a prolific composer, and his frugal habits led him to copy many of his own compositions on the backs of older works by such composers as Christian Gregor, Freydt, Geisler, and others. He was well known in Germany and was offered the position of music teacher and organist at Gnadenfrei in 1859, but chose to remain at Christiansfeld. His later service included work at Gnadenberg (1894), Kleinwelka (1895), and Neudietendorf (1898), where he remained until his death.[8]

Petrus (Peter) Herbert (d. 1571) was a bishop of the *Unitas Fratrum* and one of the three editors of the 1566 German-language hymnal. This hymnal contained some ninety of his hymns, which are noted as "distinguished by simplicity and beauty of style."[9] He was also a translator of hymns and of the Unity's confession of faith and served as the Unity's emissary in theological discussions with John Calvin and others in Switzerland.

Johannes Herbst (1735–1812) was born at Kempten, Swabia, and joined the Moravian Church in 1748. He first served the church as bookkeeper and teacher, and especially as an organist, before coming to America in 1785 to be a pastor in Lancaster and Lititz, Pennsylvania. In his spare time he was a prolific composer, producing over one hundred anthems and two hundred sacred songs. He was also an avid copier of other composers' music, and his personal collection of over one thousand anthems and many larger works is a source of incalculable value for the study of Moravian music. He was consecrated a bishop in Lititz on May 12, 1811, two days before leaving to take up new work in Salem, North Carolina. He brought his precious music collection with him, but served only a few months before his death there on January 15, 1812. He is buried in God's Acre in Salem.

John Horn: *See* Jan Roh.

Jan Hus (ca. 1372–1415) was born in Husinec in southern Bohemia. During his student years he earned money by singing in choirs. He was attracted to the priesthood because of the benefits it carried of fine clothing, food, and a secure and honored life. In the years that followed, however, he experienced a change of heart and became a true priest to his people. He received the BA in 1393 and the MA in 1396 from the University of Prague (Charles University). In 1398 he was appointed to the faculty of this institution, and began signing his name simply "Hus" (rather than "John of Husinec"). He was installed as preacher of the Bethlehem Chapel in Prague in 1402, soon after his ordination, and became very popular.[10] Within a very few years he began to be outspokenly critical of abuses within the Catholic church and was embroiled in conflict with the church and political authorities. When in late 1412 Pope John XXIII threatened an interdict against the entire city of Prague because of Hus's outspoken preaching, he departed on a voluntary exile to spare his people.[11] Hus "powerfully united the popular and the academic streams of the Czech reform movement. . . . He turned to the practical things which needed to be done to reform the church from top to bottom."[12] He advocated congregational singing and preaching in the language of the people, which became a hallmark of the Unitas Fratrum. In 1414 he was summoned to appear before the Council of Constance and chose to go, having been promised safe conduct. However, he was arrested and imprisoned on November 28, 1414. After more than six months imprisonment, his trial before the council began on June 5, 1415. He was urged to recant, which he refused to do, asking only that his supposed errors be proven to him from the Scriptures. He was condemned and burned at the stake on July 6, 1415.

Christian David Jaeschke (1755–1827) came from one of the early Czech immigrant families who renewed the old Unitas Fratrum under the patronage of Count Zinzendorf. He was born in Herrnhut. He was a teacher and organist at Ebersdorf and later a copyist of the *Gemein-Nachrichten* in Barby. He served as organist and choirmaster at Herrnhut for forty years, from 1786 to 1826, composing many anthems and vocal solos. C. F. Hasse, writing in 1829, called him a "musical Genius" and lamented that his works had not become more widely known. He was the maternal grandfather of Woldemar Voullaire (see below). Jaeschke died in

Herrnhut in 1827 after an illness of a year and a half; the *Dienerblätter* notes that he had wanted to compose the music for his own funeral, but was unable to do so.

Thor Martin Johnson (1913–75) was the son of a Moravian minister. Born and raised in Winston-Salem, North Carolina, he was nurtured in the Moravian faith and life, and with unusual musical talent, was deeply aware of the rich musical heritage of the church. He was appointed conductor of the Cincinnati Symphony in 1947, as the first American-born and trained conductor of a major symphony orchestra. He later served the Interlochen Arts Academy, Northwestern University, was founding director of the Moravian Music Festivals and the Peninsula Music Festival, and was music director of the Nashville Symphony from 1967 until his death. When invited to direct the Festival and Seminar of Early American Moravian Music in Bethlehem in 1950, he eagerly accepted. His infectious interest and enthusiasm and the quality of the musical experience led to subsequent festivals in 1954 and 1955. This momentum was the impetus for the 1956 formation of the Moravian Music Foundation. He went on to conduct the first eleven Moravian Music Festivals.

Johann Gottlob Klemm (1690–1762) seems to have been the first person in the American colonies to devote himself solely to the making of keyboard instruments. The son of an organist, organ builder, and schoolmaster, he was born near Dresden, and studied theology at Freiberg and at the University in Leipzig. He returned to Dresden, probably around 1710, to pursue a career in instrument making, and may have met the noted organ builder Gottfried Silbermann during this time. He came to know Zinzendorf, for whom he built a harpsichord, and he also built a clavichord for Tobias Friedrich. He moved to Herrnhut and joined the Moravians in 1726, and was present during the renewal service of August 13, 1727.[13] He is known to have led some services and taught the boys during his time in Herrnhut. For a while Klemm followed Moravian ways, but soon became disillusioned and left for America with the Schwenkfelders in 1733.[14] He settled outside Philadelphia and lived as a Separatist, without any religious affiliation. Klemm changed the spelling of his name to John Clemm and began work as the first professional organ and keyboard builder in America. Returning to his union with the Moravians, he moved to Bethlehem in 1757, where the younger David Tannenberg worked with him on a number of organs.

Christian Ignatius LaTrobe (1758–1836) was born on February 12, 1758, in Fulneck, England. He was the son of an English Moravian minister, Benjamin H. LaTrobe, Sr., and an American mother, Margaret Antes LaTrobe, the sister of John Antes. LaTrobe was educated in Moravian schools in Germany from 1771 to 1778, where he received sound advice on how to play an organ in church from Bishop August Spangenberg. After teaching at the Moravian school at Niesky from 1779 to 1784, he returned to London and served many years as an administrator of Moravian mission work. He was acquainted with Haydn and other leading musicians of the day and was the only Moravian composer to receive wide recognition outside the church during his lifetime. He retired at Fairfield (near Manchester), England, in 1834, where he died on May 6, 1836.

Edward William Leinbach (1823–1901) was born in Salem, North Carolina, and devoted his life to the Moravian community there. As a child he displayed great musical talent and was given training in piano, organ, and cello. He studied music in Boston with Henry Kemble Oliver. Returning to Salem, he served as organist and choir director of the Home Church, organized the Classical Music Society, developed the Salem Band, and became professor of music at Salem Female Academy (now Salem Academy and College). Leinbach was known for his performing and teaching abilities in addition to his talent as an orchestrator and composer. He is regarded as the most influential musician in Salem in the last half of the nineteenth century. He died in Salem on February 18, 1901.

Heinrich Lonas (1838–1903) was born in Herrnhut and studied music there and in nearby Zittau. He became the organist in Herrnhut in 1856, but in 1870 went to Berlin as the Moravian Church organist and instructor in the Schmidt Conservatory. In 1873 he became organist in Neuwied, a position he held for almost thirty years. In addition to writing a number of choral anthems, he produced a chorale book for use in Germany. He died on March 30, 1903.

Lukáš (Luke) of Prague (ca. 1458–1528) was born and raised in Prague. He became acquainted with the Unitas Fratrum through a friend and joined the Unity shortly after his graduation from the University of Prague (Charles University) in 1481. Throughout the remainder of his life he served as the Unity's most influential theologian and writer, assisting the young church in its search for identity and stability. His writings shaped the Unity's theology and practice for many years to come. He traveled extensively, making contact with the Eastern Orthodox and the Roman Catholic churches. He was the head of the Unity at the outbreak of the Protestant Reformation and corresponded with Martin Luther. He was probably one of the editors of the first Unitas Fratrum hymnal of 1505, and he was the editor of the hymnal of 1519. He was himself a hymn writer, and a few of his hymns have been translated into English.[15]

John Christian Malthaner (1810–73), a piano builder, was born at Leonbrunn, Würtemberg, and came to the United States in 1828.[16] He attempted to establish a piano factory in New York, but few details survive regarding this endeavor. Malthaner moved to Bethlehem in 1837 at the encouragement of Christian A. Lukenbach, the owner of a local grist mill. Malthaner first settled on Lukenbach's property and established a piano manufacturing firm. The first piano he produced in Bethlehem was a partially completed instrument he had brought from New York. He had become familiar with current practices in piano building while in New York and likely brought a number of parts with him when he moved to Bethlehem. In 1842 he moved to New Street, where he built his factory, and remained there until his death.[17] His pianos became widely known. His sons carried on the trade after his death in 1873.

Johan Hermann Mankell (1763–1835) was a Moravian church musician and composer and the father of seven sons, six of whom became musicians. The Mankell family may be a branch of the German musical family Mangold. Born in Germany, Mankell served in Christiansfeld and then in Sweden from 1823. He was the composer of works for piano, voices, and woodwind sextet.

Christian Friedrich Martin (1796–1873) was born in Markneukirchen in Germany and worked as a cabinetmaker and guitar maker with his father, Johann Georg Martin. He is known to have made guitars from before 1826. In 1833 he emigrated to New York and set up a store and workshop there. He moved to the Nazareth area in 1839 and established his guitar-making company there, where it is still in business. The New York firm of C. A. Zoebisch and Sons (see below) was the Martin company's distribution center until 1898.

Matěj (Matthias) of Kunwald (d. 1500) was one of the first ministers ordained by the Unitas Fratrum in 1467, at the age of twenty-five or thirty. The son of a farmer, he was elected a bishop and served as the Unity's sole bishop for thirty-two years (1467–99). He led the Unity with courage and endurance through its initial struggles for identity in the face of persecution.

Lisette (Lizette) Marie Van Vleck Meinung (1830–1914) showed remarkable musical talent at the age of two, when she sang a solo in the church where her father (Carl Anton Van Vleck) was the minister. She attended the Moravian Young Ladies' Seminary in Bethlehem, Pennsylvania. In 1846 Lisette came to reside with her mother, sisters, and brother in Salem, North Carolina. (Her father had died in December 1845.) She began teaching piano at the age of sixteen and in 1852 joined the faculty of the Salem Female Academy as a music teacher, a position she held for sixteen years until her marriage to Alexander C. Meinung. Her husband was also a gifted musician, and for many years their home was a music center in the community. The Meinungs gave numerous young people in Salem their first music instruction and inspired them to further study.[18] Lisette's piano compositions include short pieces such as the polka, waltz, march, and galop.

David Moritz Michael (1751–1827) was born in Kühnhausen (near Erfurt in Thuringia), Germany, and did not become a Moravian until he was thirty years old. He taught in the Moravian school at Niesky and came to America in 1795. His official church position was as a worker with the young men of the congregations in Nazareth and Bethlehem, but his contributions to the musical life of the settlements were great. He revitalized the Bethlehem *collegium musicum* and conducted the performance of Haydn's *Creation* that may have been its American premiere. He is well known as a composer of wind ensembles, especially his fourteen *Parthien* and the two "Water Music" suites, written for excursions on the Lehigh River. His other works include seventeen anthems for four-part choir (SATB or SSAB) with accompaniment by strings and organ (and in some cases winds), two soprano solos with string accompaniment, two duets for sopranos with string accompaniment, and an eleven-movement setting of Psalm 103. Johann Friedrich Peter also attributed four songs with piano accompaniment to Michael in his personal manuscript copybook.[19] Michael may well have written more such short and relatively simple works, but they have not yet been identified. He returned to Germany in 1815 and died in Neuwied, Germany, on February 26, 1827.

Philipp Heinrich Molther (1714–80) studied at the University of Jena and was a teacher of Zinzendorf's son Christian Renatus, instructing him in French and music. He was received into the Moravian Church in 1738. He helped establish the Moravian work in England, where he served as a pastor. Ill health prevented him from traveling with Zinzendorf to Pennsylvania in 1741. He was the composer of several cantatas, including one for the laying of the foundation for the Single Brothers House in Herrnhaag. He translated a number of hymns into French and served the Moravian congregation in Montmirail, Switzerland. He later served in Dublin, Ireland, and Bedford, England. He was elected a bishop in 1775 and died in Bedford in 1780.

James Montgomery (1771–1854) was born at Ayr, Scotland. His parents left him and two younger brothers in Moravian schools when they went to the West Indies to begin work in Tobago, where they later died. He pursued a literary career and was twice imprisoned for his liberal views. He returned to the Moravian Church in 1812. He championed the causes of Sunday schools and missions and received a royal pension. His poetic output includes some four hundred hymns, many of which are beloved in many denominations.

Peter Mortimer (1750–1828) was an English-born Moravian who, as a boy, was sent to Germany to complete his education at the Moravian school in Niesky. He remained in Germany for the remainder of his life, serving a number of Moravian congregations as a teacher, organist, and secretary. He also worked on books and translations involving church history.

Georg Gottfried Müller (1762–1821), a son of Bishop Buchard Müller, was born in Gross Hennersdorf, near Herrnhut, and was educated at Barby. He came to America in 1784, where he married Johanna Levering of Jamaica. He taught at the Moravian school at Nazareth, Pennsylvania, and then served in Lititz, where he was head of the *collegium musicum* and reorganized the congregation's music collection. Following additional service in Bethlehem, from 1805 to 1814 he served at Beersheba and Gnadenhutten in Ohio. He composed at least one of his works, *Lamb of God, Thou Shalt Remain Forever,* while in Ohio. After serving as pastor in Philadelphia and Newport, Rhode Island, Müller retired to Lititz in 1819 and died there of consumption on March 19, 1821.

Joseph Theodor Müller (1854–1946) was a German Moravian pastor, seminary instructor and archivist who specialized in the history of the Bohemian Brethren. His *Hymnologisches Handbuch zum Gesangbuch der Brüdergemeine* (1916) is the only published work of its kind for German Moravian hymnody. He was also the author of the three-volume *Geschichte der Böhmischen Brüder* (1922–31).

Immanuel Nitschmann (1736–90) was born in Herrnhut and came to Bethlehem in 1761. He served as a minister and diarist and was able to devote significant time to music. An organist and violinist, he copied a great deal of instrumental music that was of benefit to the *collegium musicum* in Bethlehem, including string quartets and symphonies by Franz Joseph Haydn. He also arranged arias from operas by Hasse and Graun for three violins, viola, and figured bass.

Johann Friedrich Peter (1746–1813) was born in Heerendijk, Holland, to German Moravian parents. He was educated in Holland and Germany, and came to America with his brother Simon in 1770. Peter appears to have begun composing very shortly after his arrival in the New World. He served the Pennsylvania Moravians in Nazareth, Bethlehem, and Lititz, and was sent to Salem, North Carolina, in 1780. There, among other duties, he assumed the position of music director for the community. In 1786 he married Catharina Leinbach, a leading soprano in the church choir. Under Peter's energetic and capable leadership, a musical tradition was established in Salem that benefited the community long after his departure in 1790. He afterward served Moravians in Graceham, Maryland; Hope, New Jersey; and Bethlehem, Pennsylvania, where he was a clerk, secretary, and organist at the Central Church. J. F. Peter's many works have earned him the reputation of being the most gifted of Moravian composers in America. His six string quintets, written in Salem and dated 1789, are the earliest known chamber music written in this country. He died in Bethlehem on July 13, 1813, almost literally at the organ bench, shortly after playing for a children's service.

Simon Peter (1743–1819) was born in Heerendijk, Holland, and was the elder brother of Johann Friedrich Peter. They came to America together in 1770. Simon served in Pennsylvania until coming to North Carolina in 1784, where he remained for the rest of his life as a pastor and church administrator. His musical compositions, though few in number, demonstrate a high degree of musical talent and skill.

Bessie Whittington Pfohl (1881–1971) was the wife of Bishop J. Kenneth Pfohl. A graduate of Salem College, she served as the organist and choir director at Home Moravian Church in Winston-Salem for eighteen years. She was active in the North Carolina Federation of Music Clubs. Her memoir identifies her as one of the earliest persons to rediscover the rich treasury of Moravian anthems from the eighteenth century, and her efforts were instrumental in making this music collection known.[20]

James Christian Pfohl (1912–97), a son of J. Kenneth and Bessie W. Pfohl, received early musical training at home, along with his two brothers and three sisters. He attended the University of North Carolina and the University of Michigan, where he received degrees in organ performance and musicology. He was conductor of the symphony orchestras in Jacksonville, Florida, Charlotte, North Carolina, and York, Pennsylvania; and taught music at Davidson College. He was the founder of Transylvania Music Camp and the Brevard Music Center and was noted as the inspiration for the founding of the North Carolina School of the Arts in Winston-Salem, North Carolina. He edited the first publication of a number of Moravian anthems from the eighteenth century.[21]

Johann Christopher Pyrlaeus (1713–85) was the first Moravian musician to serve in the Native American mission field. In addition to learning music as a youth, he studied theology at Leipzig University, where he may well have taken advantage of the opportunity to observe Johann Sebastian Bach's work with the Leipzig *collegium musicum.* Pyrlaeus first came into contact with the Moravians during his time at Leipzig and joined the Moravian Church, being selected to serve in Pennsylvania. The quality of his work among the Native Americans led Spangenberg to select him to organize the first Moravian Indian-language school, and he translated many hymns into the Mohican language. His most significant contribution to the music of the Moravians in America was the establishment of the Bethlehem *collegium musicum* in December of 1744. He was proficient as a singer, instrumentalist, and organist, and gave Moravian composer John Antes his early musical education. He returned to Europe in 1751.[22]

Peter Ricksecker (1791–1873) was born in Bethlehem. After attending the seminary at Nazareth, Pennsylvania, he served as a teacher at the boys' school at Nazareth. He was proficient as a violinist, organist, and singer, and it is likely that during his time teaching at Nazareth he studied composition with Johann Christian Bechler, who was then principal of the school. Ricksecker composed choral and instrumental music, including a piano *Battle of New Orleans* and six band marches. After completing his assignment at Nazareth in 1821, he taught at Lancaster, Pennsylvania. Following his ordination in 1826, he was called to service in Tobago in the West Indies. Because of health problems, he returned to Bethlehem in 1848, and in 1854 was assigned to mission work among the Native Americans near Leavenworth, Kansas, along with his daughter and son-in-law, both also accomplished musicians. This mission was established as the music center of the western Indian territory, and *Singstunden* were conducted there in both English and the Delaware language. Ricksecker composed a number of sacred songs based on hymn tunes for his Indian scholars. After leaving this mission station, Ricksecker established a music school at Leavenworth, Kansas, in 1857.[23]

Abraham Ritter (1792–1860) was born in Philadelphia to a Moravian family and was active in the church there throughout his life. He served as organist from 1811 to the time of his death and wrote a history of the Moravian work in Philadelphia. Ritter contributed two tunes to a supplement to the Episcopal hymnal (1839) and composed three short anthems for Holy Week. He died on October 8, 1860, after a lengthy illness.

Jan Roh (ca. 1485/90–1547) was ordained in 1518. He was one of the Unity's representatives in early conversations with Martin Luther. He drew up the Unity's confessions of faith of 1532 and 1535. In 1541 he published a revised edition of the hymnal of 1501. He also edited the 1544 German-language hymnal, particularly significant for its revision of some of the hymns to bring the theology back to the central tenets of the Moravian faith.

Ludolph Ernst Schlicht (1714–69) attended the theological seminary at Jena. He came to Herrnhut in 1738, where he served with his musical gifts primarily with the young. He was officially received into the Moravian Church in 1739. He served as accompanist for worship and wrote a number of anthems and cantatas as well as hymn texts. He was ordained in 1742 and served in several congregations in England and Ireland. He was probably the editor of the 1746 English Moravian hymnal. In 1753 he was called to Bedford, England, where he worked on the translation of the hymnal into English. He also worked on an English translation of the liturgy book.

Václav Solín (1527–95) was a printer and minister of the Unitas Fratrum who assisted Jan Blahoslav with editing the 1561 Czech hymnal. It is possible that he was the author of the 1561 treatise, *Musica*, published under the pseudonym Jean Josquin dez Prez.[24]

Johannes Sörensen (1767–1831) was educated at the Moravian schools in Christiansfeld (Denmark), Niesky, and Barby, Germany, and received a medical degree in 1794. Alongside his medical practice he engaged in musical activity, composing a number of beloved anthems. He had to retire in 1829 because of ill health.

August Gottlieb Spangenberg (1704–92) was the son of a Lutheran minister. He went to the University of Jena beginning in 1721, where he studied theology, and taught at Halle. He became a trusted assistant to Zinzendorf. In 1735 he led the first group of Moravians to Georgia, and he saw to that party's relocation to Pennsylvania in 1740. He also led the exploration of the colony of North Carolina in search of land to purchase for the Moravians' settlement there. He took a detailed interest in the new settlement of Wachovia in North Carolina. He returned to Europe in 1762, following Zinzendorf's death, becoming a member of the governing board of the Moravian Church. His careful and wise leadership helped stabilize the church after Zinzendorf's death, and his advice to the young Christian LaTrobe ("keep it simple") had a long-lasting influence on Moravian organ playing. His many hymn texts express his tender pastoral concern for the Moravian Church as well as his love for Christ. He was known as "Brother Joseph," after the biblical Joseph who cared for his brothers and sisters in exile in Egypt.

Jiří Strejc (1536–99) was a highly educated and literate priest of the Unitas Fratrum. He was a hymn writer (under the name Georg Vetter) and a translator for the Unity, rendering, among other things, Calvin's works from Latin into Czech. He produced a paraphrase of the Psalms in Czech in 1587, set to French melodies. First issued as a separate book, this was popular beyond the Unitas Fratrum and was included in the Unity's hymnals after 1615. He also continued Jan Blahoslav's work of translating the Bible into Czech and supervised the 1596 single-volume printing of the entire Bible in Czech (called the Kralice Bible beginning in the nineteenth century).

John Swertner (1746–1803) was born in Haarlem, the Netherlands, and attended the Moravian school in Zeist. Following his theological education at the Moravian Theological Seminary in Barby (1771–75), he was called to England to work with the boys and single brothers in Fulneck, England. He was ordained in 1779, and served in a variety of positions in Yorkshire, London, Fairfield, and Bristol, England, and Dublin, Ireland. He was the editor of the 1789 English Moravian hymnal, and translated and wrote several hymn texts included in that and later hymnals.

David Tannenberg (1728–1804) was born in Berthelsdorf, Germany, the son of members of the Unitas Fratrum who came to Germany from Moravia. He had no formal training in organ building, but worked as a joiner and came to Bethlehem in 1749. On Johann Gottlob Klemm's move to Bethlehem in 1757, Tannenberg became his assistant. He moved to Lititz in 1765, where he set up a workshop. He built organs for Moravian, German Lutheran, Reformed, and Catholic churches, as well as for some private individuals. In 1793, at Tannenberg's request, Philip Bachman, a Moravian trained in musical instrument manufacture, arrived from Germany to serve as his assistant; Bachman married Tannenberg's youngest daughter. Tannenberg died in 1804 after suffering a fall while tuning an organ. A partial list of his organs indicates that he and Klemm built five instruments working together; an additional forty-two Tannenberg instruments are documented, of which nine survive.[25]

Jacob Christian Till (1799–1882) studied piano building in Philadelphia, and after 1810 built pianos with his father Johann Christian Till as their primary source of income. The Tills received piano contracts for the parlors of the Sun and Eagle hotels in Bethlehem.[26] Since Jacob's name is on the nameplate of the Till pianos, it seems likely that he constructed the mechanism while his father built the cabinets. In 1834 he moved to Easton, approximately ten miles from Bethlehem; after that time it is not known whether he continued in the family business or made pianos on his own.[27]

Johann Christian Till (1762–1844) was born May 18, 1762, at Gnadenthal near Nazareth, Pennsylvania. Educated at Nazareth Hall, he was taught by Simon Peter. A full-time career in music for him was out of the question, and so he learned nail making and woodworking. Through Simon Peter's intercession, however, he was allowed to take part of his lunch hour for musical instruction and practice. In 1793 he became the organist and schoolmaster in Hope, New Jersey, but when that congregation closed in 1808, he had to return to woodworking in Bethlehem and later supported himself by building pianos with his son Jacob. Finally, in 1811, his musical talent was given more scope when he succeeded Johann Friedrich Peter as organist at the Central Church. Till copied many anthems for the use of the church and produced several anthems of his own for the Bethlehem collection. Examples of his work are in the Nazareth and Salem collections as well. He also wrote musical settings for the "Liturgical Hymns" of 1823, and at least one of these found its way to Europe for use in Herrnhut. He died in Bethlehem on November 19, 1844.

Johannes Renatus Verbeek (1748–1820), composer and pastor, was born in Amsterdam. He attended Moravian schools in Zeist, Gross Hennersdorf, and Niesky, and the theological seminary in Barby. After serving as a teacher in Niesky and worker with the single brothers in Barby, he was ordained in 1777. He served as scribe for the Unity Elders Conference in Barby and Herrnhut and served as a missions administrator, traveling to the West Indies in 1796–98 and to Pennsylvania and North Carolina in 1806. He was the composer of a great many anthems, many of which found their way into the American Moravian collections.

Georg Vetter: *See* Jiří Strejc.

Amelia Van Vleck (1835–1929), known as "Miss Amy," was born in Lancaster, Pennsylvania, one of the three daughters of Carl Anton Van Vleck. At eighteen Amy entered the Salem Female Academy, where her maternal grandfather was the first president. After completion of her studies, she became a professor at the academy. According to an article in a Winston-Salem newspaper, Amy was highly regarded for her musical abilities: "Her rare artistic temperament has made her throughout the years a figure of note in musical circles of the city."[28] Her memoir also testifies to her remarkable talent: "She was a rarely talented musician, a brilliant pianist, a composer of real merit, and one who used her talent in unstinted measure for the glory of God and the enjoyment and entertainment of her many friends."[29] In addition, she was the organist at Home Moravian Church in Salem, North Carolina for fifty years.[30] Amy composed several pieces for piano solo and voice with piano accompaniment.

Carl Anton Van Vleck (1794–1845) was born in Bethlehem, Pennsylvania, where his father, the pastor and composer Jacob Van Vleck, was the superintendent of the Moravian Young Ladies' Seminary. He received his education at Nazareth Hall and the Theological Institute, both in Nazareth, Pennsylvania. Van Vleck was a teacher and minister in the Moravian Church. He was a gifted musician, serving as organist, giving public recitals, and teaching music.[31] He devoted most of his musical ability to teaching and performing, rather than composing. His only known piano composition is a short rondo in F major.

Jacob Van Vleck (1751–1831) was born to a Dutch family in New York. He was educated in Nazareth and went to Germany for theological training at Barby. He returned to America in 1778 to serve as assistant pastor in Bethlehem and from 1790 to 1800 was inspector of the girls' school there. He then served in Nazareth, Lititz, and Salem, where he succeeded Bishop Herbst in 1812. He himself was consecrated a bishop in 1815. Van Vleck was a fine performer on the violin and keyboard instruments, and his keyboard style was complimented by the marquis de Chastellux, a French aide to General Washington during the Revolution. Van Vleck also contributed to the development of the *collegium musicum* in Bethlehem. His few compositions evidence considerable talent, though his church duties seem to have left little time for music in his later years. He died in Bethlehem in 1831 at the age of eighty.

Henri Marc Hermann Woldemar Voullaire (1825–1902), a grandson of Christian David Jaeschke, was born in Neuwelke in the Baltic region. Like so many Moravian composers before him, he taught in the school at Niesky, Germany (1846–55). He also served as minister of several Moravian congregations in Europe, including Zeist (Holland), Neudietendorf (Germany),

Gothenburg (Sweden), Christiansfeld (Denmark), and Neusalz, Gnadenberg, and Gnadau (Germany). His music reflects the influence of the romantic music of his time, particularly that of Brahms. He retired to Herrnhut after 1891 and died there on June 12, 1902.

Wilhelm Heinrich Wauer (1826–1902) was born in Herrnhut, where he lived for his entire life except for two and a half years of schooling in Niesky. He worked for almost fifty years in the Herrnhut manufacturing and distribution firm of Abraham Dürninger & Co., managing correspondence and transactions in English and Spanish, having learned those languages thoroughly enough to take joy in English and Spanish literature. He wished to study music, and although he continued to work in the business, he dedicated his free hours to music study, composition, and singing in the Herrnhut choir. He composed several small cantatas and songs, as well as an oratorio that was performed in Herrnhut and in other towns in Germany. Some of his works were published during his lifetime. He particularly revered the works of Bach, Handel, Haydn, Mozart, Beethoven, and especially Mendelssohn, and was influential in introducing their works and those of contemporary composers to the musicians in Herrnhut.

Johann Gottfried Weber (1740–97) was born in Herrnhut and was received into the Moravian Church in 1754. He learned music as well as his father's linen and weaving trade. He served as organist at Kleinwelka from 1766 to 1769 and in Neudietendorf in 1769–72. He served as organist in Herrnhut from 1772 to 1785. He was ordained in 1785 and served in Barby and in Gothenburg, Sweden. He returned in Herrnhut in 1788. He was the composer of many anthems and possibly the composer of six sonatas for four trombones.

Jedediah Weiss (1796–1873) was a gifted clock maker and musician, playing trombone, trumpet, violin, and bassoon. He was known for his powerful and versatile bass voice, as well as for his service for more than fifty years as one of a quartet of trombonists who were active in Bethlehem. He was one of the musicians who traveled to Philadelphia in 1822 to assist the Musical Fund Society of Philadelphia in their performance of Haydn's *Creation*. The Philadelphia composer Charles Hommann dedicated his Overture in D Major to Weiss.

Michael Weisse (ca. 1480–1534), a German monk, was accepted into the Unitas Fratrum in 1517. With Jan Roh, he served as a representative of the Unity in conversations with Martin Luther. He edited the Unity's first German-language hymnal in 1531, incorporating his own theological leaning into a number of the hymns; this hymnal was revised by Jan Roh in 1544. He also served as a translator for the Unity, translating the 1532 confession of faith from Czech to German, again interpolating his own ideas.

John Frederick [J. Fred] Wolle (1863–1933) was born in Bethlehem to a Moravian ministerial family and was the grand-nephew of Bishop Peter Wolle. He learned to play the organ as a child and studied music in Munich, Germany. Wolle served for some years as head of the music department at the University of California at Berkeley, but is best known as the founder of the Bethlehem Bach Choir (1898), which gave the first complete American performance of the Mass in B Minor in 1900. He also composed pieces for the organ, wrote alternate tunes for familiar hymn texts, and produced a limited number of choral works.

Peter Wolle (1792–1871) was born on St. Thomas in the West Indies to Moravian missionary parents but was sent at age three to Pennsylvania for his education. In 1807 he became one of the first three students at Moravian Theological Seminary and later taught in Moravian schools in Nazareth, Pennsylvania, and Salem, North Carolina. He also served pastorates in North Carolina and Pennsylvania. While serving in Lititz, Pennsylvania, he was consecrated a bishop in 1845. From 1853 to 1855 he served an interim pastorate in Dover, Ohio, and then served on the Provincial Board until his final retirement in 1861. He died in Bethlehem. In addition to composing anthems, he compiled the first Moravian tune book published in America (1836).

John Worthington (1725–90) was born in Dublin, Ireland, and was a child singer in the Anglican cathedral there. After his voice changed, he lost his choir position and turned to gambling and instrumental performances in coffeehouses. After being hired as a music teacher by Benjamin LaTrobe, he joined the Moravians and later served numerous pastorates in Great Britain after 1763. He died in his native Dublin as pastor of the Moravian church there in 1790. Only one musical arrangement by him is known to be extant, but Christian LaTrobe speaks of other compositions by Worthington which he said were praised for their "simplicity and elegance."

Nicholas Ludwig von Zinzendorf (1700–1760) was born in Dresden and raised by his grandmother, Countess von Gersdorf. He was educated at the Halle *Paedogogium* from 1710 to 1716 and studied law at Wittenberg. In 1722 he allowed exiles from Moravia to settle on his Berthelsdorf estate. He gradually came to identify more and more with these exiles and in 1727 formulated the "Brotherly Agreement" to reconcile differences among them.[32] He was ordained a Lutheran minister in 1735 and was consecrated a bishop of the renewed Moravian Church in 1737. He was banished from Saxony in 1736, making numerous journeys to visit Moravian settlements around the world, including a trip to America in 1741–43. He was the author of numerous works, including sermons, Bible commentaries, and a great many hymns, so that the theology of the eighteenth-century Moravian Church was essentially that of Zinzendorf.

Charles Augustus Zoebisch (1824–1911) was born in Markneukirchen, Germany, and came to America in 1842. He became a successful manufacturer and importer of musical instruments in New York City. He was very active in the Moravian Church in New York and served on a number of provincial boards, as well as being president of the board of the Seminary for Young Ladies in Bethlehem. His memoir cites him as the best-known layman in the Moravian Church in America. For many years until 1898, his company, C. A. Zoebisch and Sons, had exclusive rights to sell the guitars made by the Martin Guitar Company of Nazareth, Pennsylvania.[33]

Notes

1. Summary of Bachmann's life taken from William H. Armstrong, *Organs for America: The Life and Work of David Tannenberg* (Philadelphia: University of Pennsylvania Press, 1967), 48–53.

2. "Memoir of the Rt. Rev. John C. Bechler, translated by Samuel Reinke, one of his former pupils," *The Moravian* (June 26, 1857), 1.

3. Rudolf Říčan, *The History of the Unity of Brethren*, trans. by C. Daniel Crews (Bethlehem and Winston-Salem: Moravian Church in America, 1992), 220.

4. James Boeringer, "Sources for the Moravian Tunes in Gregor's 1784 *Choral-Buch*," in *Choralbuch by Christian Gregor, Facsimile of the First Edition of 1784* (Winston-Salem and Bethlehem: Moravian Music Foundation Press, 1984), 36, 41.

5. Hans T. David, *Musical Life in the Pennsylvania Settlements of the Unitas Fratrum* (reprinted from *Transactions of the Moravian Historical Society*, 1942, as Moravian Music Foundation Publications No. 6, Winston-Salem, 1959), 9.

6. James Boeringer, "Sources for the Moravian tunes," 40.

7. Bernard Adam Grube, *Lebenslauf*, trans. John T. Hamilton. Moravian Archives, Bethlehem.

8. Christina Ekström graciously supplied this information, translated from Sybille Reventlow, "Musik og Sang," in Anders Pontoppidan Thyssen, ed., *Herrnhuter-samfundet i Christiansfeld* (Åbenrå: Historisk Samfund for Sønderjylland, 1984), 684–90.

9. John Julian, *A Dictionary of Hymnology*, 2nd ed. (New York: Dover Publications, 1907), vol. 1, 512.

10. The erection in 1391 of the Bethlehem Chapel, as a place where the gospel was to be preached to the people in their own language, was a key event in the Czech reform movement of the early fifteenth century.

11. An interdict was an ecclesiastical punishment imposed by the Pope prohibiting the faithful from participating in spiritual things; an interdict applied to a region or town also forbade the administration of sacraments and solemn services. This John XXIII was later declared an "anti-pope," and his name and number were reused in the twentieth century. See F. L. Cross and E. A. Livingstone, ed., *The Oxford Dictionary of the Christian Church*, 2nd edition (Oxford, Oxford University Press, 1983), s.v. "Interdict," 708–9.

12. Říčan, 5.

13. See chapter 1, pp. 11–12.

14. The Schwenkfelders were a Protestant sect arising from followers of the Silesian Reformed theologian Caspar Schwenkfeld (1490–1561), who could not

accept the Lutheran doctrine of Holy Communion or of salvation by grace. Following persecution in the seventeenth and early eighteenth century, several hundred of the Schwenkfelders found temporary refuge in Saxony, aided by Zinzendorf, and then migrated to Pennsylvania in 1734. Howard Wiegner Kriebel, *The Schwenkfelders in Pennsylvania* (Lancaster: Pennsylvania German Society, 1904).

15. C. Daniel Crews, "Luke of Prague: Theologian of the Unity," *The Hinge: A Journal of Christian Thought for the Moravian Church* 12/3 (Autumn 2005): 21–54.

16. Augustus Schultz, *The Old Moravian Cemetery of Bethlehem, Pa., 1742–1897* (N.p., n.d.), 258.

17. Joseph Mortimer Levering, *A History of Bethlehem, Pennsylvania 1741–1892 with Some Account of Its Founders and Their Early Activity in America* (Bethlehem: Times Publishing Co., 1903), 717.

18. "Memoir of Sr. Lizette Marie Meinung," Moravian Archives (Southern Province), Winston-Salem.

19. Jeannine Ingram, "A Musical Potpourri: The Commonplace Book of Johann Friedrich Peter," *Moravian Music Foundation Bulletin* 24/1 (Spring/Summer 1979): 2–7.

20. Memoir of Bessie Whittington Pfohl, Moravian Archives, Winston-Salem.

21. Memoir of James Christian Pfohl, Moravian Archives, Winston-Salem.

22. Lawrence W. Hartzell, "Musical Moravian Missionaries, Part I: Johann Christopher Pyrlaeus," *Moravian Music Journal* 29/4 (Winter 1984): 91–92.

23. Lawrence W. Hartzell, "Musical Moravian Missionaries, Part V: Peter Ricksecker," *Moravian Music Journal* 32/1 (Spring 1987): 14–15.

24. Edmund deSchweinitz, *The History of the Church Known as the Unitas Fratrum, or The Unity of the Brethren*, 2nd ed. (Bethlehem: Moravian Publication Concern, 1901), 424. See also Thomas Sovík, "Music of the American Moravians: First Tradition," *Czechoslovak and Central European Journal* (formerly *Kosmas*) 9/1–2 (Summer/Winter 1990): 35–46, and "Music Theorists of the Bohemian Reformation: Jan Blahoslav and Jan Josquin," *Journal of Czechoslovak and Central European Studies* (formerly *Kosmas*) 8/1 (January 1989): 105–45.

25. William H. Armstrong, "David Tannenberg: An Organ Builder's Life," in Gary Albert, ed., *Splendid Service: The Restoration of David Tannenberg's Home Moravian Church Organ* (Winston-Salem: Old Salem, Inc., 2004).

26. Levering, 716.

27. Folder 17, "Instruments—Other," Collections Office, Moravian Museum, Bethlehem.

28. "Miss Amy Van Vleck," *Winston-Salem Journal*, October [19], 1926. This article was in praise of Amy as she celebrated her ninety-first birthday.

29. "Memoir of Sr. Amelia Adelaide Van Vleck," Moravian Archives (Southern Province), Winston-Salem.

30. "Memoir of Sr. Amelia Adelaide Van Vleck."

31. "Memoir of our Married Brother Carl Anton Van Vlec[k], who blessedly fell asleep in Greeneville, Tennessee, on 21 December, 1845," Moravian Archives (Southern Province), Winston-Salem.

32. See chapter 1, pp. 11–12, for a discussion of the events of 1727.

33. Harry Emilius Stocker, *A History of the Moravian Church in New York City* (New York: n.p., 1922), 318–21; "Notes and Queries," *Moravian Music Journal* 27/2 (Summer 1982): 54, 57. Stocker indicates that C. A. Zoebisch's son was Clemence Theodore, not C. A., Jr., as the *Journal* article states.

Appendix Two

A Moravian Musical Timeline

1372 (ca.)	Jan Hus born (d. 1415)
1393	Jan Hus receives bachelor's degree
1396	Jan Hus receives master's degree
1398	Jan Hus appointed to the faculty of the University of Prague (Charles University)
1402	Jan Hus installed as preacher at Bethlehem Chapel, Prague
1412	Jan Hus begins voluntary exile after pope threatens interdict against city of Prague
1415	Jan Hus martyred July 6
1457 (or 1458)	Unity of Brethren founded; first congregation in Kunvald with Utraquist pastor Michal
1458 (ca.)	Lukáš of Prague born (d. 1528)
1467	Matěj of Kunwald, Eliáš of Chřenovice, and Tůma Přeloucký ordained as Brethren's first priests at Lhotka, near Rychnov; Matěj is chosen as senior (bishop)
1480 (ca.)	Michael Weisse born (d. 1534)
1481	Lukáš of Prague joins Unity
1485/90	Jan Roh born (d. 1547)
1500	Jan Augusta born (d. 1572)
1501	Czech hymnal produced (not by Unitas Fratrum), contains eleven of Lukáš's hymns
1505	Czech-language Unity hymnal, probably edited by Lukáš and his brother Jan Černy; reported to have contained some four hundred hymns; no surviving copy known
1517	Michael Weisse accepted into Unitas Fratrum
1518	Jan Roh ordained
1518	Lukáš becomes head of Unity
1519	Czech hymnal, edited by Lukáš; no surviving copy known
1521	Czech collection of funeral hymns, edited by Lukáš
1523	Jan Blahoslav born (d. 1571)
1524	Jan Augusta joins Unitas Fratrum
1528	Lukáš dies

1531	*Ein new Gesengbuchlen*, first German-language Unitas Fratrum hymnal, edited by Michael Weisse; has Zwinglian tendencies; contains 157 hymns; reprinted at least four times over next ten years (see 1544 below)
1532	Jan Augusta elected bishop
1532, 1535	Unity's confessions of faith drawn up by Jan Roh
1534	Michael Weisse dies
1536	Jiří Strejc born (also known as Georg Vetter; d. 1599)
1541	Czech hymnal, edited by Jan Roh; 482 hymns, 300 melodies; about one-quarter of the hymns are by Lukáš; one copy known to exist
1544	German hymnal, Jan Roh revision of Weisse 1531; three known surviving copies (one at Moravian Music Foundation); reprinted/reissued at last twelve times over sixty-five-year period
1547	Jan Roh dies
1548	Jan Augusta imprisoned (until 1564)
1554	first Polish Brethren's hymnal; edited by Izrael; revised and enlarged 1569
1557	Jan Blahoslav elected bishop
1558	*Musica* (1558) by Jan Blahoslav (1523–71), the first of the only two music treatises known to have been written by Czech Protestants during the Renaissance and Reformation years
1561	*Muzika*, written by "Jan Josquin," whose true identity remains unconfirmed, the second Czech Protestant music treatise (see above); "Jan Josquin" was most likely a pseudonym for Václav Solín (1527–95), who helped Blahoslav edit the 1561 hymnal
1561	Czech hymnal edited by Blahoslav; contains 735 hymn texts, over 450 melodies, including 60 from 1501 book; copy preserved in Unity Archives, Herrnhut; reissued 1564; reprinted or reissued at least nine times over fifty-year period
1564	Jan Augusta released from prison
1566	German *Kirchengesang*, edited by Petrus Herbert, Michael Tham, and Jan Jelecký; contains 348 hymns, with appendix containing an additional 108 hymns by Lutheran authors; reprinted 1590; later editions 1606, 1639, 1661 (this last edited by Komenský), 1694
1571	Petrus Herbert dies; Jan Blahoslav dies
1572	Jan Augusta dies
1579–94	Publication of Kralice Bible (in parts)
1587	Jiří Strejc's paraphrase of Psalms, set to French tunes
1592	Jan Amos Comenius (Komenský) born
1596	Kralice Bible printed in single volume

1599	Jiří Strejc dies
1618	May 23: nobles invade royal castle of Hradcany, throw regents and secretary out the window; Thirty Years' War begins
1620	November 8: battle of White Mountain; Catholic forces win; Unity is outlawed
1648	Peace of Westphalia; no provision for the Unity
1659	Czech hymnal edited by Comenius (Komenský), *Kancionál*; includes preface important for music as well as for hymn texts
1670	Comenius dies November 15, Amsterdam; buried in Naarden
1690	Johann Gottlob Klemm born May 12, near Dresden (d. 1762)
1700	Nicholas Ludwig von Zinzendorf born May 26 (d. 1760)
1704	August Gottlieb Spangenberg born July 13 (d. 1792)
1706	Tobias Friedrich born (d. 1736)
1711	Karl Otto Eberhardt born August 31 (d. 1757)
1713	Johann Christian Pyrlaeus born April 25 (d. 1785)
1714	Ludolph Ernst Schlicht born November 4 (d. 1769)
1714	Philipp Heinrich Molther born December 28 (d. 1780)
1715	Bernard Adam Grube born, Walschleben, June 21 (d. 1808)
1718	John Cennick born December 12, Berkshire, England (d. 1755)
1719	Johann Daniel Grimm born October 5, Stralsund (d. 1760)
1722	Zinzendorf allows exiles from Moravia to settle on his estate at Berthelsdorf; Herrnhut founded
1723	Christian Gregor born January 1, Silesia (d. 1801)
1725	Jeremias Dencke born October 2, Silesia (d. 1795)
1725	John Worthington born November 3, Dublin (d. 1790)
1726	Johann Gottlob Klemm joins Moravian Church, moves to Herrnhut
1727	Herrnhut: Zinzendorf draws up Brotherly Agreement to assist in quelling dissent among residents
1727	August 13, Herrnhut: Spiritual renewal of Moravian Church
1728	David Tannenberg born March 21, Berthelsdorf (d. 1804)
1728	Herrnhut: beginning of daily watchwords
1729	Johann Christian Geisler born March 13, Silesia (d. 1815)
1730	Christian Gottfried Geisler born October 10, Silesia (d. 1810)
1731	Herrnhut: first printing of Daily Texts
1731	Herrnhut *collegium musicum* started
1732	Herrnhut: Easter dawn service first celebrated
1732	Moravian Church begins mission work, with first mission to St. Thomas, Virgin Islands
1733	Johann Gottlob Klemm moves to Philadelphia
1733	Greenland mission started
1735	Nicholas Ludwig von Zinzendorf ordained Lutheran minister

1735	March 13: David Nitschmann consecrated bishop by Daniel Jablonski, a grandson of Comenius and one of two surviving bishops of ancient Unitas Fratrum
1735	Johannes Herbst born July 23, Swabia (d. 1812)
1735	*Gesangbuch der evangelischen Brüder-Gemeinen in Herrn-Huth* printed, known as *Herrnhuter Gesangbuch*; twelve appendices produced over the next twelve years
1735	August Gottlieb Spangenberg leads first group of settlers to Savannah, Georgia, the Moravians' first settlement in North America
1735	Suriname mission started
1736	Tobias Friedrich dies
1736–47	Heerendijk, Holland, settlement started
1737	Nicholas Ludwig von Zinzendorf consecrated bishop of Renewed Moravian Church
1737	Gnadenthal, South Africa, mission started
1738	Amsterdam, Holland, congregation started
1738	Fetter Lane, London, congregation started
1738	Herrnhaag settlement started (abandoned 1750)
1738	Philipp Heinrich Molther received into Moravian Church
1739	Ludolph Ernst Schlicht received into Moravian Church
1740	Christian Gregor received into Moravian Church
1740	Karl Otto Eberhardt received into Moravian Church
1740	John Antes born March 24, Frederick Township, Pennsylvania (d. 1811)
1740	Johann Gottfried Weber born October 7, Herrnhut (d. 1797)
1740	Moravians in Georgia relocate to Pennsylvania; found Nazareth settlement in 1741
1741–43	Zinzendorf travels to America
1741	August Spangenberg present at "renewal" of Herrnhaag *collegium musicum*
1741	Bethlehem, Pennsylvania, settlement started
1742	Ludolph Ernst Schlicht ordained
1742	Bethlehem, Pennsylvania, girls' school started (see 1785)
1742	Bedford, England, congregation started
1742	Cape Town, South Africa, congregation started
1742	Gnadenfrei congregation started
1742	Neudietendorf congregation started
1742	Niesky congregation started
1742	Niesky *Paedogogium* (boys school) started
1743	Simon Peter born April 2, Heerendijk, Holland (d. 1819)
1744	Haarlem, Holland, congregation started

1744	January 25: Spinet arrives in Bethlehem, one of the first instruments the Moravians transported to the New World; it suffered damage during the voyage, but was repaired for use in following day's service
1744	Bethlehem, Pennsylvania, *collegium musicum* begun, directed by Johann Christopher Pyrlaeus
1745	John Cennick received into Moravian Church
1745	Johann Christian Geisler starts trombone choir for Gnadenfrei congregation
1746	Johann Friedrich Peter born May 19, Heerendijk, Holland (d. 1813)
1746	Christian Ludwig Brau born October 10, Drammen, Norway (d. 1777)
1746	English-language Moravian hymnal, probably edited by Ludolph Ernst Schlicht
1746	Fulneck, England congregation started
1746	Zeist, Holland congregation started
1746	Ebersdorf congregation started
1747	Johann Daniel Grimm joins Moravian Church
1748	First mention of *collegium musicum* in Zeist records
1748	Bernard Adam Grube comes to Bethlehem as missionary to Native Americans
1748	Jeremias Dencke organist at Herrnhut
1748	Johann Ludwig Freydt born February 18, Aschersleben, Germany (d. 1807)
1748	Johannes Renatus Verbeek born November 17 (d. 1820)
1748	Johannes Herbst joins Moravian Church
1749	Neuwied congregation started
1749	David Tannenberg comes to Bethlehem
1750	Dublin, Ireland, congregation started
1750	Herrnhaag settlement abandoned; residents disperse, some two hundred or more to Bethlehem, Pennsylvania
1750	Peter Mortimer born December 5, England (d. 1828)
1750s	John Worthington serves Fulneck, England congregation as pastor
1751	Ockbrook, England, congregation started
1751	Jacob Van Vleck born March 24, New York (d. 1831)
1751	David Moritz Michael born October 21, Germany (d. 1827)
1751	Johann Christopher Pyrlaeus returns to Germany
1752	John Antes comes to school at Bethlehem, Pennsylvania
1753	Wachovia, North Carolina: first settlement at Bethabara
1754	Barby, Germany, theological seminary started
1754–55	*Alt und Neuer Brüder Gesang* printed in London

1754	*A Collection of Hymns of the Children of God in All Ages, From the Beginning till now. Designed chiefly for the Use of the Congregations in Union with the Brethren's Church* printed in London
1754	Johann Gottfried Weber received into Moravian Church
1755	Johann Daniel Grimm compiles manuscript chorale book, establishes tune-numbering system
1755	Johann Friedrich Peter enters boarding school at Niesky, Germany; possibly received musical training from Johann Daniel Grimm
1755	John Cennick dies July 4, London
1755	Johann Gottfried Gebhard born August 2 (d. after 1799)
1755	Christian David Jaeschke born December 29, Herrnhut (d. 1827)
1757	Christian Gottfried Geisler at Zeist; school and church organist till end of life
1757	Karl Otto Eberhardt dies December 16, Herrnhut, where he was serving as organist
1757	Johann Gottlob Klemm moves to Bethlehem, reunites with Moravian Church; Tannenberg becomes his assistant
1758	Kleinwelke congregation started
1758	Christian Ignatius LaTrobe born February 12, Fulneck (d. 1836)
1759	John Antes makes one of first violins made in U.S. (Bethlehem?)
1759	Christian Gregor begins arranging "Psalms" (odes), writing anthems
1759	Nazareth Hall Academy founded; temporarily closed and students moved to Bethlehem; reopened in Nazareth 1785
1760	Johann Christian Geisler begins composing
1760	Zinzendorf dies May 9
1760	Johann Daniel Grimm dies August 20, Gross Hennersdorf
1760	John Gambold, Jr., born November 15, London (d. 1795)
1761	Jeremias Dencke comes to America
1761	Immanuel Nitschmann comes to Bethlehem, aids *collegium musicum* by copying music and leading rehearsals
1762	John Antes opens instrument-making shop, Bethlehem
1762	Johann Gottlob Klemm dies May 4
1762	Georg Gottfried Müller born May 22, Gross Hennersdorf (d. 1821)
1762	Johann Christian Till born May 18, Gnadenthal (near Nazareth), Pennsylvania (d. 1844); educated at Nazareth Hall, student of Simon Peter
1762	August Gottlieb Spangenberg returns to Europe to help stabilize Moravian Church following Zinzendorf's death

1763	"Boarding School for Girls" started in Lititz, Pennsylvania; later Linden Hall
1763	Carl Bernhard Garve born January 24 (d. 1841)
1763	Johan Hermann Mankell born September 19, Germany (d. 1835)
1764	John Antes lives in Herrnhut
1765	John Antes moves to Neuwied
1765	Johan Friedrich Peter enters seminary at Barby, Germany; begins copying music; completed seminary 1769
1765	David Tannenberg moves to Lititz, Pennsylvania; sets up workshop
1765	May: Bernard Adam Grube arrives as pastor in Lititz; serves through 1785, organizes choir and *collegium musicum* (first documented in diary for 17 November 1765).
1766	Jeremias Dencke writes anthem for Provincial Synod in Bethlehem—earliest known Moravian concerted church music written in America
1766–69	Johann Gottfried Weber organist at Kleinwelka
1767	Gracehill, Ireland, congregation started
1767	Johannes Sörensen born May 18 (d. 1831)
1769	Ludolph Ernst Schlicht dies March 4
1769	John Antes sent as missionary to Egypt
1769–72	Johann Gottfried Weber organist at Neudietendorf
1769–77	John Worthington serves Ockbrook, England, as pastor
1770	Carl Bernhard Garve received into Moravian Church
1770	Johann Friedrich Peter comes to America, begins work in boys' school in Nazareth, Pennsylvania
1770	Simon Peter comes to America, serves in Pennsylvania
1770–72	Christian Gregor visits Pennsylvania and North Carolina
1771	James Montgomery born November 11, Ayr, Scotland; son of Moravian missionary parents (d. 1854)
1771	Labrador mission started
1771	Christian Friedrich Hasse born in Sarepta, Russia (d. 1831)
1771–75	Christian Ignatius LaTrobe attends Moravian school at Niesky
1772	Jacob Van Vleck sent to Barby, Germany, to school
1772	Salem, North Carolina: beginning of school for girls; first boarding program begun 1802
1772–85	Johann Gottfried Weber serves as organist at Herrnhut
1773	Christiansfeld, Denmark congregation started
1773	Johann Friedrich Peter comes to Bethlehem to work with boys and keep books; leads *collegium musicum* in rehearsals and makes it part of regular worship services
1773–81	John Antes in Egypt

1774	John Gambold is sent to school at Niesky, then Barby
1775	Philipp Heinrich Molther elected bishop
1776–79	Christian Ignatius LaTrobe attends seminary at Barby
1777	Johannes Renatus Verbeek ordained
1777	Johann Gottfried Gebhard at seminary in Barby
1777	Johann Ludwig Freydt joins Moravian Church, teaches at Niesky
1777	Christian Ludwig Brau dies February 4, Barby
1778	*Gesangbuch* edited by Christian Gregor; becomes standard for the next century
1778	Jacob Van Vleck returns to America after theological education in Barby, Germany; serves as assistant pastor in Bethlehem
1779	Johann Friedrich Peter called to Lititz, Pennsylvania, as record keeper and secretary
1779–84	Christian Ignatius LaTrobe teaches at Moravian school at Niesky
1780	Philipp Heinrich Molther dies September 9, Bedford, England
1780 (ca.)	Nazareth, Pennsylvania, *collegium musicum* founded
1780–90	Johann Friedrich Peter called to Salem as record keeper and music director; later serves as interim pastor and supervisor of boys' school
1780	Immanuel Nitschmann resumes leadership of Bethlehem *collegium musicum*
1781	Gnadenfeld congregation started
1781	David Moritz Michael joins Moravian Church; serves as copyist of *Gemeinnachrichten*
1781	John Antes recalled to Germany; arrives Herrnhut 1782
1781	December 19: First reference to *collegium musicum* in Salem (North Carolina) records, Elders Conference
1783–95	David Moritz Michael teaches at Niesky boys' school
1783	John Antes serves as Single Brethren's warden (business manager), Neuwied
1783	First documented celebration of July 4 takes place in Salem; including lovefeast ode entitled *Freudenpsalm* (Psalm of Joy)
1784	Christian Ignatius LaTrobe begins service in London as head of Single Brothers Choir
1784	Simon Peter comes to North Carolina
1784	*Choralbuch* edited by Christian Gregor
1784	Georg Gottfried Müller comes to America, teaches at Nazareth

298   A MORAVIAN MUSICAL TIMELINE

1784–90	Johann Gottfried Gebhard serves as music instructor at seminary in Barby
1784	Johann Christian Bechler born January 7, on the Baltic island of Oesel (modern Saaremaa) (d. 1857)
1785	Johann Gottfried Weber ordained; serves in Barby and Gothenburg, Sweden
1785	March 9: Simon Peter begins pastorate at Friedberg; April 24: begins to give music instruction
1785	Johann Christopher Pyrlaeus dies May 28
1785	Bethlehem, Pennsylvania, Boarding School for Young Ladies opened (see 1742)
1785	Fairfield, England congregation started
1785	Johannes Herbst comes to America as pastor at Lancaster, Pennsylvania (later Lititz)
1785–86	John Worthington serves Fairfield, England, as pastor
1785–88	Georg Gottfried Müller at boys' school in Nazareth
1785–1809	John Antes serves as warden (business manager) at Fulneck, England
1786	Christian David Jaeschke begins forty years' service as organist and choirmaster at Herrnhut
1787	John Antes becomes head of Fulneck overseers' board
1787	Christian Ignatius LaTrobe becomes secretary of Society for Propagation of the Gospel (London)
1788	Johann Gottfried Weber returns to Herrnhut
1788	Christian Ignatius LaTrobe ordained
1788	John Gambold's six keyboard sonatas published in Leipzig
1788–91	John F. Früeauff at boys school in Nazareth
1789	Christian Gregor consecrated bishop
1789	English-language Moravian hymnal edited by John Swertner
1789	Johann Friedrich Peter's Six String Quintets completed, Salem; score is dated January 9, 1789; parts dated February 28, 1789
1790	Johann Gottfried Gebhard leaves seminary at Barby; no mention of him in Moravian records after 1799
1790	Johann Friedrich Peter arrives at Graceham, Maryland, as interim pastor
1790	John Worthington dies March 12, Dublin
1790–1800	John Swertner serves as pastor at Fairfield, England
1790–1800	Jacob Van Vleck serves as inspector of girls' school, Bethlehem; leads collegium musicum
1791	Peter Ricksecker born, Bethlehem (d. 1873)
1791	Johann Friedrich Peter recalled to Bethlehem
1791	Johann Friedrich Peter comes to Hope, New Jersey, to supervise school

1792	Peter Wolle born January 5, St. Thomas (d. 1871)
1792	August Gottieb Spangenberg dies July 18, Berthelsdorf
1792	Abraham Ritter born, Philadelphia (d. 1860)
1793	Philip Bachman arrives from Germany to serve as David Tannenberg's assistant
1793	Johann Friedrich Peter called to Bethlehem as bookkeeper, diarist, musician
1793–1808	Johann Christian Till serves as organist and schoolmaster, Hope, New Jersey
1794	Johannes Sörensen receives medical degree
1794	Carl Anton Van Vleck born November 4, Bethlehem, Pennsylvania (d. 1845)
1794–95	Henry Christian Müller at boys' school in Nazareth
1795	Peter Wolle sent to Pennsylvania for education
1795	Jeremias Dencke dies May 28, Bethlehem
1795	John Gambold, Jr. dies June 21, Barby
1795–1804	David Moritz Michael at boys' school in Nazareth
1796	Christian Ignatius LaTrobe becomes secretary of the Unitas Fratrum in England
1796	Christian Friedrich Martin born January 31, Markneukirchen, Germany (d. 1873)
1796	Jedediah Weiss born February 21, Bethlehem (d. 1873)
1796–98	Johannes Renatus Verbeek travels to West Indies
1797	Johann Gottfried Weber dies March 30, Gnadau
1797	Heinrich Gottlob Gütter born June 23, Germany (d. 1847)
1799	Jacob Christian Till born July 15 (d. 1882)
1799	Carl Bernhard Garve ordained
1801	Christian Gregor dies November 6, Berthelsdorf
1802	Johann Friedrich Peter serves as pastor, Mountjoy, Pennsylvania
1802–9	Jacob Van Vleck teaches at boys' school in Nazareth
1803–5	Gottlob Friedrich Hillmer assembles selection of Moravian sacred music in two volumes: *Sammlung einiger musikalischen Fest-Gesänge der evangelischen Brüdergemeine zum Singen am Klavier eingerichtet* (Breslau: Grass und Barth)
1804	David Tannenberg dies May 19, after a fall sustained while tuning organ
1804	David Moritz Michael becomes overseer of Nazareth Single Brothers Choir
1804	Johann Friedrich Peter recalled to Bethlehem
1804–31	Christian Friedrich Hasse serves as music director at Fulneck
1805	David Moritz Michael's Psalm 103 presented for first time, Nazareth

1805	Johann Ludwig Freydt retires in Niesky
1805–14	Georg Gottfried Müller serves at Beersheba and Gnadenhutten, Ohio
1806	Johannes Renatus Verbeek travels to Pennsylvania, North Carolina
1806–12	Johann Christian Bechler teaches at boys' school in Nazareth
1807	Königsfeld congregation started (Black Forest, Germany)
1807	Peter Wolle is one of first three students at Moravian Theological Seminary, Nazareth, Pennsylvania
1807	Johann Ludwig Freydt dies January 4, Niesky
1808	David Moritz Michael becomes overseer of Bethlehem Single Brothers Choir
1808	John Antes retires to Bristol
1808	Hope, New Jersey, congregation closes; Johann Christian Till recalled to Bethlehem, where he serves as woodworker
1808	Bernard Adam Grube dies March 20, Bethlehem
1809	David Moritz Michael writes *Die Wasserfahrt* for Whitmonday celebration
1810	Christian Gottfried Geisler dies June 3, Zeist
1810?	David Moritz Michael writes *Suiten bey einer Quelle zu blasen* for Whitmonday celebration
1810	John Christian Malthaner born, Leonbrunn, Würtemberg (d. 1873)
1810 on	Johann Christian Till and son Jacob Christian Till build pianos as primary source of income
1810–16	Samuel Reinke instructor at boys' school in Nazareth
1810–14	Peter Wolle instructor at boys' school in Nazareth
1811	May 12: Johannes Herbst consecrated bishop; called to Salem; May 14: leaves Lititz for Salem
1811	John Antes dies December 17, Bristol
1811	Early American performance of Haydn's *Creation*, Bethlehem, with David Moritz Michael conducting and Johann Friedrich Peter playing violin
1811	Johann Christian Till becomes organist at Central Church, Bethlehem, succeeding Johann Friedrich Peter
1811	Christian Ignatius LaTrobe publishes *Anthems, for one or more Voices, sung in the Church of the United Brethren*, London; includes pieces by Gregor, Grimm, Graun, Antes, Naumann, and LaTrobe
1811–21	Peter Ricksecker teaches at boys' school in Nazareth
1811–60	Abraham Ritter organist at Moravian church in Philadelphia
1812	Johannes Herbst dies January 15, Salem
1812	James Montgomery returns to Moravian Church

1812	Jacob Van Vleck moves to Salem, succeeds Johannes Herbst
1813	Johann Friedrich Peter dies July 13, Bethlehem
1815?	Lititz *collegium musicum* changes name to Lititz Philharmonic Society (date uncertain)
1815	Johann Christian Geisler dies April 14, Berthelsdorf
1815	Francis Florentine Hagen born October 30, Salem (d. 1907)
1815	Jacob Van Vleck consecrated bishop
1815	David Moritz Michael retires to Neuwied, teaches music in boys' school
1815–17	Christian Ignatius LaTrobe travels to South Africa
1817	Heinrich Gottlob Gütter comes to Bethlehem
1817–22	Johann Christian Bechler principal at boys' school in Nazareth
1819	Heinrich Gottlob Gütter joins Moravian Church
1819	Georg Gottfried Müller retires to Lititz
1819	Simon Peter dies May 29, Salem
1820	Johannes Renatus Verbeek dies July 13, Herrnhut
1820	Bethlehem *collegium musicum* reorganizes; takes the name Philharmonic Society of Bethlehem; reorganizes again in 1858, 1869; ceases activity in late 1870s or early 1880s
1821	Georg Gottfried Müller dies March 19, Lititz
1822	Musicians from Bethlehem travel to Philadelphia to assist Musical Fund Society performance of Haydn's *Creation*
1823	Edward William Leinbach (Lineback) born November 4, Salem (d. 1901)
1823	Carl Bernhard Garve edits new edition of *Liturgical Hymns*
1824	Charles Augustus Zoebisch born May 9, Germany (d. 1911)
1825, 1827	Carl Bernhard Garve's collections of sacred songs published
1825	Henri Marc Hermann Woldemar Voullaire born July 29, Neuwelke (d. 1902)
1825	Georg Friedrich Hellström born December 7 (d. 1912)
1826	Christian David Jaeschke retires as organist-choirmaster at Herrnhut
1826	Wilhelm Wauer born June 23 (d. 1902)
1826	Peter Ricksecker ordained, called to Tobago, West Indies
1827	David Moritz Michael dies Neuwied, February 26
1827	Christian David Jaeschke dies October 22, Herrnhut
1828	John Christian Malthaner arrives in New York
1828	Peter Mortimer dies January 8, Herrnhut
1829–32	Christian Friedrich Hasse publishes *Sacred Music: partly original; partly selected from the works of the chief of the most modern German composers, by C. F. Hasse, the Vocal parts as in the Original Score, and adapted exclusively to English Words. The Instrumental*

Parts arranged for the Piano Forte, 2 vols. (Leeds: J. Muff), including works by John Gambold and C. D. Jaeschke in addition to some of his own and works of non-Moravian composers (final volume published after his death)

1830	Lisette (Lizette) Marie Van Vleck Meinung born April 13, Newport, Rhode Island (d. 1914)
1831	Johannes Sörensen dies April 29
1831	Christian Friedrich Hasse dies May 1
1831	Jacob Van Vleck dies July 3, Bethlehem
1833	Christian Friedrich Martin moves to New York
1834	Christian Ignatius LaTrobe retires to Fairfield, England
1835	Amelia Van Vleck born October 18, Lancaster, Pennsylvania (d. 1929)
1835	Johan Hermann Mankell dies November 4
1836	Peter Wolle compiles first Moravian tune book published in America
1836	Johann Christian Bechler called to Sarepta, Russia
1836	Christian Ignatius LaTrobe dies May 6, Fairfield, England
1836	Carl Bernhard Garve retires
1837	John Christian Malthaner moves to Bethlehem
1837	Nazareth *collegium musicum* is reorganized as Musical Society of Nazareth
1837–41	Francis Florentine Hagen teaches at boys' school in Nazareth
1838	Heinrich Lonas born March 26, Herrnhut (d. 1903)
1839	Christian Friedrich Martin moves to near Nazareth; establishes guitar-making company
1841	Carl Bernhard Garve dies June 21, Herrnhut
1842	Charles Augustus Zoebisch arrives in America
1844	Johann Christian Till dies November 19, Bethlehem
1845	Carl Anton Van Vleck dies December 21, Greenville, Tennessee
1845	Peter Wolle consecrated bishop
1846	Van Vleck sisters move with their brother and mother to Salem, following father, Carl Anton Van Vleck's death
1847	Heinrich Gottlob Gütter dies July 8
1848	Peter Ricksecker returns to Bethlehem
1849	Gottfried Theodor Erxleben born June 15 (d. 1931)
1849	Johann Christian Bechler retires to Herrnhut
1850	Joseph Theodor Müller born May 14 (d. 1946)
1852	Georg Friedrich Hellström called to Christiansfeld
1852	Lisette Van Vleck joins faculty at Salem Female Academy, stays until her marriage to Alexander Meinung in 1868
1853–55	Peter Wolle serves as interim pastor in Dover, Ohio

1854	Peter Ricksecker assigned to Native American mission near Leavenworth, Kansas
1854	Ernst Immanuel Erbe born December 30, Bern, Switzerland (d. 1927)
1854	James Montgomery dies
1856	Heinrich Lonas becomes organist in Herrnhut
1857	Peter Ricksecker starts music school at Leavenworth, Kansas
1857	Johann Christian Bechler dies April 18, Herrnhut
1858	Theodor Liley Clemens born December 8, Yorkshire (d. 1933)
1860	Abraham Ritter dies October 8, Philadelphia
1861	Peter Wolle retires
1863	John Frederick Wolle born April 4, Bethlehem (d. 1933)
1870	Heinrich Lonas becomes organist at Moravian congregation in Berlin, instructor in Schmidt Conservatory
1871	Peter Wolle dies November 14, Bethlehem
1873	Christian Friedrich Martin dies February 16, Nazareth
1873	Heinrich Lonas becomes organist at Neuwied
1873	John Christian Malthaner dies
1873	Peter Ricksecker dies July 13
1873	Jedediah Weiss dies September 3, Bethlehem
1873	Rufus Alexander Grider prepares catalog of Philharmonic Society of Bethlehem music and property
1881	Bessie Whittington Pfohl born July 28 (d. 1971)
1882	Jacob Christian Till dies April 9
1886	Theodor Liley Clemens ordained and called to Antigua
1888	Theodor Liley Clemens called to Tobago (to 1917)
1889	Ernst Immanuel Erbe arrives in America (St. Louis)
1891	Henri Marc Hermann Woldemar Voullaire retires to Herrnhut
1894	Georg Friedrich Hellström moves to Gnadenberg
1895	Georg Friedrich Hellström moves to Kleinwelka
1898	Georg Friedrich Hellström moves to Neudietendorf
1898	Bethlehem Bach Choir founded, John Frederick Wolle, director
1900	Bethlehem Bach Choir gives first complete American performance of Bach's Mass in B Minor, under direction of John Frederick Wolle
1901	Edward William Leinbach dies February 18, Salem
1902	Wilhelm Wauer (Herrnhut composer) dies January 3, Herrnhut
1902	Henri Marc Hermann Woldemar Voullaire dies June 12, Herrnhut

1903	Heinrich Lonas dies March 30
1907	Francis Florentine Hagen dies Lititz, Pennsylvania, July 7
1911	Charles Augustus Zoebisch dies May 13
1912	James Christian Pfohl born September 17 (d. 1997)
1912	Georg Friedrich Hellström dies, Neudietendorf
1913	Thor M. Johnson born June 10 (d. 1975)
1914	Lisette (Lizette) Marie Van Vleck Meinung dies
1916	Joseph Theodor Müller publishes *Hymnologisches Handbuch zum Gesangbuch der Brüdergemeine*
1917–19	Theodor Liley Clemens on disability leave
1919–21	Theodor Liley Clemens serves in Trinidad
1922–31	Joseph Theodor Müller, *Geschichte der Böhmischen Brüder*, three volumes
1927	Ernst Immanuel Erbe dies March 6
1929	Amelia Van Vleck dies August 20, Salem
1931	Gottfried Theodor Erxleben dies December 12, Herrnhut
1933	John Frederick Wolle dies January 12
1933	Theodor Liley Clemens dies July 23, Eydon, England
1946	Joseph Theodor Müller dies August 6
1950	First Early American Moravian Music Festival, Bethlehem, Pennsylvania, conducted by Thor Johnson
1956	Moravian Music Foundation established, headquarters in Winston-Salem
1971	Bessie Whittington Pfohl dies November 23, Winston-Salem
1975	Thor M. Johnson dies January 16
1997	James Christian Pfohl dies March 28

Bibliography

Adams, Charles B. "Contemporary Hymnological Practice in the Moravian Church in the United States." BD thesis, Moravian Theological Seminary, 1934.
———. *Our Moravian Hymn Heritage.* Bethlehem: Department of Publications, Moravian Church in America, 1984.
Albert, Gary J., ed. *Splendid Service: The Restoration of David Tannenberg's Home Moravian Church Organ.* Winston-Salem: Old Salem, Inc., 2004.
Albright, S. C. *The Story of the Moravian Congregation at York, Pennsylvania.* York: Maples Press, [1927].
Allen, Walser H. "Three Musical Moravians Named Wolle." *Moravian Music Foundation Bulletin* 18/2 (Fall–Winter 1973): 2–7.
Alt- und neuer Brüder-Gesang von den Tagen Thenochs bisher, für alle Kinder und Seelen Gottes. London, 1753.
"An Organ of 1819: Built by Philip Bachman." *The American Organist* 16/5 (May 1933): 262.
Anburey, Thomas. *Travels Through the Interior Parts of America*, vol. II. Boston and New York: Houghton Mifflin Co., 1923.
Anderson, Thomas Jerome. "The Collegium Musicum Salem, 1780–1790: Origins and Repertoire." PhD diss., Florida State University, 1976.
Antes, John. *Three Trios for Two Violins and Violoncello.* Edited by D. Keneth Fowler. Winston-Salem and Bethlehem: Moravian Music Foundation, 1998.
Armstrong, William H. *Organs for America: The Life and Work of David Tannenberg.* Philadelphia: University of Pennsylvania Press, 1967.
Atwood, Craig D. "Blood, Sex, and Death: Life and Liturgy in Zinzendorf's Bethlehem." PhD diss., Princeton Theological Seminary, 1995.
———. *Community of the Cross: Moravian Piety in Colonial Bethlehem.* University Park: Pennsylvania State University Press, 2004.
Atwood, Craig D., and Peter Vogt, eds. *The Distinctiveness of Moravian Culture: Essays and Documents in Moravian History in Honor of Vernon H. Nelson on His Seventieth Birthday.* Nazareth: Moravian Historical Society, 2003.
Auszug aus dem bisher in den evangelischen Brüder-Gemeinene gebräuchlichen Choral-Buche mit ausgeschribenen Stimmen der Choral-Melodien. Gnadau: Evangelische Brüder-Unität, 1831.
Bach, Carl Philipp Emanuel. *Carl Philip Emauel Bach Edition.* Rachel W. Wade, general editor; E. Eugene Helm, coordinating editor. Oxford and New York: Oxford University Press, 1989.

Bach, Johann Christoph Friedrich. *Four Early Sinfonias.* Edited by Ewald V. Nolte. Recent Researches in the Music of the Classical Era 15. Madison: A-R Editions, 1982.

Bach, Johann Sebastian. *Neue Ausgabe Sämtlicher Werke,* Serie IV: *Orgelwerke,* Band 3: *Die einzeln überlieferten Orgelchoräle.* Edited by Hans Klotz. Basel: Bärenreiter, 1961.

Barnes, Alan, and Martin Renshaw. *The Life and Work of John Snetzler.* Brookfield, VT: Scholar Press–Ashgate Publishing Company, 1994.

Bauer, Emil. *Das Choralbuch der Brüdergemeine von 1784, nach seiner Abfassung und seinen Quellen mit dazu gehörigen biographischen Notizen.* Gnadau: Verlag der Buchhandlung der evangelischen Brüder-Unität, 1867.

Bechler, John Christian. "Memoir of the Rt. Rev. John C. Bechler, translated by Samuel Reinke, one of his former pupils." *The Moravian* (June 26, 1857), 1.

[Bechler, Johann Christian]. "Rules for Interludes." Undated, unpublished manuscript. Historical Society Museum, Lititz.

Beck, Abraham R. "David Tannenberg." *Pennsylvania German* 10/7 (July 1909): 339–41.

Beck, Hartmut. "Entstehung und Ausbreitung der Herrnhuter Brüdergemeine vom 15.–18. Jahrhundert nach dem gegenwärtigen Stand der Forschung, mit Bezug auf die kirchliche Blasmusik." In *Musikgeographie. Weltliche und geistliche Bläsermusik in ihren Beziehungen zueinander und zu ihrer Umwelt,* edited by Manfred Büttner, Wolfgang Schnabel, and Klaus Winkler, 137–50. Abhandlungen zur Geschichte der Gewissenschaften und Religion/Umwelt-Forschung Bd. 6, Tl. 2. Bochum: Universitätsverlag Dr. N. Brockmeyer, 1991.

Beck, Paul E. "David Tannenberger, Organ Builder." *Papers Read Before the Lancaster County Historical Society* 30/1 (1926): 3–11.

Benda, Franz. *Six Sonatas for Solo Violin and Continuo.* Edited by Douglas A. Lee. Recent Researches in Music of the Classical Era 13. Madison: A-R Editions, 1981.

Bethlehem Female Seminary Records, Moravian Archives, Bethlehem:
    Expense Journal January 1, 1814–March 31, 1819, FemSem20
    Bills for tuning instruments, folder FemSem 187.4
    Bill for Till piano, No. 395, folder FemSem 187.6.1
    Folder "Musical Entertainments and Public Examinations 1838–1846," box "Musical Entertainment"

Bettermann, Wilhelm. "Wie das Posaunenblasen in der Brüdergemeine aufkam." *Jahrbuch der Brüdergemeine* 33 (1937/1938): 24–26.

Biggs, E. Power. "Welcome Back American Trackers." *Diapason* 51/10 (September 1, 1960): 18–19.

Bird, Ruth Holmes (Scott). "Music Among the Moravians: Bethlehem, Pennsylvania, 1741–1816." Master's thesis, Eastman School of Music, 1938.

———. "My Moravian Studies." *Moravian Music Journal* 26/2 (Summer 1981): 35–42.

Blahoslav, Jan. *Musika (1558).* Translated by Thomas Sovík. Denton, TX: Czech Historical Society, 1991.

Blandford, Frances. "A Portrait of Christian Ignatius La Trobe." *Moravian Music Foundation Bulletin* 10/2 (Spring 1966): 1–4.

Blankenburg, Walter. "Die Musik der Brüdergemeine in Europa." In *Unitas Fratrum. Herrnhuter Studien. Moravian Studies,* edited by Mari P. van Buijtenen [e.a.], 351–86. Utrecht: Rijksarchief, 1975.

Blankenburg, Walter. "The Music of the Bohemian Brethren." In *Protestant Church Music*, edited by Friedrich Blume, 591–607. New York: W. W. Norton, 1974.

Bleyle, Carl Otto. "Georg Andreas Sorge's Influence on David Tannenberg and Organ Building in America During the Eighteenth Century." PhD diss., University of Minnesota, 1969.

Blume, Friedrich, ed. *Geschichte der evangelischen Kirchenmusik.* Kassel: Bärenreiter-Verlag, 1965.

Boalch, Donald H. *Makers of the Harpsichord and Clavichord 1440–1840*, 3rd ed. Edited by Charles Mould. Oxford: Clarendon Press, 1995.

Boand, Jillian. "The Road Not Taken: A Discourse on Moravian Deviation from Romanticism in the Nineteenth Century." Unpublished paper presented at the Sixth Bethlehem Conference on Moravian Music, October 23, 2004. Filed at the Moravian Music Foundation.

Boeringer, James. "A Guide to the Moravian Lovefeast." *Moravian Music Journal* 26 (Fall–Winter 1981): 86–87.

———. *I Will Sing a New Song Unto the Lord: The Works of Richard T. Gore.* Chantry Music Press, 1974.

———. "Preface," *Six Little Keyboard Sonatas Dedicated to Lady Schönberg by John Gambold, Schoolteacher and Organist at Niesky.* Winston-Salem: Moravian Music Foundation, n.d.

Bosch, Ben van den. *The Origin and Development of the Trombone-Work of the Moravian Churches in Germany and All the World.* Translated by C. Daniel Crews. Winston-Salem: Moravian Music Foundation, 1990. Originally published as "Entstehung und Entwicklung der Posaunenarbeit der Brüdergemeinen in Deutschland und in aller Welt." In *Posaunen in der Bibel und bei uns vor 1843*, edited by Horst Dietrich Schlemm, 43–65. Beiträge zur Geschichte Evangelischer Posaunenarbeit 1. Gütersloh: Gütersloher Verlagshaus Gerd Mohn, 1989.

———. "Was blies man bei den Herrnhuter Bläserchören?" In *Was wurde wann und wo von wem geblasen? Die Literatur der Posaunenchöre einst und jetzt*, edited by Horst Dietrich Schlemm, 13–23. Beiträge zur Geschichte Evangelischer Posaunenarbeit 4/1. Gütersloh: Gütersloher Verlagshaus Gerd Mohn, 1997.

Bowne, Eliza Southgate. *A Girl's Life Eighty Years Ago.* New York: Charles Scribner's Sons, 1887.

Bratrský Zpěvník. Nové Pace: Jednota bratrská, 1957.

Brown, Dale. *Understanding Pietism.* Grand Rapids: William B. Eerdmans Publishing Company, 1978.

Brunner, Raymond J. "The Tannenberg Organ at Nazareth Moravian Church." *Dieffenbuch* 4/1 (1981): 4–7. Publication of the Tannenberg Chapter of the Organ Historical Society.

———. *That Ingenious Business: Pennsylvania German Organ Builders.* Birdsboro: Pennsylvania German Society, 1990.

Bunners, Christian. "Pietismus und Musik im 18. Jahrhundert. Eine Problemskizze." *Unitas Fratrum* 47 (2000): 1–11.

Butt, John. *Music Education and the Art of Performance in the German Baroque.* Cambridge: Cambridge University Press, 1994.

Büttner, Manfred, "Bethlehem (USA) und der älteste noch heute existierende 'richtige' Posaunenchor." In *Musikgeographie. Weltliche und geistliche Bläsermusik in ihren Beziehungen zueinander und zu ihrer Umwelt*, edited by Manfred Büttner, Wolfgang Schnabel, and Klaus Winkler, 253–59. Abhandlungen zur Geschichte der Geowissenschaften und Religion/Umwelt-Forschung Bd. 6, Tl. 2. Bochum: Universitätsverlag Dr. N. Brockmeyer, 1991.

Caldwell, Alice M. "Music of the Moravian *Liturgische Gesange* (1791–1823): From Oral to Written Tradition." PhD diss., New York University, 1987.

———. "Zwischenspiele im Herrnhuter Choralgesang." *Unitas Fratrum* 47 (2000): 107–20.

Camus, Raoul F. *Military Music of the American Revolution.* Chapel Hill: University of North Carolina Press, 1976.

Cansler, Jeannine Ann. "An Annotated Listing of Organists Flourishing in Five American Cities Between 1700 and 1850." DMA diss., University of Oregon, 1984.

Carter, Stewart. "The Gütter Family: Wind Instrument Makers and Dealers to the Moravian Brethren in America." *Journal of the American Musical Instrument Society* 27 (2001): 48–83.

———. "The Salem Cornetts." *Historic Brass Society Journal* 14 (2002): 279–308.

———. "Trombone Ensembles of the Moravian Brethren in America: New Avenues for Research." *Brass Scholarship in Review: Proceedings of the Historic Brass Society Conference, Paris 1999.* Bucina: The Historic Brass Society Series No. 6. Hillsdale, NY: Pendragon Press, 2006.

Chase, Gilbert. *America's Music, from the Pilgrims to the Present.* New York: McGraw-Hill, 1955.

Choralbuch der evangelischen Brüdergemeine. Gnadau: Verlag der Unitätsbuchhandling, 1893.

Choralbuch der evangelischen Brüdergemeine. Gnadau: Verlag der Unitätsbuchhandling, 1927.

Choralbuch der evangelischen Brüdergemeine. Berlin: Verlag Merseburger, 1960.

"Christian Ignatius Latrobe, 1758–1836." *Moravian Music Foundation Bulletin* 10/1 (Fall 1965): 1.

Christianson, Thomas. "Four-Hand Piano Transcription and Geographies of Nineteenth-Century Musical Reception." *Journal of the American Musicological Society* 52, no. 2 (1999): 255–98.

Church Music and Musical Life in Pennsylvania in the Eighteenth Century. Vol. 2, 115–271. Lancaster: Pennsylvania Society of the Colonial Dames of America, 1927.

Clark, David Runner. "Music in the Moravian Community of Lititz." DMA diss., University of Rochester, 1976.

Clark, J. Bunker. "American Organ Music Before 1800." *Diapason* 72/11 (November 1981): 1, 3, 7.

Claypool, Richard D. "Archival Collections of the Moravian Music Foundation and Some Notes on the Philharmonic Society of Bethlehem." *Fontes Artes Musicae* 23/4 (October–December 1976): 177–90.

Claypool, Richard D. "The Bethlehem Musical Societies." Unpublished paper presented at the Moravian Museum of Bethlehem, March 17, 1975. Moravian Music Foundation Vertical Files, Winston-Salem.

———. "Mr. John Antes: Instrumentmaker." *Moravian Music Foundation Bulletin* 23/2 (Fall–Winter 1978): 10–13.

Claypool, Richard D., ed. "Catalog of the Lititz Collegium Musicum Collection." Typescript, 1980. Moravian Music Foundation, Winston-Salem.

Clinkscale, Martha Novak. *Makers of the Piano*. Vol. 2, 1820–1860. New York: Oxford University Press, 1999.

A Collection of Hymns of the Children of God in All Ages, From the Beginning till now. In Two Parts Designed chiefly for the Use of the Congregations in Union with the Brethren's Church. London: 1754.

A Collection of Hymns for the Use of the Protestant Church of the United Brethren. London: 1789.

Comenius, Jan [John] Amos. *The Bequest of the Unity*. Translated and edited by Matthew Spinka. Chicago: National Union of Czechoslovak Protestants in America, 1940.

———. *The School of Infancy*. Edited with introduction by Ernest M. Eller. Chapel Hill: University of North Carolina Press, 1956.

Comenius, Jan [John] Amos, ed. *Kancionál* (1659). Reprinted with introduction by Olga Settari. Kalich: Kultur Kontakt, 1992.

"Composers—Francis Florentine Hagen (1815–1907)." *Moravian Music Journal* 26/1 (Spring 1981): 21.

Cooper, Philip T. D. "A History of the Tannenberg Organ in York." *Diapason* 85/12 (1994): 12–14.

Cranz, David. *The History of Greenland: containing a description of the country, and its inhabitants; and particularly, a Relation of the Mission, carried on for above these Thirty Years by the Unitas Fratrum, at New Herrnhuth and Lichtenfels, in that Country*. 2 vols. London: Brethren's Society for the Furtherance of the Gospel among the Heathen, 1767.

Crawford, Richard. "The Moravians and Eighteenth-Century American Musical Mainstreams." *Moravian Music Journal* 21/2 (Fall–Winter 1976): 2–7.

Crews, C. Daniel. *Confessing Our Unity in Christ: Historical and Theological Background to the "Ground of the Unity."* Winston-Salem: Moravian Archives, 1994.

———. "Die Stellung der Musik im gottesdienstlichen Leben der Brüdergemeine." *Unitas Fratrum* 47 (2000): 12–28.

———. *The Development of Moravian Worship: A Report to the Hymnal Committee*. Unpublished paper, August 1987. Moravian Music Foundation Vertical Files, Winston-Salem.

———. "The Hymnal of 1754: A Search for Identity and Respectability." Unpublished paper presented at the Fifth Bethlehem Conference on Moravian Music, October 2002. Moravian Music Foundation Vertical Files, Winston-Salem.

———. *Johann Friedrich Peter and His Times*. Winston-Salem: Moravian Music Foundation, 1990.

Crews, C. Daniel. *John Antes.* Winston-Salem: Moravian Music Foundation, 1997.

———. "Luke of Prague: Theologian of the Unity." *The Hinge, A Journal of Christian Thought for the Moravian Church* 12/3 (Autumn 2005): 21–54.

———. *Moravian Meanings: A Glossary of Historical Terms of the Moravian Church, Southern Province.* 2nd ed. Winston-Salem: Moravian Archives, 1996.

———. "Questions of Moravian Identity." *TMDK (Transatlantic Moravian Dialog Korrespondenz),* 9 (July 1996): 26–32.

———. "The Theology of John Hus, With Special Reference to His Concepts of Salvation." PhD diss., University of Manchester, 1975.

———. *This We Most Certainly Believe: Thoughts on Moravian Theology.* Winston-Salem: Moravian Archives, 2005.

Crews, C. Daniel, and Nola Reed Knouse. "Questions of Music in the Church: As Seen by the Unity Elders' Conference, May 1790." *Moravian Music Journal* 44/2 (Fall 1999): 5–6.

Crews, C. Daniel, and Richard W. Starbuck. *With Courage for the Future: The Story of the Moravian Church, Southern Province.* Winston-Salem: Moravian Church in America, Southern Province, 2002.

Cross, F. L., and E. A. Livingstone, eds. *The Oxford Dictionary of the Christian Church,* 2nd ed. Oxford: Oxford University Press, 1983.

Cumnock, Frances. "The Lovefeast Psalm: Questions and a few Answers." *Moravian Music Foundation Bulletin* 23/1 (Spring–Summer 1978): 2–9.

———. "The Salem Congregation Collection: 1790–1808." *Moravian Music Foundation Bulletin* 17/1 (Spring–Summer 1972): 1–4.

———. "The Salem Congregation Music: Problems Then and Now." *Moravian Music Foundation Bulletin* 19/2 (Fall–Winter 1974): 1–4.

Cumnock, Frances, ed. *Catalog of the Salem Congregation Music.* Chapel Hill: University of North Carolina Press, 1980.

David, Christian. *Beschreibung und Zuverläßige Nachricht von Herrnhut in der Ober-Lausitz.* Leipzig, 1735.

David, Hans T. "Music of the Early Moravians in America." *Musical America* 59 (September 1939): 5–6, 33.

———. "Musical Life in the Pennsylvania Settlements of the Unitas Fratrum." *Transactions of the Moravian Historical Society* 13 (1942). Reprinted as Moravian Music Foundation Publications No. 6. Winston-Salem: Moravian Music Foundation, 1959.

David, Hans T., and Arthur Mendel, eds. *The New Bach Reader: A Life of Johann Sebastian Bach in Letters and Documents.* Revised and enlarged by Christoph Wolff. New York: W. W. Norton, 1998.

Davis, Ronald L. *A History of Music in American Life.* Vol. I, *The Formative Years, 1620–1865.* Malabar, FL: Robert Krieger Publishing Company, 1982.

Davison, Archibald T. *Protestant Church Music in America.* Boston: E. C. Schirmer Music Co., 1933.

Dean, Talmadge Whitman. "The Organ in Eighteenth Century English Colonial America." PhD diss., University of Southern California, 1960.

Dencke, Jeremias. *Personalien.* Undated manuscript in Moravian Archives, Bethlehem. Unpublished translation in Moravian Music Foundation Vertical Files, Winston-Salem.

deSchweinitz, Edmund. *The History of the Church Known as the Unitas Fratrum, or The Unity of the Brethren,* 2nd ed. Bethlehem: Moravian Publication Concern, 1901.

deSchweinitz, Paul. "The Old Tanneberger Organ at Nazareth." *The Moravian* (May 11, 1898).

Dickinson, Clarence, ed. *Early American Moravian Church Music.* New York: H. W. Gray Co., Inc., n.d.

Dir, o Herr, sei Lob gegeben: Mit Comenius singen und beten. Herrnhut: Direktion der Evangelische Brüder-Unität, 1992.

Dodge, Alfred. *Pianos and Their Makers.* Covina, CA: Covina Publishing Co., 1911. Reprint, New York: Dover, 1972.

Dreger, Wilfred L. "The Celebration and Doctrine of Holy Communion in the Ancient Unity." BD thesis, Moravian Theological Seminary, 1945.

Dreydoppel, Otto, Jr. "The Intentions of Our Founders: A Historical Review of Moravian Worship." Unpublished paper presented at Symposium on Moravian Theology, Moravian Theological Seminary, November 18, 1988. Moravian Music Foundation Vertical Files, Winston-Salem.

Drummond, Robert R. *Early German Music in Philadelphia.* New York: Da Capo Press, 1970.

Duncan, Timothy P. "The Organ in Moravian Choral Anthems." *Moravian Music Journal* 37/1 (1992): 5–9.

———. "The Role of the Organ in Moravian Sacred Music between 1740–1840." DMA diss., University of North Carolina at Greensboro, 1989.

Eader, Thomas S. "David Tannenberg's Last Organ." *Tracker* 4/3 (1960): 3–4.

Ein New Gesengbuchlen, ed. Michael Weisse. 1531. Reprint, edited by Wilhelm Thomas. Kassel: Bärenreiter, 1931.

Erbe, Ernst Immanuel. *Seventeen Organ Chorales.* Edited by James Boeringer. Charlotte: Brodt Music Co., 1983.

Erbe, Ernst Immanuel, ed. *Auszug zu dem Choralbuch der evangelischen Brüdergemein für Clavier, Harmonium oder Hausorgel.* Ebersdorf: 1885.

Erxleben, Theodor. *Hilfsbuch für Liturgen und Organisten in den Brüdergemeinen.* 2nd ed. Gnadau: Verlag der Unitäts-Buchhandlung, 1891.

———. "Kleine Choralkunde zum Choralbuch der Brüdergemeine 1917." Unpublished manuscript. Moravian Archives, Herrnhut.

Falconer, Joan O. "Birthday Songs for Polly Heckewelder." *Moravian Music Foundation Bulletin* 19/1 (Spring–Summer 1974): 1–3.

———. "Bishop Johannes Herbst (1735–1812), an American-Moravian Musician, Collector, and Composer." PhD diss., Columbia University, 1969.

Finney, Theodore M. "The Collegium Musicum at Lititz, Pennsylvania, During the Eighteenth Century." *Papers of the American Musicological Society,* 1937: 45–55.

Finscher, Ludwig, ed. *Die Musik in Geschichte und Gegenwart.* Kassel: Bärenreiter, 1994, s.v. "Collegium musicum," "Divertimento," "Harmoniemusik," "Partita."

Fox, Pauline M. "Parodies for Piety: 'aus Naumanns Cora,'" *Moravian Music Journal* 42/2 (Fall 1997): 6–14; 43/2 (Fall 1998): 11–21.

———. "Reflections on Moravian Music: A Study of Two Collections of Manuscript Books in Pennsylvania ca. 1800." PhD diss., New York University, 1997.

Frank, Albert H. *Companion to the Moravian Book of Worship.* Winston-Salem: Moravian Music Foundation, 2004.

———. "Johann Christian Bechler." *Unitas Fratrum* 47 (2000): 83–88.

Franklin, Benjamin. *The Autobiography of Benjamin Franklin.* New Haven: Yale University Press, 1964.

Freeman, Arthur J. *An Ecumenical Theology of the Heart: The Theology of Count Nicholas Ludwig von Zinzendorf.* Bethlehem and Winston-Salem: Moravian Church in America, 1998.

Freylinghausen, Johann Anastasius. *Geistreiches Gesang-Buch, den Kern alter und neuer Lieder in sich haltend.* Halle: in Verlegung des Wäysenhauses, 1741.

Fries, Adelaide, ed. and trans. *Records of the Moravians in North Carolina.* Vols. 1–5. Raleigh: North Carolina Historical Commission, 1922–41.

———. *The Moravians in Georgia, 1735–1740.* Raleigh: Edwards & Broughton, 1905.

Frischmann, Charles. "Organs and Organ Music in Colonial America." *Journal of Church Music* 17 (December 1975): 2–4.

Gambold, John. *Sechs kleine Klavier-Sonaten.* Leipzig: For the author, 1788. Reprint edited by James Boeringer, *Six Little Keyboard Sonatas Dedicated to Lady Schönberg by John Gambold, Schoolteacher and Organist at Niesky.* Winston-Salem: Moravian Music Foundation, n.d.

Gaustad, Edwin Scott. *A Religious History of America,* rev. ed. San Francisco: Harper & Row, 1990.

Gebhard, Johann Gottfried. *Eine Sonate für das Klavier.* Barby: For the composer, 1784.

Gesangbuch der Evangelischen Brüdergemeine. Gnadau: Verlag der Unitäts-Buchhandlung, 1917.

Gesangbuch der Evangelischen Brüdergemeine. Hamburg: Friedrich Wittig Verlag, 1927.

Gesangbuch der Evangelischen Brüdergemeine. Herrnhut and Bad Boll: Direktionen der Evangelische Brüder-Unität, 1967.

Gesangbuch der Evangelischen Brüdergemeine, Teil II. Herrnhut and Bad Boll: Evangelische Brüder-Unität, 1998.

Das Gesangbuch der Gemeine in Herrnhuth. 12 Anhänge + 4 Zugaben. Herrnhut: Evangelische Brüder-Unität, 1735[–48].

Gesangbuch zum Gebrauch der evangelischen Brüdergemeinen. Barby: Friedrich Spellenberg, 1783.

Gesangbuch zum Gebrauch der evangelischen Brüdergemeinen. Barby: Conrad Schilling, 1805.

Gezangboek ten Gebruik der Gemeenten der Moravische Broederkerk in Zuid-Afrika, 7th ed. Genadendal: Evangeliese Broederkerk, 1914.

Giesler, John H. "Bicentennial of Gregor's Hymnal of 1778." *Moravian Music Foundation Bulletin* 23/2 (Fall–Winter 1978): 15–16.

Giesler, John H. "Musical Ministers of the Moravian Church." *Hymn* 29/1 (January 1978): 6–14.

———. "A Study in the Sources of the Ancient Unitas Fratrum Hymnals." BD thesis, Moravian Theological Seminary, 1958.

Gleason, Harold, and Warren Becker. *Early American Music—Music in America from 1620–1920*, 2nd ed. Bloomington: Frangipani Press, 1981.

Goldman, Richard Franks. *Landmarks of Early American Music, 1760–1800*. New York: AMS Press, 1974.

Gollin, Gillian. *Moravians in Two Worlds*. New York: Columbia University Press, 1967.

Gombosi, Marilyn. *A Day of Solemn Thanksgiving: Moravian Music for the Fourth of July, 1783 in Salem, North Carolina*. Chapel Hill: University of North Carolina Press, 1977.

Gombosi, Marilyn, ed. *Catalog of the Johannes Herbst Collection*. Chapel Hill: University of North Carolina Press, 1970.

Gordon, Tom. "Seal Oil and String Quartets: Moravian Music Among the Labrador Inuit." Lecture presented at the Sixth Bethlehem Conference on Moravian Music, October 23, 2004.

Gould, Nathaniel Duren. *Church Music in America*. Boston: A. N. Johnson, 1853.

The Graceham Organ Book. Compiled by Bishop Samuel Reinke. Manuscript, Graceham Moravian Church, Thurmont, MD, 1830.

Graun, Karl Heinrich. *Geistliche Oden in Melodien gesetzt von einigen Tonkünstlern in Berlin*. Berlin: Christian Friedrich Voss, 1758.

Gregor, Christian. *Choral-Buch, enthaltend alle zu dem Gesangbuche der Evangelischen Brüder-Gemeinen vom Jahre 1778 gehörige Melodien* (Leipzig: Breitkopf, 1784). Facsimile edition, edited by James Boeringer. Bethlehem and Winston-Salem: Moravian Music Foundation Press, 1984.

Grider, Rufus A. *Historical Notes on Music in Bethlehem, Pa. (from 1741–1871)*. Philadelphia: John L. Pile, 1873. Reprinted as Moravian Music Foundation Publications No. 4. Winston-Salem: Moravian Music Foundation, 1957.

Griffin, Frances. *Less Time for Meddling: A History of Salem Academy and College, 1772–1866*. Winston-Salem: John F. Blair, 1979.

———. "The Moravian Musical Heritage." *Moravian Music Foundation Bulletin* 12/2 (Spring 1968): 1–3.

Grimm, Johann Daniel. *Handbuch bey der Music-Information im Paedagogio zu Catharinenhof, besonders auf das Clavier applicirt, in vier Lehr-Classen und einem Supplement, nebst einer Beylage, die Zeichen und Aufgaben in sich enthalten (Manuskript, Grosshennersdorf bei Herrnhut 1758)*. Edited by Anja Wehrend. Tübingen: Max Niemeyer GmbH, 2002.

Grout, Donald Jay, and Claude V. Palisca. *A History of Western Music*, 4th ed. New York: W. W. Norton, 1988.

Grube, Bernard Adam. *Lebenslauf* (Memoir). Undated. Translated by John T. Hamilton. Moravian Archives, Bethlehem.

Gura, Philip F. *C. F. Martin and His Guitars, 1796–1873*. Chapel Hill and London: University of North Carolina Press, 2003.

Haeussler, Armin. *The Story of Our Hymns: The Handbook to the Hymnal of the Evangelical and Reformed Church.* St. Louis: Eden Publishing House, 1952.

Hagen, Francis Florentine. *Church and Home Organist's Companion.* 2 vols. Philadelphia: Fred. Williams, 1880, 1881.

———. *Unitas Fratrum in Extremis; or, Thoughts on the Past and Present Condition of the Moravian Church in America, Respectfully Submitted to the Provincial Synod of 1893, at Bethlehem, Pa.* Bethlehem: Moravian Publications Office, 1893.

Hahn, Hans-Christoph, and Hellmut Reichel. *Zinzendorf und die Herrnhuter Brüder: Quellen zur Geschichte der Brüder-Unität von 1722 bis 1760.* Hamburg: Friedrich Wittig Verlag, 1977.

Hahn, Katherine Ann. "The Wind Ensemble Music of David Moritz Michael." Master's thesis, University of Missouri-Columbia, 1979.

Haldeman, Eliza Jacobs. "Seventy-seven Years Ago." *Linden Hall Echo* 1/5 (May 1877); 2/1 (September 1877).

Hall, Harry H. *A Johnny Reb Band from Salem,* rev. ed. Raleigh: Office of Archives and History, North Carolina Department of Cultural Resources, 2006.

———. "Moravian Music Education in America, ca. 1750 to ca. 1830." *Journal of Research in Music Education* 29/3 (Fall 1981): 225–34.

———. "The Moravian Trombone Choir: A Conspectus of its Early History and the Traditional Death Announcement," *Moravian Music Journal* 26/1 (1981): 5–8.

———. "The Moravian Wind Ensemble: Distinctive Chapter in America's Music." PhD diss., George Peabody College for Teachers, 1967.

———. "The Moravian Wind Ensemble Tradition in America." *Moravian Music Foundation Bulletin* 9 (Spring 1965): 1–4.

Haller, Mabel. "Early Moravian Education in Pennsylvania." PhD diss., University of Pennsylvania, 1953. Reprinted in *Transactions of the Moravian Historical Society* 15 (1953), 1–409.

Hamilton, J. Taylor and Kenneth G. Hamilton. *History of the Moravian Church: The Renewed Unitas Fratrum, 1722–1957.* Bethlehem and Winston-Salem: Interprovincial Board of Christian Education, Moravian Church in America, 1967.

Hamilton, Kenneth G., trans. and ed. *The Bethlehem Diary.* Vol. I, 1742–1744. Bethlehem: Archives of the Moravian Church, 1971.

Hamilton, Kenneth G., and Lothar Madeheim, trans. *The Bethlehem Diary.* Vol. II, 1744–1745. Edited by Vernon H. Nelson, Otto Dreydoppel, Jr., and Doris Rohland Yob. Bethlehem: Moravian Archives, 2001.

Hart, Joanne S. *American Organ Music: A Glance at the Past 100 Years.* Dayton: Sacred Music Press, 1975.

Hartmann, Andrea. "Musik zu den Festtagen der Brüdergemeine 1759–1800." *Unitas Fratrum* 47 (2000): 29–40.

Hartzell, Lawrence W. "Musical Moravian Missionaries, Part I: Johann Christopher Pyrlaeus," *Moravian Music Journal* 29/4 (Winter 1984): 91–92.

———. "Musical Moravian Missionaries, Part V: Peter Ricksecker." *Moravian Music Journal* 32/1 (Spring 1987): 14–15.

Hartzell, Lawrence W. *Ohio Moravian Music.* Winston-Salem: Moravian Music Foundation Press, 1988.

———. "Trombones in Ohio." *Moravian Music Journal* 28 (1983): 72–74.

Hasse, Christian Friedrich. *Sacred Music: partly original; partly selected from the works of the chief of the most modern German composers, by C. F. Hasse, The Vocal parts as in the Original Score, and adapted exclusively to English Words. The Instrumental Parts arranged for the Piano Forte.* Leeds: J. Muff, [1829].

Haydn, Franz Joseph. *Kritische Ausgabe sämtlicher Symphonien.* Edited and with introduction by H. C. Robbins Landon. Vienna: Universal Edition, 1965–68.

———. *Works.* Edited and with introduction by Jens Peter Larsen. Koh: Joseph Haydn-Institut. Munich: G. Henle Editions, 1958f.

Heckewelder, John. *A Narrative of the Mission of the United Brethren among the Delaware and Mohegan Indians.* Philadelphia: M'Carty & Davis, 1820.

Henkelmann, Brian G. "Early Reformation Christology: The 1544 Hymnal of the Unity of the Brethren." MATS thesis, Moravian Theological Seminary, 1983.

Henry, James. *Sketches of Moravian Life and Character.* Philadelphia: J. B. Lippincott & Co., 1859.

Hensel, W. U. "A Famous Organ Builder." *Historical Papers and Addresses of the Lancaster County Historical Society* 11 (1907).

Herbst, John. *Hymns to Be Sung at the Pianoforte.* Edited by Monica Schantz. Bethlehem: Moravian College, 1973.

Herbst, Johannes. *Lebenslauf* (Memoir). Undated manuscript. Moravian Archives, Winston-Salem. Unpublished translation in Moravian Music Foundation Vertical Files, Winston-Salem.

Herrnhut, Wochenblatt aus der Brüdergemeine 35/2 (January 10, 1902): 12–13.

Hertel, Marilyn. "The Development of the Moravian Sacred Music as Typified in the Sunday Musical Services of the Early American Moravian Congregations." MM thesis, Bob Jones University, 1968.

Hickel, Helmut. *Das Abendmahl zu Zinzendorfs Zeiten.* Hamburg: Ludwig Appel, 1956.

———. *Lebenserinnerungen.* Herrnhut: 1992.

Hiller, Johann Adam. *Allgemeine Choral-Melodienbuch.* 1793.

Hillmer, Gottlob Friedrich. *Sammlung einiger musikalischen Fest-Gesänge der evangelischen Brüdergemeine zum Singen am Klavier eingerichtet.* 2 vols. Breslau: Grass und Barth, 1803–5.

Hoople, Donald Graham. "Moravian Music Education and the American Moravian Music Tradition." EdD diss., Teachers College, Columbia University, 1976.

Howard, John Tasker. *Our American Music,* 3rd ed. New York: Thomas Y. Crowell, 1954.

Howard, John Tasker, and George Kent Bellows. *A Short History of Music in America.* New York: Thomas Y. Crowell, 1957.

Huebener, Mary Augusta. *History of the Moravian Congregation of Lititz, Pa.* Bethlehem: Times Publishing Co., 1949.

Hutton, James. *The tunes for the hymns in the collection with several translations from the Moravian hymnbook.* London: Bible and Sun, [1742]; part II, 1746; part III, 1749.

Hymnal and Liturgies of the Moravian Church. Bethlehem: Board of Elders of the Northern Diocese of the Church of the United Brethren in the United States of America, 1923.

Hymnal and Liturgies of the Moravian Church. Bethlehem and Winston-Salem: Moravian Church in America, 1969.

Ingram, Jeannine S. "Music in American Moravian Communities: Transplanted Traditions in Indigenous Practices." *Communal Societies. The Journal of the National Historic Communal Societies Association* 2 (1982): 39–51.

———. "A Musical Potpourri: The Commonplace Book of Johann Friedrich Peter." *Moravian Music Foundation Bulletin* 24/1 (Spring/Summer 1979): 2–7.

———. "Reflections on the Salem Collegium Musicum." *Moravian Music Foundation Bulletin* 20/1 (Spring–Summer 1975): 8–11.

"Instruments–other." Folder 17, Collections Office, Moravian Museum, Bethlehem.

The Johannes Herbst Collection. Microfiche. New York: University Music Editions, 1974.

Johansen, John. "Moravian Hymnody." *Hymn* 30 (July 1979): 167–77. Reprinted as Moravian Music Foundation Publications No. 9. Winston-Salem: Moravian Music Foundation, 1980.

Johns, Michael. "Collauf and His Contribution to Moravian Music." DMA diss., Temple University, 1996.

———. "A Second Look at Collauf." *Moravian Music Journal* 41/2 (Fall 1996): 7–15.

Josquin, Jan. *Muzika (1561).* Translated by Thomas Sovík. Denton, TX: Czech Historical Society, 1991.

Jueckstock, John Douglas. "The Complete Works of Jeremias Dencke (1725–1795)." DMA diss., Southwestern Baptist Theological Seminary, 1984.

Julian, John. *A Dictionary of Hymnology.* New York: Dover, 1907.

Jüngerhaus-Diarium. Unpublished manuscript. Moravian Archives, Herrnhut. Copies also in Moravian Archives, Bethlehem and Winston-Salem.

Kares, Martin H. H. "Orgelbau in den U.S.A. Deutsche und deutschstämmige Orgelbauer und ihre Instruments des 18. und 19. Jahrhunderts in Pennsylvania." Master's thesis, Philipps-Universität Marburg/Lahm, 1988.

Kästner, Carl A., ed. *Auszug aus dem Choral-Buch der Evangelischen Brüdergemein.* Niesky: 1841.

Kauffmann, George Friedrich. *Harmonische Seelenlust (1793): Präludien über die bekanntesten Chorallieder für Orgel.* Edited by Pierre Pidoux. Kassel: Bärenreiter, 1967.

Keehn, David P. "The Trombone Choir of the Moravian Church in North America." Master's thesis, West Chester State College, 1978.

Kleine Gesangbuch der Brüdergemeine. Gnadau: Verlag der Unitätsbuchhandling, 1870.

Knapp, Albert. *Geistliche Gedichte des Grafen von Zinzendorf . . . Mit einer Lebensskizze und des Verfassers Bildniss.* Stuttgart and Tübingen: J. G. Gotta'scher Verlag, 1845.

Knouse, Nola Reed. "Die *Moravian Music Foundation* und brüderische Musikforschung in Amerika." *Unitas Fratrum* 47 (2000): 121–27.

———. "The American Moravian Brass Players: What Did They Play?" *Moravian Music Journal* 43 (1998): 11–21.

———. "Moravian Music and the Organ." *Tracker* 48/3 (Summer 2004): 22–26.

Knouse, Nola Reed. "'Not to Glory, But to Serve': The Musical Gifts of Johann Friedrich Peter." *Unitas Fratrum* 47 (2000): 41–60.

———. "The Organ in Moravian Church Music." *Moravian Music Journal* 44/1 (Spring 1999): 3–11.

Knouse, Nola Reed, and C. Daniel Crews. *Moravian Music: An Introduction*. Winston-Salem: Moravian Music Foundation, 1996.

Koch, Heinrich Christoph. *Musikalisches Lexikon* (1802). Reprint edition, Hildesheim: Georg Olms Verlagsbuchhandlung, 1964.

Kortz, Edwin W. "The Liturgical Development of the American Moravian Church." STD diss., Temple University, 1955.

Kottick, Edward L. *A History of the Harpsichord*. Bloomington: Indiana University Press, 2003.

Kratzenstein, Marilou. *Survey of Organ Literature*. Ames: Iowa State University Press, 1980.

Kriebel, Howard Wiegner. *The Schwenkfelders in Pennsylvania*. Lancaster: Pennsylvania German Society, 1904.

Kroeger, Karl. "A Core Repertory of American Moravian Hymn Tunes." *Moravian Music Journal* 31 (Spring 1986): 3.

———. "David Moritz Michael's Psalm 103: An Early American Sacred Cantata." *Moravian Music Foundation Bulletin* 21/2 (Fall–Winter 1976): 10–12.

———. "An Eighteenth-Century English-Moravian Repertory," *Moravian Music Journal* 27/2 (Fall 1992): 9, 13–22.

———. "Ernst Immanuel Erbe: A Forgotten Moravian Composer." *Moravian Music Foundation Bulletin* 24 (Spring–Summer, 1979): 9–12.

———. "Moravian Music in America. A Survey." In *Unitas Fratrum. Herrnhuter Studien. Moravian Studies*, edited by Mari P. van Buijtenen [e.a.], 387–400. Utrecht: Rijksarchief, 1975.

———. "Moravian Music in 19th-Century American Tunebooks." *Moravian Music Foundation Bulletin* 18/1 (Spring–Summer 1973): 1–3.

———. "The Moravian Tradition in Song." *Moravian Music Foundation Bulletin* 20/2 (Fall–Winter 1975): 8–10.

———. "New Light on Early Bethlehem Music." *Moravian Music Foundation Bulletin* 19/1 (Spring–Summer 1974): 4–5.

———. "On the Early Performance of Moravian Chorales." *Moravian Music Foundation Bulletin* 24 (Fall–Winter 1979): 2–8.

———. "A Preliminary Survey of Musical Life in the English Moravian Settlements of Fulneck, Fairfield, and Ockbrook During the 18th and 19th Centuries." *Moravian Music Journal* 29/1 (Spring 1984): 20–25.

———. "What Happened to the Antes String Quartets?" *Moravian Music Journal* 41/1 (Spring 1996): 23–26.

Kroeger, Karl, ed. *A Moravian Music Sampler*. Moravian Music Foundation Publication No. 7. Winston-Salem: Moravian Music Foundation, 1974.

Landenberger, G. F., ed. *Choral-Buch für die Orgel mit zwischenspielen versehen und für den vierstimmigen Gesangeingerichtet Enthaltend*. Mercersburg: Deutschen Evangelisch–Lutherischen Synode von Pennsylvanien, 1862, 1870, 1879.

Lang, Paul Henry. *Music in Western Civilization.* New York: Norton, 1941.

Larson, Paul S. *An American Musical Dynasty: A Biography of the Wolle Family of Bethlehem, Pennsylvania.* Bethlehem: Lehigh University Press, 2002.

Larson, Paul, and Carol Traupman-Carr, eds. *The Square Piano in Rural Pennsylvania, 1760–1830.* Catalog of an exhibition, October 19–November 26, 2000. Payne Gallery, Moravian College, Bethlehem.

LaTrobe, Christian Ignatius. *Anthems for One, Two, or more Voices performed in the Church of the United Brethren, Collected and the Instrumental parts adapted for the Organ or Piano Forte, Composed by various Authors.* London: Printed for the Editor, 1811.

———. *Hymn-tunes sung in the Church of the United Brethren.* London: J. Bland, for the author, [ca. 1790].

———. *Letters to My Children; Written at Sea During a Voyage to the Cape of Good Hope, in 1815.* Edited and with an introduction by J. A. LaTrobe. London: Seeley's, 1851.

———. *Nine Preludes for Organ.* Edited by Karl Kroeger. Charlotte: Brodt Music Company, 1978.

———. *Three Sonatas for the Pianoforte, Composed & Dedicated, by Permission, to Mr. Haydn, Op. III.* London: J. Bland, for the Author. Reprint, edited by Charles E. Stevens. New York: Boosey & Hawkes, 1970.

LaTrobe, Christian Ignatius, ed. *Hymn Tunes sung in the Church of the United Brethren.* London: J. Bland, for the author, ca. 1790.

———, ed. *Hymn-Tunes sung in the Church of the United Brethren, Collected by Chrn. Igns. LaTrobe. A New Edition revised & corrected with an Appendix.* London: 1826.

———, ed. *Original Anthems for One, Two, or More Voices Adapted for Private Devotion or Public Worship Composed and the Accompaniments Arranged for the Piano Forte or Organ.* London: Printed for the Author, 1828.

LaTrobe, Peter, *Hymn-Tunes sung in the Church of the United Brethren first collected by Chr. Ign. La Trobe. An enlarged edition, Arranged in Parts for the Use of Choirs.* London: William Mallilieu, ca. 1854.

Laubenstein, Sarah. "Two Early American Organ Builders." *Music, the A.G.O. Magazine* 9/12 (1975): 39–40.

Laudate. Gesangboek van die Evangeliese Broederkerk in Suider-Afrika. Genadendal: 1983.

Leaman, Jerome. "The Trombone Choir of the Moravian Church." *Moravian Music Foundation Bulletin* 20/1 (1975): 2, 7.

Leaver, Robin. "Two Pupils of Rheinberger and Their Use of the Organ in Performance of Bach's *St. John Passion.*" *Tracker* 33/2 (1989): 18–23.

Leonard, Bill J. *Baptist Ways: A History.* Valley Forge: Judson Press, 2003.

———. *God's Last and Only Hope: The Fragmentation of the Southern Baptist Convention.* Grand Rapids: W. B. Eerdmans, ca. 1990.

———. "Perspectives on Baptist Denominationalism: Anticipating the Future." In *Findings: A Report of the Special Study Commission to Study the Question: "Should the Cooperative Baptist Fellowship Become a Separate Convention?"* ed. Randall C. Lolley. Atlanta: Cooperative Baptist Fellowship, 1996, 102–11.

Levering, Joseph Mortimer. *A History of Bethlehem, Pennsylvania: 1741–1842 with Some Account of Its Founders and Their Early Activity in America.* Bethlehem: Times Publishing Co., 1903.

Libin, Laurence. *American Musical Instruments in the Metropolitan Museum of Art.* New York: W. W. Norton, 1985.

————. "Commercial Accounts of Early Moravian-American Music." In *Land Without Nightingales: Music in the Making of German-America,* edited by Philip V. Bohlman and Otto Holzapfel, 99–110. Madison: University of Wisconsin Press, 2002.

————. "John Huber's Pianos in Context." *Journal of the American Musical Instrument Society* 19 (1993): 5–37.

————. "The Memoirs of David Tannenberg." *Journal of Moravian History* 2 (2007).

————. "Nazareth Piano May Be Among America's First." *Moravian Music Journal* 33/1 (Spring 1988): 1–6.

————. "New Facts and Speculations on John Clemm." *Tracker* 31/2 (1987): 18–24.

————. "New Insights to Tannenberg's Clavichords." In *De Clavicordio VII: Proceedings of the VII International Clavichord Symposium, Magnano, 6–10 September 2005,* 129–55. Magnano: Musica Antica a Magnano, 2006.

————. "Organ History, with Strings Attached." *Tracker* 49/3 (Summer 2005): 3–5.

Linyard, Fred, and Phillip Tovey. *Moravian Worship.* Bramcote, Nottingham: Grove Books Limited, 1994.

Das Litaneyen-Büchlein nach der bey den Brüdern dermalen hauptsächlich gewöhnlichen Singe-Weise . . .. Barby: 1757.

The Litany-Book according to the Manner of Singing at present mostly in Use among the Brethren. London: 1759.

Liturgienbuch der evangelischen Brüdergemeine. Gnadau: Verlag der Buchhandlung der evangelischen Brüder-Unität, 1873.

Liturgische Gesänge der evangelischen Brüdergemeinen, aufs neue revidirt und vermehrt. Barby: 1793.

The Liturgy and Hymns of the American Province of the Unitas Fratrum. Bethlehem: Moravian Publication Concern, 1876.

The Liturgy and the Offices of Worship and Hymns of the American Province of the Unitas Fratrum. Bethlehem: Moravian Publication Concern, 1908.

Lob und Anbetung des Gottmenschen, am Tage der Einweihung der neuen Orgel in der Deutschen Evangelisch Lutherischen Zions Kirche in Philadelphia, October 19. Germantown: Michael Billmeyer, 1790.

Lonas, Heinrich, ed. *Choralbuch der evangelischen Brüdergemeine zum Gebrauch in Kirche, Schule und Haus.* Herrnhut: n.d.

————, ed. *Choralbuch der evangelischen Brüderkirche, enthaltend 123 der bekannten Melodien mit Text und als Anhang neun der beliebtesten Arien.* Gnadau: C. A. Seiler, n.d.

Longworth, Mike. *Martin Guitars: A History,* rev. ed. Philadelphia: Falcon Press, 1980.

Luth, Jan Roelof. " 'Daer wert om't uitgekregen . . .' Bijdragen tot een geschiedenis van de gemeentesang in de Nederlands Geregormeerde protentantism ca. 1550–ca. 1852." PhD diss., Kampen, Netherlands.

————. "Some Data concerning Organ-accompaniment and Organ-Registration in Germany during the Nineteenth Century." In *Ars et Musica in Liturgia,* edited by Frans Browaer and Robin A. Leaver. N.p.: 1993.

Lütjeharms, W. *Het philadelphisch-oecumenisch striven der hernhutters.* Zeist, 1935.

Maurer, Joseph A. "Central Moravian Church: Center of Moravian Music." *American Organist* 41/11 (November 1958): 407–12.

———. "Moravian Church Music: 1457–1957." *American Guild of Organists Quarterly* 2 (1957): 3–6, 16–19, 30–32.

———. "The Organs in Central Moravian Church." *American Organist* 41/11 (November 1958): 412–18, 420–22.

Mayes, Curtis S. "A Descriptive Catalogue of Historic Percussion, Wind, and Stringed Instruments in Three Pennsylvania Museums." MM thesis, Florida State University, 1974.

McCorkle, Donald M. "The Collegium Musicum Salem: Its Music, Musicians, and Importance." North Carolina Historical Review (October 1956). Revised and reprinted as Moravian Music Foundation Publications No. 3. Revised edition, Winston-Salem: Moravian Music Foundation, 1979.

———. "The Moravian Contribution to American Music." *Music Library Association Notes*, 13/4 (September 1956), 597–606. Reprinted as Moravian Music Publications No.1. Winston-Salem: Moravian Music Foundation, 1956.

———. "Moravian Music in Salem: A German-American Heritage." PhD diss., Indiana University, 1958.

———. "Prelude to a History of American Moravian Organs." *American Guild of Organists Quarterly* 3/4 (October 1958): 142–48.

M'Culloch, William. *Selected Music.* Philadelphia, 1807.

[McFarland, James R.]. *Services of Rededication of the 1787 Tannenberg Organ in the Gallery of the Brothers' House, April 17 and 24, 1983.* Lititz: Lititz Moravian Congregation, 1983.

McGeary, Thomas. "David Tannenberg and the Salem 1800 Organ." *Moravian Music Journal* 31/2 (Fall 1986): 18–23.

———. "David Tannenberg's Directions for Organ Tuning." *Organ Yearbook* 16 (1985): 78–79.

McManis, Charles W. "David Tannenberg and the Old Salem Restoration." *American Organist* 48/5 (May 1965): 15–20.

———. "Restoration of Tannenberg Organ at Old Salem." *Diapason* 56/4 (March 1965): 36–37.

McManis, Charles W., and Frank P. Albright. "Tannenberg Restoration: Presenting Two Interesting Views." *Tracker* 9/2 (Winter 1965): 1–2, 7–8.

"McManis to Restore Tannenberg." *Moravian Music Foundation Bulletin* 7/2–3 (Spring–Summer–Fall 1963): 1, 6.

Meigen, Siegfried. "Die Anfänge wurden aufgeschrieben: 175 Jahre Bläserchor Königsfeld." *Der Brüderbote. Mitteilungen aus der Brüdergemeine* 454 (May 1987): 10–13.

Meinecke, C. *A New Instruction for the Piano Forte Containing the Rudiments of Music explained in a concise manner, and a Sett of Lessons Calculated to establish the True Method of Fingering And afford an agreeable Study for Pupils,* 2nd ed. Philadelphia: Willig, 1823.

Meinung, Lisetta Maria Van Vleck. Memoir, prepared by J. Kenneth Pfohl. Moravian Archives, Winston-Salem.

Meyer, Dieter. "Christian Gregor als Kantor, Liederdichter und Bischof der Brüdergemeine." *Unitas Fratrum* 47 (2000): 61–82.

———. *Der Christocentrismus des späten Zinzendorf.* Frankfurt am Main: Peter Lang, 1973.

Michael, David Moritz. *Complete Wind Chamber Music.* Edited by Nola Reed Knouse. Recent Researches in American Music 59; Music of the United States of America 16. Middleton, WI: A-R Editions, 2006.

Michael, David Moritz. *Lebenslauf* (Memoir). Unpublished manuscript. R.22.40.29, Moravian Archives, Herrnhut. Unpublished translation by Donald M. McCorkle. Moravian Music Foundation Vertical Files, Winston-Salem.

Miller, Theodore B. *A History of St. Michael's Union Church, 1769–1969.* N.p., n.d.

"A Modern 'Singstunde.'" *Moravian Music Foundation Bulletin* 14/2 (Spring 1970): 6.

Montgomery, James. *Original Hymns for Public, Private and School Devotion.* London: Longman, Brown, Green and Longmans, 1853.

Moravian Book of Worship. Bethlehem and Winston-Salem: Moravian Church in America, 1995.

Moravian Daily Texts. Bethlehem and Winston-Salem: Moravian Church in North America, 2007.

The Moravian Hymn Book and Liturgy. London: Moravian Book Room, 1975.

The Moravian Hymn Book with Tunes authorized for use in The Moravian Church [Unitas Fratrum] in Great Britain and Ireland with the Liturgy and Canticles. London: Moravian Publication Office, 1914.

Moravian Youth Hymnal. Bethlehem and Winston-Salem: Interprovincial Board of Christian Education, Moravian Church in America, 1942.

Müller, Joseph Theodor. *Geschichte der Böhmischen Brüder.* Band I, 1400–1528. Herrnhut: Verlag der Missionsbuchhandlung, 1922.

———. *Hymnologisches Handbuch zum Gesangbuch der Brüdergemeine.* Herrnhut: Verlag des Vereins für Brüdergeschichte in Kommission der Unitätsbuchhandlung in Gnadau, 1916.

Music of the Ephrata Cloister, Harmonists, and Moravians. Chesterhill, OH: Quakerhill Enterprises, ca. 1985.

"Musical Instruments—Winston-Salem: Ardmore Moravian." *Moravian Music Journal* 26/1 (Spring 1981): 19.

The Musical Journal for the Piano Forte. Vols. 3 and 5. Philadelphia: B. Carr, 1803–4.

Mussulman, Joseph A. *Official Programme of Exposition Concerts Chicago May-October, 1893.* N.p., n.d.

Myers, Richmond E. *Sketches of Early Bethlehem.* Bethlehem: Moravian College Alumnae Association, 1981.

Nachrichten aus der Brüder-Gemeine. Various years. Gnadau: Verlag der Unitäts-Buchhandlung.

Nelson, James D. "Herrnhut: Friedrich Schleiermacher's Spiritual Homeland." PhD diss., University of Chicago, 1963.

Nelson, Vernon H. "The Bethlehem Choir and Orchestra, 1812–1816." In *Proceedings of the Seventh Bethlehem Conference on Moravian Music, October 12–14, 2006.* Edited by Nola Reed Knouse. Winston-Salem: Moravian Music Foundation, 2007.

Nieuwenhuizen, Frederick. *Koraal-Boek inhoudende alle de melodijen der Evangelische Gezangen, in gebruik bij den Openbaren Godsdienst, van de Nederduitsche Hervormde Gemeenten, geschikt voor het orgel en Klavecimbaal.* Amsterdam: 1821.

Nitschke, A. *Choral-Buch der Evangelischen Brüdergemeine, Auszug aus dem, dem Choralgesang in den Brüdergemeinen zu Grunde gelegten Choralwerk von Chr. Gregor, vierstimmig arrangirt und mit leichten doppleten Zwischenspielen versehen.* Königsfeld: 1868.

Nolte, Ewald V. "Christian Ignatius LaTrobe's Letter to His Daughter Agnes." *Moravian Music Foundation Bulletin* 10/1 (Fall 1965): 2–4.

———. "Publications: The New Grove Dictionary and Moravian Music," *Moravian Music Journal* 26/2 (Summer 1981): 29–31.

"Obituary [Abraham Ritter]." *The Moravian* (November 8, 1860), 358–59.

Ochse, Orpha Caroline. *The History of the Organ in the United States.* Bloomington: Indiana University Press, 1975.

The Offices of Worship and Hymns of the American Province of the Unitas Fratrum. Bethlehem: Moravian Publication Concern, 1891.

Ogasapien, John. "New Data on John Geib." *Tracker* 23/4 (1979): 12–14.

———. *Organ Building in New York City: 1700–1900.* Braintree, MA: Organ Literature Foundation, 1977.

Ogden, John C. *An Excursion into Bethlehem and Nazareth in Pennsylvania in the Year 1799.* Philadelphia: Charles Cist, 1805.

Oldendorp, C. G. A. *Historie der caribischen Inseln St. Thomas, St. Crux und St. Jan* [unabridged edition]. Vol. 2/1. Dresden: 2002.

"Organ of 1804 Restored." *Diapason* 51/4 (March 1, 1960): 6.

The Orphean Lyre. Vol. 1. Boston, S. H. Parker, [1816].

Owen, Barbara. "American Organ Music and Playing From 1700." *Organ Institute Quarterly* 10 (1976): 10–15.

———. "A Salem Chamber Organ." *Essex Institute Historical Collections* 110/2 (1974): 111–19.

———, comp. and ed. *A Century of American Organ Music 1776–1876.* Vol. 4. Miami: McAfee Music, 1991.

Pachelbel, Johann. *Ausgewählte Orgelwerke, Zweiten Teil der Choralvorspiele.* Vol. 3. Kassel: Bärenreiter, 1950.

Palmer, Christian. *Evangelische Hymnologie.* Stuttgart: 1865. Reprint, Leipzig: 1978.

"Performers." *Moravian Music Journal* 26/1 (Spring 1981): 22.

Perrin, Irma C. "The History of Organ and Organ Builders in America Before 1900." PhD diss., Northwestern University, 1953.

Peter, Johann Friedrich. *Lebenslauf* (Memoir). Unpublished manuscript. Moravian Archives, Bethlehem. Unpublished translation by Donald M. McCorkle. Moravian Music Foundation Vertical Files, Winston-Salem.

Peucker, Paul M. "Findbuch zu R.28: Manuskripte von teils gedruckten, teils ungedruckten Werken über die Brüdergemeine." Typescript, 1997. Filed at Moravian Music Foundation, Winston-Salem.

———. "Music in the Moravian Archives, Herrnhut." Typescript list, October 2002. Filed at Moravian Music Foundation, Winston-Salem.

Pfohl, Bernard J. "The Home Moravian Church Organ." Bernard J. Pfohl Collection, no. 11: a. Letter of 1948, b. Paper of 1947, c. Letter of 1915. Moravian Music Foundation, Winston-Salem.

―――. *The Salem Band*. Winston-Salem: [Wachovia Historical Society], 1953.

―――. "The Salem Band." *Moravian Music Foundation Bulletin* 18/1 (Spring–Summer 1973): 5–8.

Pfohl, Bessie Whittington. Memoir, prepared by James C. Hughes. Moravian Archives, Winston-Salem.

Pfohl, James Christian. Memoir, prepared by Gerald R. Harris. Moravian Archives, Winston-Salem.

Phelps, Roger P. "The History and Practice of Chamber Music in the United States from Earliest Times up to 1875." PhD diss., State University of Iowa, 1951.

Písně duchovné evangelické. Kralice: 1615.

Písně duchovné evangelické. Kralice: 1618.

Plitt, Johannes. "Denkwürdigkeiten aus der Geschichte der Brüder-Unität." Manuscript, 1841. Copies in Moravian Archives, Herrnhut, and Moravian Archives, Bethlehem.

Podmore, Colin. *The Moravian Church in England 1728–1760.* Oxford: Clarendon, 1998.

Pressley, Ernest Wayne. "Musical Wind Instruments in the Moravian Musical Archives, Salem, North Carolina: A Descriptive Catalog." DMA diss., University of Kentucky, 1975.

Pyatt, Janet Best. "Johann Heinrich Rolle: A Non-Moravian Composer in the Moravian Music Foundation." *Moravian Music Journal* 38/1 (Spring 1993): 7–13.

―――. "Music and Society in Eighteenth-Century Germany: The Music Dramas of Johann Heinrich Rolle (1716–1785)." PhD diss., Duke University, 1991.

Rath, Richard Cullen. *How Early America Sounded.* Ithaca, NY: Cornell University Press, 2003.

Rau, Albert G. "John Frederick Peter." *Musical Quarterly* 23 (1937): 306–13.

Rau, Albert G., and Hans T. David. *A Catalogue of Music by American Moravians, 1742–1842.* Bethlehem: Moravian College and Seminary for Women, 1938. Reprint ed., New York, AMS Press, 1970.

Readings for Holy Week, 2nd printing. Bethlehem: Interprovincial Board of Communication, 2000.

Reed, Nola Jane. "The Theories of Joseph Riepel as Expressed in His *Anfangsgründe zur musicalischen Setzkunst* (1752–1768)." PhD diss., University of Rochester, 1983.

Reichardt, Johann Friedrich. *Briefe eines aufmerksamen Reisenden die Musik betreffend.* Vol. 1. Frankfort und Leipzig: 1774. Reprint Hildesheim: Olms, 1977.

Reichel, Gerard. *The Story of the Thirteenth of August 1727.* Translated by Douglas L. Rights (1927). Revised edition, Winston-Salem: Moravian Archives, 1994.

Reichel, William C. *Bethlehem Seminary Souvenir: A History of the Rise, Progress, and Present Condition of the Moravian Seminary for Young Ladies, at Bethlehem, Pa., with a catalogue of its pupils, 1785–1858.* 4th ed, revised and enlarged by William H. Bigler. Bethlehem: Published for the Seminary, 1901.

―――. *Historical Sketch of Nazareth Hall 1755–1869.* Philadelphia: J. B. Lippincott & Co., 1869.

Reichel, William C. *Something About Trombones, and the Old Mill at Bethlehem*. Edited by John W. Jordan. Bethlehem: Moravian Publication Office, 1884.

Reventlow, Sybille. "Musik og Sang." In *Herrnhuter-samfundet i Christiansfeld*, edited by Anders Pontoppidan Thyssen, 684–90. Åbenrå: Historisk Samfund for Sønderjylland, 1984.

Reventlow, Sybille, and Suzanne Summerville. "Die Christiansfelder Musikkataloge—Neues Forschungsunternehmen in Dänemark." *Unitas Fratrum* 3 (1978): 65–69.

Reynolds, Jeffrey C. "The Trombone in Moravian Life." *Moravian Music Journal* 32 (1987): 7–11.

Říčán, Rudolf. *The History of the Unity of Brethren*. Translated by C. Daniel Crews. Bethlehem and Winston-Salem: Moravian Church in America, 1992.

Rierson, Charles F., Jr. "The Collegium Musicum Salem: The Development of a Catalogue of Its Library and the Editing of Selected Works." EdD diss., University of Georgia, 1973.

Ripin, Edwin M., et al. *The New Grove Piano*. New York: W. W. Norton, 1988.

Ritter, Abraham. *History of the Moravian Church in Philadelphia from its Foundation in 1742 to the Present Time*. Philadelphia: Hayes and Zell, 1857.

Roberts, Charles R. and J. D. Schindel. *History of Egypt Church*. Allentown: Lehigh County Historical Society, 1908.

Roberts, Dale Alexander. "The Sacred Vocal Music of David Moritz Michael: An American Moravian Composer." DMA diss., University of Kentucky, 1978.

Rosetti, Francesco Antonio. *Five Wind Partitas: Music for the Oettingen-Wallerstein Court*. Edited by Sterling E. Murray. Recent Researches in Music of the Classical Era 30–31. Madison: A-R Editions, 1989.

Rothrock, Donna Kaye. "Moravian Music Education: Forerunner to Public School Music." *Bulletin of Historical Research in Music Education* 8/2 (July 1987): 63–82.

———. "The Perpetuation of the Moravian Music Tradition: Bernard Jacob Pfohl and the Salem, North Carolina, Bands, 1879–1960." EdD diss., University of North Carolina at Greensboro, 1991.

Runner, David C. "Music in the Moravian Community of Lititz." DMA diss., Eastman School of Music, 1976.

Sablosky, Irving. *What They Heard: Music in America, 1852–1881*. Baton Rouge: Louisiana State University Press, 1986.

Sadie, Stanley, ed. *The New Grove Dictionary of Music and Musicians*. 2nd ed. London and New York: Macmillan, 2001, s.v. "Collegium musicum," "Divertimento," "Harmoniemusik," "Partita," "Zinzendorf, Nikolaus Ludwig von (1700–1760)."

Sammartini, G. B. *The Symphonies of G. B. Sammartini*. Edited by Bathia Churgin. Cambridge, MA: Harvard University Press, 1968.

Schmauk, Theodore E. "The Church Organ and Its History." Lebanon: [1896]. Manuscript in Archives of the Ministerium of Pennsylvania, Lutheran Theological Seminary, Philadelphia.

Schönleber, Albert, and Hans-Michael Wenzel. "Seit mehr als 250 Jahren wird geblasen: von der Bedeutung der Bläserchöre im Gemeinleben." *Der Brüderbote* 454 (May 1987): 5–10.

Schultze, Augustus. *Guide to the Old Moravian Cemetery of Bethlehem, Pa., 1742–1897.* Bethlehem: Comenius Press, n.d.

Schulze, Adolph. *200 Jahre Brüdermission.* Vol. II. Herrnhut: 1932.

Selch, Frederick R. "Some Moravian Makers of Bowed Stringed Instruments." *Journal of the American Musical Instrument Society* 19 (1993): 38–64.

Services for Holy Communion. Bethlehem and Winston-Salem: Interprovincial Board of Publications and Communications, Moravian Church in America, [1996].

Shawe, Clarence H. *The Spirit of the Moravian Church.* Bethlehem and Winston-Salem: Interprovincial Board of Christian Education, Moravian Church in America, 1957.

Shields, T. Edgar. "Two Eighteenth-Century Organ Builders." *American Organist* 27/6 (June 1944): 129–30.

Smaby, Beverly Prior. *The Transformation of Moravian Bethlehem: From Communal Mission to Family Economy.* Philadelphia: University of Pennsylvania Press, 1988.

Smith, Jewel Ann. "Music, Women, and Pianos: The Moravian Young Ladies' Seminary in Antebellum Bethlehem, Pennsylvania (1815–1860)." PhD diss., Cincinnati College–Conservatory of Music, 2003.

Smither, Howard E. *A History of the Oratorio.* Vol. 3, *The Oratorio in the Classical Era.* Chapel Hill: University of North Carolina Press, 1987.

Snyder, Howard Albert. "Pietism, Moravianism, and Methodism as Renewal Movements: A Comparative and Thematic Study." PhD diss., University of Notre Dame, 1983.

Sommer, Elisabeth W. *Serving Two Masters: Moravian Brethren in Germany and North Carolina, 1727–1801.* Lexington: University Press of Kentucky, 2000.

Sonneck, Oscar. *A Bibliography of Early Secular American Music.* Revised and enlarged by William Treat Upton. Washington, D.C.: Library of Congress, 1945. Reprint, New York: Da Capo Press, 1964.

Sorge, Georg Andreas. *The Secretly Kept Art of the Scaling of Organ Pipes.* Translated and edited by Carl O. Bleyle. Bibliotheca organologica 33. Buren: Frits Knuf, 1978.

Sovík, Thomas. "Music of the American Moravians: First Tradition." *Czechoslovak and Central European Journal* (formerly *Kosmas*) 9/1–2 (Summer/Winter 1990): 35–46.

———. "Music Theorists of the Bohemian Reformation: Jan Blahoslav and Jan Josquin." *Journal of Czechoslovak and Central European Studies* (formerly *Kosmas*) 8/1 (January 1989): 105–45.

Spacht, Thomas. "Toward an Understanding of Some Hymn Accompaniment Practices in Germany and Pennsylvania around 1850." *Tracker* 42/1 (1998): 14–17.

Spangenberg, August Gottlieb. *Kurzgefasste historische Nachricht von der gegenwärtigen Verfassung der evangelischen Brüderunität.* Berlin: August Mylius, 1796.

———. *Leben des Herrn Nicolaus Ludwig Grafen und Herrn von Zinzendorf und Pottendorf.* 3 vols. Barby: Zu finden in der Brüder-Gemeinen, 1772–74.

Speller, John L. "A Double Tannenberg Legacy: Restoration of the 1787 and 1793 Organs in Lititz, Pennsylvania." *Tracker* 31/3 (1987): 24–31.

Spinka, Matthew. *John Amos Comenius: That Incomparable Moravian,* rev. ed. New York: Russel and Russell, 1967.

Steelman, Robert. *Catalog of the Lititz Congregation Collection.* Chapel Hill: University of North Carolina Press, 1981.

———. "The First Trombone Choir of Lititz." *Moravian Music Journal* 27/1 (1982): 4–6.

———. "A Source of Some Early Moravian Chorale Melodies." *Moravian Music Foundation Bulletin* 21/2 (Fall–Winter 1976): 7–9.

Stevens, Charles E. "Christian Ignatius Latrobe's Music at York Minster." *Moravian Music Foundation Bulletin* 25/1 (Spring–Summer 1980): 10–12.

———. "The Musical Works of Christian Ignatius Latrobe." PhD diss., University of North Carolina at Chapel Hill, 1971.

Stevenson, Robert. *Protestant Church Music in America: A Short Survey of Men and Movements from 1564 to the Present.* New York: W. W. Norton, 1966.

Stocker, Harry Emilius. *A History of the Moravian Church in New York City.* New York, 1922.

Stockton, Edwin L., Sr. "A Brief Sketch of the Twenty-Sixth Regimental Band North Carolina Troops C.S.A., 'The Pride of Tarheelia.'" *Moravian Music Journal* 26/3 (Fall 1981): 52–55.

Stoeffler, F. Ernest. *German Pietism During the Eighteenth Century.* Studies in the History of Religions 24. Leiden: E. J. Brill, 1973.

———. *The Rise of Evangelical Pietism.* Studies in the History of Religions 9. Leiden: E. J. Brill, 1971.

Stoeffler, F. Ernest, ed. *Continental Pietism and Early American Christianity.* Grand Rapids: William B. Eerdmans Publishing Company, 1976.

Stolba, K. Marie. "Evidence for Quartets by John Antes, American-Born Moravian Composer." *Journal of the American Musicological Society* 33/3 (Fall 1980): 565–74.

———. "From John Antes to Benjamin Franklin—A Musical Connection." *Moravian Music Foundation Bulletin* 25/2 (Fall–Winter 1980): 5–9.

Strauss, Barbara Jo. "A Register of Music Performed in Concert, Nazareth, Pennsylvania, from 1796–1845: An Annotated Edition of an American Moravian Document." MM thesis, University of Arizona, 1976.

Summerville, Suzanne. "Music in Christiansfeld, Denmark, Yesterday and Today." *Moravian Music Foundation Bulletin* 22/2 (Fall–Winter 1977): 10–12.

Supplement to the Moravian Hymn Book. London: Moravian Book Room, 1940.

Suttoni, Charles. "The Moravians Make Music." *Moravian Music Foundation Bulletin* 23/2 (Fall–Winter 1978): 13–14.

Swaim, Lewis B. "The Theology of James Montgomery as Revealed in His Hymns." BD thesis, Moravian Theological Seminary, 1955.

Swasta, Susan M., and Richard D. Krohn. *Mind, Body, and Spirit: Moravian Academy, 1742–1992.* Bethlehem: Moravian Academy, 1991.

Sweet, William Warren. *The Story of Religion in America.* New York: Harper & Brothers, 1950.

Sweitzer, Vangie Roby. *Tuned for Praise: The Bethlehem Area Moravian Trombone Choir, 1754–2004.* Bethlehem: Central Moravian Church, 2004.

Tagg, Barbara, and Linda Ferreira. "Fourteen Conductors Speak About American Choral Music." *Choral Journal* 48/8 (March 2003): 9–25.

Tannenberg, David. Letters. Moravian Music Foundation, Winston-Salem.

Thomas, J., and T. Baldwin, eds. *Complete Pronouncing Gazetteer, or Geographical Dictionary, of the World.* Philadelphia: J. B. Lippincott & Co., 1855.

Tollefsen, Randall H. *Catalogue of the Music Collection of the Moravian Congregation at Zeist.* Utrecht: Rijksarchief, 1985.

Traupman-Carr, Carol A., ed. *Pleasing for Our Use: David Tannenberg and the Organs of the Moravians.* Bethlehem: Lehigh University Press, 2000.

Twelve Little Ballads and a Favorite Lesson. Book 2. Philadelphia: G. E. Blake, 1810–14.

Uttendörfer, Otto. *Zinzendorfs Gedanken über den Gottesdienst.* Herrnhut: Gustav Winter, 1931.

Van Vleck, Amelia Adelaide. Memoir, prepared by J. Kenneth Pfohl. Moravian Archives, Winston-Salem.

Van Vlec[k], Carl Anton. Memoir. Moravian Archives, Winston-Salem.

Van Vleck, Jacob. *Lebenslauf.* Printed in *Gemein-Nachrichten,* 1833/4: 651–66.

Van Vleck, Louisa Cornelia. Memoir, prepared by Edward Rondthaler. Moravian Archives, Winston-Salem.

Vardell, Charles G., Jr. *Organs in the Wilderness.* Winston-Salem: Salem Academy and College, 1944. Reprint, edited by Nola Reed Knouse. Winston-Salem: Moravian Music Foundation, 1991.

Vanhall, Johann Baptist. *Six Symphonies.* Edited by Paul Bryan. Recent Researches in Music of the Classical Era 17–18. Madison: A-R Editions, 1985.

Verzeichnis des Musik-Archivs Neuwied. Typescript. Copies in Moravian Music Foundation, Winston-Salem and Bethlehem, July 1995.

Vogt, Peter. "Bibliographie und Discographie zur Herrnhuter Musik." *Unitas Fratrum* 47 (2001): 128–36.

———. "A Bibliography of German Scholarship on Moravian Music." *Moravian Music Journal* 42/2 (Fall 1997): 15–22.

———. "A Codified Repertoire? The Scope and Character of Moravian Music According to the *Hilfsbuch* of 1865, 1891 and 1907." Unpublished paper presented at the Sixth Bethlehem Conference on Moravian Music, October 7, 2004.

———. "Listening to 'Festive Stillness': The Sound of Moravian Music According to Descriptions of Non-Moravian Visitors." *Moravian Music Journal* 44/1 (Spring 1999): 15–23.

———. Review of *Musikanschauung, Musikpraxis, Kantatenkomposition in der Herrnhuter Brüdergemeine,* by Anja Wehrend. *Moravian Music Journal* 42/2 (Fall 1997): 3–5.

Walker, Williston, Richard A. Norris, David W. Lotz, and Robert T. Handy. *A History of the Christian Church.* 4th edition. New York: Charles Scribner's Sons, 1985.

Warner, Paul T. "History of the First Moravian Church of Philadelphia, Penna." *Transactions of the Moravian Historical Society.* Nazareth: Moravian Historical Society, 1942.

Wehrend, Anja. "Gottesdienstliches Musizieren als Vorspiel zur himmlischen Harmonie: Der Einfluß der barocken Musikanschauung auf Zinzendorfs Abbild- und Harmoniebegriff." *Unitas Fratrum* 47 (2000): 89–106.

———. *Musikanschauung, Musikpraxis, Kantatenkomposition in der Herrnhuter Brüdergemeine.* Frankfurt am Main: Peter Lang, 1995.

Wehrend, Anja. "Zinzendorfs Musikverständnis." In *Graf ohne Grenzen. Leben und Werk von Nikolaus Ludwig Graf von Zinzendorf,* edited by Dietrich Meyer and Paul Peucker, 101–7. Herrnhut: Unitätsarchiv, 2000.

Weinlick, John R. "Moravian Music: A Way of Life." *Moravian Music Foundation Bulletin* 14/2 (Spring 1970): 1–5.

Wellesz, Egon, and Frederick Sternfeld, eds. *The New Oxford History of Music.* Vol. 7, *The Age of Enlightenment.* London: Oxford University Press, 1973.

Whelan, Frank. "Professor gives New Insight into Wolle family." *Morning Call* (Allentown, January 25, 2004), E3.

Wied, Maximilian. *Travels in the Interior of North America.* Translated by H. Evans Lloyd. London: Ackerman & Co., ca. 1843.

Williams, Henry L. "Centennial of a Transitional Hymnal: The Offices of Worship and Hymns, 1891." *Moravian Music Journal* 37/1 (Spring 1992): 3ff.

———. "The Development of the Moravian Hymnal." *Transactions of the Moravian Historical Society,* 18/2 (1962).

Williams, Peter. *A New History of the Organ from the Greeks to the Present Day.* Bloomington: Indiana University Press, 1980.

Willig's Juvenile Instructor. [ca. 1835].

Winkler, Klaus. "Entstehung und Ausbreitung der Bläsermusik bei der Herrnhuter Brüdergemeine im 18. Jahrhundert." In *Musikgeographie. Weltliche und geistliche Bläsermusik in ihren Beziehungen zueinander und zu ihrer Umwelt,* edited by Manfred Büttner, Wolfgang Schnabel, and Klaus Winkler, 123–75. Abhandlungen zur Geschichte der Gewissenschaften und Religion/Umwelt-Forschung Bd. 6, Tl. 2. Bochum: Universitätsverlag Dr. N. Brockmeyer, 1991.

———. "Zur Entwicklung der Blasmusik bei den Herrnhutern im 18. Jahrhundert: Quellenkundliche Studien zu Instrumentarium, Zeremoniell und Repertoire der ersten Posaunenchörem." In *Posaunen in der Bibel und bei uns vor 1843,* edited by Horst Dietrich Schlemm, 66–96. Beiträge zur Geschichte Evangelischer Posaunenarbeit 1. Gütersloh: Gütersloher Verlagshaus Mohn, 1989.

Wolf, Edward C. "Music in Old Zion, Philadelphia, 1750–1850." *Musical Quarterly* 58/4 (October 1972): 648–50, 623–26.

———. "The Organs at St. Michael's and Zion Lutheran Churches, Philadelphia." *Tracker* 6/3 (April 1962): 7.

———. "Sequel to Journey to Pennsylvania." *Tracker* 17/3 (1973): 12.

———. "The Tannenberg Organ at Old Zion Church, Philadelphia." *Journal of Church Music* 3/4 (April 1961): 2–5.

Wolfe, Richard J. *Early American Music Engraving and Printing.* Urbana: University of Illinois Press, 1980.

———. *Secular Music in America 1801–1825: A Bibliography.* 3 vols. New York: New York Public Library, 1964.

Wolle, Peter. Diary. Unpublished manuscript. Moravian Museum, Lititz.

———. *Hymn tunes used in the Church of the United Brethren, Arranged for Four Voices and the Organ or Piano-Forte; to which are added Chants for the Litany of that Church, and a Number of Approved Anthems for Various Occasions.* Boston: 1836.

Wolle, Peter. *Moravian Tune Book arranged for four voices with accompaniment for organ and piano.* Bethlehem: Moravian Publication Office, 1889.

Zahn, Johannes. *Die Melodien der deutschen evangelischen Kirchenlieder, aus den Quellen geschäpft und mitgeteilt von Johannes Zahn.* 6 vols. Gütersloh: C. Bertelsmann, 1889–93.

Zedler, Heinrich. *Grosses vollständiges Universal-Lexicon aller Wissenschaften und Künste.* Vol. 28. Leipzig und Halle: 1741.

Zeisberger, David, ed. *A Collection of Hymns for the Use of the Christian Indians, of the Missions of the United Brethren, in North America.* Philadelphia: Henry Sweitzer, 1803.

Zinzendorf, Nicholas Ludwig von. *Summarischer Unterricht in Anno 1753 für reisende Brüder.* London: 1755.

Contributors

ALICE M. CALDWELL has been engaged in research on various aspects of Moravian music history for over twenty years, including liturgical music, sacred vocal music, keyboard music, and music education. In 2006 she delivered the Walter Vivian Moses Lectures in Moravian Studies, sponsored by Moravian Theological Seminary. She holds a degree in organ performance from the Oberlin Conservatory of Music and a PhD in musicology from New York University. Dr. Caldwell lives in Connecticut, where she is active as a music educator and church musician.

C. DANIEL CREWS is the archivist of the Moravian Church in America, Southern Province, and is the author of numerous publications on Moravian history and theology. He holds doctorates from the University of North Carolina at Greensboro and the University of Manchester in England, and has done post-doctoral studies at the University of Prague in the Czech Republic. In addition, he is an ordained Moravian minister and has served congregations in North Carolina, England, and the Virgin Islands.

LOU CAROL FIX received the BM and MM degrees in organ performance from Salem College, North Carolina, and Indiana University at Bloomington, respectively. She also holds the MA degree in musicology from Indiana University. She has taught music history, organ, recorder, and church music at Moravian College in Bethlehem since 1985. Currently she is also the organist and music director at Peace-Tohickon Lutheran Church in Perkasie, Pennsylvania, and teaches music at Moravian Academy in Bethlehem. Her research interests include seventeenth-century organ performance practice and Moravian music in America.

PAULINE M. FOX holds the BM in piano performance from Houghton College, an MA in music history from Marywood College, and a PhD in historical musicology from New York University. She is pursuing an interest in the music of Moravians in eastern Pennsylvania, where she has resided for many years. Previous projects include papers for several of the Bethlehem Conferences on Moravian Music; "Parodies for Piety," a two-part article for the *Moravian Music*

Journal that discusses the appropriation by Herrnhut Moravians of the Dresden composer J. G. Naumann's popular 1780 opera *Cora*; and a survey of Bethlehem Moravian musical heritage for the Northeast Regional Conference of the College Music Society in February 2004. She serves as director of music at East Stroudsburg United Methodist Church and is active in the Lehigh Valley Chapter of the American Guild of Organists, holding the Guild Associateship diploma (A.A.G.O.). Since 1998, she also has been a member of the Monroe County Open Space Advisory Board, concerned with environmental preservation. She is also fond of bluegrass music. In 2007 she completed the cataloguing of records from the Female Seminary in Bethlehem.

ALBERT H. FRANK retired in 2007 as the assistant director of the Moravian Music Foundation. He is the author of the *Companion to the Moravian Book of Worship* (2004). He holds the BA from Moravian College, the MDiv from Moravian Theological Seminary, and the DMin from Drew University. An ordained Moravian minister, he has served congregations in Tobago, West Indies, Philadelphia, and Dover, Ohio. He also served as a faculty member at Moravian Theological Seminary and an adjunct staff member of the Unity Archives in Herrnhut, Germany.

NOLA REED KNOUSE is the director of the Moravian Music Foundation, a position she has held since 1994, serving as Director of Research and Programs from 1992 to 1994. She holds the BA from Wake Forest University and the MA and PhD from the Eastman School of Music of the University of Rochester. She served as the music editor of the 1995 *Moravian Book of Worship* and as the editor of *Moravian Chorales and Music*, Volume 2, and has prepared scholarly editions of many Moravian anthems. She is the editor of *David Moritz Michael: Complete Wind Chamber Music*, published in 2006 as Volume 16 of the American Musicological Society's Music of the United States of America (MUSA) series. Prior to her work at the Moravian Music Foundation, she held teaching positions at Oregon State University and Salem College.

LAURENCE LIBIN is emeritus Research Curator at the Metropolitan Museum of Art, Honorary Curator of Steinway & Sons, and currently the vice president of the Organ Historical Society. A Life Fellow of the Royal Society of Arts, he received the Anthony Baines Memorial Award from the Galpin Society (UK) in 2006 for services to organology. Mr. Libin is a widely published scholar and has taught in the graduate schools of Columbia and New York universities. He is a consultant to international cultural institutions, especially on issues of conservation of historic musical instruments. In 2004 he identified a clavichord in the Moravian Historical Society as the earliest extant work of David Tannenberg.

PAUL PEUCKER is the director of the Moravian Archives in Bethlehem, Pennsylvania. He holds the PhD from the Rijkuniversiteit at Utrecht, the Netherlands, with his dissertation on the first Moravian settlement in the Netherlands. Prior to coming to the United States, he was the director of the Unitätsarchiv (archives of the worldwide Moravian Church) in Herrnhut, Germany. He has published articles in Germany, the Netherlands, and the United States, focusing primarily on aspects of Moravian history. He has played the French horn in Moravian brass choirs in Zeist, the Netherlands; Herrnhut, Germany; and Bethlehem, Pennsylvania.

JEWEL A. SMITH received a PhD in musicology from the University of Cincinnati. Her areas of specialty are nineteenth-century music, American music, and women's music education in antebellum America. She has presented papers and lecture-recitals based on her research at meetings of the American Musicology Society, the Society for American Music, the Bethlehem Conferences on Moravian Music, the College Music Society Great Lakes Chapter, the Women in the Arts Conference, and the International Alliance for Women in Music Congress; and at Salem College, Mt. Holyoke College, and Amherst College. Her forthcoming book *Music, Women, and Pianos in Antebellum Bethlehem Pennsylvania: The Moravian Young Ladies' Seminary* documents not only the academic and music curricula offered at a distinguished seminary, but also the importance of piano study from a sociological viewpoint, music making in a gendered environment, and performance opportunities available for nineteenth-century women. She is currently beginning a sequel that explores women's music education in prominent nineteenth-century American female seminaries, such as Troy Female Seminary, Mt. Holyoke Female Seminary, Ipswich Female Seminary, Litchfield Female Seminary, and Music Vale Seminary.

Index

Smither, Howard, 92
Snetzler, John, 152
Snipes, Jayson, xviii, 109–11
Solín, Václav, 8, 282, 291
sonatas, piano. *See* piano, Moravian music
for
Sörensen, Johannes, 282–83, 296, 299,
302
Sorge, Georg Andreas, 134, 152–53, 154
sources, Moravian music, 88–89, 94–97
South Africa, xv, 5, 13, 22n13, 89, 179,
196, 259
Sovík, Thomas, 8
Spangenberg, August Gottlieb, 12, 35,
139–40, 176, 192; life, 267, 276, 281,
283, 292, 293, 295, 299
speaking, 35
specifications, organ. *See* organ,
specifications
Spener, Philip Jakob, 10
spinet, xii, 228, 229, 242, 294
Sprechen. See speaking
St. Thomas, Virgin Islands, 13, 178, 292
Stadtmusiker, 173
Stadtpfeifer, 4, 173
Stamitz, Johann, 195, 196, 197, 219
Stamitz, Karl [Carl], 197, 219
Star-Spangled Banner, 260
Staten Island, 220, 268
Stefan, Andrew, 44
Steinhauer, Henry, 215
stops, organ. *See* organ, stops
strangers' service. *See Fremdenstunde*
Strejc, Jiří, 283, 291
Suite: bey einer Quelle zu blasen. See Michael,
David Moritz
Sun Inn, 242
Suppé, Franz von, 197
Suriname, 13, 179, 222, 293
Swertner, John, 51, 283, 298
Synod: 1750, 17, 253; 1764, 174; 1775,
17, 48; 1782, 17, 48, 214; 1893, 73

Tannenberg, David, xiii, 134, 137; clavi-
chord and harpsichord, 242; life, 268,
283–84, 292, 294, 295, 296, 299;
organs, 149–55, 159, 167n97
Tannenberg, Jr., David, 156
Tanzania, 5
Taylor & Boody Organbuilders, 159
Te Deum, 136, 176
Te Jehovah, 176
temperament, 152

temperament, equal, 152–53, 166n87
texture: in Antes trios, 199–200; in
anthems, 98–101; in Michael wind
pieces, 204–6; in piano music, 229–40
Tham, Michael (the Elder), 45
theological seminary, Barby. *See* Barby
theology, 12, 14, 32, 33, 38, 160; ancient
Unity, 7–8, 277, 286; "blood and
wounds," 14; in hymns, 45, 47, 51,
56–57, 62, 64, 65, 69, 71, 72, 75, 76;
and music, 90, 91, 126, 172, 262–63
Thirty Years' War, 9, 45, 263, 292
Till, Jacob Christian, 242–44; life, 284,
299, 300, 303
Till, Johann Christian, 95, 101, 106, 198,
242–44; life, 284, 295, 299, 300, 302
Tod Jesu, Graun. *See* Graun
Tomochichi, 178
transcriptions, piano, 235
treatises, music. *See* music treatises
Trinity Church, New York City, 153
trombone, xiv, xv, 169–70, 172–73; in
anthems, 97–98; with organ, 137
trombone choir, 178, 261–62; Bethlehem
Area Moravians, 179, 181; Downey,
California, 179; Glenwood Moravian,
179; Salem, North Carolina, 179
trombone hill, 178
trumpet, xiii, 172, 173
tune book. *See* chorale book; hymnal
tune numbering. *See* hymns, tune
numbering system
tunes, hymn. *See* chorale book; hymnal;
hymns, tunes; hymns, tune numbering
system
tuning, xiv, 228. *See also* temperament
Türk, Daniel Gottlieb, xi, 90, 95
Twelve Little Ballads and a Favorite Lesson
(1810–14), 224
26th N. C. Regimental Band, xii, 239,
249n16, 259

Unitas Fratrum, 5, 7, 76. *See also* Ancient
Unity; Moravian Church, names for
Unitäts-Archiv. See Moravian Archives,
Herrnhut
Unity of the Brethren, 5, 7. *See also*
Moravian Church, names for
upper congregation, 66, 149

valve instruments, 177, 181, 259
Van Vleck, Amelia Adelaide, 233, 238–39,
285, 302, 304

Van Vleck, Arthur Laurence, 140
Van Vleck, Carl Anton, 233, 234, 278, 285, 299, 302
Van Vleck, Jacob, 19, 193, 195, 285, 294, 296, 297, 298, 299, 301, 302
Van Vleck, Lisetta. *See* Meinung, Lisetta Van Vleck
Van Vleck, Louisa Cornelia, 140
Verband der Posaunenchöre der Brüdergemeine, 180
Verbeek, Johannes Renatus, 284, 294, 297, 299, 301
Verzeichniß derer Musicalien welche in Concert sind gemacht worden. See Register of Music Performed in Concert, Nazareth
Vetter, Georg. *See* Strejc, Jiři
Vierling, Johann Gottfried, *Orgel Stücke,* 146
visitors, reactions to music by, 135, 136, 207, 255
Vogt, Peter, 255, 256
Voullaire, Henri Marc Hermann Woldemar, 275, 285–86, 301, 303

Wachet auf, ruft uns die Stimme, 65, 67–69
Wachovia Historical Society, xviii
Wachovia, North Carolina, 176, 283, 294. *See also* Bethabara, Bethania, Salem
Wagner, Richard, 158
Wanhal, Johann Baptist, 195, 197
Washington, George, 219, 285
Wasserfahrt. See Michael, David Moritz
Watchnight. *See* New Year's Eve service
watchword, daily. *See* Daily Text
Watteville, Benigna von, 175, 213
Watteville, Johannes von, 66, 175
Watts, Isaac, 51
Wauer, Wilhelm Heinrich, 286, 301, 303
Weber, Johann Gottfried, 182, 286, 293, 295, 296, 298, 299
Wehrend, Anja, 4, 93, 258
Weiss, Jedediah, 197, 286, 299, 303
Weisse, Michael, 45, 59, 76, 172, 286, 290, 291
Wesley, Charles, 51, 259
Wesley, John, 2

Westmann, Johann, 174
Westphalia, peace of, 292
White Mountain, battle of, 9, 45, 292
Whitefield, George, 13
Whitmonday, 204, 300
Wied, Maximilian, 228
Wierzbicki, James, xvii
Winston-Salem, North Carolina, 181. *See also* Salem, North Carolina
Wolf, Ernst Wilhelm, 196, 198
Wolfley, Eric, 228n
Wolle, Francis, 247
Wolle, James, 247
Wolle, John Frederick, xii, 158, 257, 287, 303, 304
Wolle, Lisetta, 221
Wolle, Peter, 52, 73, 156–57, 195, 247, 287, 299, 300, 302, 303
Wolle, Theodore F., 157–58
worship, 5, 29–40, 56, 75, 135, 253–55, 260–62; music and, in England, 18, 254
Worthington, John, 287, 292, 294, 296, 298

York, Pennsylvania, 155, 222
Young Ladies' Seminary, Bethlehem, xii, 194, 213–15, 219, 285, 288; piano at, 228–47

Zeisberger, David, 53
Zeist, The Netherlands, 89, 94, 169, 182, 192, 271, 294
Zinzendorf, Christian Renatus, 14, 64–65, 94, 279
Zinzendorf, Erdmuth Dorothea von Reuss, Countess von, 64–65, 74
Zinzendorf, Nicholas Ludwig, xiii, 10–14, 31, 32, 38, 47, 94, 98, 134, 137, 153, 172, 176; hymns of, 64; life, 283, 287, 292, 293, 295
Zion Lutheran Church, Philadelphia, 154, 155
Zoebisch, C. A. & Sons, xiv, 278, 288
Zoebisch, Charles Augustus, xiv, 288, 301, 302, 304
Zwischenspielen. See interludes, organ

Eastman Studies in Music